# MINNEAPOLIS AND THE AGE OF RAILWAYS

# MINNEAPOLIS

## AND THE AGE OF RAILWAYS

DON L. HOFSOMMER

University of Minnesota Press
Minneapolis • London

*The University of Minnesota Press gratefully acknowledges assistance provided for the publication of this volume by the John K. and Elsie Lampert Fesler Fund.*

*The publication of this book is supported in part by a grant from the St. Cloud State University Foundation.*

*Illustrations in the book are courtesy of the author, unless otherwise credited.*

Published by the University of Minnesota Press
111 Third Avenue South, Suite 290
Minneapolis, MN 55401-2520
http://www.upress.umn.edu

Library of Congress Cataloging-in-Publication Data

Hofsommer, Donovan L.
    Minneapolis and the age of railways / Don L. Hofsommer.
        p. cm.
    Includes bibliographical references and index.
    ISBN 0-8166-4501-9 (hc/j : alk. paper)
    1. Railroads—Minnesota—Minneapolis—History.
    2. Minneapolis (Minn.)—History.
    I. Title.
    HE2781.M6H64 2005
    385′.09776′57909034—dc22

                                        2005012410

Printed in the United States of America on acid-free paper

The University of Minnesota is an equal-opportunity educator and employer.

12  11  10  09  08  07  06  05          10  9  8  7  6  5  4  3  2  1

**For Sandra**

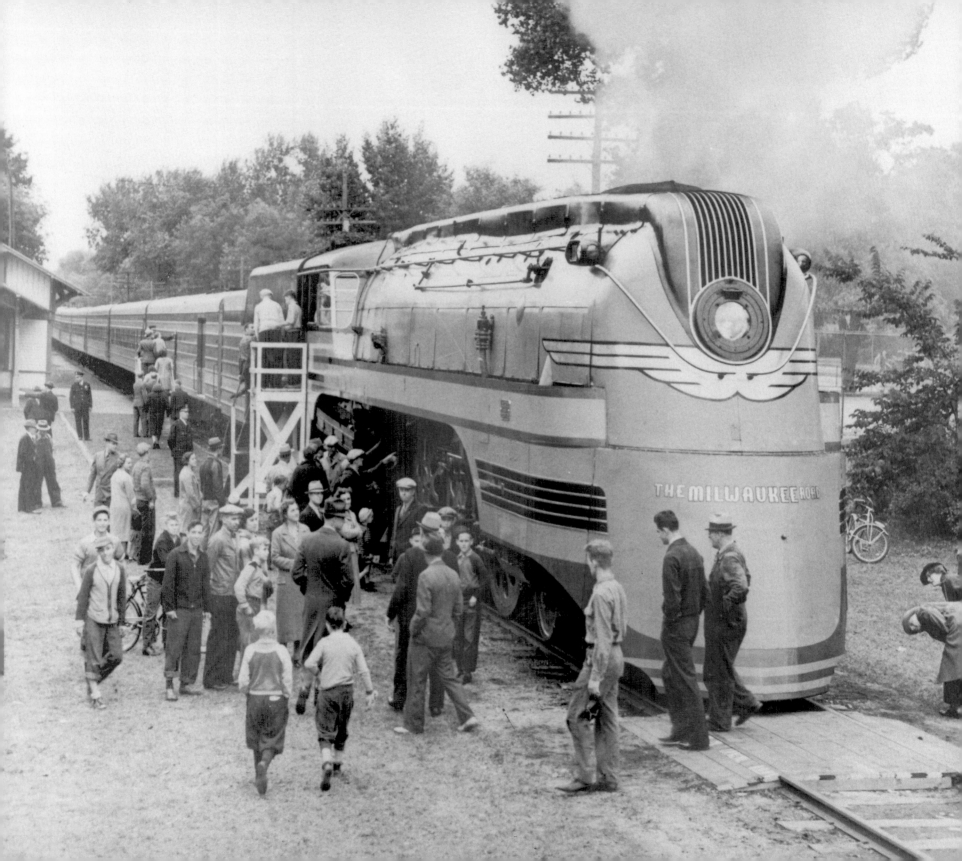

# CONTENTS

# Abbreviations and Acronyms

| | | | |
|---|---|---|---|
| AC | Author's collection | M&D | Minneapolis & Duluth Railroad |
| Alton | Chicago & Alton | M&StL | Minneapolis & St. Louis |
| BCR&M | Burlington, Cedar Rapids & Minnesota | MHS | Minnesota Historical Society |
| BCR&N | Burlington, Cedar Rapids & Northern | Milwaukee Road | Chicago, Milwaukee & St. Paul (or) Chicago, Milwaukee, St. Paul & Pacific |
| BNSF | Burlington Northern Santa Fe | | |
| Burlington Route | Chicago, Burlington & Quincy | MPL | Minneapolis Public Library |
| C&NW | Chicago & North Western | North Western | Chicago & North Western |
| C&RI | Chicago & Rock Island | NP | Northern Pacific |
| CB&Q | Chicago, Burlington & Quincy | Omaha | Chicago, St. Paul, Minneapolis & Omaha |
| CGW | Chicago Great Western | PRR | Pennsylvania Railroad |
| Clover Leaf | Toledo, St. Louis & Western | Railway Transfer | Railway Transfer of the City of Minneapolis |
| CM&StP | Chicago, Milwaukee & St. Paul | Rock Island | Chicago, Rock Island & Pacific |
| CMStP&P | Chicago, Milwaukee, St. Paul & Pacific | RPO | Railway Post Office |
| CRI&P | Chicago, Rock Island & Pacific | StP&D | St. Paul & Duluth |
| CStP&KC | Chicago, St. Paul & Kansas City | StP&P | St. Paul & Pacific |
| CStPM&O | Chicago, St. Paul, Minneapolis & Omaha | StP&SC | St. Paul & Sioux City |
| GN | Great Northern | StPM&M | St. Paul, Minneapolis & Manitoba |
| IC | Illinois Central | Soo Line | Minneapolis, St. Paul & Sault Ste. Marie |
| ICC | Interstate Commerce Commission | SP | Southern Pacific |
| JJHRL | James J. Hill Reference Library | USRA | United States Railroad Administration |
| LCL | Less-than-carload | WC | Wisconsin Central |
| LS&M | Lake Superior & Mississippi | WM&P | Wisconsin, Minnesota, & Pacific Railway |
| Manitoba | St. Paul, Minneapolis & Manitoba | | |

# PREFACE

For a people well and completely accustomed to Boeing 747s and Ford SUVs, when Amtrak handles a scant 1 percent of intercity passenger miles, when nearly two-thirds of intercity ton miles move by highway, air, water, or pipeline, it is nearly impossible to imagine a time, not long removed, when locomotives and rails utterly dominated the domestic landscape—creating the age of railways, the steamcar civilization.

The word *revolutionary* is overworked in contemporary conversation and writing, but it is the absolutely correct term in defining the astonishing impact of railroads on American society late in the nineteenth century and into the next—roughly 1860 to 1920. The industry helped lay the foundation for the modern American economy and pioneered many of the systems by which it was organized: advanced methods of finance and management, means of regulating labor relations and competition, and new fields of operation for financiers, bankers, and speculators. The expanded and expanding network connected manufacturer and consumer, and, as the services offered became more dependable, enabled inventory practice to be changed, aided in the rise of the factory system, and offered huge new opportunities for wholesalers. (Indeed, the industry also provided an impressive market in its own right.) In short, the railroad—and its ally, the telegraph—were at center stage throughout the years when the United States was extending its agricultural frontiers to the farthest corners of the West while simul-

taneously undergoing a transformation that would see it become a most powerful and vibrant urban and industrial nation.

The country's early carriers constructed their primary arteries to link established cities, or to enable them to make claim to substantial underdeveloped areas, which they could promote and prosper later. A fleshing-out process followed with the opening of secondary lines and branches. These were built to open farmland, to access stands of timber, to serve mines and quarries, to outflank pretenders, to make territorial claims, or to achieve a combination of these objectives. In 1860, America's railroads were not integrated, nor were they efficient. Systemization soon followed, however, and railroads swiftly became the nation's first big business.

During the tumultuous years from 1860 to America's involvement in World War I, the country's population nearly tripled—from 35,700,000 to 103,400,000. At the same time, the American rail network increased by a factor of seven—to 253,626 miles—while gross operating revenues rose spectacularly—thirteenfold, from $300 million in 1865 to $4 trillion in 1917. In fact, American trackage exceeded that of Europe even before the turn of the century.

Minneapolis was a full player in all of this, alert to its prospects as part of the steamcar civilization but surprisingly slow to receive those benefits and even clumsy in the early process of reaching for them. Nearby St. Paul, by comparison, flowered early and brightly. Head of navigation on the Mississippi, territorial and then state capital, St. Paul was central to pioneer plans for a rail system serving the region as well as transcontinental aspirations. Indeed, Minnesota's first train steamed out of St. Paul under the proud and expansive banner of St. Paul & Pacific. When Lake Superior & Mississippi spiked down rails to link the Great Lakes chain with the heartland's primary riverway, St. Paul predictably was the focal point. And when rails pushed off to the southwest, they were owned by St. Paul & Sioux City. Eventually St. Paul would be the head-quarters city for giants Great Northern and Northern Pacific and for important regional Chicago, St. Paul, Minneapolis & Omaha. For that matter, powerful Chicago-based Chicago, Milwaukee & St. Paul early was known as "the St. Paul Road."

Minneapolis could boast no such primacy. There was joy, of course, when the first train puffed into St. Anthony—but it had come *from* St. Paul, and it returned *to* St. Paul. And St. Paul & Pacific was hardly content with a tiny ten-mile route from St. Paul to St. Anthony and soon pushed on through Minneapolis to the west and north-west. There was joy, too, when a predecessor of Chicago, Milwaukee & St. Paul reached Minneapolis in 1865, but it was a mere stub from Mendota off what became the pioneer route from Chicago and Milwaukee to St. Paul. Leaders at the Falls of St. Anthony had mixed opinions about all of this, their collective egos bruised, but they had not acted affirmatively with any degree of energy or enthusiasm on their own behalf—not matching earnest and calculated efforts by counterparts at St. Paul and seemingly naive as to the intentions of bold entrepreneurs at Chicago and Milwaukee who saw so clearly utility in iron rails as effective tools of urban economic imperialism. Finally, businessmen and other public figures at the falls awakened to twin needs of protection and promoting their growing interests by fostering a home road—Minneapolis & St. Louis—which, they hoped, would provide an all-season, reliable means of countering the influence of St. Paul and circumventing the escalating muscle of roads representing Chicago and Milwaukee. But even the home road was often referred to as "the St. Louis Road," and later on an-other locally sponsored enterprise, Minneapolis, St. Paul & Sault

Leaders at the Falls of St. Anthony were reactive, not proactive. To maximize the industrial potential at the falls, they needed a locally owned railway that could bring in necessary raw materials and carry away finished product—a railway that would serve their own ends in a campaign of urban economic imperialism. In the process, the raw village of St. Anthony, from where this photograph was taken in 1865, and the equally raw village of Minneapolis would be transformed. Photograph courtesy of the Minneapolis Public Library, Minneapolis Collection.

Ste. Marie, took the nickname "Soo Line" to imply a focus away from Minneapolis.

Yet M&StL and Soo Line were effective tools in promoting Min-neapolis interests even as the city's importance grew. Just as rails provided the nation with its cardiovascular system, just as rails turned Chicago into "nature's metropolis," so did rails provide as-cendancy for Minneapolis. Rails brought logs and wheat and car-ried away lumber and flour; cars arrived with a bewildering array of consumer goods to stock wholesale houses and then delivered those same goods to outlying retailers; rails provided coal and cordwood to the fuel-starved city and took away a wide assortment of locally manufactured goods, from paint to farm implements; cars brought immigrants for the local labor force and agriculturalists for nearby and distant hinterlands; depots thronged with passengers arriving from or departing for faraway places, who mixed with commuters from Minnetonka and elsewhere; excursionists arrived by the trainload to "see the sights"; mail and express moved to destinations on intricate schedules; railroad time became standard time; and, to be sure, railroads set the tempo at Minneapolis just as they did all across the country during the age of railways.

Minneapolis became a powerhouse in lumber, flour, and other manufacturing as well as a growing center of wholesale distribution. Its population surpassed St. Paul, established railroad companies increased their presence, new roads sought entry, and Minneapolis extended its influence to a huge hinterland—north, west, and south. By 1920, the city was served by a dozen railroads including three with arteries all the way to Puget Sound, seven combinations to and from Chicago, three options to St. Louis, in addition to portals for Omaha and Kansas City—offering, in the aggregate, outlet to every location served by rail throughout North America. And while the age of railways was passing by the third decade of the twentieth century, the broad contours of the country were fixed—its industries and manufacturing centers, its metropolises, its huge and productive agricultural regions, its lines of transportation and communication, its flows of commerce and culture. The experience of Minneapolis during the years 1865–1920 reflected as much.

This is not a history of Minneapolis, nor is it a record of every railroad that entered or served the city. Rather it is a study, on the one hand, of the relationship between Minneapolis and its railroads, and, on the other, of the symbiosis that developed between the city and its railroads with a huge hinterland stretching from the Canadian border to northern Iowa and west as far as central Montana—all of it reflecting the steamcar civilization, the age of railways. The Minneapolis experience is framed here in substantial part by the Minneapolis & St. Louis Railway—the early local favorite, the home road. Brief portions of this work appeared earlier in *The Tootin' Louie: A History of the Minneapolis & St. Louis Railway*.

Many persons gave generously of time and resources to bring this project to fruition. Among these were Jim Scribbins, Edward W. Solberg, Gregory P. Ames, Todd Orjala, Pieter Martin, Susan Motin, Joan O'Driscoll, Ann E. Anderson, Richard B. Peterson, Douglas E. Welch, Peter J. Rickershauser, Aaron Isaacs, JoEllen Haugo, Natalie Hart, Todd Mahon, Patrick D. Hiatte, Stan Kistler, and Suzanne Burris. H. Roger Grant, W. Thomas White, and James A. Ward read all or parts of the manuscript, and each one offered invaluable suggestions for improvement. For errors of fact and infelicities of style that remain, I alone am responsible.

April 2005

# Steamcars at Last

Oh, it's once I made money by driving my team,
But now all is hauled on the railroad by steam.
May the devil catch the man that invented the plan,
For it's ruined us poor wagoners, and every other man.

CHAUTAUQUAN, MARCH 1900

They gathered at the American House—"one of the largest hotels north of St. Louis," the *Pioneer* enthused in praise of the three-story frame structure at the corner of St. Anthony and Washington Streets not far from steamboat landings along the Mississippi River in the raw but fully confident village of St. Paul.[1] The setting was absolutely fitting. After all, the Minnesota Territorial legislature had chosen the American House for its assemblage in 1851. Now, two years later, on November 26, 1853, eight earnest stalwarts of the territory met in this same hotel to draw plans for the essential transportation requirements of the future state. Specifically they composed the directorate of the recently chartered Minnesota Western Rail Road, one of several such enterprises authorized in the same season. And these men were well chosen. Among them was Henry Rice, former trader and future U.S senator; Franklin Steele, earlier sutler for the frontier post at Fort Snelling and soon to be prominent in nearly all matters at nearby St. Anthony and Minneapolis; Canadian-born Martin McLeod, another former trader, whose commanding pres-

ence would grace the first four terms of the Minnesota Legislature; Morton S. Wilkinson, future member of the legislature and the U.S. Senate; Socrates Nelson, a lumberman from neighboring Stillwater, who also served in the territorial legislature; and Alexander Wilkin, U.S. marshal for the territory and then territorial secretary, who as colonel of the Ninth Minnesota Infantry would perish at the Battle of Tupelo during the Civil War.[2]

There was not a railroader in the bunch, and for that matter there was not one foot of rail anywhere in the broad expanse of the future state at that time. Yet each one of these men well understood the potential represented by railroad technology—growth, dominion, prestige, power—and each pledged himself earnestly to such a new civilization carved out of the western wilds.

All of it represented optimism and confidence typical of America's frontier regions during the early 1850s. The Minnesota story was different only in that the federal government had but recently, on March 3, 1849, bestowed territorial status. At that time fewer than four thousand Euro-Americans claimed residence in the area, and trapping and trading, the economic and cultural activity that had dominated the landscape for a century and a half, remained an important element. Precipitous change was in the offing, however. Territorial Governor Alexander Ramsey enthusiastically prophesied that Minnesota would be "peopled with a rapidity exceeding anything in the history of western colonization." Predictable western boosterism, yes, but Ramsey quickly and successfully lobbied Washington for treaties of removal that would at once terminate the "Indian menace" and clear title to the public domain. A trickle of early settlers changed to a steady flow—to 150,092 nine years later when statehood was obtained. "No longer 'outside barbarians,' we are within the Chinese wall of the confederacy . . . " exclaimed the *St. Paul Daily Minnesotan* for May 14, 1858. "We are a State of the Union."[3]

Yet there was a serious damper on this understandable elation. Word of statehood had reached Minnesota in a depressingly tedious fashion—by wire to the nearest telegraph office, Prairie du Chien, Wisconsin, nearly 190 miles downstream on the Mississippi River from St. Paul, and then relayed northward by the next available steamboat for delivery to St. Paul newspapers, which spread the news—seventy-two long hours after President James Buchanan affixed his signature to the bill of admission.[4]

Indeed, Minnesota remained a raw frontier, devoid of the railroad and its handmaiden the telegraph. Many new arrivals to the area—arguably most—were delivered by water. In 1844, forty-one steamboats had landed at Fort Snelling; three years later regular packet service was established to nearby St. Paul. Steamers also crept up the Minnesota River to Mankato and New Ulm and even beyond. But waterborne commerce was subject in Minnesota climes to the "ice king," and, of course, broad areas of the state were devoid of navigational opportunities of any kind. Alternatives ameliorated only slightly. Crude stage roads linked St. Paul with Stillwater, on

During the mid-1850s, St. Anthony was a raw frontier village. This view looks downriver past Hennepin Island to the southeast. The large brick building in the foreground is the Upton Block, which still stands at 129 Main Street Southeast. Photograph by Benjamin Franklin Upton; courtesy of the Minnesota Historical Society.

the St. Croix River to the east, and with St. Anthony, to the northwest. And Pembina carts were employed in freighting between the head of navigation on the Mississippi at St. Paul and the Red River of the North. None of this, however, was remotely adequate to realizing Ramsey's great dream of rapidly peopling Minnesota.[5]

Only railroads could accomplish Ramsey's "manifest destiny." Twin rails, a growing chorus shouted, alone could alleviate the tyranny of distance, provide all-season, low-cost, high-speed, efficient delivery of passengers and freight. This revolutionary technology derived from England but enjoyed a huge embrace in the United States. By 1850 more than 9,000 miles of track reached westward and southwestward from Atlantic port cities. That was only the beginning. During the 1850s, a total of 21,605 miles of line were placed in service around the country.[6]

The collective impact of railways on the national fabric was nothing less than dramatic. Locomotives quickly eclipsed steamboats as the centerpiece of what historian George Rogers Taylor called the "transportation revolution" of 1815–60, in the process greatly accelerating the country's westering process. Rails overcame geographic challenges, offered reliable service with calculated periodicity, had an almost limitless capacity, and quickly became the nation's basic means of transport. Railroads also became America's first big business. They simultaneously gave rise to all sorts of manufacturing and commerce, changed warehousing traditions, and spawned regionally specialized factory production. The net result was an integrated national economy blending city and countryside as one.[7]

Many early promoters of railroads saw them as vibrant and effective tools of urban economic imperialism—means by which to hold substantial outlying territories subservient to the commercial and financial interests of a particular city. Thus, for example, the Baltimore & Ohio, sponsored by Baltimore's economic elites, was deployed as the appropriate device to claim and hold the broad expanse of the Ohio River valley for that aggressive eastern metropolis. It was much the same in the interior, where the early importance of St. Louis would be thoroughly challenged by Chicago and to a lesser extent by Milwaukee. Strategically located on the Mississippi

just below confluences with the Illinois and Missouri and above the confluence of the Ohio, St. Louis earned dominion over a huge hinterland. By 1840, the "Gateway City" provided about half the marketing and supply needs of Illinois and had forged significant trade patterns in what would become the states of Iowa, Wisconsin, and Minnesota. Milwaukee, too, had great aspirations, but Chicago—located at the base of Lake Michigan and thus at the farthest inland point to take advantage of water transport to and from the Atlantic—quickly rose to contend for the nation's broad heartland.[8]

Yet none of the railroads representing imperial instincts of St. Louis, Chicago, or Milwaukee evinced urgent interest in Minnesota Territory, occupying themselves instead with more densely settled areas of Illinois, Wisconsin, and Iowa. With good reason. Railroad ventures were both capital intensive and labor intensive—expensive undertakings fraught with financial risk of great magnitude. That reality escaped frustrated residents of thinly populated Minnesota Territory. "We must have an outlet, *and an outlet by rail*, and this as speedily as possible, or we are nowhere," wailed the *St. Anthony Express* for February 18, 1854. Yet those same residents had no capital reservoir adequate to satisfy such grand aspirations. They were aware, though, of government policy that had been generous in support of transportation ventures elsewhere—public lands in favor of the great Sault Canal, for example. More specifically, they pointed to congressional support of the Illinois Central Railroad, designed to link Lake Michigan to the Gulf of Mexico.[9]

Thus informed, territorial assemblymen boldly petitioned Congress for liberal assistance in forging a strong Minnesota rail net. It was not forthcoming, not immediately at least. Nevertheless, territorial solons authorized incorporation of a number of companies, Minnesota Western among them—all of which were projected well ahead of justifiable demand, and none of which had the ability to attract financial capital to bring about construction. But as territorial population increased, and as Congress moved to consider and to authorize statehood, Minnesotans took heart that federal lands might come their way. That optimism was rewarded when Congress did, in fact, set aside a handsome grant of the public domain to aid

in construction of railroads for the new state. With this tantalizing promise, a general strategy took form, one designed to open primary production areas of the new state: the near Mississippi River valley, the Minnesota River valley, and the Red River valley. Another part of the general strategy was to tie those three regions of the state to St. Paul, Minneapolis, and St. Anthony. To that end, the territorial assembly allocated lands to four specific rail projects:

1. Minnesota & Pacific (Stillwater, St. Paul, St. Anthony, and Minneapolis to Breckenridge with a branch shooting northwestward to the Canadian boundary).

2. Transit (Winona, Rochester, and St. Peter westward to the Big Stone River).

3. Root River & Southern Minnesota (La Crescent to Rochester—connection with Transit—and St. Paul, St. Anthony, Minneapolis, and Shakopee as well as Mankato—connecting with Transit again—to Iowa near the mouth of the Big Sioux River).

4. Minnesota & Cedar Valley (Minneapolis southward to the Iowa border).

"Minnesota wants these roads commenced at once," demanded the *Frontiersman* at Sauk Rapids. It would not be that easy. Lands given by the federal government to the territory and then reallocated to private railroad concerns to encourage construction certainly were attractive but quite insufficient in and of themselves. Huge sums of investor capital also would be required. Money in such amounts was always scarce and always competitive—a problem severely exacerbated by the Panic of 1857, which put a chill on nearly all western railroad projects. Railroad construction in Minnesota "commenced at once" would be delayed accordingly.[10]

Finally, however, but ever so gradually it seemed to Minnesotans, the railroad age unfurled in their state. Private bankers and other investors continued to take careful note of the high cost of railroad construction everywhere and were predictably skeptical of overly optimistic schemes from developmental roads popping up across the broadening western frontier. Minnesota was no exception. Monied interests in the East and abroad also understandably favored established companies that had passed the entrepreneurial stage. Moreover, during the Panic of 1857 and throughout the awful years of civil war and even thereafter, investment capital remained scarce compared to demand and expensive as a result. Eventually, though, a combination of government land grants and private investment ended the lengthy gestation. Utterly frustrated with rail organizations to which land earlier had been given without precipitating

---

FACING PAGE: Industrial potential at the Falls of St. Anthony was already tapped as the Panic of 1857 eased. A substantial bridge linked St. Anthony with Hennepin Island. Photograph by Beal's Gallery; courtesy of the Minnesota Historical Society.

RIGHT: The *William Crooks* and a short train of cars introduced the age of railways to both St. Paul and St. Anthony.

construction, the Minnesota legislature forthwith took claim to the rights and privileges of those companies under foreclosure and sale, if only on a temporary basis without outright cancellation of such benefits. In the shakeout that followed, one of the grantees, Minnesota & Pacific, regained its authority, stumbled again, and was redefined as the St. Paul & Pacific Railroad. Armed with a handsome grant of land, this high-sounding concern finally recruited requisite capital, and on June 28, 1862, its *William Crooks*, a resplendent American Standard locomotive, puffed exuberantly away from a crude little depot next to Phalen Creek in St. Paul with a few cars bound for end-of-track, an open bit of prairie on the east bank of the Mississippi River about ten miles to the northwest, just short of the falls at St. Anthony. As the diminutive train ambled haltingly down a shaky track, its engine crew waved eagerly to joyous onlookers as the locomotive's whistle sent out melodious reports boldly proclaiming a new era for Minnesota. The steamcar civilization finally had arrived.[11]

St. Paul, from which this pioneer train had just departed, quickly emerged as the region's premier urban center. In 1841, Father Lucian Galtier had blessed a humble log structure and named this "basilica" after St. Paul, "the apostle of nations." It implied much.

After all, the new but raw community stood at the head of navigation on the Mississippi, trade—even with the future Dominion of Canada—centered there, and St. Paul would become the capital of the territory and then the state. In 1850, its population stood at 850; in 1855, it grew to 4,040; and by 1860, 10,600 persons claimed residence there.[12]

St. Paul was not the sole urban oasis, however. Chief among other contenders were nearby St. Anthony and Minneapolis—both hard by a thundering sixteen-foot cataract on the Mississippi, St. Anthony on the east side, Minneapolis on the west. The army properly recognized the falls as a ready and convenient power source; as early as 1821, the post commander at Fort Snelling had ordered construction of grist and saw mills on the west bank. Soldiers soon

**ABOVE:** In 1862, St. Paul & Pacific's passenger equipment was typical of the time—elementary.

**LEFT:** Nicollet Island, with Minneapolis in the distance. At lower right can be seen St. Paul & Pacific's crude terminal at St. Anthony. Photograph by Benjamin Franklin Upton; courtesy of the Minnesota Historical Society.

were at the business of raising wheat near the fort and logging near at hand and far afield. To be sure, an immense forest stretched northward from the falls into present-day Ontario and Manitoba; in fact, at least two-thirds of Minnesota was overlaid by commercially valuable timber. Most of the remaining third was rolling prairie with rich soil—a marvelous gift of ice age glaciers. And according to conventional wisdom, the plowman followed the axman—in other words, land that produced fine trees would also produce fine crops. Agriculture, went the argument, would follow in the wake of timbering. And the Mississippi with its tributaries represented wonderfully placed natural highways to bring raw materials to the falls for processing; the Mississippi was also a beautiful artery flowing southward to any number of distant markets for value-added products manufactured at the falls.[13]

The focus was on the falls. Franklin Steele had staked a large claim on the east side in 1838 and ten years later paid the government for 332 acres, which he planned to promote. In 1848, Steele completed a dam and sawmill; before the year was out a half-million board feet of lumber produced there failed to meet an insatiable demand. A small grist and flour mill soon took up operation, and in 1854 the first merchant flour milling began. A plat was registered, and in 1855 St. Anthony was incorporated with a population of about three thousand persons.[14]

Across the way, on the west bank, land was part of the Fort Snelling preserve, and development there was slower as a consequence. In 1855 and 1857, however, investors exploited water power on that side. A small settlement of homes, stores, schools, and churches soon dotted the landscape, and in 1855 the town of Minneapolis was platted; about fifteen hundred persons lived there. In the same year, a suspension bridge over the river connected the ephebic communities of St. Anthony and Minneapolis. Together they were destined for a bright future in manufacturing made possible in the early years largely by water power at the falls. But the falls and environs were also a mixed blessing. It irked frontier residents of the two communities that while mother nature had blessed them well with the great falls as a handsome source of natural power, that same

St. Anthony Falls, a thundering sixteen-foot cataract on the Mississippi River, promised a rich future for St. Anthony and Minneapolis in 1863, but the great potential at the falls could be realized only with adequate rail service to move raw materials in and finished products out. Minneapolis, to which St. Anthony soon would be joined, was simply a way station on St. Paul & Pacific, at the end of a stub branch owned by a company whose loyalties lay elsewhere. Photograph courtesy of the Minneapolis Public Library, Minneapolis Collection.

mother nature had played a nasty trick on them by giving the downstream Mississippi a tortuous, crooked, and rock-filled channel defying navigation before broadening and slowing at St. Paul. This required that passengers and freight both move overland to and from rival St. Paul—even in the age of railroads. A downbound train from St. Anthony in April 1863, for example, handled 878 barrels of potatoes and several thousand feet of lumber and shingles—all of which had to be unloaded at St. Paul and then reloaded aboard a waiting steamboat at the levee.[15]

Minnesotans understandably hoped to control their own destinies as to the state's railroad network—to determine what intercommunity or interregional linkages were necessary, to locate specific lines of route, to determine when to start and when to complete them, and to determine financial arrangements. Just as predictably, little of it was in their province. Rather, they would, in large measure, be buffeted and their destinies molded by external forces—often distant, nearly impossible to control, and difficult to influence.

The growing prominence of Milwaukee and Chicago, both impressive port cities on Lake Michigan to the southeast, illustrated the point. Powerful trade ties long had been forged via the Mississippi River between St. Paul and St. Louis; furs, ginseng, cranberries, potatoes, and lumber moved southward, with an array of finished goods arriving from St. Louis. Other river towns downstream from Minneapolis and St. Paul—La Crosse, Dunleith, Dubuque, Rock Island, and Davenport among them—challenged this arrangement to the distress of St. Louis interests; the tide was turning against that place as early as 1850. Rails emanating from Milwaukee but especially from Chicago administered the coup de grâce.

On February 22, 1854, Chicago & Rock Island (C&RI or Rock Island) became the first railroad to link the Great Lakes chain with the Mississippi. Pointed directly toward the new state of Iowa—a lush, well-watered region of untold agricultural potential—the road's Chicago sponsors nevertheless had an even broader expanse in mind. That was reflected in June of the same year when nearly twelve hundred prominent guests from around the country were treated to a gala rail-water excursion from Chicago to Rock Island, temporary end-of-tracks, and on up to St. Paul aboard steamboats. This "grand excursion" was much more than symbolic. Clearly the leaders of Chicago were looking broadly in calculating their plans for further economic imperialism. Those plans were enhanced when Chicago & Rock Island sponsors celebrated the completion of the first bridge over the Mississippi River (linking Rock Island with Davenport) in 1856. Moreover, prominent Chicagoan William B. Ogden urged C&RI to pursue an aggressive three-pronged extension to the interior: to the Southwest, to the West, and to the Northwest. It was a bold plan from the sagacious Ogden, but one that would take time. Meanwhile, the road reached Iowa City in 1856, Des Moines in 1867, and Council Bluffs, on the Missouri River completely across Iowa, in 1869.[16]

Chicago, Burlington & Quincy (CB&Q or Burlington Route) was another early contender that came to be a primary player in heartland railroading. True to its corporate namesake, CB&Q pushed westward from Chicago to Galesburg, Illinois, where one leg tilted southwestward to strike the Mississippi at Quincy, Illinois, and from whence a physical and eventual corporate connection was made with Hannibal & St. Joseph to span northern Missouri. The other leg reached East Burlington, Illinois, and opened service on March 17, 1855; the Mississippi was not bridged by CB&Q until 1868, but a Burlington affiliate inched westward across southern Iowa during the late 1850s and throughout the next decade to reach the Missouri River in 1870.[17]

Yet another Chicago-sponsored aspirant that would loom large in Midwest railroad circles, Chicago & North Western (C&NW or North Western), through a forerunner, reached Fulton, Illinois, across from Clinton, Iowa, in 1855. Soon thereafter another predecessor began construction on the Iowa side of the Mississippi in 1857, and ten years later became the first to span the state—in the process also becoming the first railroad to connect with Union Pacific as part of the great central overland transcontinental route.[18]

Two additional east-west routes soon to be affiliated with Chicago roads likewise pushed away from the Mississippi into Iowa's interior north but parallel to C&NW. One of these, eventually settling under the Illinois Central (IC) flag, began at Dubuque in 1857, reached Cedar Falls in 1861 and Fort Dodge in 1869, and touched the Missouri River at Sioux City in 1870. The other, styled McGregor & Western, lifted itself out of the Mississippi valley in northeastern Iowa at Marquette to tap Calmar in 1866; at that point the route curved tantalizingly northwestward toward Minnesota. In 1869, another leg stretched westward from Calmar to Mason City, but not until 1878 did that the line cross into Dakota Territory.[19]

Each one of these several lines across the Hawkeye state was oriented on an east-to-west axis, and each one finally connected the Mississippi River on the east with the Missouri River on the west. In an earlier era they would have represented land bridges between natural highways—waterways—serving intermediate territory. Raw materials would have flowed to transloading points, and finished goods would have moved outbound—to and from St. Louis, for instance. No more. Iowa by 1870 boasted 2,683 miles of railroad (up from 655 in 1860). All of this mileage served in a farm-to-market fashion, of course, but three primary routes—the main lines of Burlington, Rock Island, and North Western—were also vital segments of the first transcontinental route. There was more. These new channels of transportation—the young nation's vital arteries and veins—had also irreversibly altered market relationships based on steamboat and wagon modes. Every one of the early east–west roads in Iowa was, or quickly became, an integral appendage or extension of a Chicago company. And every one of the Chicago parents shared the same impulses of urban mercantilism or urban economic imperialism. The case of CB&Q was typical. Speaking of the new giant bridge over the Mississippi at Burlington, Charles E. Perkins of that road dryly proclaimed that "besides helping us to transport all freight with greater facility and rapidity, and thereby increasing, probably, our general business . . . it will enable us to carry grain from the line of our road toward Chicago, instead of seeking the St. Louis market. . . ."[20]

Indeed, St. Louis proved the loser. The trend already had been against the Gateway City, and when Confederates blockaded the lower reaches of the Mississippi during the Civil War, St. Louis lost its southern outlet. With Chicago-based railroads in place and with the river closed to the south, business to and from St. Louis withered on the northern Mississippi. The verdict was clear: Chicago was the big winner over St. Louis, and Chicago's weapon of choice was the railroad. Moreover, as one exuberant Chicago booster observed: "And everywhere these iron arms are being rapidly lengthened out." To be sure, rails as a mode of transport scored a salient victory over steamboats.[21]

Chicago's aggressive economic instincts (and Milwaukee's, too) soon would be apparent. Meanwhile, the carnage of civil war finally ended, American industrialization shifted into high gear, emigration

picked up, and capital moved more willingly to the northwest—although never as rapidly as locals would desire. Minnesota's St. Paul & Pacific reflected as much. That premier road, completed in 1862 from St. Paul to St. Anthony and supported by generous land grants, soon bridged the Mississippi River and inched out of Minneapolis with two lines: one northwestward up the east side of the Mississippi to Elk River in 1864 and East St. Cloud in 1866, and the other westward to Howard Lake in 1867–68 and to Willmar in 1869. These two lines were bound for the Red River

St. Paul & Pacific bridged the Mississippi River and then inched out of Minneapolis with two lines reaching west and northwest. This view of Hennepin Avenue from Washington Avenue is from 1869. Note St. Paul & Pacific's bridge in the upper left. Photograph by William W. Wales; courtesy of the Minnesota Historical Society.

valley and served to open huge chunks of domain tributary to St. Paul, St. Anthony, and Minneapolis to one degree or another.[22]

Predecessors of another major player, the future Chicago, Milwaukee & St. Paul, (CM&StP or Milwaukee Road) were active severally in the same years. One of these, Minnesota Central, gradually pushed southward from Mendota toward Faribault, reached in 1865. Stages handled passengers between Mendota and Minneapolis until rails were driven around Fort Snelling to Minneapolis, also reached in 1865. A small frame depot was erected on Second Street, and a roundhouse, machine shop, and car shop quickly appeared nearby. Shortly thereafter Minnesota Central teamed with another pioneer road to open a line from Mendota to St. Paul, thereby creating a dogleg route between Minneapolis and St. Paul plied by a homely commuter train called "Old Peggy." In all of this Minnesota Central created a southern outlet for both Minneapolis and St. Paul—one that grew greatly in importance as the road pressed south through Owatonna and Austin to a junction with the McGregor & Western line in northern Iowa from Marquette to Calmar—in the process forging Minnesota's first rail link with the East over a crescent-shaped route to Milwaukee via Prairie du Chien. (Through service began on October 14, 1867.) Elsewhere, an extension from Milwaukee to Chicago and a new line up the west

FACING PAGE: St. Paul & Pacific crossed the Mississippi River with this newly completed bridge (on the left) over the east channel of the river between Nicollet Island and St. Anthony. This view of St. Anthony from the Winslow House looks up Second Street at what would become northeast Minneapolis. The church in the foreground is the First Universalist Church, now Our Lady of Lourdes Catholic Church. Photograph by Benjamin Franklin Upton; courtesy of the Minnesota Historical Society.

BELOW LEFT: The St. Paul & Pacific terminal at Washington Avenue and Fourth Avenue North, the first passenger station in Minneapolis, was a busy place.

BELOW RIGHT: Milwaukee Road's pioneer stub line into Minneapolis, shown in this view from the 1860s, skirted the escarpment below Fort Snelling after crossing the Minnesota River. Photograph courtesy of the Minneapolis Public Library, Minneapolis Collection.

bank of the Mississippi to St. Paul from La Crosse and La Crescent though the communities of Winona and Hastings, all completed in 1872, taken together with its existing line from Milwaukee to La Crosse, would give Milwaukee Road two strategic options in the vital Chicago–St. Paul-Minneapolis corridor. Additionally, others of Milwaukee's early clients were locking up substantial portions of Minnesota's farm belt—one building westward from La Crosse through the southern part of the state to Austin and Albert Lea toward Dakota Territory, and another moving westward from Hastings on an alignment south of St. Paul and Minneapolis to Chaska and beyond.[23]

One more principal pioneer railroad concern envisioned an operation from St. Paul southwestwardly along the Minnesota River to Mankato and eventual construction or connections to Sioux City and Omaha. St. Paul & Sioux City, ultimately styled Chicago, St. Paul, Minneapolis & Omaha (CStPM&O or Omaha), and headquartered in St. Paul, opened service from the state capital to Shakopee in 1866, to St. Peter in 1868, and to Sioux City in 1872. Other

elements eventually to be associated with the Omaha in Wisconsin joined with powerful Chicago & North Western "in amicable relations of interest and mutual advantage" that, in effect, would grant Chicago-based North Western in 1872 an important through route to St. Paul in close competition with Milwaukee Road.[24]

A company that would connect with the Omaha and one soon to fall into North Western's widening orbit was Winona & St. Peter. This company, in the years 1864-71, completed a line westward from the Mississippi at Winona through Owatonna and Waseca to

---

**BELOW LEFT:** Omaha's early predecessor, Minnesota Valley, operated this homely if completely functional "steam coach" in local service. Photograph courtesy of the Hennepin History Museum.

**BELOW RIGHT:** Milwaukee Road clients locked up substantial portions of Minnesota's farm belt. One of these, Hastings & Dakota, moved westward from the Mississippi River at Hastings on an alignment south of St. Paul and Minneapolis to Chaska and beyond. Photograph ca. 1868 by Benjamin Franklin Upton; courtesy of the Minnesota Historical Society.

the Minnesota River at St. Peter before stretching out in 1873 to Lake Kampeska in Dakota Territory.[25]

Elsewhere, dreamers and schemers long had recognized that the Head of the Lakes would one day emerge as an important point for transportation devices, and reflecting as much, the Minnesota territorial assembly in the 1850s had chartered the Nebraska & Superior Railroad. It was not until the war years, however, that work began, if haltingly, under the banner Lake Superior & Mississippi Railroad (LS&M).[26]

Of all aspiring enterprises bearing on Minnesota, none held more allure or drew more attention here and abroad than did Northern Pacific (NP), chartered by Congress on July 2, 1864, with authority to construct a line of road all the way from Lake Superior to Puget Sound. Despite a colossal land grant, which the *Boston Transcript* called "a territorial kingdom," great uncertainty surrounded the enterprise. Beginning and end points were not precisely defined, the entire route was through an unsettled wilderness with much of it in harsh climes and difficult terrain, and potential traffic was problematic. The charter was held by a syndicate of important investors representing several eastern roads, but the project languished until Philadelphia financier Jay Cooke took personal interest. Cooke and associates also invested in properties in and about Duluth, assuring, in effect, that it would become the eastern terminus of NP. Ground would not be broken until February 15, 1870, at Thompson Junction, near the Dalles of the St. Louis River on Lake Superior & Mississippi, twenty-four miles west of Duluth. (NP acquired use of LS&M trackage into and out of Duluth, thus avoiding unnecessary duplication.) Construction would take rails westward to Brainerd in 1870 and then toward the Red River valley.[27]

So the railroad era had finally come to Minnesota, a greatly changed place since statehood in 1858. More than any other single factor, railroads altered the essential fabric of the youthful state. They quickly became the state's first big business, requiring massive infusions of cash and labor, and consequently gave rise to all sorts of business, commerce, and industry. In short, they provoked opportunity. In 1858, there had not been 1 mile of railroad serving the

Great allure surrounded Northern Pacific. In 1869 an NP "exploring expedition" headed west down Washington Avenue. Photograph courtesy of Burlington Northern Santa Fe.

new state's 150,000 citizens; during the 1860s, however, 766 miles of line were completed, and Minnesota's population mushroomed to 434,706.[28]

Of the total Minnesota population, 20,300 persons lived in the capital city of St. Paul. But just as importantly, St. Paul had also become the state's transportation capital—its hub, with spokes of water and rail heading to important mercantile centers and to a broad hinterland.[29]

By comparison, Minneapolis and St. Anthony had a combined population of 18,079, but they claimed only marginal transportation services, and these, city leaders testily admitted, had a distinctly St. Paul flavor. St. Anthony had served briefly as end-of-track for St. Paul & Pacific, but that road soon scurried off west and northwest. In addition, a Milwaukee Road predecessor had driven a spur up from Mendota on the original St. Paul–Milwaukee route in 1865 to

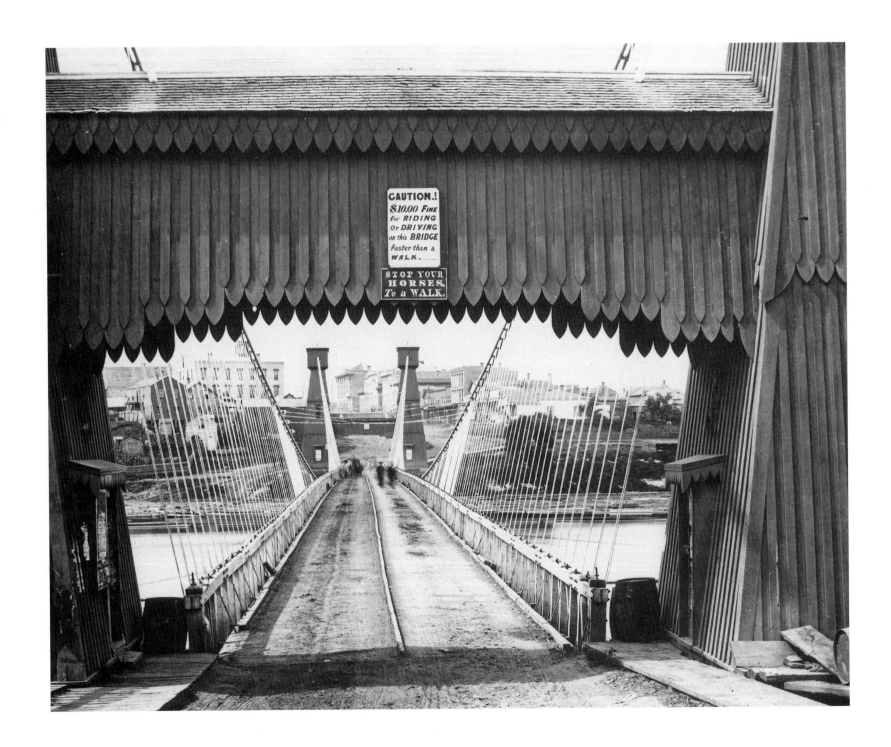

tap Minneapolis. These companies as well as the Omaha and LS&M all focused on St. Paul; St. Anthony and Minneapolis, by comparison, were mere way stations on one road, and Minneapolis was at the stub end of another's branch.[30]

Compared to St. Paul's early advantages as head of navigation on the Mississippi and capital of the territory and then state, St. Anthony and Minneapolis had offered little to entice railroad interests. And their leaders had not been bold in this regard. All of that was finally changing. The collective value of manufacturing at the falls in 1870 was an impressive $6.8 million. Lumber led in value, followed by flour; foundries, machine shops, and textile mills contributed to a mixed economy. So did wholesale firms, the professions, service companies, and retail shops. Hats, caps, and boots were available, for instance, at Gent's Furnishing Goods, while bonnets of the "latest styles and fashions" could be found at Mille Dorchester's Millinery Depot. Travelers might especially be attracted to the "renovated and refurbished" Nicollet House, which proudly advanced itself as a "first class hotel."[31]

Minneapolis, to which St. Anthony soon would be officially joined, had much to be proud of as the 1870s dawned. Nevertheless, its one conspicuous shortcoming was yet to be satisfactorily addressed: what it needed, and needed desperately, were railroads and more railroads—forged and owned locally, tightly focused on the needs of Minneapolis industry and commerce, and certainly not pets of St. Paul nor powerful economic tentacles of far-off Milwaukee and Chicago.

---

FACING PAGE: The suspension bridge across the Mississippi, completed late in 1854, was the first to span that river. This photograph, taken from Nicollet Island, looks toward the west bank and Minneapolis. Photograph courtesy of the Minnesota Historical Society.

RIGHT: The elegant Nicollet House suggested that Minneapolis was on the cusp of great development—if the city could satisfy its transportation needs.

# Nicollet House

MINNEAPOLIS, - - MINNESOTA.

## F. S. GILSON & CO.,
Proprietors.

Rates Reduced to $2.00, $2.50 and $3.00 per Day, According to Location of Rooms.

By this popular plan the public can avail themselves of First-Class Accommodations at a Moderate Price.

THE LARGEST AND BEST FURNISHED HOTEL IN THE NORTHWEST

**ROOMS ARRANGED FOR FAMILIES.**

Has all Modern Improvements, including Gas, Hot and Cold Water, Bath Rooms, etc.

Centrally Located, one block from the Post Office, and but four from either Railroad Depot, and at the Junction of all Street Railways.

**THE ONLY FIRST-CLASS HOUSE IN THE CITY.**

THE COMMERCIAL TRAVELERS' HEADQUARTERS.

# LATE TO THE PARTY

2

*. . . a Minneapolis road . . . controlled by the citizens of this place, and kept from the hands of outside parties.*

*MINNEAPOLIS TRIBUNE*, FEBRUARY 11, 1870

It was between the presidential administrations of William Henry Harrison and Warren G. Harding, roughly 1840 to 1920, that the United States was transformed from a decentralized agrarian republic into an urban and industrial nation. During those short eight decades a precipitous change occurred in the process of production and distribution. Moreover, value added by manufacture rose 76 percent from 1849 to 1859, and 25 percent from 1859 to 1869, and leaped an astonishing 82 percent between 1869 and 1879. These dramatic changes were driven, in large part, by the availability of coal as an inexpensive and flexible source of energy and by the new railroad technology that provided rapid, calculated, and all-season transport.[1]

Not surprisingly, the modern factory concept with large numbers of workers managed or supervised in central shops—an essential element in the new order—was pioneered in New England by textile manufacturers and by the Springfield Armory. Inexpensive coal in substantial quantities likewise served the needs of pig iron producers, which enjoyed a 100 percent increase in volume during the brief period 1865–70. And together with inexpensive iron, coal allowed the factory system to spread into numerous metal-working industries. Coal further provided fuel necessary in other basic industries such as refining and distilling, while also generating steam power necessary in fabricating and other manufacturing plants. Railroads could and did deliver this coal and other basic materials, and railroads could and did carry away a prodigious output from these factories. As historian Alfred D. Chandler put it, "the almost simultaneous availability of an abundant new form of energy and revolutionary new means of transportation and communication led to the rise of modern business enterprise in American commerce and industry." Mass production, of course, required mass consumption, with railroads and the telegraph as twin maidens providing the essential transportation and communication linkage. Predictably, sites of mass production and mass consumption were cities; just as predictably, the growth of cities and the dramatic expansion of the American railroad network led to creation of large, vertically integrated business concerns.[2]

Those same industries in those same cities needed at once a massive labor force and a massive body of consumers. Much of the

Lumber milling at St. Anthony Falls dated from territorial days. By 1870, the aggregate value of production on both sides of the stream was $4.3 million, and the mills employed three thousand men—all good news for railroad companies that could carry lumber from the falls and return with inbound wheat. Photograph ca. 1870; courtesy of the Minneapolis Public Library, Minneapolis Collection.

population was made up of emigrants from northern and western Europe who had studied carefully the relative opportunities before them in native lands compared to opportunities existing at the same time in the United States. The cost of oceanic passage might have circumscribed their options in an earlier day, but increased numbers of iron-hulled, steam-powered vessels in the trans-Atlantic trade beginning in the 1850s and accelerating thereafter changed all that through expanded capacity, faster turnaround times, and reduced dwell time. For aspiring emigrants it all meant a greatly reduced tariff. Annual average arrivals of immigrants to the United States for the period 1856–60 was 169,958; the Civil War predictably reduced that number, but for the first five postwar years numbers increased to 302,620 per annum. The federal government and to a much greater extent the various states, railroad companies, and steamship lines encouraged immigration. Official encouragement from Minnesota, for example, began during territorial days and continued under state auspices; several Minnesota railroads also levied impressive campaigns to populate the state with a hearty and industrious people. Much of their effort was directed to the outlands and agriculture, but the carriers were also interested in the towns and cities. The lumbering and flouring mills at the Falls of St. Anthony, for example, especially needed a workforce adequate to a surging demand.[3]

Marvelous stands of white pine had characterized a huge domain stretching eastward from Maine; Minnesota was the final outpost. No other tree was so highly prized in the production of dimension lumber—wood that was straight, strong, even-grained, and receptive to paint. Commercial interest in regional forests predated even territorial days and was reflected in a treaty dating from 1837 when one band of Ojibway ceded a giant chunk of prairie woodlands to the federal government. The first sawmill in the future state began operation two years later. Much of the early production sought a St. Louis market, right down the St. Croix and Mississippi waterways.[4]

It was Franklin Steele who envisioned the movement of pine logs from the upper Mississippi and especially its Rum River tributary to the falls at St. Anthony for milling. He had staked an early claim on the east bank of the falls, perfected that claim in 1848, and then placed a mill at that location. Other mills followed on both sides of the cataract; in 1856, there were six of them, producing 12 million board feet of lumber annually. Four years later they collectively employed 1,146 men. In 1862, millers on the St. Anthony side alone turned out 28.1 million board feet of lumber, 15.2 million shingles, and 4.5 million lath. By 1870, the aggregate value of

By 1870, thirteen mills at the falls produced 193,000 barrels of flour valued at $1.125 million. Of the several independent merchant mills, easily the most impressive were those owned by C. C. Washburn. This view is of the interior of Washburn's "A" Mill, ca. 1874. Photograph by William H. Jacob; courtesy of the Minnesota Historical Society.

production on both sides of the stream was $4.3 million, and the mills employed 3,000 men. Among those who invested in or became actual entrepreneurs in lumber milling at the falls were R. P. Russell, Isaac Atwater, Henry Titus Welles, R. J. Mendenhall, W. W. Eastman, J. R. Sidell, and William D. Washburn.[5]

Many of these same men were likewise involved in flour milling. Minnesota's settling and filling-in process moved generally from southeast to northwest, typically along water traces such as the Mississippi, St. Croix, and lower Minnesota. So, too, did the wheat culture spread northwestward to Minnesota, following a path from Illinois, Wisconsin, and Iowa. Earliest milling at the falls was by the government in 1823 to provide for the troops at Fort Snelling, but it was not until 1851 that the first grist and merchant flour mill was established on the east bank. The frenetic Franklin Steele became a partner in that enterprise a year later. But local growers could not supply an adequate flow of wheat, and the shortage required expensive imports from down river to satisfy an increased demand for flour—fueled mostly by a growing work force in the burgeoning local lumber industry. Nevertheless, some Minneapolis flour was shipped to eastern markets as early as 1858.[6]

The production of wheat in the countryside and flour milled at the falls accelerated in the 1860s. Spurred by local, national, and even international demand and coupled with a maturing rail network providing reliable transport, midwestern farmers turned increasingly from subsistence to commercial farming with wheat as the primary cash crop. It was everywhere in demand. In Minnesota, the percentage of tilled area sown to wheat grew to nearly 54 in 1860 and to 62 in 1868. A significant portion of this increased production moved to the falls, where 30,000 barrels of flour were milled in 1860, growing to 98,000 barrels in 1865. And there was profit in the manufacture of flour. Capital investment to increase production and management talent to organize larger enterprises came from lumbermen such as John S. Pillsbury, Curtis H. Pettit, William P. Ankeny, John Martin, William D. Washburn and his brother Cadwallader C. Washburn, as well as from others, Paris Gibson and William W. Eastman among them.[7]

By 1870, thirteen mills at the falls operated by as many firms produced 193,000 barrels of flour valued at $1.125 million. Of the several independent merchant mills, easily the most impressive was that owned by C. C. Washburn. Active in logging and lumbering before the Civil War, Washburn emerged from that conflict with an admirable military record and then turned his interests to flour milling and politics. "Washburn B," six stories in height with a daily capacity of 800 barrels—said to be the largest west of Buffalo—opened in 1867. Operated for two years under contract by Judd & Brackett, the enterprise failed in 1869. Many local observers believed the venture had been doomed simply because of its prodigious size; supplying a constant flow of grain to its eager millstones was admittedly a problem.[8]

Flour milling centers had moved westward across the new nation with the wheat culture; Richmond, Virginia, then Rochester, New York, and finally St. Louis, Missouri, held distinction as the largest milling center. St. Louis, of course, claimed a huge hinterland served by the Mississippi, Ohio, Illinois, and Missouri rivers, and even some of Minnesota's early wheat production moved to milling at St. Louis and then downstream as flour to various southern destinations. That pattern was jolted by the Civil War and then severely truncated by rails emanating from Chicago and Milwaukee, where railroad companies and others built, owned, and operated multistoried, steam-powered elevators with holding capacity of thousands of bushels in vertical bins. Aided by telegraphic communication, com-

Minneapolis was served only by St. Paul & Pacific, which had scurried off west and northwest, and by a mere stub of Chicago, Milwaukee & St. Paul, which reached the city with a route that skirted the base of Fort Snelling.

FORT SNELLING, MINNESOTA, ON THE CHICAGO, MILWAUKEE AND ST PAUL R. R.

modity exchanges such as the Chicago Board of Trade, founded in 1848, were established to facilitate the acquisition or sale of grain in transit or yet in the field. Even before Chicago-based rails reached Minnesota, grain from the area had moved to that place by water and then rail via Rock Island (Chicago & Rock Island), Fulton (Chicago & North Western), and Dunleith (Illinois Central). Cars with inbound grain arriving at Chicago were loaded with lumber and finished goods for the interior—loads in both directions, a formula for financial success favoring Chicago and its railroads alike.[9]

Milwaukee interests were no less advocates and practitioners of this type of urban mercantilism. Carriers from that city along with their Minnesota surrogates had an early and commanding presence via La Crosse and Prairie du Chien. Nearly all wheat that moved eastbound from Minnesota during the 1860s and well into the 1870s flowed to storage elevators or reshipment at Chicago or Milwaukee, the latter the strongest buyer until 1875.[10]

All of this was vexing and even hurtful to flour millers—and even lumber millers by indirection—at St. Anthony Falls and Minneapolis. The growing power and influence of railroads and grain handlers based in Milwaukee and Chicago at the same time irritated farmers in southeastern Minnesota, who complained of heavy tariffs and high storage charges for wheat moving eastbound. Some who criticized the arrogance of Milwaukee and Chicago actually urged returning to river transport via St. Louis as a means to counteract the power of the lake ports. Indeed, in 1865, after the Civil War ended, much of the Iowa and Minnesota crop did move that way. Even the *Chicago Tribune* complained that Illinois-based railroads were overcharging and thus driving business down the Mississippi River away from Lake Michigan. Closer to home, the *Minneapolis Tribune* counseled in favor of steamboats to defend against what it labeled railroad monopoly.[11]

Flour and lumber interests at the falls were not convinced as to steamboats, however. Rather, more railroad service, they slowly came to believe, was the right and proper remedy to satisfy their needs. But the *Minneapolis Tribune* for January 7, 1868, incomprehensibly blustered that Minneapolis was already "the acknowledged railroad center of the upper Mississippi and the state." Balderdash. The *Tribune* was simply engaging in a bit of journalistic schizophrenia that was typical of the time, boasting of something that did not exist as a camouflage to hide inadequacy. In reality, rail service at Minneapolis was modest in the extreme, and none of it emanated from or focused on that community. St. Paul & Pacific had built to St. Anthony and then through Minneapolis to the west and northwest; Minneapolis was served only by a spur from the pioneer St. Paul-to-Milwaukee line (CM&StP); Lake Superior & Mississippi had studiously avoided both St. Anthony and Minneapolis in choosing St. Paul as its southern outpost from Duluth; and St. Paul & Sioux City had likewise ignored the two communities at the falls. In short, Minneapolis remained only a way station on a through route and at the end of a stub branch.[12]

It was downstream rival St. Paul, the state capital, rising high on bluffs above the Mississippi at its head of navigation, that truly was "the acknowledged railroad center," or as one chronicler put it, "the point where merchandise is concentrated and distributed, where great railroad systems meet and connect, and where travel halts and is transferred." Minnesota's governor echoed this view: "St. Paul is the railroad and commercial center of Minnesota just as New York is for the whole country. . . ." The city's population had doubled during the 1860s to twenty thousand; it possessed a Roman Catholic cathedral, an opera house, the new Metropolitan Hotel, and three vigorous newspapers; and in addition to several regularly scheduled intercity passenger trains, St. Paul boasted three daily turns to its "enterprising suburbs," St. Anthony and Minneapolis. What explained St. Paul's primacy in railroads? The answer, said one observer, was clear: "The sagacious merchants and businessmen of the city perceived at an early day the supreme importance of promoting by all practical means the construction of these highways of commerce and possessing the courage, they did not hesitate at critical periods of its history to employ all the resources of private capital and public credit, to secure for St. Paul the prestige of becoming the railway center of the northwest. . . ." His analysis was in equal parts hyperbole and truth, but it did invite invidious comparison with the

leadership of both St. Anthony and Minneapolis—neither of which measured up to St. Paul in terms of rail service.[13]

Their pride wounded, leaders at the falls glared enviously downstream at St. Paul and continued to grumble about that city's advantages and at the diversion of wheat from what they perceived their "natural territory" to Milwaukee and Chicago. Diversion to eastern points meant, of course, that Minnesota-grown wheat was competitive and that local millers had to pay a premium for what they got. And as millers at the falls increased their capacity beyond local flour requirements, they were forced to seek alternative and distant markets for their product. This, in turn, meant that for the first time they were compelled to pay close attention to the matter of rates on transportation. What they found pleased them not at all. Railroads based at the Lake Michigan ports of Milwaukee and Chicago set very clear policies of discrimination *in favor* of those communities and *against* all others. St. Louis already had learned that harsh if predictable lesson. Said one senior manager at Chicago, Burlington & Quincy, ". . . railroad men have every inducement to advance the development of the country which their line traverses." Said another, "We are always desirous of shaping our tariff so as to build up the prosperity of those who build up our prosperity."[14]

The crunch came in the late 1860s when Milwaukee interests engaged in a series of nasty strong-arm tactics. Concerned that Minnesota wheat and flour would move eastward via Duluth if or when rail linked the Mississippi with Lake Superior, Milwaukee Road hired wheat buyers along its own lines and those of surrogates and gave them instructions to pay upward of ten cents a bushel over

Minneapolis prices. The purpose was twofold: to drive wheat toward company-owned or favored elevators in the city of Milwaukee and to delay or even stop construction of the Lake Superior & Mississippi between St. Paul and Duluth. Flour interests at the falls had to face a grim reality: they were sadly dependent on "foreign" railroads that had the power and ability to strangle them by rendering their investments valueless.[15]

A curious mixture of fear and determination slowly but finally combined to mobilize leaders in Minneapolis and St. Anthony. Milwaukee's arrogant and bullying tactics brought gloomy visions of bankruptcy to local millers, but fortunately those same rough tactics occurred during a period of general optimism at home and across the nation. Commercial activity was abundant, venture capital was available, the tide of emigration was rising, and hundreds of miles of railroad were either planned or being built. St. Paul railroad leader James J. Hill, for example, later would recall the period as one of "feverish activity." Indeed, railroad expansion and building construction drove the entire domestic economy, and railroads swiftly came to dominate national corporate finance. During the 1860s the country's mileage increased from 30,635 to 52,914 with growth in

FACING PAGE: The turntable at Milwaukee Road's passenger facility in downtown Minneapolis obliquely stated reality: the city was at the end of a mere branch operated by an important but "foreign" rail carrier. Photograph courtesy of the Minnesota Historical Society.

ABOVE RIGHT: St. Paul & Sioux City propelled a diagonal route from the state's capital city into northwestern Iowa, an important artery that, to the everlasting consternation of Minneapolis advocates, avoided the Mill City. StP&SC reached St. Peter, Minnesota, in 1870. Photograph courtesy of the Minnesota Historical Society.

1868 and 1869 especially dramatic. In Minnesota, railroad mileage increased from 210 in 1865 to 766 at the end of the decade—impressive but inadequate to the needs of Minnesota's 439,706 citizens and certainly inadequate for lumber and flour millers at the falls, who reluctantly but finally vowed to seek a means of thwarting the lusting tentacles of Milwaukee and Chicago.[16]

Timing seemed propitious. As it developed, their campaigns, their dreams, and their desires would comingle with campaigns, dreams, and desires of others in Missouri and Iowa. For instance, St. Louis, smarting acutely at Chicago's recent good fortune, looked northward to Iowa and pledged support for an assortment of

north–south rail propositions that might be linked in some way to the Gateway City. To that end they agitated for an iron appendage reaching from Burlington, on the Mississippi in southeastern Iowa, at an angle but parallel to flowage of the Iowa and then Cedar rivers, to Iowa City, Cedar Rapids, Waterloo, and on—perhaps to St. Paul. Part of this alignment included what William B. Ogden a decade earlier had proposed as part of Chicago & Rock Island's potential domain, and in any event portions of the route already had been staked out in 1865 by the Cedar Rapids & St. Paul Railway, which hoped to build up the Cedar Valley, and in 1867 by the Cedar Rapids & Burlington Road, whose backers hoped to link the cities of its namesake to a series of roads projected along the west bank of the Mississippi from St. Louis to Keokuk and Burlington. In 1867 and 1868, New York capitalists concocted a plan to unite the two Iowa companies and blend them in concert with the St. Louis, Rock Island & Chicago Railroad (using CB&Q as a traffic link between Burlington and Monmouth, Illinois), which was then contemplating a vertical-axis route in Illinois from East St. Louis to Rock Island. Nothing came of this corporate amalgam, but the St. Louis-through-Iowa-to-St. Paul dream persisted. Meanwhile, the two Iowa roads were combined with new articles of incorporation to bring forth the Burlington, Cedar Rapids & Minnesota Railway (BCR&M), which initially projected an angular line from Burlington to Cedar Falls, splitting there with one leg going on to Waverly and Charles City to a terminal in Minnesota at Austin, and with the other leg running through Mason City to Mankato. The eastern leg would connect at Austin with CM&StP for St. Paul and Minneapolis, while the western extension would meet St. Paul & Sioux City for a connection to St. Paul. In fact, BCR&M would complete its line from Burlington through Cedar Rapids (missing Iowa City) to Cedar Falls in

A curious mixture of fear and determination slowly but finally combined to mobilize leaders in Minneapolis and St. Anthony. The suspension bridge over the river between the two communities proclaimed confidence in the future. Photograph ca. 1868 by William Henry Illingworth; courtesy of the Minnesota Historical Society.

1870–71 and on to Plymouth Junction (short of Austin and far short of Mankato but hard by the Iowa-Minnesota boundary) in 1872.[17]

Another consortium of interests from Iowa and Missouri met in Cedar Rapids in 1865 to form the St. Louis & Cedar Rapids Railway, with which they planned to build a line from the Missouri border to Cedar Rapids. Connecting service to St. Louis would be provided by the North Missouri Railroad, which had been chartered in 1851 with broad powers to strike toward an Iowa connection. The Panic of 1857 and the Civil War prevented early fruition, but in 1868 the Missouri route opened to Coatesville near the state boundary, 236 miles from St. Louis. On the Iowa side, the route bent northeastward to Ottumwa, reached during the summer of 1870, but then fizzled and stubbed at that point, never to reach Cedar Rapids.[18]

Yet another Iowa operation, Cedar Falls & Minnesota, was chartered in 1858 with authorization to build from Cedar Falls to the Minnesota border, about 75 miles. Owners did some grading in 1860 and 1861, and in 1864 the road was leased to an Illinois Central predecessor, the Dubuque & Sioux City, which in the same year completed the line under the Cedar Falls & Minnesota banner to Waverly. By the end of 1869, rails were pushed on to Lyle, Minnesota, 76 miles from Cedar Falls. And in the next year, Milwaukee Road would drive a line southwestward from Austin to Mason City, 40 miles, through Lyle and Plymouth Junction, giving Cedar Falls & Minnesota as well as Burlington, Cedar Rapids & Minnesota northern connections to Austin and on to St. Paul and Minneapolis.[19]

The same Cedar Falls & Minnesota and North Missouri roads were to have been integral elements in what one booster once blithely called "the Grand Trunk Railway of the West," and another breezily labeled "the grandest railroad project of the age." This was the ill-fated Iowa Central Railroad, which pledged to link up with North Missouri on the south and Cedar Falls & Minnesota plus Minnesota Central (the Milwaukee predecessor between St. Paul and Austin) on the north to create "the new trinity—Minnesota, Iowa, and Missouri." Chartered in 1865, Iowa Central's local boosters saw in it a means by which to bypass Chicago and circumvent the increasingly powerful Chicago-based horizontal-axis roads, a means to tap St. Louis as an alternative or competitive outlet, and a means to funnel Iowa coal to northern markets and Minnesota lumber to Iowa consumers. Cooperation and assistance seemed sure among several parties. The president of Minnesota Central said that a connection with Iowa Central was "regarded as one of the first importance." Minnesota Governor William R. Marshall gave similar assurances on behalf of his state, and a resolution passed by North Missouri's board of directors pledged aid because they saw Iowa Central "as one of the most important railway enterprises to St. Louis." In fact, North Missouri expected to help—and to profit from business delivered to and received from—both Iowa Central and St. Louis & Cedar Rapids at the Iowa border. Several factors militated against the Iowa Central venture, however, and in the end it perished like so many other "paper railroads" of the time.[20]

Ever so curiously, it was not Iowa Central *Railroad* but rather a most humble operation that eventually metamorphosed into the Iowa Central *Railway* to become an essential north–south artery in the heartland. It was the presence of coal banks in the valley of the Iowa River in Hardin County that prompted organization of the Eldora Railroad & Coal Company early in 1866 for the purposes of extracting that coal and operating a road from Eldora through the coal beds to Ackley, 16 miles north, where traffic could be interchanged with the newly built Dubuque & Sioux City, soon to be leased to Illinois Central. During the summer of 1868, the Eldora Railroad & Coal Company dissolved to become the more important Iowa River Railway with power to extend down the Iowa River valley to Marshalltown and beyond. Rails reached Marshalltown in 1869, but in the next year further corporate reorganization resulted in the Central Railroad Company of Iowa, which integrated existing properties from Ackley through Eldora to Marshalltown, and in 1871 would extend the road from Marshalltown through Grinnell and Oskaloosa to Albia, one county short of Missouri, and from Ackley northward to Mason City, Manly, and Northwood, 4 miles shy of Minnesota, at the point of a triangle, southeast of Albert Lea and southwest of Austin.[21]

Henry Titus Welles and William Drew Washburn among others at the Falls of St. Anthony studied the changed and changing railroad maps of Missouri and Iowa and scrutinized wild rumors and mature plans in those parts to discover any that might provide advantage for St. Anthony and Minneapolis. They had followed with interest efforts of Cedar Falls & Minnesota promoters but were dismayed when that property fell to the clutches of those associated with Chicago-based Illinois Central, and they had watched with mixed emotions as Iowa Central Railroad blossomed only to wither. They were uncertain as to intentions and financial conditions of the distant but potentially important North Missouri and its St. Louis supporters, and they were pleased to see Burlington, Cedar Rapids & Minnesota crews bring that road from southeast Iowa to the north-central boundary of that state. Yet they wondered as to BCR&M loyalties and traffic alliances with Chicago roads it connected or crossed. Of particular interest to them was the emerging Central Railroad Company of Iowa. Surely, they concluded, a combination of symbiotic interests could be welded in a way as to simultaneously advance individual and collective purposes in Iowa, Missouri, and at the falls.[22]

What of their own intentions? Leaders at the falls were frankly late to the party—they were tardy at the national building frenzy. But they were not absent. In the summer of 1869, W. D. Washburn dickered for control of St. Paul & Sioux City, but that proved too big a bite. Moreover, Washburn and friends learned a hard lesson.

The view from the Winslow House in St. Anthony showed a bustling lumber milling enterprise on the lower part of Nicollet Island with a burgeoning Minneapolis in the background. Photograph courtesy of the Minnesota Historical Society.

None of them as individuals and not all of them as a group had the financial wherewithal adequate to sponsor their own railroad projects. And while venture capital was available, there was great competition for it among a host of candidates near and far. And it was expensive. Iowa promoters, for example, had found adequate financing for the Eldora "plug" only among monied persons in Baltimore. Nearby rival St. Paul had struggled mightily before securing life-giving financial sustenance from Philadelphia banking houses for the Lake Superior road, and as one authority noted, "St. Paul & Pacific would have been stuck on the Minnesota prairies without the millions from Amsterdam." High cost of construction coupled with the initial paucity of traffic on developmental railroads gave investors distinct pause, but Washburn and the others were confident that the several businesses at the falls could provide a substantial and growing base of traffic that would offset risk.[23]

With that in mind, and motivated further by irritation with high-handed treatment by Milwaukee interests, Welles and Washburn finally took action. A rail outlet to Lake Superior, they concluded, was absolutely essential; in fact, C. C. Washburn had entertained the idea of such a road from Hudson, on the St. Croix River east of St. Paul, to Bayfield, Wisconsin, as early as 1865. Nothing came of it. Then, when Lake Superior & Mississippi was being formed, the Washburns and associated others expended great energy to make St. Anthony the southern terminus of that road. That failed, too. And now, lacking wherewithal to build a largely parallel (and duplicative) line, W. D. Washburn and Welles (soon joined by others) argued for a short but direct connection from the falls to the Lake Superior & Mississippi above St. Paul, in that way establishing linkage with the Great Lakes chain. At the same time they pledged themselves to another line of road striking southward from the falls.[24]

During late summer of 1869 several prominent men of the area were summoned to the office of Franklin Steele, the now aging entrepreneur who had been president of the Minnesota Western Rail Road, moribund since 1854. In short order they agreed to dust off that old charter and to seek permission from the Minnesota legislature to form a new company or new companies adequate for their needs. All of it was accomplished in 1869 and 1870 when the legislature authorized the Minneapolis & St. Louis Railroad (M&StL) with rights to build and operate a line from some point on the Lake Superior & Mississippi through Minneapolis to the Iowa boundary. Even before this authority was given, W. D. Washburn pledged considerable personal support for the enterprise and purchased substantial properties for terminal facilities and trackage to and about the mills on the west bank of the falls that would give M&StL sole entrance. The first board of directors was a "who's who" of leadership at the falls: Henry T. Welles (president), William D. Washburn, John S. Pillsbury, R. J. Baldwin, R. P. Russell, W. W. McNair, Isaac Atwater, and Levi Butler. That fine directory, boasted the *Minneapolis Tribune*, made the business "a Minneapolis road . . . controlled by the citizens of this place, and kept from the hands of outside parties." These men, said the *Tribune*, most assuredly would keep "the road true to the interests of this city."[25]

# Of Champagne and Panic

Upon this enterprise more than any other hangs the future destiny, for good or for evil, of our young city.

W. D. Washburn, 1871

There was not a railroader in the lot. Membership on Minneapolis & St. Louis's initial board of directors—all local men—included two lawyers (Isaac Atwater and William W. McNair), four bankers (Rufus B. Baldwin, Richard J. Mendenhall, Jacob K. Sidle, and W. P. Westfall), two land dealers (Roswell P. Russell and Henry Titus Welles), one physician (Levi Butler), and six involved in lumber or flour milling (W. P. Ankeny, William W. Eastman, Paris Gibson, John Martin, John S. Pillsbury, and William Drew Washburn). Many were active in more than one line of endeavor, lumber milling and flour milling, for example, and several (Atwater, Baldwin, Butler, McNair, Pillsbury, Washburn, and Welles) had been, were, or would be active politically. Indeed, Atwater served on the Minnesota Supreme Court, Pillsbury was governor of Minnesota, Washburn was elected to the U.S. House of Representatives and then to the Senate, and Welles was mayor of St. Anthony and then president of the Minneapolis town council. The majority were Republicans; only McNair, Mendenhall, Sidle, and Welles were Democrats. All but one had arrived in the 1850s (Russell came as early as 1839), and all but one came from the eastern seaboard (Butler hailed from Indiana).[1]

Henry Titus Welles was M&StL's first president. A native of Connecticut, graduate of Trinity College, and admitted to the bar of Hartford County, Welles had arrived at St. Anthony in 1853. He entered the lumber business but soon gave it up for real estate investment and public service. He was elected mayor of St. Anthony in 1855, later was chosen to head the Minneapolis school board, and in 1863 received the Democratic nomination for governor. With others, Welles saw to erection of the splendid Nicollet House in 1858, and for many years he was president of Northwestern National Bank. Active and enterprising by nature, Welles was recognized for his breadth of view, his keen perception, and his imaginative resourcefulness. He was also known for his Yankee tact but could be counted on to candidly express his views on public policy. This was certainly the case in terms of expanding his adopted city's transportation options.[2]

No less than other leaders at the falls, Welles was dismayed as the railroad revolution seemed to pass by Minneapolis and St. Anthony. Hoping to rectify that circumstance, Welles had sought out E. F. Drake of nearby St. Paul and at that time president of St. Paul & Sioux City (StP&SC). Welles pointed out to Drake that StP&SC had authority and even land grant support for not only its route southwestward from St. Paul but also for a tap line into St. Anthony. Drake seemed to sneer at the notion of even a short stub, and his irritating and arrogant demeanor was offensive. Welles determined to go it alone.[3]

So did William Drew Washburn. Born in Maine, educated at Bowdoin College, member of the bar, he was one of eleven children— one of seven sons[4]—born to Israel and Martha Washburn. In 1857, at the age of twenty-six, he had gone west to make his fortune, setting himself up in the lumber milling business at St. Anthony Falls. He was staked by loans from his brothers, especially Cadwallader, gruff and taciturn, thirteen years his senior. In 1861, President Lincoln appointed him Surveyor General of Minnesota, a position that gave Washburn ample opportunity to apprise himself as to the magnificent potential of the state and to make numerous contacts that would profit him over the years. Elected to the state assembly in 1870, Washburn split his time and talents among public and private interests in a way that later would have been con-

William Drew Washburn would put his own personal stamp on M&StL.

sidered inappropriate but in those years was perfectly normal. His investments expanded in lumber milling and then flour milling at the falls and elsewhere. Mercurial, opinionated, and easily distracted, Washburn nevertheless had an unbounded faith in the future of Minneapolis and the upper Midwest. His boyish enthusiasms were infectious; his convictions became resolute. One example will suffice: a railroad controlled by Minneapolis interests and leading to a Great Lakes outlet, on the one hand, and to the southern part of the state, on the other, was essential to the control of trade. Small wonder that William Drew Washburn took 604 of the first M&StL shares sold. Welles, with only one share, was president; Washburn became vice president; Atwater, secretary; and Baldwin, treasurer; but there was never any doubt that M&StL would be a Washburn operation.[5]

That did not necessarily mean a singularly William Drew Washburn operation; gruff and plainspoken Cadwallader would have much to say about M&StL. Born in 1818, Cadwallader spent his boyhood working on the family farm and at his father's general store when not attending the district school. There would be no college opportunity for him. At the age of twenty-one, he moved west, becoming surveyor for Rock County, Illinois, studying law at Rock Island, and starting practice at Mineral Point, Wisconsin. Industrious, frugal, and self-reliant, Cadwallader Washburn invested in timber lands, got himself elected to Congress, became a general in the Civil War, and built impressive sawmills at La Crosse, Wisconsin. He also had extensive tracts of pine lands in Minnesota and investments at the falls. After the war, milling of flour increasingly captured his interest. "Washburn's folly" or "B Mill"—the largest flouring mill west of Buffalo—began production in 1866 even as he was elected again to Congress. "A Mill," dwarfing "B Mill" in size and paid for out of profits from "Washburn's folly," would commence operation in 1874. But Washburn was not interested simply in volume; he also coveted quality. That, too, would come, if later.[6]

Cadwallader Washburn was increasingly of the belief that railroads were necessary to protect and enhance his Minnesota investments, and he was sympathetic to M&StL's goals and purposes. But he would not become a member of its board of directors until 1876, and he did not involve himself immediately as an investor or in the company's management. That proved the case with others who were willing to give moral support but who were unable or unwilling to subscribe financially. M&StL promoters quickly learned hard lessons that railroads were capital intensive, that capital was expensive, and that private bankers usually chose to avoid risk—preferring to invest in established roads. All of this was reflected in M&StL's minute book late in 1870 when the secretary dolefully recorded that the company was "unable at the present time to advance money" necessary to prosecute construction.[7]

M&StL boosters had to trim sail. Independence of ownership and operation loomed large in their minds, but financial realities militated against them. For a Great Lakes outlet, they grudgingly looked to St. Paul–based Lake Superior & Mississippi. The earliest reflection of desires to link the watersheds of Lake Superior and the Mississippi River by rail was the Nebraska & Lake Superior Railroad, authorized during territorial days. Minnesota Governor Alexander Ramsey had urged the route in 1861. In that year the legislature authorized nearly 700,000 acres of swamp land in support, a $250,000 bonus from St. Paul followed, and a substantial federal land grant before the end of the Civil War added to the venture's attractiveness. Several St. Paul luminaries put their shoulders to the Lake Superior project. Among them were William L. Banning, prominent in Democratic politics and a banker; James Smith Jr., an attorney; Jacob H. Stewart, a physician who served in the state senate; and Robert A. Smith, who arrived in 1853 to serve as private secretary to Territorial Governor Willis A. Gorman, then pursued his own political career and became a banker. These men and a few others "took hold of the enterprise and put in enough money to grade about thirty miles." Then on October 20, 1865, the president of the board, Lyman Dayton, died. It fell to Banning to pick up the pieces, who "after much trouble got some Philadelphian capitalists" to provide funding adequate to complete the line.[8]

Eastern capitalists such as Erastus Corning earlier had taken interest in the venture, but the Panic of 1857, the Dakota Conflict in

Washburn's "A" Mill had a capacity of 1,200 barrels per day, a wonder for its time.

1862, and the Civil War all worked against it. Banning faced a daunting challenge, but J. Edgar Thompson finally showed an interest—a very good omen given Thompson's firm reputation in American railroad circles. Banning then turned his attention to Jay Cooke.[9]

In 1861, Cooke and his brother-in-law, William G. Moorhead, had opened up the new office of Jay Cooke & Company at 114 South Third Street in Philadelphia. Cooke was the dominant member of the firm, but Moorhead was president of the Philadelphia & Erie Railroad and well known. Soon a second office was opened in Washington, DC. Cooke earned the reputation as "financier of the Civil War," but aiding the federal government in those trying years was not his only interest. The "House of Cooke" bought and sold securities for customers on commission, and it also bought some for its own account. This pattern persisted after the war, with Cooke taking a greater interest in railroads, among them North Missouri, with which Central Railroad Company of Iowa hoped to connect. Cooke initially rebuffed Banning's overtures as to Lake Superior & Mississippi, but Banning did arrange for Cooke (and Moorhead) to acquire over 44,000 acres of pine lands around Duluth, with Banning taking a commission on the transaction. Cooke already owned lands in Iowa, Wisconsin, and Minnesota—some he had held since the 1850s—and his interest was further piqued by a trip to the upper Mississippi country during the summer of 1868. Banning again besought him, and this time Cooke agreed to take LS&M bonds, which he then sought to sell in Europe. That effort met no success, but with another Philadelphia-based banking house, E. W. Clarke & Company, the two firms sold over $2.5 million in LS&M bonds at home under a most lucrative arrangement that granted LS&M stock bonuses to the bankers. Moorhead from Cooke's firm and J. H. Clark from another major firm became directors of the road. LS&M's future was firmly hitched to a Philadelphia star.[10]

Superior City was an established settlement, while only a handful of shacks dotted the landscape across the bay. Fate, however, would smile on Duluth. LS&M was authorized a route solely in Minnesota defining its eastern terminal at Duluth, a grant proposal for a Superior City-to-St. Paul route competing with LS&M fell on

hard times, and Cooke took a most active interest in Duluth itself. W. Milnor Roberts, a trusted engineer, told Cooke that commerce to and from the Head of the Lakes was assured and that the inner bays, Superior and St. Louis, constituted one of the greatest natural harbors in the world. Cooke received similar optimistic reports from others and responded by acquiring 40,000 acres of land in and about Duluth. By the summer of 1869, its population may have been one thousand. As one visitor recorded, the place was "ringing with the noise of axes and hammers and saws, and clanking wheels, and flapping boards flung down, and scenes of busy life on every side. Wood choppers are cutting trees, piling sticks and brush, and burning log-heaps clearing the land, not for wheat and potatoes, but for the planting of a city."[11]

All of this was good news for LS&M, if not for local control of that road. Corporate offices were established at 424 Walnut Street in Philadelphia, although Banning remained nominally as president in St. Paul. Membership on the board's executive committee was entirely of Philadelphians, and money flowed regularly from that place for construction purposes. The line from St. Paul to White Bear Lake, 12 miles, opened on October 12, 1868, and another 18 miles, to Wyoming, was placed in service at year's end. The next summer saw nearly two thousand men at work on the line, and English colonizing agents were hired to recruit settlers for LS&M's service area. The line opened to Hinckley, 77 miles north of St. Paul, on January 1, 1870, and on September 15 of that year the entire 155-mile route was officially turned over to operation. Before that, however, special trains, such as that of August 1, headed by the locomotive *W. L. Banning* and bearing among other notables Banning and his family, Chief Justice Salmon P. Chase, and his daughter Kate Chase Sprague, toured the line. Another, late in August, took seven carloads of persons representing St. Paul, Minneapolis, St. Anthony, Stillwater, Hastings, and Red Wing to celebrate what one journalist jubilantly labeled uniting "in the bands of iron wedlock the mightiest river of the nation and the greatest lake of the continent—the 'Father of Waters' and the 'King of the Lakes.'" The same writer waxed eloquent as to the Dalles of the St. Louis River—"one of nature's ruggedest and most romantic scenes"—through which the line passed in its descent from Thompson to Duluth. In fact, the line through the 10-mile gorge required heavy work of cuts and fills with accompanying high and lengthy trestlework attended by a most difficult westbound grade. In all, it was expensive to build and to maintain.[12]

Even as the Philadelphians took control of LS&M in 1869 they sought to expand traffic options. Banning was given terse instruc-

tions to see if bonds of the Minnesota Valley Railroad (soon to be St. Paul & Sioux City) could be acquired, to see if the debt of that company could be paid off and a new mortgage arranged, and to

In 1870, Lake Superior & Mississippi completed its important strategic route between St. Paul and Duluth. Business prospects for the road remained unclear: how much work would there be for the 0-6-0 switcher at Duluth, especially when Lake Superior was icebound? Photograph courtesy of the Minnesota Historical Society.

see if a through route to Sioux City could be consummated under one organization. Combination of Minnesota Valley and LS&M made good sense in terms of traffic, with lumber that could move from the timber-rich environs of LS&M and wheat returning from the expanding agricultural region southwest of St. Paul—loads in both directions.[13]

Like LS&M, St. Paul & Sioux City (née Minnesota Valley) was of local extraction, but inexplicably there was little if any duplicate support in St. Paul for the two roads. Among local players in the St. Paul & Sioux City camp were John S. Prince, who arrived in 1854, became active in lumber milling, real estate, and banking, and served as mayor during the 1860s; A. H. Wilder, who laid up wealth through various undertakings including general contracting; C. H. Bigelow, secretary of St. Paul Fire & Marine Insurance Company; Horace Thompson, a prominent banker; Russell Blakely, leading Republican and operator of freight and staging lines; John L. Merriam, also active in Republican politics and the staging business and eventually in general contracting; and, J. C. Burbank, president of Minnesota Stage Company and future president of St. Paul Fire & Marine. E. F. Drake, who arrived in St. Paul in 1861, quickly became involved in Republican matters and would serve as president of StP&SC. Despite the logic of amalgamating LS&M and StP&SC, it did not happen. For those in charge of LS&M, this failure to gain broader traffic support for their pioneer line to Lake Superior made Minneapolis and proposals of Washburn and crew attractive in the extreme.[14]

Competitive pressures and financial stress at LS&M also worked to bring comity between Philadelphia and Minneapolis. A writer for the *Atlantic Monthly* in 1870 wrote that "civilization is attracted to the line of railroad like steel-filings to a magnet." Beautifully prosaic and marvelously true—depending on time and place. Insofar as it pertained to LS&M's service area, the prognosis was less sanguine. The editor of the *St. Anthony Democrat* groused that the country through which the LS&M line passed was "by no means attractive." Further, he said, "the soil is poor as a general rule, the country flat—often swampy." "So long as the state abounds in good, fertile unsettled lands, this portion will remain comparatively neglected,"

he gloomily predicted. The editor was not completely on the mark, but there was truth in what he said. Except for timber resources, the line would produce little traffic on its own. But the *Atlantic* writer pointed to Minnesota-produced grain, much of which moved out of state to Milwaukee, Chicago, or down the Mississippi, and urged diversion of it to Duluth—tending, as a consequence, "to raise the price of wheat in Minnesota and to lower the price of flour in Boston . . ." while "the great returning tide of Eastern merchandise flowing to the far Northwest will be sure to pass this way." To that end Jay Cooke and friends spent mightily at Duluth to improve the harbor and to provide easy and efficient means of transshipment. Over one hundred men (in the summer of 1870) hurrying to complete a 900,000-bushel grain elevator—Duluth's first—was graphic testimony to Cooke's dream.[15]

None of this was lost on competitors. A rate war had broken out among Mississippi River steamboat interests in 1868 as they moved to combat diversion of traffic by rail, especially to Milwaukee and Chicago. More importantly, LS&M in possible alliance with other local operations excited the active irritation of Lake Michigan port cities, particularly Milwaukee. In a decision that was typical of fledgling roads built ahead of demand, LS&M management immediately adopted a policy of "taking its just proportion of the freight at best obtainable prices," that is, dramatically dropping rates to procure traffic. (In 1871, LS&M would handle an amazing 2.25 million bushels of wheat.) This prompted Milwaukee interests to lower their rates, to which LS&M responded by hauling wheat to Duluth without charge. These chaotic conditions benefited Minneapolis not at all. The Washburns and associates redoubled efforts to secure rail outlets to Lake Superior and to the south that would serve their needs.[16]

Finance remained the bugaboo. Money was tight. The old Minnesota Western was to have received land grant support, but that enterprise had languished, and those rights had been effectively picked up by others. For that matter, public sympathies regarding land grants had ebbed and then stopped. Nevertheless, special legislation did authorize communities to bond themselves in support of rail projects. Interest was especially strong in St. Anthony and

Minneapolis, where newspaper support was general and intense. The *Weekly Democrat* at St. Anthony was typical. If completed, said the *Democrat*, M&StL would be controlled "by our citizens" and "run in the interests of our cities, bringing competition and reducing the tariff on both freight and passengers." Vote in favor of a bond issue was his emphatic advice. Across the way, the editor of the *Minneapolis Tribune* took a similar view, saying that completion of rail outlets to the Great Lakes and to the south were essential "if we are to hold our own; or better than that—win in our race with rival cities and towns in gaining population and wealth." In the end, Minneapolis voted $250,000 in support—1,086 for the measure and 112 against; in St. Anthony, a $50,000 issue failed, mostly because of parochialism that would soon doom that community as an independent entity. Meanwhile, M&StL issued two thousand special shares that were taken by Henry T. Welles and W. D. Washburn to pay for construction of a line northeastwardly from Minneapolis to White Bear Lake, about 14 miles. M&StL's board authorized Welles and Washburn to form a new company, Minneapolis & Duluth Railroad (M&D), to own and operate that line; articles of incorporation were filed on May 16, 1871.[17]

Construction had begun even before legal niceties were in place. By February 1871 the *Minneapolis Tribune* reported one hundred men working on cuts and fills. On the Minneapolis side, M&D would own (with M&StL) trackage securing the mills on the west bank and would gain access to St. Anthony by rights over St. Paul & Pacific's bridge. In July workmen were completing most segments of the road.[18]

Meanwhile, another company, not corporately connected with M&StL or M&D, had planned and completed a line from Stillwater, on the St. Croix River east of St. Paul, northwestward to White Bear Lake, about 13 miles. This company, Stillwater & St. Paul, began service in January 1871, and when M&D would complete its line, the two in combination would afford a direct link to and from Minneapolis via White Bear Lake, avoiding rival St. Paul, would also connect St. Paul with Minneapolis and Stillwater through LS&M, and would provide a through route from Minneapolis and Stillwater to Duluth,

Minneapolis & Duluth, sponsored by M&StL, utilized Lake Superior & Mississippi's facilities at White Bear Lake. Minneapolitans were pleased with the new direct access to Duluth and the Great Lakes chain. Photograph by William Henry Illingworth; courtesy of the Minnesota Historical Society.

linking water (Lake Superior) with water (St. Croix-Mississippi). This was extremely important to Cooke and others who controlled LS&M's destiny because, in addition to their investment in the railroad, they also owned vast properties at Duluth—among them the huge Union Improvement & Elevator Company, which, incidentally, owned satellite elevators at Hastings (on the Mississippi) and Stillwater (on the St. Croix) that now could feed LS&M and the Duluth facilities. Small wonder that Philadelphia-directed LS&M quickly leased Stillwater & St. Paul to become one of its integral parts.[19]

All of this put a broad smile on the faces of Minneapolitans. Indeed, five hundred of them were in an exuberant mood on July 22 as they boarded a special train for the opening run to White Bear Lake and then on down to Stillwater. W. D. Washburn was euphoric. He recalled that a Milwaukee representative had told him that he was "insane" for promoting local railroad ventures, but "this road [M&D]," he exclaimed, "is everything to us." And, he beamed, "It will make Minneapolis the great railroad and commercial center west of Chicago." Welles, too, was expansive. "This connection with Lake Superior," he observed, "puts us upon a par with all other points in the state, and by giving us completed lines of railway, makes us comparatively independent." Regularly scheduled service from Minneapolis to White Bear Lake began on August 7, and beginning ten days later trains would commence and terminate at the "plat-

form of the St. Paul & Pacific Depot." Freight business was handled at the same place initially and would be "forwarded without delay," promised W. W. Hungerford, superintendent.[20]

The profound value to Minneapolis of the newly completed M&D line to White Bear Lake was fully apparent. But that was hardly to slight M&StL—"the St. Louis road." Indeed, said Washburn, "upon this enterprise more than any other hangs the future destiny, for good or for evil, of our young city." Typical boosterism of the time, yes, but Minneapolis did hang its hat on M&StL to provide an independent outlet for its flouring and lumbering interests and to bring a large and predictable flow of wheat from southern Minnesota and northern Iowa. To that end Washburn and Welles had repaired to Mason City, Iowa, early in 1870 to talk with representatives of the Central Railroad Company of Iowa, who pledged to provide a cross-Iowa bridge between M&StL and the North Missouri road.[21]

Meanwhile, M&StL made but measured progress. Chief Engineer Clough suggested a route southwestward from the west bank mills in Minneapolis toward Cedar Lake and beyond. That would require the good humor of and even cooperation from St. Paul & Pacific, which already owned land and operated its line toward Willmar in that corridor. A contract was drawn on May 10, 1871, leasing rights to construct and operate a line parallel to StP&P from near that company's Minneapolis station (Holden Street) to Cedar Lake station. From there Clough's survey continued southwestward through what later became the village of Hopkins, then gingerly down a brow of bluffs into the valley of the Minnesota River through Chaska to a crossing of that stream at Carver, and then more or less south to meet St. Paul & Sioux City's angular line from St. Paul toward northwest Iowa. Bids for grading were solicited in mid-1870, and some heavy work was done yet that year.[22]

The *Minneapolis Tribune* asserted that M&StL would "solve the railroad problem of this city." Indeed, it would, when completed,

M&StL began track laying on August 14, 1871. Before the year was out, rail would reach Carver and slightly beyond, 27 miles from the Falls of St. Anthony. Photograph by Benjamin Franklin Upton; courtesy of the Minnesota Historical Society.

secure "to Minneapolis the railroad supremacy of the state. . . ." None of this was well received by neighboring St. Paul. Neither was it welcome news for St. Paul–based St. Paul & Sioux City nor for railroad interests of Milwaukee, both of which set irritating traps to delay or even derail M&StL. The *Tribune* reported early in 1871 that considerable strife had broken out among property owners along M&StL's proposed route at the southwest edge of the city. It turned out that one very significant parcel was owned by T. A. and H. G. Harrison, both heavily involved with St. Paul & Sioux City. H. G. Harrison also bellowed that the bond issue so recently voted in Minneapolis was without constitutional validity. One alderman saw through that facade, declaring StP&SC's real intent was to "embarrass the business of this city, diverting it to St. Paul. . . ." That barrage died down and finally expired, but another flamed up when Milwaukee and M&StL jousted for position south of the Minneapolis milling district. In the end, M&StL got the better of that contest.[23]

Tracklaying began August 14. Construction already had commenced on a six-stall roundhouse "in the lower part of the city," and on a two-story building containing offices, a passenger station, and a freight house "at the corner of Second and Marshall" streets. On November 14, a special train was run to end-of-track, 1 mile south of Carver, for the purpose of allowing members of the Minneapolis City Council a personal examination of the road prior to issuance of municipal bonds in support. The mood was celebratory, and after lunch sponsored by townspeople of Carver, "a heavy fire from champagne corks was commenced," as one reporter observed. The return trip of 25 miles was made in a mere 55 minutes.[24]

But the great day of celebration was reserved for Saturday, November 25. And what a day it was, with special trains, festivities at Carver and Minneapolis, and speeches ad nauseam. One train, headed by M&D locomotive number one, elegantly bedecked with evergreens and flags, handled eight cars—including a commissary "being well stocked with everything necessary to add spirit to the occasion"—filled with excursionists from Duluth, Stillwater, and Minneapolis to Sioux City Junction, 2.5 miles south of Carver, and return. Meanwhile, another train, this one from rival St. Paul, brought

dignitaries to Minneapolis for a gala bash at Harmonia Hall, "where the ladies of our city had spread," reported the *Tribune*, "a most plenteous and bountiful collation" for about four hundred guests. No fewer than nine toasts followed. It took four full columns in the *Tribune* to relate the exciting events of that day.[25]

There was good reason for local pride. With M&D and M&StL in place, Minneapolis had "passed the years of infancy and adolescence," crowed one city journalist, "and now rejoices like a strong man to run a race—is no longer dependent, no longer 'suburban,' but stands up in the full vigor of conscious strength, able and willing to assert his qualities." There was an intoxicating quality to the moment. But there also were notes of caution for those who chose to hear them. At the great Harmonia fest, H. T. Welles had proved to be anything but effusive. It was the intention of M&StL to push the road on south to Iowa "as rapidly as possible," said Welles, but "its further completion was dependent somewhat on circumstances." What did that mean?[26]

In short, it meant that despite the inflated rhetoric of building the two roads with only local money, private investment plus municipal aid from Minneapolis ($250,000) and Carver ($20,000), and despite the constant admonition that the roads were to be locally owned and locally operated, reality was otherwise. Local boosters, frank to say, were either unwilling or unable to carry the burden. As early as March 1870, Welles had said, "We have behind us the whole Northern Pacific Company." That expansive and tantalizing statement was less than completely true, yet it was accurate in part. In fact, the life and times of Jay Cooke & Company, Lake Superior & Mississippi, Minneapolis & Duluth, and Minneapolis & St. Louis were destined to be linked with Northern Pacific.[27]

The fabled Northern Pacific enterprise had languished until Cooke took an interest. In 1869 he agreed to get money for building the road; on February 15, 1870, ground was finally broken at Thompson, 23 miles west of Duluth on LS&M. W. D. Washburn, his cousin Dorillus Morrison, and William W. Eastman—all of Minneapolis—were with others associated as contractors for NP's Minnesota Division, and Washburn and Isaac Atwater were among those who labored unsuccessfully in 1870 to convince NP to fix Minneapolis (then off-line) as its headquarters city. Even as construction crews inched west toward the Red River valley, Cooke gathered in the pioneer St. Paul & Pacific and placed its existing twin lines leading out of Minneapolis to the west and northwest under NP's flag. Then, early in 1871, NP purchased half-interest in LS&M's line from Duluth to Thompson. NP was a colossus—the biggest single business enterprise undertaken in the United States to that time.[28]

M&StL's star would be part of NP's constellation. Welles had sought to distance himself from his own forthright statement of association back in March 1870, but to no avail. The truth was out. On May 1, 1871, M&StL's board heard a proposal from LS&M for lease of M&StL and two days later agreed to a "Philadelphia proposition" on the line from Minneapolis to Sioux City Junction. Secretary Atwater was exceedingly spare with detail, but perhaps there were little hard data to spread upon the minute book as yet. And when Minneapolis & Duluth had opened to White Bear Lake during the summer of 1871, W. D. Washburn provided only skimpy but nevertheless profound information. He revealed that he had held early and energetic talks with Philadelphia financiers regarding the M&D and M&StL ventures, but they had urged delay. Washburn would have none of it; the roads had to be built now. "They helped us" with M&D, said Washburn, and, he went on, "they are going to help us build" M&StL "to Carver, and then on to the state line." He was ready to drop the other shoe. "We shall transfer the road to them, and I can assure you . . . that they will run it on liberal principles." Even that was unclear, for he spoke of the two roads as one. The picture soon cleared. Talks were held with Frank H. Clark, S. M. Felton, and William G. Moorhead representing Cooke & Company, and E. E. Clarke & Company, another Philadelphia banking firm, and in the end M&D, like M&StL, was leased to LS&M. Washburn would serve nominally as M&D's president, and Welles would be on its board, but the three remaining members—a majority—were Clark, Felton, and Moorhead.[29]

The situation for M&StL was rather more complicated, but with the same result. The company was responsible for placing its own bonds and did so through the good efforts of local board member Rufus J. Baldwin, who disposed of them mainly in Holland. These forty-year first mortgage bonds earned 7 percent and were endorsed by LS&M, to which M&StL was leased on October 24, 1871. But unlike the M&D arrangement, M&StL retained its full complement of officers and directors—all local—and, said *American Railroad Manual*, "this company maintains an independent organization." M&StL, nevertheless, was very much in NP's camp through LS&M. Over the next two years, Welles, as president of M&StL, worked diligently with Charles C. Gilman of Central Railroad Company of Iowa to coax Cooke and NP into a massive plan to finish the missing links in the Minneapolis-to-St. Louis route, to consolidate the corporate entities, and to have NP take the entire completed package. To no avail.[30]

What was in it for LS&M, NP, and the Philadelphia bankers? Security. LS&M's success, its president had freely admitted, was predicated on that road's "extension into the settled and developed sections of the country." With leases of M&D and Stillwater & St. Paul, LS&M now had lines from White Bear Lake equidistant to Stillwater, St. Paul, and Minneapolis—"arms resting on the Mississippi, Minnesota, and St. Croix rivers," as its annual report for 1871 spelled out. Lumber could flow southward on M&StL from mills on LS&M or at St. Anthony and Minneapolis; grain could move variously to milling at Minneapolis to St. Anthony if not to Duluth for transshipment; flour from Chaska and flour from the falls could move in all directions, as could manufactured goods to and from local points. It was a good plan and bound to get better if M&StL could be pushed to completion to a southern connection, adding range but also coal from Iowa to the traffic mix. NP needed LS&M as a funnel for construction materials, especially in the hard months when Duluth was icebound, and Cooke needed a constant and growing volume of businesses to protect his investments in and about Duluth, not to mention LS&M, NP, and other assorted ventures. Cooke had rolled dice in a giant crap game. He was in too far in too many interconnected ventures to do anything but press onward. For Cooke it was go for broke.[31]

Northern Pacific was at center stage. Gaining control of marginally established St. Paul & Pacific was in part an admission that St. Paul and Minneapolis were much more logical starting points than Duluth for any transcontinental road. But two completed lines of StP&P spanning a rich portion of Minnesota—opening the Red River valley and pointed toward Canada—intersected by a completed Northern Pacific from Duluth through Dakota Territory and beyond to Puget Sound, linked by LS&M between St. Paul and Minneapolis to Duluth, and supplemented by a completed and welded M&StL–Central Railroad Company of Iowa–North Missouri route to St. Louis made strategic sense and promised balanced traffic flows.[32]

Meanwhile, Minneapolis took time to bask in the warm rays of its early railroad era. In 1870, St. Paul & Pacific offered a daily passenger train northwestward to Anoka, Elk River, and St. Cloud, and another on its line westward to Litchfield. Milwaukee Road's predecessor advertised its *Owatonna Accommodation* as well as its *Eastern Express*. It also scheduled two "Minneapolis & St. Paul trains," which St. Paul & Pacific bettered with three of its own between those cities. Additional service was obtained when Milwaukee completed its line up the Mississippi through Winona and Red Wing. And Minneapolis & Duluth added to the mix in 1871 with four daily turns between Minneapolis and White Bear Lake—two connections to Stillwater and two for Duluth.[33]

Business was good and growing, the cars filled with a polyglot of customers from all walks of life. They brought one B. B. Miller to ballyhoo his dreamy and ill-fated "Air and Hour Line Railway" project, and they delivered Vice President Schuyler Colfax, who came from Winona and Owatonna, stayed over at the splendid Nicollet House, and departed for Morris and the Red River valley on a St. Paul & Pacific special train. Aboard the cars were also those who traveled to hinterlands and reported what they had seen. One voluble itinerant visited the "picturesque village of Dassel," west of Minneapolis on StP&P, to find, apparently to his amazement, "clever businessmen" making their mark in the midst of a "howling wilderness" with erection of a lumber mill to process native hardwoods into lumber for nearby farmers and other customers. The implication was clear:

building up of the outback could only redound positively for Minneapolis. A similar message came from a passenger on a Milwaukee train in southern Minnesota who made a glowing report of that

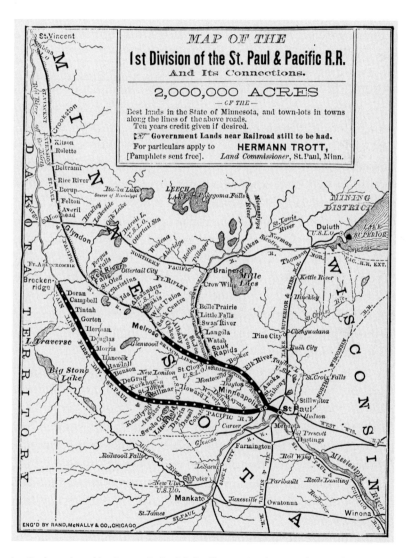

Jay Cooke gathered in pioneer St. Paul & Pacific, a tacit admission for Northern Pacific that St. Paul and Minneapolis were better starting points than Duluth for a transcontinental venture.

area: "On either side we look upon the broad rolling prairie, and see farm-houses, school-houses, barns, straw-stacks, and all the substance and surroundings necessary for successful farming. There lies the soil for which a New Englander would give his last dollar." And, he went on, "All the towns along the line are thrifty, growing, promising places. No man can ride through this portion of the state and doubt the future greatness of Minnesota."[34]

That greatness was sure to be reflected in a large way at Minneapolis. Evidence was found variously. In the month of March 1870, Milwaukee Road alone shipped from Minneapolis 11,454,550 pounds of freight (principally flour, wool, hides, mill feed, merchandise, and lumber) and received for unloading 1,704,290 pounds of miscellaneous freight. StP&P's Dassel station to the west in two months of 1871 dispatched about five thousand pheasants, ducks, and prairie chickens plus several tons of venison—much of it billed to Minneapolis. The monthly arrival of Milwaukee's pay car was joyous news for that company's growing body of employees at Minneapolis, StP&P handled the Westminster Presbyterian Sunday School—260 children and adults—to Lake Minnetonka to introduce the "excursion and picnic season of 1870," and a year later M&D had the honor of delivering the Baptist Sunday School excursion to White Bear Lake for "good fishing, superb dinner, pleasant sailing, and lots of fun."[35]

All of it represented change—exhilarating and discomfiting at once. A single incident serves to illustrate. When a train unfortunately collided with a team and wagon in St. Anthony, the *Weekly Democrat* in 1871 complained that "trains frequently come sweeping down the track at eight or nine miles an hour, and it is common for them to come into the city at the rate of even 15 miles per hour." This was unconscionable, the editor hissed: "It is about time this recklessness was stopped by some authority. The outrage has been tolerated too long."[36]

As summer passed to fall in 1872, local focus again attached to prospects for the St. Louis road. The air was abundant with rumor regarding M&StL under NP's broad banner. The local press reported that NP had authorized one survey from Sioux City Junction southward to Albert Lea and another from the Central Railroad of Iowa at Northwood, Iowa, also to Albert Lea. The shorter section, from Northwood to the Southern Minnesota Rail Road at Albert Lea, would be rushed to completion yet in 1872, said *Minneapolis Tribune*; the longer segment would be done "within a year."[37]

It was not to be. Construction on NP west from Thompson to the Mississippi River at Brainerd, 90 miles, was difficult and costly without benefit of adequate offsetting traffic. Rails did not reach Brainerd until March 1871. To the west the country began to open up a bit, making it more attractive to agriculturists. But NP did not attain the Missouri River at Bismarck, 455 miles from Duluth, until June 3, 1873. "All that this country needs now," Milnor Roberts had told Cooke a few days earlier, "is settlers." True, but there was no time. Cooke's legendary colonization campaign to people such a vast domain in such a short time was doomed to failure. Neither had Duluth grown as fast as Cooke hoped, nor had traffic on LS&M increased in a profitable way. LS&M sought shelter by offering itself for sale to NP early in January 1872, but NP agreed only to lease the road. A year later NP nervously agreed to LS&M's guarantee of Central Railroad Company of Iowa bonds, but only if North Missouri joined in agreement and then took a lease to operate the Iowa road. That did not happen. On September 13, 1873, NP's executive committee considered a curious request from W. D. Washburn offering to "rent" M&StL to NP. Washburn feared that Cooke's house of cards would collapse. It did—the next day, precipitating the awful Panic of 1873.[38]

Perhaps there had been omens of impending disaster. Near at home, St. Anthony Falls "went out" (collapsed) in October 1869, and fire destroyed lumber mills on the St. Anthony side in 1870. A severe blizzard hit Minnesota early in January 1873, ice lay in the lake at Duluth until July 1, and the first of several grasshopper invasions hit the state that summer. Financial markets had turned skittish in 1871 after the terrible Chicago fire, were nervous again the next fall, and showed real alarm as Grangers pushed legislation hostile to railroads. Financial panics typically had sprung from seeds long germinating, but the fall of Cooke set off this one. Great financial houses in addition to Cooke's went under, factories failed for want of orders, construction all but ceased, and the national orgy of railroad building ground to a halt. All of this was devastating to workers in basic industry who lost earning power or even jobs, and that, in turn, caused a decline in demand for products of food and fiber. Multipliers kicked in immediately. In good times, industrialists sought funds from bankers to expand or improve, and in bad times they looked to bankers to help save companies or reorganize them. But there were so many supplicants and bankers who had been badly bruised, maimed, and traumatized by recent events. They were wary. With a shortage of available capital, businessmen scaled back or eliminated spending plans.[39]

The railroad industry had fueled much of the expanding national economy following the Civil War. The years 1868-73 had been a period of particularly intense speculation and rapid railroad construction—much of it ahead of demand. Prudence was an uncommon commodity. That was as true in Minnesota as elsewhere when mileage in the state increased from 1,092 in 1870 to 1,902 in 1873. And it was just as true that Minnesota suffered as much as any state during the Panic. One close observer of the Minneapolis scene wrote starkly that the Panic "temporarily blighted" the "prosperity of the city" like "a late-sown field of wheat by an August frost." But perhaps no Minnesota community was hit harder than Duluth, which lost half of its five thousand inhabitants in less than two years.[40]

These circumstances quickly embraced Northern Pacific and those around it. On November 1, 1873, NP defaulted payments on M&D's bonds; LS&M bondholders met the same fate. NP tried to hold on and, in the case of M&D, asked for new leases—with financial obligations guaranteed personally by Henry T. Welles, W. D. Washburn, and C. C. Washburn, a burden totally unacceptable to those

men. NP shuddered. It would surrender its lease of LS&M on February 1, 1874, and give up stock control of the larger St. Paul & Pacific later that year. Receivership would follow on April 22, 1875.[41]

The fallout for M&StL and M&D was swift. A special meeting of the M&D board was held in Philadelphia, and the LS&M agreement was terminated. NP formally turned over M&StL and M&D to their owners on December 11, 1873. M&D then was leased "in perpetuity" to M&StL with M&StL promising to pay interest on M&D's bonds. In the process, M&D effectively—if not legally or corporately—lost identity, with the entire operation from White Bear Lake through Minneapolis to Sioux City Junction henceforth identified as M&StL. Monumental problems remained, however. Under the old arrangement, LS&M had supplied management, maintenance, and equipment, all of which M&StL now had to provide for M&D and for itself, too. M&D owned "two fine Baldwin locomotives," 4-4-0s, and they were returned. M&StL then leased additional motive power and rolling stock from NP, which, under the circumstance, it had in great excess.[42]

M&StL's bubble had burst. It had succeeded in securing rail outlet for milling and manufacturing interests of Minneapolis and St. Anthony (which was joined to Minneapolis in 1872), it had an outlet to the Great Lakes chain via LS&M, and it had a connection to St. Paul & Sioux City (which by now had completed its line through rich agricultural country to Sioux City, Iowa). But the great goal of reaching St. Louis remained unmet. Moreover, absent Cooke and Northern Pacific there seemed no white knight to salvage that dream. Those who had given birth to M&StL and M&D now had those properties back in their laps; they would be obliged to play the part of owner-operators—and in the swirl of the worst depression to hit the American people to that time.

# THE ST. LOUIS ROAD

4

Minneapolis greets St. Louis . . . the metropolis of the
upper Mississippi and the "Queen City" are separated
by but 26½ hours time.

*MINNEAPOLIS TRIBUNE*, NOVEMBER 13, 1877

The short lines of road making up both Minneapolis & St. Louis
and Minneapolis & Duluth had not been built ahead of need as had
been the case with so many other lines in Minnesota. If anything
they lagged behind demand. Their supporters were left to shake
their heads and mutter of lost opportunities. Indeed, if M&StL had
been completed to hook up with Central Railroad Company of Iowa
and/or Burlington, Cedar Rapids & Minnesota, traffic expansion to
and from St. Louis as well as intermediate points could only have
strengthened all constituent roads against vicissitudes resulting
from the Panic of 1873. But M&StL had not been expanded southward from Carver under NP's flag, and while M&D had secured connection to Duluth and the Great Lakes chain, that company's earnings had proved seasonal and woefully inadequate. M&StL's treasure,
shared with M&D, was access to and near transport monopoly of
mills and manufacturing plants along the west bank of the Mississippi River at Minneapolis. That asset had to be held at all cost.

The Washburns and associates were interested in railroads only
tangentially, seeking with M&StL and M&D means to protect non-
rail assets closest to their hearts. But to protect those assets and
investments, they were obliged to defend and nurture "their" railroads—without assurance of success. The fixed debt of the two companies, which had seemed modest in upbeat days before the Panic,
now seemed monstrous. By May 1874, a sense of desperation seized
the Minneapolis board, a mood somberly reflected in minutes of
its meeting on May 2: "Earnings of said lines of road are wholly
insufficient at present to defray the current operating expenses and
provide a sum sufficient to meet interest." In other words, dire circumstance of depression and crop failure "threatened foreclosure
of its [M&StL's] mortgaged indebtedness." Nevertheless, the board
agreed that "certain stockholders" would "make good." To "make
good," M&StL issued stock, which was taken, for the most part, by
W. D. Washburn, who had replaced Henry T. Welles as president
in January, by his brother Cadwallader, by Welles, and by Robert
B. Langdon.[1]

This was adequate, barely, to maintain a tolerable status quo
for M&StL and M&D—actually M&StL, for M&D was operated by

M&StL more or less as a wholly controlled subsidiary. Other Minnesota roads were less fortunate. "Two are in the hands of receivers, three others have defaulted in interest upon their debt, and two have resorted to funding interest for a term of years, while the remainder of the roads in Minnesota [including M&StL] have maintained their credit by continued assessment upon stockholders in one form or another." Such was the droll report of Minnesota's Railroad Commission at mid-year 1874. These nasty circumstances were reflected in an immediate way: bankruptcy claimed M&StL board members Paris Gibson and Richard J. Mendenhall, and even W. D. Washburn late in 1874 was compelled to assign certain of his properties "for the

benefit of his creditors." Washburn survived financially, propped up by brother Cadwallader, and continued as M&StL's majordomo.[2]

Even as fiscal calamity rained down about him, W. D. Washburn boldly reasserted that M&StL would be driven southward to meet Central Railroad Company of Iowa and in that way realize the much longed for but sadly delayed Minneapolis-to-St. Louis dream. Yet the Iowa road itself remained without connection to the North Missouri road on the south and in truth was little more than an isolated vertical axis route across Iowa. It stumbled into receivership in mid-1874. Another attractive candidate, Burlington, Cedar Rapids & Minnesota, also stood beckoning at the Iowa border and, in fact, had joined with Chicago, Milwaukee & St. Paul and others in 1872 to provide through if doglegged service between St. Louis and Minneapolis. Nevertheless, BCR&M early in 1874 continued to woo Washburn, promising to guarantee M&StL's construction bonds on an extension from Carver to Albert Lea. Like Central Railroad Company of Iowa, BCR&M was itself desperate for traffic and, like Central Railroad, offered M&StL impressive synergies. But also like the other Iowa road, BCR&M was financially embarrassed, defaulting on interest due late in 1873 and headed for receivership in 1875.[3]

These two Iowa companies were hardly distinctive in looking for means to expand on their own, to seek traffic alliances adequate to maintain independence, or to make themselves attractive to others. Such was the case of other allied Iowa concerns, Clinton, Iowa & Dubuque and Chicago, Dubuque & Minnesota, building up the west side of the Mississippi River from Clinton, Iowa, to La Crescent, Minnesota, across from La Crosse, Wisconsin. Behind these two ostensibly local roads was Chicago, Burlington & Quincy, which

Prosperity for Duluth and its Lake Superior & Mississippi Railroad is implied in this view of a locomotive shoving a long line of boxcars for loading or unloading at the Duluth freight terminal. Yet prosperity for both city and railroad was elusive during the financial Panic of 1873. In the end, Cooke & Company failed, Northern Pacific stumbled, and NP leases were abrogated. Consequently LS&M, M&StL, and M&D all were again independent—and very frightened. Photograph by Whitney & Zimmerman; courtesy of the Minnesota Historical Society.

Cadwallader Washburn more than once was compelled to bail out brother William Drew. Photograph courtesy of the Minneapolis Public Library, Minneapolis Collection.

also, interestingly, had financial investment in BCR&M. By 1869, CB&Q, under the leadership of James F. Joy, an able lawyer and brilliant strategist, had bridged the Mississippi at both Burlington and Quincy, and with its own lines or those of surrogates had linked Chicago with Council Bluffs and with Kansas City. Fleshing out followed; by 1872, CB&Q had 800 miles of line in Illinois alone. "It is impossible to remain stationary," Joy had told shareholders in 1869. "If the companies owning and managing roads there do not meet the wants of the adjoining country and aid in its development, other alliances are sure to be found which end in rival roads and damage to existing interests." CB&Q's concern in expanding northwestward and particularly in gaining an independent route to St. Paul and Minneapolis was logical and likely inevitable. The twin roads along the west bank of the Mississippi in Iowa were crucial pieces in that puzzle. Another piece was Southern Minnesota Railroad, stretching westward from La Crescent to Austin, Albert Lea, and beyond. So, too, in this scenario was the as yet incomplete M&StL, which could supply the northernmost link between Albert Lea and Minneapolis. Joy and certain directors at CB&Q reasoned that all of this plus modest construction by Burlington in Illinois and a contract with Chicago & North Western for use of its bridge at Clinton would provide them a fine new service area. It was not to be. C&NW adamantly refused to contract for use of the Clinton bridge, the two Iowa roads and Southern Minnesota alike were financially shaky and thus vulnerable to the Panic, and M&StL showed no ability to complete its own road to Albert Lea.

A new Burlington management reassessed the plan and, in 1877, would pull the plug on the twin Iowa roads, which were then reorganized and, like Southern Minnesota, fell into Milwaukee's orbit. Burlington squandered a decade in this quest, but its dream of a strong incursion to Minneapolis remained bright.[4]

There is no evidence that Washburn had financial interest in the Southern Minnesota road, but he certainly pondered what that company's performance implied in terms of an M&StL completed to Albert Lea. On the positive side, he would have noted that Albert Lea received and dispatched more tonnage than any other station on Southern Minnesota's line and that it also earned more freight revenues than any other single station. That augured well in terms of a productive local service area for M&StL. Moreover, Southern Minnesota's chief tonnage was wheat—subject to competition and diversion to Minneapolis for milling. On the other hand, Southern Minnesota's experience suggested that Mother Nature could play dirty tricks along M&StL's potential route. The winter of 1874–75 was punishing, with snow blockages closing Southern Minnesota's line for protracted periods (the road's revenue for February 1874 was a scant $26,420), and spring floods and summer storms tore at the roadway. Heavy rains in the summer of 1875 reduced the wheat crop, and a long siege of the "locust pest" (grasshoppers) began in 1876. Two years earlier, Southern Minnesota had suffered foreclosure, the result of the financial panic gripping the country and the vicissitudes of nature.[5]

The unfortunate experience of Southern Minnesota illustrated a broader picture. The financial performance of Minnesota's railroads for 1874 was pathetic, and the 1875 performance was poorer by $1.24 million. Nationally, only 1,711 miles of new road were built in 1875, compared to 5,878 in 1872, and in Minnesota a mere 57 miles were constructed in the three-year period 1873–75. John J. Randall, Minnesota's railroad commissioner, said, "the cause of this falling off is accounted for by the general depression of business and light crop of 1874." That was only partially correct. Another factor was investor concern over well-intentioned but usually wrongheaded railroad regulation.[6]

For those without railroad service, nothing was so devoutly to be hoped for. Steamcars would, they knew, provide all-weather, regularly scheduled, and inexpensive transportation. Such were the reasons for the existence of railroads, they judged. But for those who financed, owned, and operated railroads, they existed as profit-making business ventures. With such a basic difference in perspective, a collision was easily predicted. Moreover, as the nation's first big industry, railroads were at the eye of change—change that was rapidly transforming the country from one that was rural and agrarian to one that was urban and industrial. As an agent of profound change, the railroad industry was something to behold but also something that many found fearsome and worthy of scapegoating—especially during the 1870s, when discontented farmers complained of low grain prices, high rail rates, and an uncharitable Mother Nature. Their cause was picked up by a number of journalists, such as the editor of the *St. Anthony Democrat*, who blathered:

> We say, now, to the railroads, your days of evil are numbered.
> Just so soon as an outraged people can speak and act through
> their representatives, you will be shorn of power to swindle and
> fleece them. The legislature will most certainly establish rules
> and regulations for you.

This particular journalist was especially vexed by St. Paul & Pacific— "owned and controlled beyond the limits of the State . . . an enemy to our people from one end of the line to the other. . . it is among us without having any interest in common with us." Two issues seemed paramount at the *Democrat*: absentee ownership and high rates charged by StP&P. "The cost of getting wheat to market is so enormous as to deter our farmers from attempting it. It would seem that this road is made to play into the hands of Eastern speculators who come out here and purchase the products of our farmers for a mere song, thus enriching themselves at the expense of the bone, sinew, flesh and blood of our toil-worn people." This was certainly no way to run a railroad, the editor concluded. What should be the proper course? He offered no response, except to say, "The people

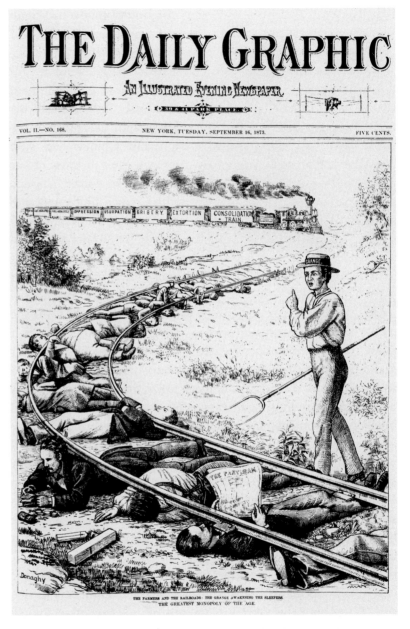

According to this political cartoonist, railroads were killing farmers and small businessmen and were responsible for the Panic of 1873. Photograph courtesy of Burlington Northern Santa Fe.

have every reason to suppose that the various roads will be run in their interest and for their accommodation, and not for the purpose of filching from them their last hard-earned dollar."[7]

The editor and kindred spirits found Oliver H. Kelly's Patrons of Husbandry (the Grange) a useful vehicle for their deliberations and then their actions. Much of the heated debate as to railroads and their place and responsibility in American society centered on the upper Midwest, and by 1874, Illinois, Iowa, Wisconsin, and Minnesota all had enacted restrictive railroad regulations, uniformly labeled "Granger Laws." A Minnesota rate law had been established in 1871, but the law of 1874 declared certain acts of rate discrimination to be unjust, regardless of competitive factors. The new law also established a three-man commission with power to fix maximum rates that state courts should assume as reasonable.[8]

Railroaders and their supporters saw matters differently. The carriers had unusually high fixed costs, were capital intensive, were labor intensive, required large volumes of business to spread costs and to avoid excess capacity, could not easily relocate plant once put down, and could not store their service. The need to adjust rates according to local requirements and/or to supply and demand led to a policy practiced by most railroad managers of making deals with individual shippers, offering whatever rate would obtain the traffic. This led to discrimination in *favor* of somebody or some place, and *against* somebody or some place—discrimination, incidentally, that was often demanded as a concession by powerful shippers and opposed to the best interests of the railroad companies.[9]

Grangers and allied interests were voluble on the matter of rates as a means of establishing equity and heartily supported more rail lines as another magical nostrum. Tradition taught them that the absence of competition, or even too little competition, was a great evil. But it was not possible—any more than it was desirable—to supply every nook and cranny of any state with multiple lines of railroad. Even Minnesota's railroad commission had to admit that "the building of railroads in this State . . . has not proven remunerative to the companies" and that "our railroads [are] too large and have cost too much money for the wants of our State." But that same

body nevertheless complained that Minnesota suffered from an inadequate development of railroads in proportion to its size. Massachusetts had 1 mile of railroad for 4.70 square miles, and Ohio had 1 mile for 7.07 square miles. Closer to home, Illinois had 1 mile of railroad to 5.38 square miles compared to 1 mile for 43.45 square miles in Minnesota; that is, Illinois had "very nearly *ten times* the extent of railroad in proportion to the area that Minnesota has," sobbed the regulatory authority, ignoring in Illinois earlier settlement, a larger population, urban influence, and other significant variables.[10]

No less a mind than E. L. Godkin summed up the matter in *The Nation* for April 10, 1873. Said Godkin, "The contest now going on . . . is one of the early skirmishes of the impending war, which, unless we greatly err, is destined to produce industrial, social, and above all, political changes in this country of the most startling description." Indeed, wrote Godkin, "the locomotive is coming in contact with the framework of our institutions. In this country of simple government, the most powerful centralizing force which civilization has yet produced has, within the next score years, yet to assume its relations to that political machinery which is to control and regulate it."[11]

Minneapolis & St. Louis was not immune from scattergun attack, but as a tiny local road operated for local interests, it was sheltered in a way that St. Paul & Pacific, Northern Pacific, and the Chicago and Milwaukee roads were not. When M&StL and M&D properties had been returned to the owners, there was but one officer of the company, A. H. Bode, who received $1,500 per year for performing his duties as secretary, superintendent, general ticket agent, and general freight agent. Bode was in charge of 42 miles of railroad, the engineering for which had been "economically done"—a track structure that was innocent of ballast except for dirt and very light (49 pounds per yard) iron rail. Equipment consisted of two M&D locomotives and two others leased from Northern Pacific as well as five cars for passenger business plus 68 pieces of freight equipment, likewise leased from NP. Even before the Panic neither M&D nor M&StL had earned income over operating expenses—explaining, no doubt, why NP through Lake Superior & Mississippi had been so eager to end the leases. For instance, M&StL in the last five months of lease (July–November 1873) had operating expenses tallying 134.9 percent of earnings—a dismal record indeed. M&StL's operating revenues for fiscal 1875 exceeded operating expenses by 20 percent, but after paying taxes and interest on bonds, the road was in the red by nearly $30,000. The next two years proved no better.[12]

Casual is the word that sums up early M&StL operations. Under NP's banner, M&StL and M&D had operated two mixed trains (freight and passenger) daily-except-Sunday from Minneapolis to White Bear Lake and Minneapolis to Sioux City Junction. That pattern continued under independent management. For a while M&StL trains utilized the St. Paul & Pacific station in Minneapolis, but to save money M&StL moved to meager quarters across from Milwaukee's station on Second Street in 1874. Boardings were modest: 7,858 in 1873, but rising to 30,855 in 1875, and to 40,709 in 1876. Passenger hauls were short, 15.4 miles on average in 1875, and revenue thin, $24,570 for the same year.[13]

Freight was and always would be most important at M&StL. Daily switching was necessary in and about the mills, but except for extras when demand required, billings were handled by the regularly scheduled mixed trains. Lumber and wood led all commodities in volume, followed by grain, flour, and merchandise. In 1875, M&StL moved 136,958 tons earning $98,186 in revenue; the record for 1876 was marginally higher. Wheat moved to Minneapolis from LS&M at White Bear Lake, from on-line stations, and from St. Paul & Sioux City at Sioux City Junction. Minneapolis-milled flour, on the other hand, moved mostly northbound to Duluth for transshipment; indeed, in 1876, every barrel of it billed on M&StL moved thusly.[14]

Of the eight M&StL stations from White Bear Lake to Sioux City Junction, Minneapolis was clearly the largest and the best established. Others, like Eden Prairie and Hopkins, were given life by the railroad, and still others, Chaska and Carver, as examples, were nourished by the new service. Carver, named for Jonathan Carver, a Connecticut-born explorer and author, had been platted as early as 1857 but did not thrive until the coming of the railroad. By 1875, it claimed about one thousand inhabitants, and area farmers used

M&StL to ship an average of 187,406 bushels of wheat to Minneapolis for the 1875–76 seasons. The town boasted four general stores and one each drug, hardware, grocery, harness, and boot and shoe store, all of which received stock from wholesalers in Minneapolis. In addition to grain, Carver also shipped brick in carload lots, much of it to Minneapolis. Three hotels, including the Railroad House, "convenient to the Minneapolis & St. Louis depot," served the needs of the traveling public, while other local entrepreneurs handled local express and omnibus requirements. The strong and growing commercial ties between Minneapolis and Carver as part of the larger community's hinterland were typical. So, too, were the railroad and its trackside cohabitant, the telegraph line, providing the necessary umbilical cord.[15]

What M&StL needed was more traffic on that umbilical cord. Such an increase *from* Minneapolis, flour as the easy example, depended on an increase *to* Minneapolis, wheat as the corollary example. But M&StL's tiny service area could not, of itself, generate adequate additional traffic. "The Minneapolis & St. Louis is now in the hands of gentlemen of Minneapolis whose first thoughts are for the best interests of the city," intoned the *Minneapolis Tribune* when reporting that the road had been returned to its owners late in 1873. To make good on that great claim, however, Minneapolis-based M&StL was obliged to expand. And the owners boldly claimed that they had such a plan " . . . to extend their railroad . . . to a connection . . . with the Central Railroad Company of Iowa . . . this making a direct line . . . from Duluth, Minneapolis and St. Paul, to St. Louis and New Orleans." A bold plan, to be sure. Vicissitudes of the Panic held otherwise. The Iowa concern remained dormant at Northwood, just south of the Iowa border, and M&StL was utterly without ability to complete its own leg. In 1875, however, M&StL received authority to thrust a "branch" *westward* to Green Lake or New London in Kandiyohi County, perhaps 100 miles. Then, two

FACING PAGE: M&StL shared the Minneapolis railroad scene with St. Paul & Pacific and Chicago, Milwaukee & St. Paul.

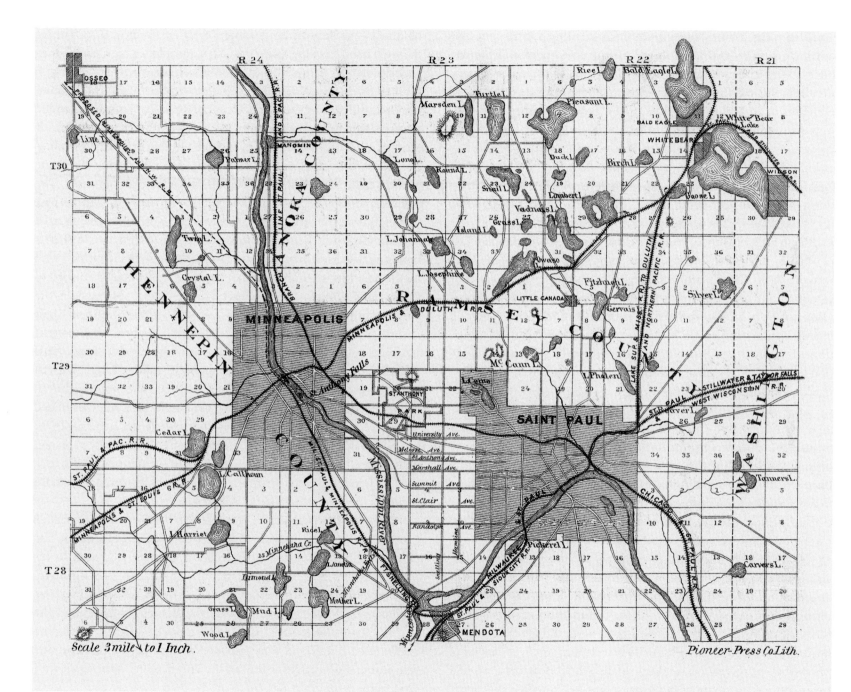

Scale 3 mile to 1 Inch.

Pioneer-Press Co. Lith.

years later, the Minnesota legislature passed other special laws permitting governmental units to aid "in the construction of branch lines," in this case by M&StL northwestward about 100 miles to Sauk Center in Stearns County, and westward approximately 60 miles to Hutchinson, in McLeod County. At all events, Washburn and crew were fishing for local support in regions they perceived subject to the wheat culture and receptive to Minneapolis jobbers. The notion of building to Sauk Center seemed curious at first blush, since St. Paul & Pacific long had planned to complete one of its pioneer lines through that place en route from Minneapolis via St. Cloud to the Red River valley. This would not be completed until 1878, however, and Henry Titus Welles, Isaac Atwater, and R. J. Mendenhall—all of M&StL persuasion—were at the same time directors of the Minneapolis & St. Cloud Railroad, a paper outfit that held a collection of potentially valuable rights including authority for a line from Minneapolis to St. Cloud along the west bank of the Mississippi (St. Paul & Pacific went up the east side). Nothing ever came of any of these dreams for M&StL, but the desire to build westward in addition to the original goal of building south remained well embedded in corporate memory.[16]

That Henry T. Welles and others were active severally in business was typical of the time. For example, seven of the ten men who formed the Minneapolis Street Railway in 1873 were likewise members of M&StL's directory, and one of these men was W. D. Washburn who, with two additional M&StL directors, joined six others to form the Board of Trade of Minneapolis in 1872. Six years later Washburn would be president of that group, and seven of the thirty-one members of its board were also M&StL directors.[17]

Neither was it unusual for leading businessmen of the time to be active politically. Cadwallader C. Washburn's Civil War army career spliced a five-term presence in Congress, and he was elected to one term as governor of Wisconsin before turning his entire energy to the business field. William D. Washburn never did get the political bug out of his system. After his Civil War stint as surveyor general of Minnesota, he served on the Minneapolis School Board, was elected to the Minnesota House of Representatives, and sought—and nearly obtained—the Republican nomination for governor in 1873. The humorless, hard-working, plain-spoken Cadwallader took personal responsibility very seriously, and he became increasingly irritated with William Drew, who did not have his older brother's financial acumen, who held increasing ambition for a public career, and who tended toward dogmatic and arrogant ways and was not easy to work with. Most of all, Cadwallader was disgusted with his brother's unwillingness to devote full attention to business matters during the Panic and his apparent inability to keep his financial affairs in order. The solemn Cadwallader had saved his younger brother from bankruptcy earlier, but he smarted at that necessity and at the continuing need to maintain family honor by paying his own assessment on M&StL's bonds as well as that of William Drew. "Strange that railroad, with all the business it is doing, cannot pay . . . ," Cadwallader growled to W. D. Hale, William Drew's secretary, late in 1875. Meanwhile, the younger brother was touring Europe with another brother, Elihu, cavorting about, or frolicking, the humorless Cadwallader thought. "You had better write WD to come home," he ordered Hale. "It is disgraceful that he should be away spending money while his creditors are waiting for him to pay." More payments were coming due on William Drew's "paper," and Cadwallader knew he would be obliged to cover them. "It is an outrage to ask me to do it . . . ," he fumed. Cadwallader may have detected a darker side of William Drew's persona, and, in fact, the younger man was on a bit of a frolic, but he also took time in London to make contact with bankers regarding bonds for M&StL's proposed extension to Albert Lea.[18]

Cadwallader Washburn's perturbation and frustration with his brother and especially with M&StL were easily understood. The elder Washburn's interest in railroads was merely adjunct to his main concerns, lumber and flour; he saw M&StL as a means to protect and advance them, not an end in itself. Yet M&StL proved expensive and given Northern Pacific's financial debacle and the revoked leases on M&StL and M&D, unlucky. M&StL opened an abbreviated hinterland that provided modest agricultural production and marketing opportunities for Minneapolis, although significant tonnage in grain did come off St. Paul & Sioux City at Sioux

City Junction, presently renamed Merriam, and flour moved to the Head of the Lakes in season. Shipments of flour from Minneapolis mills had accelerated nicely from 1873 to 1876, but the short crop of 1876 significantly reduced receipts of wheat, serving to magnify M&StL's truncated reach. So, too, did high rates on flour demanded by railroads leading eastward to Chicago and beyond to seaboard. Cadwallader Washburn groused that M&StL was, as presently constituted, inadequate, but he was in too deeply to get out. To protect his investment in the road, he was obliged to spend even more on it. The same was true for William Drew. By the end of 1877, Cadwallader would own 1,321 shares, and by 1879 he would hold 5,742; William Drew would own 959 shares at the end of 1877, and 5,926 two years later. Nobody else came close in terms of stock ownership.

Cadwallader Washburn recognized that M&StL had to expand, but he was irritated at the drain that the railroad put on his time and on his pocketbook. Construction southward to Albert Lea would require huge expenditures for excavation, bridges, culverts, ties, rail, and fasteners as well as new cars and locomotives, such as this handsome American Standard 4-4-0. Photograph from the collection of Paul H. Stringham.

In addition, Cadwallader became a board member in 1876. His brother remained president, but the imperious Cadwallader clearly determined to keep a steely eye on his often arrogant and dogmatic younger brother.[19]

M&StL finally would build south. By 1876 there were modest signs of financial recovery, investment capital began to seek outlet, and the Washburns took on new resolve. They had given up on linking with Central Railroad Company of Iowa, which remained in receivership with competing groups of eastern bondholders squabbling over control and direction. Rather, the Washburns turned to Burlington, Cedar Rapids & Minnesota, which also had fallen on hard times, but which was reorganized by bondholders and sold, and on June 27, 1876, restyled itself as Burlington, Cedar Rapids & Northern Railway (BCR&N). The old company had financial and traffic support from large and powerful Chicago, Burlington & Quincy, with which it connected at Burlington, Iowa, and ownership of the new company was mostly in eastern hands, investors who had substantial stakes in CB&Q as well as Chicago, Rock Island & Pacific. Although bitter rivals in a later time, these two strong roads in the mid-1870s to the end of the decade had harmonious relations. BCR&N profited from this cordiality. Rock Island fed and received traffic at West Liberty, Iowa, and CB&Q reciprocated at Burlington.

Elsewhere, CB&Q was building or buying line segments that, when stitched together, would eventually create a direct route down the west side of the Mississippi from Burlington to St. Louis. BCR&N was attractive to both Rock Island and Burlington—its southeast-to-northwest route across Iowa likened as a funnel for business to or from St. Louis and Chicago.

The old BCR&M had urged M&StL southward in 1874 to no avail, but early in 1877 the reorganized and rejuvenated BCR&N extended its line from Plymouth to Manly, 5 miles, from whence it secured operating rights over crestfallen rival Central Railroad Company of Iowa to Northwood, 11 miles, and only 4 miles from

Completion of M&StL's line to Albert Lea was good news for the Minneapolis flour millers. Many new country elevators built along the southern extension would soon provide thousands of bushels of wheat, billed to the hungry mills at the falls. Photograph courtesy of the Minneapolis Public Library, Minneapolis Collection.

the state boundary. As these developments were unfolding, W. D. Washburn was in New York City making arrangements with BCR&N President Fred Taylor for construction and lease of a 12-mile stub from the Iowa boundary to Albert Lea and for joint traffic programs. (BCR&N would build the short link from Northwood to the border on its own account.)[20]

On April 11, 1877, M&StL asked for bids on grading a line from Merriam to Albert Lea. The route selected lifted out of the Minnesota River valley to traverse young glacial plain typified by lakes and moraines through established if yet small communities—Jordan, New Prague, Waterville, Waseca, Hartland, and Manchester—and creating new villages of Montgomery, Kilkenny, Palmer, Otisco, and New Richland. By late August tracklayers were south of Montgomery; two months later construction crews reached New Richland.[21]

On the south end, BCR&N crews pushed across the state line in mid-August and reached Albert Lea on September 6. Two days later the first revenue freight arrived, and on September 9, BCR&N inaugurated daily-except-Sunday passenger service featuring "Palace sleeping cars owned by this line."[22]

Finally, on November 12, workmen laid the last rail and drove the final spike at Albert Lea on the M&StL segment from the north, shortly before arrival of a splendidly appointed excursion train from Minneapolis, which stopped only briefly before hurrying on to ceremonies at the state line and then returning to a "sumptuous repast" and jovial "speech-making" at the Hall House. W. D. Washburn exclaimed that "it was the happiest day of his life." Back in Minneapolis, the editor of the always friendly *Tribune* puffed out his chest and boldly proclaimed, "Minneapolis greets St. Louis . . . the metropolis of the upper Mississippi and the 'Queen City' are separated by but 26½ hours time." And then, in a great sigh of relief, he said, "We have got the road, and we are happy over the fact . . . ," a gross understatement. It was a great day for Minneapolis and especially for the celebrants, whose euphoria continued as the two-car excursion train went "bounding home through the moonlight."[23]

"Minneapolis & St. Louis Railway. The Shortest and Most Direct Line to St. Louis, New Orleans and Galveston. Making Quicker Time than by any other Route, and Carrying the Great Southern Mail." The new order was heady stuff, and M&StL's advertising reflected as much. Two express trains daily "With Pullman's Palace Sleeping Cars" plied the Minneapolis-to-St. Louis route daily via M&StL/BCR&N to Burlington, thence CB&Q eastward to Monmouth, and then southward to St. Louis, 571 miles.[24]

Not nearly as flashy and appealing as express train passenger service, freight, nevertheless, paid most of the bills. As quickly as the line to Albert Lea was open, M&StL dispatched daily "flour express" trains from the milling district eastward over BCR&N—to the immense satisfaction of the two railroad companies and shippers alike. In 1877, M&StL moved more than half of the Minneapolis flour production. Moreover, the many new country elevators built along the Albert Lea extension soon disgorged thousands of bushels of wheat, billed to the hungry mills at the falls, and as on-line communities grew so did their need for lumber and other building materials as well as the full range of mercantile goods, supplied by Minneapolis industrialists and wholesalers.[25]

Those who backed M&StL spiritually and/or financially had been slow to act in the fast-changing environment following the Civil War. Indeed, they had reacted instead of initiating—they had responded instead of acting. M&StL, as a consequence, was slow out of the blocks. Bad fortune had followed with NP's financial debacle and the awful Panic of 1873. But in finally deciding to move in 1877, M&StL's boosters chose well. The grasshopper menace passed, growing conditions were superb, and the year's crop was heavy. Confidence enveloped the national economy and the state's as well. M&StL caught a powerful wave of optimism. In 1875, Minnesota's population stood at 597,407, and in the fall of 1877, the *Minneapolis Tribune* reported that immigrants were "pouring into the state from all directions." One source contended that more than 1.250 million acres of land was taken "by actual settlers in Minnesota" in that year alone. All of this was reflected by new rail lines—212 miles in 1877, raising the state's total to 2,199. But in 1878, another 350 miles would be added, more miles opened than in any other state.[26]

# PULLING AND HAULING

5

Judicious managers will not fail to adopt the best available measures for increasing the productive powers of their customers.

*RAILWAY WORLD*, AUGUST 7, 1880

Three days after the joyous excursion to Albert Lea, the Washburn brothers made their own personal inspection of the new line. They must have taken pride in their accomplishment. Certainly those who were partial to them or to Minneapolis were proud as well as pleased. Said a special correspondent for the *Minneapolis Tribune*, "These long years of doubt and discouragement . . . have now passed away, and General W. D. Washburn and his public spirited associates, after their untiring labors and great sacrifices, have now the proud satisfaction of witnessing the full realization of their most enthusiastic and sanguine expectations." Nevertheless, as the inspection train rolled onward, the solemn and humorless Cadwallader may have blurted out his growing irritation and frustration with the whole M&StL affair. During the summer the older brother again had covered William Drew's "paper"—"so that it would not be protested." Governor Washburn was clearly agitated and, as he said at the time, "driven into a heap by the demand of the R.R. and to meet my own paper." Indeed, he had growled, "the drafts are coming in on me so fast for the Albert Lea extension and the payments for my bonds, that I must ask for an extension on my notes." His patience was thin. "Before these notes fall due," he snarled, "I shall hope to get the road off my hands. . . ."[1]

William Drew may have ignored those outbursts from his broad-shouldered brother, at least in the euphoria of the moment, but Cadwallader was truly in earnest. There were other problems, too. M&StL's directory was made up of Minneapolis men tied directly or indirectly to the milling district, and their loyalty to the road could be assumed, but not every person from the city's primary industrial center was on that board. There were others, competitors and detractors, who resented the Washburns and resented the "Washburn road," as M&StL often was called. They could make trouble. So could competing railroads, which had never looked kindly on the Minneapolis company and which bitterly resented its primacy in the milling district and now despised its new outlet via Albert Lea. And, as it developed, the late 1870s and early 1880s would witness a veritable explosion of railroad construction. Some of it was well reasoned; some reflected corporate one-upmanship; some was the elixir of powerful personal egos; some reflected innate instinct for survival. A move by one company triggered a response

**CHICAGO AND ST. PAUL**

THROUGH LINE,

VIA THE

"ELROY ROUTE,"

West Wisconsin & Chicago & Northwestern

RAILWAYS.

*The only Line Running THROUGH TRAINS between ST. PAUL and CHICAGO WITHOUT CHANGE OF CARS.*

Making this the Most Comfortable, Expeditious,

**SHORTEST AND ONLY DIRECT ROUTE**

To MADISON, BELOIT, JANESVILLE,

**Chicago, New York, Boston,**

**PHILADELPHIA,**

And all Points East and South.

THE PIONEER ROUTE, RUNNING

**2** **EXPRESS TRAINS DAILY FROM ST. PAUL TO CHICAGO,**
Carrying all Classes of Passengers through without Change of Cars.

The traveling public will find this New Line in every respect a FIRST-CLASS ROAD, all trains being fully equipped with New and Elegant

**PULLMAN PALACE DAY & NIGHT COACHES,**

**WESTINGHOUSE AIR BRAKE,**

AND

**MILLER PLATFORMS.**

Passengers taking this Route will secure to themselves advantages afforded by no other Line.

**THROUGH TICKETS** to all points East and South for sale at the Company's Office, Third Street, corner Jackson, same side as Merchants' Hotel.

☞ SLEEPING CAR BERTHS can be secured at same place. ☜

BAGGAGE CHECKED THROUGH TO ALL PARTS OF THE UNITED STATES.

Buy your Tickets via the WEST WISCONSIN RAILWAY.

| CHAS. THOMPSON, | JOHN H. HULL, | WM. JAMES, | F. B. CLARKE, |
| Ticket Agent. | Superintendent. | Gen. Pass. Agt. | Gen. Freight Agt. |

*Third Street, cor. Jackson, same side Merchants' Hotel, St. Paul, Minn.*

Chicago & North Western and surrogates together combined in strong competition in the Chicago–St. Paul corridor but did not yet reach Minneapolis.

by another; reaction bred predictable reaction, ad infinitum. Often these episodes took the character of war. All of it was as typical in the upper Midwest as elsewhere, and the Washburns—whether they liked it or not—were swept up by the tide. Cadwallader could dream of dumping his interest in M&StL, but he could not do it—for now, at least. The Washburns found no opportunity to rest on their oars. Completion of the road to Albert Lea and into the waiting arms of Burlington, Cedar Rapids & Northern opened new vistas for M&StL but simultaneously activated determined hostility from powerful quarters. M&StL found itself in an exciting but utterly volatile environment.[2]

For the Minneapolis road, Chicago, Milwaukee & St. Paul always represented a distinct and disturbing thorn in the side. A relative newcomer, Chicago & North Western, also stirred the pot. These two roads once briefly shared common management and directory, but more usually—as was now the case—were fierce competitors. C&NW had pushed westward and northwestward from Chicago by construction for its own account, through acquisitions, and through clients. For instance, in a bold strategic move, C&NW had acquired Winona & St. Peter in 1868, snatching it away from Milwaukee's eager clutches. That pioneer road linked valleys of the Mississippi and Minnesota with a line built haltingly from 1864 to 1873 through Rochester, Owatonna, Waseca, St. Peter, and New Ulm before dashing on to Lake Kampeska in Dakota Territory. Even earlier a series of predecessors had completed a marvelously located line across Iowa through Cedar Rapids and Marshalltown to become the first connection with Union Pacific and the central overland route to Pacific tidewater. C&NW was no less active in Wisconsin, where it went head-to-head with Milwaukee Road and even claimed certain portions of the state for its own. Indeed, in 1872 the West Wisconsin Railway and a friendly associate had completed a line into St. Paul and with C&NW commenced through operations to Chicago. The authoritative *Railroad Gazette* concluded a year later that, at least in the short term, there was "little need of new construction by the company."[3]

Milwaukee Road was a colossus. That company, of course, owned two routes from Milwaukee to St. Paul and Minneapolis, the pioneer line via Austin, northeast Iowa, and Prairie du Chien, plus the newer, river route from La Crosse through Winona and Hastings; after 1872, CM&StP also had its own thoroughfare from Milwaukee to Chicago, giving it a marvelous position in the 400-mile Chicago–Minneapolis corridor. Under the aggressive leadership of Alexander Mitchell and Sherburne S. Merrill, it always was in position to flex its muscles and did so when it wanted. That had happened early in 1877 when CM&StP announced that it would no longer interchange business at Chaska, where a good volume of wheat from its Hastings & Dakota moved to M&StL for Minneapolis millers. Hastings & Dakota, of course, stretched westward from Hastings, on the Mississippi, along a path south of St. Paul and Minneapolis to Chaska, and had pressed on through excellent farm country to Glencoe, 54 miles away from Hastings, in 1872. Minneapolis-bound traffic from the west always could have been taken on through Chaska to Farmington and then backhauled by CM&StP to Minneapolis, if at a senseless waste of ton miles, but M&StL had provided the most direct hookup. Now, however, Mitchell bowed his back and absorbed the inefficiency to maintain line-haul all the way to Minneapolis. W. D. Washburn perceived this turn of events "as a declaration of war on Minneapolis & St. Louis" and retaliated by closing off Milwaukee's access to M&StL's dominant trackage in the milling district. Said an angry Washburn, " . . . your cars will not be transferred to our tracks." Those cars now would have to be unloaded on CM&StP sidings and the contents drayed to the mills, a process as inconvenient as it was expensive. Millers watched nervously. Three months passed before the two roads patched things up and restored operations to the status quo ante. "Like all wars," said a local newspaper, "it ended in peace." Not necessarily. In 1877, CM&StP did more business in Minneapolis and in Minnesota than any other railroad, and its managers remained determined to maintain that domination—M&StL notwithstanding.[4]

Mitchell and Merrill likewise were doggedly committed to expanding service opportunities elsewhere within the state. In 1879, CM&StP would take stock control of Southern Minnesota, with which M&StL connected at Albert Lea, draining off traffic east-

ward to Milwaukee's line that previously had gone northward on the Minneapolis road. Mitchell and Merrill also angled for rights to build up the west bank of the Mississippi River toward St. Cloud—effectively extending their river line from La Crosse—parallel to St. Paul & Pacific, soon to be invigorated as St. Paul, Minneapolis & Manitoba (StPM&M or Manitoba) by James J. Hill and his associates. The Milwaukeeans would lose that campaign, but they confirmed CM&StP's intentions of nipping at Manitoba's flanks by acquiring all assets of Hastings & Dakota, which pressed westward to Montevideo and Ortonville with clear designs on Dakota Territory. Mitchell and Merrill also authorized beefing up Milwaukee's presence in and about Minneapolis and St. Paul with a 10-mile "short line" between those cities (the old route via Mendota was indirect, 15 miles) and by a 31-mile cutoff from Minneapolis southwestward to Hastings & Dakota at Cologne. That cutoff, crossing M&StL west

Milwaukee Road was a colossus and a constant irritant to the much smaller and weaker M&StL, particularly in the west-bank milling district, where M&StL dominated. Here a Milwaukee switch crew poses for a photograph with Washburn's "B" Mill in the background. Photograph courtesy of the Hennepin History Museum.

of Hopkins, was clearly a shot across M&StL's bow, pointedly announcing that Milwaukee would control as much business as possible in and out of Minneapolis, and when completed, would obviate the need for most interchange at Chaska. Indeed, under Mitchell and Merrill the Milwaukee Road during the 1870s became one of the strongest—if not in fact the strongest—competitors in the Midwest. By the end of the decade the road would operate nearly 4,000 miles of line.[5]

Before all of this was public information, Charles F. Hatch, M&StL's general manager, reported to stockholders with great relish that Hastings & Dakota's westward extension had taken it through "fine wheat growing land" and that "wheat from this section would naturally come to the flour mills at Minneapolis, and the return cars can be loaded with lumber for that section" under "a satisfactory arrangement . . . with the CM&StP . . . to bring business of this section over our line of road via Chaska." Hatch also confidently told M&StL's owners that "traffic arrangements with the St. Paul & Sioux City R.R. for hauling the Minneapolis business of that line via Merriam Junction over our line continued to be satisfactory and to the mutual advantage of both companies." Hatch saw only a mirage that quickly evaporated when CM&StP announced its cutoff and short line and when local control of St. Paul & Sioux City passed to others of a more aggressive bent. In fact, M&StL was caught in a vise with powerful players at the lever—a reality that got plainer with every passing day.[6]

Much speculation surrounded the question of ownership and allegiance of several prominent area railroads. West Wisconsin, as an example, often was considered a client for Chicago & North Western, and West Wisconsin did connect with C&NW and did have a traffic agreement with C&NW bearing on business between Chicago and St. Paul. Furthermore, control of West Wisconsin and its neighbor, North Wisconsin, had passed to a syndicate headed by H. H. Porter, a Chicagoan and on the board of C&NW, and the Porter clique was rumored to have its eye on St. Paul & Sioux City. Did all of that confirm that C&NW was orchestrating from behind the scene? Many Minnesotans thought so.[7]

These unstable variables were swiftly manifest at Minneapolis. In fact, serious problems had surfaced earlier when millers in

M&StL enjoyed supremacy in the west-bank milling district—a cramped and crowded area that at some locations required heavy trestle work to match shipper needs with railroad technology. This view looks west through the flour mill row along the trestle above the First Street canal, which delivered the water that powered the mills. The Crown Roller Mill can be seen in the distance. Photograph ca. 1878; courtesy of the Minnesota Historical Society.

competition with the Washburns, and even some who were friendly, worried over M&StL's practical monopoly in the west-bank milling district and over M&StL's modest route structure, which they felt restricted an adequate supply of wheat as well as their ability to move finished product to expanding markets. They were motivated variously by jealousy and legitimate fears, egged on by powerful Chicago, Milwaukee & St. Paul and those behind plans for St. Paul & Sioux City and West Wisconsin plus opportunistic surrogates. In any event, the dissidents, led by Joel Bassett, a man long hostile toward the Washburns, discovered and dredged up an old charter that had given Minneapolis Eastern Railroad authorization to build and operate a line between Minneapolis and St. Paul. Articles of incorporation claiming those rights and using that name were filed on June 17, 1878. On the surface Minneapolis Eastern appeared as nothing more than an unnecessary nuisance, but there was more

here than met the eye, and for M&StL the stakes were enormous. The Washburns were in a state of high dudgeon. Soon the environment was so explosive that a "railroad conference" was scheduled in the "gentlemen's parlors of the Nicollet." Present were W. D. Washburn (M&StL), Alexander Mitchell and S. S. Merrill (CM&StP), H. H. Porter (West Wisconsin), and C. B. Wright (NP). A majority of these men urged pooling of all railroad property and trackage in and about the mills under a "stock company to consist of the various railroad companies and the mill owners." It seemed a most democratic solution, but there was nothing in it but loss for the

Milwaukee Road's impressive passenger station at Third and Washington was a profound statement of that company's affluence and its prominence in and about Minneapolis. Photograph ca. 1878; courtesy of the Hennepin History Museum.

Washburn mills and for M&StL; William Drew Washburn said as much. Brother Cadwallader, who as governor of Wisconsin had witnessed firsthand the power of CM&StP and C&NW in that state, was even more adamant, growling that M&StL's "property shall not be confiscated for the benefit of two alien corporations" to advance their own mendacious inclinations. Nevertheless, as consequence of difficult and contentious legal proceedings, Minneapolis Eastern was awarded certain property rights in the west-bank milling district, and M&StL was forced into "the exchange and leasing of tracks." It was a stunning victory for the big roads; it was a stinging loss for the Washburns and M&StL.[8]

M&StL's strong position in the west-side milling district was effectively broken; bad news would follow bad news. Minneapolis Eastern built about 3 miles of track in and about the milling district but never more. In fact, that is all its promoters ever wanted. M&StL expanded its own switching network and in the future would still handle a plurality of line hauls to and from the district. But for M&StL, the worst news was yet to come: early in the fall of 1878, Minneapolis Eastern announced that it was owned in equal parts by Chicago, Milwaukee & St. Paul and Chicago, St. Paul,

Minneapolis & Omaha (West Wisconsin's successor). The camel's nose was forever more under M&StL's tent. Operations began in midsummer 1879 and included both plant switching and interchange of cars to and from CM&StP. In another numbing blow to M&StL, Minneapolis Eastern gained track connection with St. Paul, Minneapolis & Manitoba, allowing interchange with that major road as well. Moreover, St. Paul & Sioux City was enthusiastically agitating for rights to run its trains directly to Minneapolis over M&StL from Merriam just as West Wisconsin gained running rights over Manitoba from St. Paul to Minneapolis.[9]

Meanwhile, traffic arrangements for M&StL's outlet to Duluth became confused. Lake Superior & Mississippi was always a close working partner, and after NP's lease of it ended early in 1874, M&StL poured even more flour over that road to Lake Superior. LS&M stumbled through the Panic of 1873 as a stand-alone carrier if still controlled by Philadelphia interests. The intervening country between Duluth and St. Paul remained thinly settled and produced marginal traffic, and Duluth was particularly hard hit during the Panic of 1873. Grain, flour, and merchandise moved northbound to the lake, while coal, salt, and miscellaneous freight passed southward. Finally, in 1876 LS&M bondholders announced intentions of foreclosing, a process culminated in 1877 by creation of the St. Paul & Duluth Railroad (StP&D) as successor. The "new" road had several former LS&M directors, a clear Philadelphia flavor, and continuing if less tangible financial linkage to Northern Pacific.[10]

LEFT: Minneapolis Eastern joined CM&StP in threatening M&StL's premier presence in the west-bank milling district. Seen here is Washburn's massive original "A" Mill, which would be destroyed along with several neighboring mills in a catastrophic explosion in 1878. Photograph courtesy of the Minneapolis Public Library, Minneapolis Collection.

FACING PAGE: After a lengthy legal battle with Minneapolis Mill, Minneapolis Eastern constructed a massive trestle on the river side of the mills along the First Street canal, effectively breaking M&StL's dominance of the west-side milling district. The trestle ran from the Palisade Mill on the left to a bridge shared with Manitoba that spanned the head of the canal. M&StL's trestle above the First Street canal can be seen behind the Palisade Mill. Photograph by Henry R. Farr; courtesy of the Minnesota Historical Society.

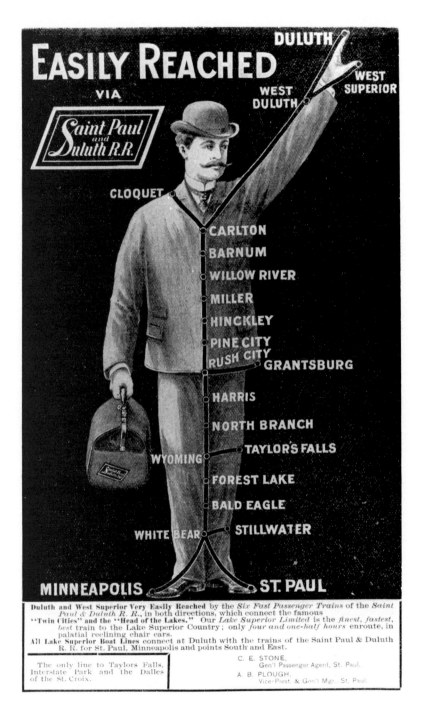

Duluth and West Superior Very Easily Reached by the *Six Fast Passenger Trains* of the *Saint Paul & Duluth R. R.*, in both directions, which connect the famous "Twin Cities" and the "Head of the Lakes." Our *Lake Superior Limited* is the *finest, fastest, best* train to the Lake Superior Country; only *four and one-half hours* enroute, in palatial reclining chair cars.
All Lake Superior Boat Lines connect at Duluth with the trains of the Saint Paul & Duluth R. R. for St. Paul, Minneapolis and points South and East.

The only line to Taylors Falls, Interstate Park and the Dalles of the St. Croix.

C. E. STONE,
Gen'l Passenger Agent, St. Paul.

A. B. PLOUGH,
Vice-Prest. & Gen'l Mgr., St. Paul.

By mid-1879, rumors circulated to the effect that control of St. Paul & Duluth had changed. The rumors proved founded. New directors included David Dows and R. P. Flower, closely connected with Chicago & North Western as well as Chicago, Rock Island & Pacific, and Jeremiah Milbank and Peter Geddes, directors of Chicago, Milwaukee & St. Paul. The *Railroad Gazette* blandly but correctly speculated that the new owners hoped to "prevent any conflict between the line to Lake Superior and those to Lake Michigan." This news set off a wave of consternation across Minnesota, where concern over "railroad excesses" and the power of the "Chicago pool roads" remained pronounced. Some of it was Granger hysteria, but some was closely reasoned. Millers friendly to the Washburns as well as those hostile to them jointly feared that control of St. Paul & Duluth by Chicago and Milwaukee interests would effectively limit their options. The potential impact on M&StL was obvious; StP&D interchanged more freight with M&StL than any other road, and M&StL was hostage to it for any movement to and from Lake Superior. Cadwallader Washburn was irritated and frustrated, for M&StL's relationship with LS&M and StP&D under previous owners had been mutually advantageous if not always cordial. Furthermore, with historic agreements between them, M&StL, never financially robust, had been spared the need to consider its own expansion beyond White Bear Lake to Duluth. Now, however, Cadwallader leaked rumors that M&StL would make surveys to the northeast. At the same time, William Drew Washburn and John Martin quietly purchased shares of Taylor's Falls & Lake Superior Railroad, a company that had its own aspirations but one the Washburns thought might be useful in levering M&StL's strategic options.[11]

There seemed no end of concerns. Minnesota farmers had heartily embraced the wheat culture; M&StL's service area reflected as much. During the first three days of 1878, M&StL delivered to the mills 35,000 bushels from along its line; during one April day alone,

Of the several railroads serving Minneapolis, none was more creative in its advertising than St. Paul & Duluth.

18,000 bushels were dispatched from on-line stations. Yet demand exceeded supply, and those millers friendly to Washburn—and others, too—worried even more openly and loudly that the country tributary to M&StL was inadequate to need. Moreover, they brooded, M&StL remained a conspicuously modest operation laboring within shadows of hostile imperial giants and against the growing need to cover overhead expenses and to service debt. Like it or not, M&StL's owners had to confront reality: expansion was essential.[12]

Iowa beckoned. That state had been well blessed by ice age gifts: especially rich soils abroad the earth's rolling crust that proved utterly irresistible to the plowman. Iowa's population had expanded by nearly 58 percent in the five years following the Civil War to 1.2 million persons, and in the decade of the 1870s would grow by 36 percent to 1.6 million. During the same decade the number of farm units increased from 116,000 to 185,000, and by 1880 farmers would have nearly 25 million acres under cultivation. Among the classes of freight handled by Iowa railroads, grain led with a prodigious 31 percent, followed by merchandise (16 percent), lumber (15 percent), coal (11 percent), and livestock (10 percent). It was a traffic mix that had great allure for Minneapolis and M&StL. Agriculture produced significant tonnage in rye, barley, and oats, but corn flourished everywhere, and wheat, noted the eager millers, was the leading staple crop and was especially popular in northern counties. Coal, of which Minnesota had none, was found near Fort Dodge and to the south among other locations. What Iowa had, Minnesota needed. Conversely, much of Iowa was without timber to produce milled lumber, and the state's merchants complained that they were dependent on goods supplied from Chicago and to a lesser extent from St. Louis. Minnesota—and particularly Minneapolis—could meet Iowa's needs. The potential synergies were obvious: coal and grain northbound; lumber, flour, and merchandise southbound—loads in both directions. The always expansive Minneapolis Board of Trade predictably took a shine to the notion. "Nature has so located Minneapolis that it may be the great market for all this territory and the source from which the population shall draw their supplies." M&StL could provide the necessary link, could prosper

both states in the bargain, and could prosper itself in the process. "The welfare of all railways companies is so closely interwoven with the prosperity of their tributary districts," chipped in the editor of *Railway World*, "that judicious managers will not fail to adopt the best available measures for increasing the productive power of their customers. . . . " M&StL's prescription for that was to extend a "metropolitan corridor" southward into Iowa using rails as "the energizing spine of that corridor."[13]

None of this was new to the Washburns, who long had been alert to possibilities in Iowa. After M&StL reached Albert Lea in 1877, Cadwallader made a personal reconnaissance of the territory southwest of Albert Lea, found it scarcely settled, but declared that the Clarion-Webster soils in the headwaters country of the Cedar and Iowa rivers held great promise. Furthermore, if they pressed onward to Fort Dodge and environs, coal fields of considerable value could be tapped.

In any event, by midsummer 1880 rails were joined at Livermore, Iowa, and a 210-mile route from Minneapolis to Fort Dodge was complete. The *Minneapolis Tribune* took appropriate pride in the event, pointing out that "Iowa and Minnesota have many mutual and reciprocal interests" and underscored the fact that M&StL was "proving a powerful agency in developing those interests and drawing the two great commonwealths into a close union which is equally beneficial to both."[14]

No doubt. But it also awakened the active hostility of other railroads. They saw that not only would M&StL tap Webster County coal fields, but it would also make connection at Fort Dodge with an Illinois Central client from Sioux City and connection there for Omaha as well as with Des Moines & Fort Dodge for Des Moines. Moreover, predicted *Railway World* in parroting St. Paul's *Pioneer Press*, M&StL soon would announce plans for its own independent extension to Omaha "and a direct connection with Union Pacific."[15]

Other forces took note. James J. Hill, prominent citizen of St. Paul and one whose fortunes would rise with those of St. Paul, Minneapolis & Manitoba, watched M&StL with great interest. So did those in charge of affairs at St. Paul & Sioux City, who had planned their own "Fort Dodge Branch" and in 1879 authorized and began construction of it from Lake Crystal to Blue Earth. M&StL's move sorely aggrieved this rival, which saw the Washburn thrust into Iowa as a trespass on "their" territory. StP&SC's E. F. Drake sourly complained that M&StL's Iowa incursion should have been at least 20 miles to the east.[16]

The presence of coal-bearing lands near Fort Dodge was especially attractive to the Washburns and other Minneapolitans. In 1880, Webster County pits produced 128,712 tons, some of it billed to Northwestern Fuel Company of Minneapolis, and more of it to M&StL as locomotive fuel. Other shipments derived at Rippey, a station on Des Moines & Fort Dodge, with which M&StL now connected at Fort Dodge, but the total was sadly inadequate to need. "There is not half-coal enough on our line to supply the demand," admitted M&StL's Charles F. Hatch, general manager. "The wonderful growth and extension of railroads throughout the West in the last year, and the opening up and settlement of a large amount of new territory," said Hatch, "have caused a largely increased demand for fuel and particularly coal. . . ." There were additional beds of coal south of Kalo, Hatch and others at M&StL knew; they would be pursued in good time.[17]

M&StL now had an acceptable connection at Albert Lea with BCR&N for traffic to and from the east and southeast as well as its own new artery into a fertile and productive hinterland. To the north, however, M&StL faced a growing dilemma with its only outlet, St. Paul & Duluth, in the hands of a consortium representing Minneapolis rivals Chicago and Milwaukee. M&StL was hardly alone in indignation. Public irritation continued high, and criticism of the ownership arrangement shrill. In St. Paul, the *Pioneer Press* declared that eastern interests "now held Minnesota in capitalistic subjection," that Minnesota had "lost its only competing outlet upon lake navigation," and that dual membership on boards of competing companies was in violation of Minnesota law. Others in St. Paul and Minneapolis advocated an international all-rail route to the east by way of Sault Ste. Marie as the ultimate way to break the backs of the Lake Michigan roads.[18]

The whole matter was adequate to an outbreak of acute dyspepsia among Minneapolis millers who long had valued the Lake Superior chute as a useful, proper, and effective defense against the aggressive instincts of railroads based in Milwaukee and Chicago. Cadwallader Washburn demanded to know St. Paul & Duluth's intentions toward the historic arrangements M&StL had with predecessor Lake Superior & Mississippi on Duluth traffic via White Bear Lake. That traffic was appreciable, StP&D admitted; M&StL remained its most lucrative interchange partner by far. Nevertheless, St. Paul & Duluth waffled on any long-term arrangement, reflecting, without doubt, the determination of new owners to neutralize the Duluth road against their own, greater interests. The Washburns were in another tough spot. William Drew had made investments in Taylor's Falls & Lake Superior, of course, but that may have been merely a feint. Now, however, the two brothers were forced as to the issue of an independent route to Lake Superior. Cadwallader dispatched surveyors into the field northeast from Taylors Falls across Wisconsin.[19]

Interest in a rail line from the St. Croix River to Lake Superior dated from the early 1850s when Congress had granted land to the State of Wisconsin in support of such a venture. A decade later the Wisconsin legislature had awarded rights and lands to the St. Croix & Lake Superior Railroad for a line from Hudson, on the St. Croix, to Superior, with a branch to Bayfield, both on Lake Superior. That outfit failed, but the idea lived on.[20]

None of this found favor with owners of Lake Superior & Mississippi or its St. Paul & Duluth successor, who pointed out that there had been—and there continued to be—inadequate demand for transportation in that region. But residents of Taylors Falls, a small village lying east of StP&D—25 miles north of Stillwater at the head of navigation on the St. Croix, about 52 miles from

---

FACING PAGE: Construction train at Lindstrom, ca. 1880. M&StL and StP&D would jointly construct and operate the new line between Wyoming and Taylors Falls. Photograph by Sanford C. Sargent; courtesy of the Minnesota Historical Society.

Minneapolis—desperately yearned for rail service and in 1875 had seen to incorporation of the Taylor's Falls & Lake Superior Railroad and even wrested a grant of swamp land in support from the Minnesota Legislature. Timing was not propitious; the Panic of 1873 yet reigned, and the forty-one local shareholders were inadequate to mount any construction campaign. But in 1879, the needs of the Washburns and M&StL and those of Taylors Falls meshed. And, said the *Minneapolis Tribune*, "If the sale of the Duluth Road to the Chicago combination hastens another rail connection with Lake Superior, it will prove a blessing in disguise." M&StL sought local bonus support for a direct extension of the old Minneapolis & Duluth from White Bear Lake to Taylors Falls, about 26 miles, but St. Paul & Duluth—controlled by "capitalists of the pooled lines" of Chicago, the local press reminded—countered with a plan of its own to

The Taylors Falls line was picturesque, but would it generate traffic volumes? This view is about a mile and a half west of the Taylors Falls depot. Photograph from Northern Pacific.

build a branch from Wyoming, 30 miles north of St. Paul, to Taylors Falls. StP&D's response was clearly aimed at heading off a rival peddling the powerful elixir of competition. Yet the actual intentions of the Washburn brothers were clouded in mystery. In the fall of 1879, William Drew quietly urged James J. Hill, whose star in regional railroad matters clearly was rising, to build an improved line from Minneapolis to the northeast, a line, Washburn suggested, jointly operated by St. Paul, Minneapolis & Manitoba, with which Hill was closely associated, and Northern Pacific, Manitoba's traditional rival. Why? Was Washburn admitting that his financial capacity, that of his brother, and that of M&StL were collectively stretched? Did he wish to entice Hill, a local leader, against the pool roads? Hill was known to have his own strong views toward those companies, but in this case he did not rise to Washburn's bait.[21]

In February 1880 came word that Taylors Falls had voted $23,700 in aid of M&StL and that William Drew had successfully arranged for additional financing from Central Trust of New York. Work began initially above the rocky escarpment near Taylors Falls on what M&StL confidently labeled its "Lake Superior Extension." The line was to be built by Taylor's Falls & Lake Superior under M&StL's supervision; on May 1, 1880, William D. Washburn assumed full stock ownership of the Taylor's Falls road. St. Paul & Duluth cried "uncle." Negotiations followed. A covenant was made with M&StL whereby M&StL agreed to terminate construction on its "Lake Superior Extension" except the heavy work in the rock-walled gorge near Taylors Falls; M&StL and StP&D would jointly construct and operate a line from Wyoming to Taylors Falls; and M&StL would enjoy perpetual running rights over StP&D from White Bear Lake to Wyoming. Moreover, StP&D grudgingly agreed to allow M&StL overhead or operating rights for three years all the way to Duluth from White Bear Lake. The contract spoke to "common benefits," which were obvious, but the news was a shock and great disappointment in both Minneapolis and St. Paul, where leaders had pinned their hopes on M&StL to provide a new outlet to Lake Superior. The *Minneapolis Tribune*, usually a Washburn booster, wailed that M&StL could not "on any consideration, afford to permanently abandon" the goal "of its own independent line to the lake," an integral part of a glorious plan to gain the "Atlantic coast via Sault Ste. Marie," which "when consummated, must make it one of the most important trunk lines on the continent."[22]

During the ensuing spring and summer, work progressed on the new route from Wyoming to Taylors Falls, and M&StL commenced through-freight operations, actually mixed trains with very little passenger business, to and from Duluth. Several factors militated against timely completion of the new line, but finally the 20-mile route serving the villages of Chisago City, Lindstrom, Center City, Shafer, and Franconia was opened. Ringing church bells and the "boom" of cannon greeted the first passenger trains to creep into the Dalles of the St. Croix and roll to a stop in the picturesque community of Taylors Falls. The date was November 8, 1880, a perfect Indian summer day, by one account. Nine carloads of "railroad dignitaries" and other "honored guests" from Minneapolis and St. Paul quickly adjourned to Folsom's Building on First Street to enjoy a home-cooked meal of chicken pie and listen to long-winded speeches, which always seemed to attend such festivities. The guests eventually reboarded the cars, and the trains chugged upgrade and out of sight. Despite the disappearance of the trains, the track remained to promise that Taylors Falls was finally connected to the age of railways. That was ample reason for locals to dance the night away at the Dalles House.[23]

William D. Washburn was richly praised for his efforts in bringing rail service to Taylors Falls, and in the course of speeches on that rich autumnal day, he thanked village citizens for their hospitality and urged them to turn to the task of developing water power and building up "manufacturing institutions" that would, although he did not plainly say so, justify his personal investment and that of M&StL. Indeed, his thoughts must have been mixed on the return trip to Minneapolis. The short, new 20-mile service area offered limited traffic potential that had to be shared with StP&D, and M&StL's "Lake Superior Extension" was stalled in the valley of the St. Croix—far short of its stated goal and now pledged under agreement with StP&D not to go any farther. But, Washburn may have sighed, at least M&StL had rights for three years to operate its own trains over StP&D to Duluth. That place had suffered acute reverses in the Panic of 1873 but presently seemed poised for dramatic recovery. Its population in 1880 stood at a mere 3,483 inhabitants but would quadruple in only thirty-six months. In 1882 alone, 508 new buildings—including 5 sawmills—would be erected, grain receipts would double over 1881, and 569 steamers and 277 sailing vessels would call there in that season. Duluth, at the Head of the Lakes, held great potential. So the Washburns had always believed. And now M&StL could participate in that potential in a direct way. Extension beyond Taylors Falls? It would have to wait for another day.[24]

# OPTIMISM AND REALISM  6

The great Northern Pacific Railroad which will find its terminus
at Puget Sound—the best harbor on the whole Pacific Coast—
and through the great chain of lakes terminate at Portland, Maine,
*must* pass through the very heart of this State, and at this very
point—the falls of St. Anthony—will be the most important
depot between the two oceans.

*MINNEAPOLIS TRIBUNE*, MAY 25, 1867

A spirit of optimism swirled with winds of change as the decade of
the 1880s unfurled. The country's population stood at 50 million,
New York was first among states with over 5 million residents, and
the center of population had moved to a few miles west by south of
Cincinnati. Rutherford B. Hayes chose not to seek a second term
as president, and the Republicans picked James A. Garfield, who
won over Democrat Winfield Scott Hancock in the general election
that fall. In the area of technology, Thomas Edison took patent on
the incandescent light bulb and shortly would design a system for
efficient distribution of electrical power from a central generating
station. Standard Oil and Carnegie Steel were well established in
the fields of petroleum refining and steel manufacturing. But above
all this was the age of railroads—the country's first big business. Aggregate mileage stood at 93,296, up from 52,922 in 1870.[1]

The transformation of the United States to an urban, industrial
nation—under way for three decades or more—was greatly accelerated during these years by revolutionary changes in production
and distribution. Value-added manufacturing would rise by an astonishing 112 percent during the period 1879–89. Mass production
and mass consumption were inextricably linked by the railroad and
the telegraph. The growth of cities and the spread of a national rail
network led to large vertically integrated business concerns, many
of which adopted brand names, embraced massive advertising campaigns, and established national sales and marketing operations
with regional offices and traveling salesmen aided by the invention and application of the typewriter, adding machines, scales, the
mimeograph machine, and the cash register.[2]

All of this was reflected locally to one extent or another. Minnesota's population in 1880 stood at 780,773, up from 439,706 in 1870.
Acreage in farmlands had more than doubled in the 1870s, and the
average farm now was 145 acres. The state's primary cities showed
similar growth; Minneapolis, with 46,887 persons, had surpassed

St. Paul, with 41,473. In Minnesota, like the nation at large, a revival of business prosperity had followed the Panic of 1873.[3]

All of this, too, was reflected at the Falls of St. Anthony. In 1870, sawmilling had been premier, employing more persons and yielding more value than even flour milling; pineries tributary to the Mississippi River still furnished all the logs the Minneapolis mills could use. Hard times in the 1870s reduced production, but Minneapolis mills distributed to a wide area including Minnesota, Iowa, Missouri, Kansas, and Dakota Territory. In 1877, twenty mills scored combined sales of $2.4 million. Yet change was afoot. Despite increased annual production and sales to an expanded hinterland, demand exceeded capacity, and Minneapolis itself began to import lumber for local trade as well as resale. Moreover, there were problems at the falls, and some millers chose to relocate to the northern part of the city and powered their saws by steam. Still, Minneapolis in 1880 ranked third among American cities in production of sawed lumber.[4]

Change also was part of the local flour milling scene. In 1870, flour production in Minneapolis had been 193,000 barrels, but in 1875 production jumped to 843,000 barrels. In 1877, 4.5 million bushels of wheat arrived in Minneapolis, and the mills shipped 935,544 barrels of flour in 5,218 carloads. By 1880, production topped 2,051,840 barrels, and flour milling surpassed sawmilling in terms of annual value of product. Indeed, Minneapolis ranked first among all American cities in flour production.[5]

---

FACING PAGE: Industry at St. Anthony Falls was crucial to railroad interests. This photograph looking toward the west bank from the Winslow House Hotel shows the density of the mills jostling for access to the hydropower of the falls.

RIGHT: Ownership and operation of flouring enterprises on both sides of the river were characterized by convolution, but one constant was the frenetic activity in and about the milling district. Railways were at center stage, the essential intermediary between farmers who produced the wheat and millers who processed the wheat into flour, and between millers and consumers near and far. The Palisade Mill stood at what would become West River Road and Chicago Avenue. Photograph courtesy of the Minneapolis Public Library, Minneapolis Collection.

Change was similarly occurring in the very milling process and in the size and scope of operation. The Washburns, not surprisingly, were in the thick of it. The short, broad-shouldered, deep-chested Cadwallader long since had determined to become the low-cost producer through economy of scale, innovation, and talented associates. In the flour milling business, William Drew Washburn seemed only to get in the way, forcing his older brother to rely instead on George H. Christian and then John Crosby and William Hood Dunwoody. It was scientifically minded George Christian who had adopted the middlings purifier and the Hungarian roller method and who with others operated the great Washburn A mill under lease. Crosby, married to the sister of Mrs. W. D. Washburn, and like the Washburns also from Maine, gave the company an honest, steady hand at operations and in 1879 became a principal in the Washburn-Crosby Company. Dunwoody, originally from Pennsylvania, had earlier experience as a flour merchant and proved to be an excellent salesman. It was Dunwoody who in 1877 landed a

contract in Scotland and who laid foundation for the great export trade in Minneapolis flour that followed. With an adequate supply of hard spring wheat, with economy of scale and the force of innovation, with demand and profit high, all looked well for the Washburn flouring activity in the spring of 1878.[6]

On May 2, 1878, Washburn A exploded. The concussion and fire claimed eighteen lives and ruined six flour mills and several other businesses in the immediate vicinity. Minneapolis was stunned; it was a terrible disaster by any standard. But Cadwallader and others turned the disaster to advantage. Work on Washburn C, already under way, continued, and a new, larger, more modern Washburn A was designed on the site of the old.[7]

Even as plans went forward on the new Washburn A, word circulated about Pillsbury A, a truly formidable rival mill. A native of New Hampshire, Charles A. Pillsbury in 1869 had followed the lead of his uncle, John S. Pillsbury, and moved to Minnesota. Soon the younger man was engaged in flour milling. In 1874, he founded C. A. Pillsbury & Company, a family partnership, one expanded in 1878 when his father, George A., brought additional talent and capital to the enterprise. Pillsbury proved a strong competitor and would help push Minneapolis to first rank in the flouring trade. When the handsome, seven-story Pillsbury A began production across the river from the Washburn operation in 1881, it would have capacity to turn out 4,000 barrels of "Pillsbury's Best" each day.[8]

But taciturn Cadwallader Washburn had shown the way. The Washburn company had recognized the great potential in marketing abroad and had cracked that market; in 1878 over 100,000 barrels of Minneapolis flour moved to Europe, primarily the United Kingdom. And it was the Washburn company that recognized utility in direct sales to merchants instead of consignment of flour in the East. In 1877, a traveling salesman was employed for that purpose; his first customer was in Chicago, where the famous Palmer House purchased a carload and began a long run of buying flour exclusively from Washburn. Personalized sales in the East also reflected Washburn's understanding that the United States had the fastest growing market of any industrialized nation and that his company had to maximize domestic as well as international sales in order to enjoy the fruits of the large scale, automatic, continuous-process, gradual-reduction roller mills that had been built in Minneapolis. He also appreciated the need for establishing a reputation for producing a high-quality product. That recognition came in 1880, when Washburn-Crosby entered three brands of spring wheat process flour at the Millers' International Exhibition at Cincinnati and came away with gold, silver, and bronze awards. On August 19, 1880, the first flour was packed and shipped under the now famous "Gold Medal" brand name. Finally, Washburn clearly understood the crucial relationship that transportation played in all of this. That, of course, was where railroads—especially M&StL—fit in.[9]

From the very beginning of the company in 1870, M&StL had been the tender handmaiden of the Minneapolis flour millers, the Washburns in particular and, by extension, those whose fortunes

When Washburn "A" exploded in 1878, Cadwallader Washburn determined to rebuild on the same site but with a larger and more modern mill. Photograph courtesy of the Minneapolis Public Library, Minneapolis Collection.

This promotional illustration would have viewers believe that Pillsbury had exclusive provenance on both sides of the milling district. Washburn and others would have taken exception.

were tied in one way or another to those flour millers. There was a distinct symbiosis that all could see and understand. Flour millers needed a constant and reliable source of wheat, and they needed constant and reliable avenues to move flour to markets near and far. Flour millers also needed favorable rates on both raw material and finished product. Indeed, favorable rates were crucial to their financial success. Fortunately, the millers had an ace in the hole in this regard—moving flour to hinterlands that produced the very wheat they milled. Another head haul, lumber, likewise protected the back haul, wheat, through indirect subsidy. The same effect might be had by merchandise billed to Minneapolis wholesalers in cars that carried flour outbound. All of this explained M&StL's early plan to link up with St. Paul & Sioux City at Merriam, to reach the Great Lakes chain at Duluth, to push on to Albert Lea and a grand union there with Burlington, Cedar Rapids & Northern, and finally to drive into Iowa with a line to Fort Dodge. Each one of these campaigns had mirrored the flour millers' need for supply as well as outlet and a need for balance of traffic that would provide the lowest possible rates on both wheat and flour. But the decline of lumber milling at the falls threatened this delicate arrangement. Small wonder that the Washburns and those associated with them looked so often and so longingly to the country northeast of Minneapolis to Lake Superior, not merely to guarantee a seasonal Great Lakes chute for flour but also to tap immense stands of commercially valuable timber that could provide lumber shipments offsetting those lost as the era of sawmilling at the falls gradually tailed off. Flour millers also had to confront another troubling reality: the locus of the wheat belt was shifting. In fact, the shift was ongoing. The "old" wheat belt once had been in Ohio, Indiana, and Illinois, but as the westering process had accelerated, the wheat culture moved west and north to Iowa and southern Minnesota. And the shift continued. In its wake came the corn belt or, more correctly, the corn and hog belt. Increasingly wheat production moved to western and northwestern Minnesota and into Dakota Territory, away from M&StL's service area and into those of comparative giants, all of which, it seemed, were constantly expanding their reach.[10]

One of these, the historic St. Paul & Pacific, had limped ahead of demand, survived the Panic of 1873, thrust twin arteries west and northwest into the Red River valley and, in 1879, emerged as the St. Paul, Minneapolis & Manitoba (StPM&M or Manitoba). Led by four talented and experienced businessmen, the "associates" as they were called, the Manitoba prospered especially under leadership provided by James J. Hill of nearby St. Paul. Manitoba held a fine franchise, its service area was only now blooming, and it had an alert and aggressive management team. Neither was the road hesitant as to its intentions. Late in 1880, the local press reported that StPM&M planned to "branch about generally" in Minnesota,

Manitoba, and Dakota Territory. Reality quickly followed rhetoric. Manitoba's strategic plans continued to focus west by north of Minneapolis, and the company labored diligently to create a fire wall between itself and powerful and aggressive Chicago, Milwaukee & St. Paul, which at one point seemed poised to build up the west side of the Mississippi opposite the Manitoba from Minneapolis to St. Cloud. None of this seemed a threat to M&StL and its primacy at Minneapolis, but when Hill contemplated a diagonal route from St. Cloud northeastward to Duluth—a line sure to drain wheat eastward to the lake head instead of to Minneapolis mills—W. D. Washburn complained privately to Hill, forecasting damage beyond measure to both Minneapolis and St. Paul if that line were built. Hill was not dissuaded, and Manitoba eventually completed a 66.5-mile route from St. Cloud to a junction with St. Paul & Duluth at Hinckley, 77 miles above St. Paul and 76 miles below Duluth. And to forever seal off CM&StP, Manitoba itself began to occupy the west bank of the Mississippi in 1881–82, starting a new line from near Minneapolis to St. Cloud, duplicating its earlier route on the other side of the river.[11]

Hill also became a force to reckon with right in Washburn's backyard. "Our business is increasing very rapidly in Minneapolis," Hill told a correspondent in 1880. "We are bringing to the millers about 70 cars of wheat daily and I think it safe to say that we have during the past year hauled as much lumber away from Minneapolis as all other roads combined." He was well off the mark in terms of lumber movement, but there was no gainsaying Manitoba's growing presence in the affairs of Minneapolis millers. StPM&M, after all, served the giant new Pillsbury mill, had connection with west-bank millers via tiny Minneapolis Eastern, and its service area was expanding synonymously with the wheat culture. Despite completion of its new southwest-to-northeast route from St. Cloud to Duluth—which did in fact carry wheat away from Minneapolis as Washburn had feared—Manitoba would, nevertheless, handle a prodigious tonnage of wheat to the Mill City. Meanwhile, Manitoba's elderly passenger station at Minneapolis—one used by others including M&StL off and on—was simply inadequate. Some railroaders including Washburn urged a union passenger facility, but Hill said no and announced his own plans for a new Manitoba station that he expected to share with other roads. In this, as was so often the case, Hill had stolen the march on the others. Yet his plan would require a substantial bridge to bring Manitoba's main line to the west side of the river in Minneapolis—hard by the Washburn milling area and M&StL itself. There was no way to gracefully resist this bold incursion, for a new passenger station was critical to the city's welfare, and moreover, the Washburns and friends had civic as well as business responsibilities, even if they might be at M&StL's expense. Thus, Henry Titus Wells and C. C. Washburn quietly aided Hill in gaining approaches necessary to the famous Stone Arch Bridge. Irksome delays followed, but the die was cast: Manitoba's aggressive nose would be well under M&StL's tent.[12]

Hill's Manitoba was not the region's sole contender. Indeed, Manitoba would be forced to share a huge domain with now revived Northern Pacific, which had stumbled to collapse on the banks of the Missouri River at Bismarck in the Dakota Territory when Jay Cooke failed in 1873. NP's line westward from Duluth had been ahead of demand, but it offered great potential. And, of course, the company held franchise to a route all the way to Puget Sound. With the return of prosperity, NP crews moved haltingly to complete the transcontinental promise. Closer to home, NP had lost control of Lake

Manitoba's famous Stone Arch Bridge, seen here in two stages of its construction, provided access to and egress from the road's new Minneapolis passenger station. Photograph on left ca. 1883 by H. R. Farr; courtesy of the Minnesota Historical Society.

Superior & Mississippi, which had become St. Paul & Duluth, but presently looked to find another—and perhaps even more advantageous route—to St. Paul and Minneapolis. To be sure, NP managers had a clear understanding of the assets and liabilities of Duluth as its eastern terminus—the harbor was icebound large portions of the year and devoid of rail service from the east, save indirectly from St. Paul—and aspired to augment its traffic potential by direct connection with friendly or at least not hostile roads such as CM&StP, C&NW surrogates, and M&StL. Thus motivated, NP in 1877 gained charter rights to complete a partially graded route southward from Brainerd, on its main line between Duluth and Moorhead, to Sauk Rapids, across the Mississippi from St. Cloud on the then St. Paul & Pacific, about 64 miles. When completed in the same year, NP angled for and eventually got operating rights over Manitoba (née St. Paul & Pacific) from Sauk Rapids to St. Paul, although its dream to work with CM&StP on a west-side line from Minneapolis to St. Cloud seemed to go for naught as Hill finally clamped off that avenue.[13]

Northern Pacific's activities predictably excited the most active interests of Minneapolitans. Said the *Tribune*, "the great Northern Pacific . . . will soon be able to pour into the lap of Minneapolis the treasures which lie on either side of a route across the continent." That assumed, of course, that NP wisely would choose Minneapolis and not St. Paul as its "new" eastern terminus. But NP secured valuable lands without cost in St. Paul and chose that place to locate the bulk of its facilities. In any event, Northern Pacific in Minneapolis was an accomplished fact, at least as a tenant when the decade of the 1870s ended, but with promise for a greater presence in time. NP was not a threat to M&StL, and M&StL was not a threat to NP; indeed, the two had had a close association earlier when both M&D and M&StL had been leased to NP through LS&M. And in a few years they would work closely together again.[14]

Meanwhile, Chicago, Milwaukee & St. Paul continued to expand its influence across the southern third of Minnesota. Although outmaneuvered by James J. Hill on the west-bank matter, Milwaukee's patient, determined, and unsentimental Alexander Mitchell charted his own imperial path. Of particular note for both the short term and the long term was westward extension of what locally was still called the Hastings & Dakota, but which everybody knew was CM&StP, reaching Montevideo in 1878, Ortonville in 1879, and Aberdeen, Dakota Territory, in 1881. Moreover, Milwaukee's long anticipated 33-mile "Hastings Cut-off"—a direct line to Minneapolis from Hastings & Dakota at Cologne via Hopkins—became fact in 1880. So, too, did the 10-mile "Short Line" between St. Paul and Minneapolis. Collectively this gave CM&StP a complete thoroughfare from Chicago to Aberdeen via Milwaukee, La Crosse, St. Paul, and Minneapolis—a route poised for further expansion to the Missouri River and beyond. Elsewhere, Milwaukee had gobbled up Chicago, Clinton, Dubuque & Minnesota, which rival Chicago, Burlington & Quincy once had hoped to use along the Iowa side of the Mississippi for its approach to St. Paul and Minneapolis, and CM&StP likewise acquired lines in the Wisconsin River valley, tweaking another rival, Chicago & North Western. By 1881, *Railroad Gazette* claimed that Milwaukee had "a larger mileage than is worked by any other in the world directly by a single management." And more acquisitions and more construction were planned or under way—a new wholly owned line from Chicago across Iowa to Council Bluffs, for instance. By 1882, Milwaukee would be, as one press account put it, "recognized as the greatest railroad corporation in the world. . . ."[15]

Milwaukee's chief rival, Chicago & North Western, was equally active, acquiring existing properties or sponsoring new construction for its own account. C&NW was particularly expansive in north-central and northwest Iowa and in the eastern portion of what would become South Dakota. To be sure, C&NW was a full player in the "Great Dakota Boom" of the late 1870s and 1880s; by 1881, C&NW's influence was established all the way to Pierre, on the Missouri River, 785 miles northwest of Chicago. As *Railway World* admiringly pointed out, C&NW's Dakota domain was a vast

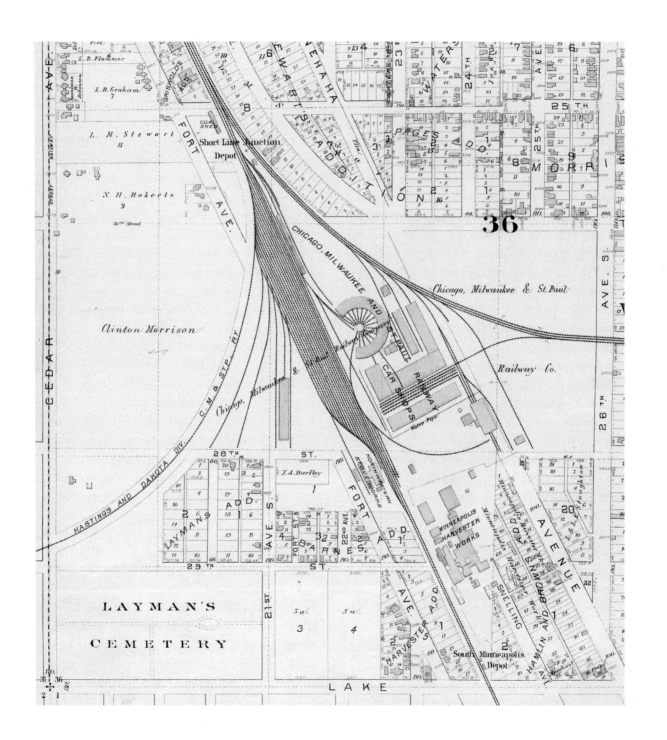

"unsettled country" now open "to homestead, timber culture, and pre-emption entries."[16]

Chicago & North Western's allegiance was always with Chicago, from which point entire trainloads of building materials were dispatched to the lumber-starved prairies and plains in its sprawling service territory. "Every new settler upon the fertile prairies means one more added to the vast army of lumber consumers," the *Northwest Lumberman* gleefully observed in 1880. And a critical mass of such settlers implied establishment of small villages with stores, schools, churches—all requiring building materials. When made empty, cars that had carried lumber westbound could be reloaded with grain billed to Chicago dealers—long-haul loads in both directions, good for C&NW, good for those who paid the transportation bills, and good for consumers because lower transit rates meant lower retail prices.[17]

None of this was lost on the Washburns and other business leaders at Minneapolis, who understood that loads leaving Minneapolis needed to be matched by loads arriving from the hinterland. That would keep rates down; that would tie surrounding areas to Minneapolis; that would profit manufacturing, jobbing, and banking interests; and that would make M&StL viable as a "home" road. More easily said than done. The prescription was accurate in all its parts, but the administration of it would be difficult in the best of circumstances, but even more so in the 1880s as the big roads fastened their grips on service areas with blankets of branch lines.

As Cadwallader Washburn considered all of this, he saw what had to be done: M&StL had to expand, again. It was a gamble,

FACING PAGE: Chicago, Milwaukee & St. Paul located impressive engine facilities and car shops at the junction of its pioneer route and new "short line" in south Minneapolis near Minnehaha Avenue and East Twenty-eighth Street. Nearby were important shippers Minneapolis Harvester and Northwestern Stove Works. Map from *A Complete Set of Surveys and Plats of Properties in the City of Minneapolis, Minnesota* (Philadelphia: C. M. Hopkins, 1885); courtesy of the Minneapolis Public Library.

RIGHT: Chicago, Milwaukee & St. Paul, not to be outdone by Northern Pacific, followed its own imperial path and reached Aberdeen, South Dakota, in 1881.

Milwaukee's long-anticipated "Short Line" between St. Paul and Minneapolis, including a substantial bridge crossing the Mississippi River (near the present-day Shriners Hospital), became fact in 1880. Photograph courtesy of the Minnesota Historical Society.

especially when the giants were venting their imperial instincts, but the Washburns were in too deeply to get out, and once more they would be required to step forward in order to protect earlier investments of time, talent, and treasure. Plainly stated, M&StL needed a greater range to disperse products and goods of Minneapolis and to gather in a greater volume of grain. There was another element in this mix. The winter of 1880-81 was unusually brutal, with blizzards and bitter cold setting in early and staying long. Rail lines were blocked, cleared, blocked again by capricious and vicious storms. All served to exacerbate the area's chronic fuel scarcity; railroads themselves were forced to cancel runs for want of coal. Of course, one of the reasons given for M&StL building on to Fort Dodge had been to tap Webster County coalfields. Some shipments were made that hard winter, but those billings were inadequate to need, and furthermore, the Webster County fields were not large. M&StL managers considered both strategic and immediate options. But for the moment, M&StL managers focused only on additional coal beds 49 miles south of Fort Dodge at Coaltown, an established community on the Des Moines & Fort Dodge Railroad, 36 miles from Des Moines.[18]

Others were watching with great interest. Before he had gained his reputation as a railroad man, James J. Hill was, among other things, a leading fuel merchant in St. Paul. This led him understand-ably to take interest in Iowa coalfields and introduced him to a long association in that regard with Hamilton Browne of Des Moines, a man who owned considerable experience as a land broker and developer of coalfields. Before 1880, Hill had invested in Webster County and to the south, collecting "about 2,300 acres of land . . . which the State Geologist pronounces the best coal field in Iowa." Even as M&StL had been driving its line southwestward to Fort Dodge in 1880, Hill curiously had undertaken to lure Milwaukee into building a vertical axis route from its soon-to-be-completed line across Iowa to Council Bluffs through Hill's land holdings to Mason City on CM&StP's well-established line across northern Iowa and served also by a Milwaukee route to Austin and on to St. Paul. To such a north–south line from central Iowa, Hill promised traffic in coal that would fuel St. Paul and Minneapolis, as well as new markets to the northwest as his Manitoba Road opened up more of Dakota Territory. Advantages to CM&StP were apparent, although such traffic would not have been oriented to its Chicago and Milwaukee bases, and nothing came of it. W. D. Washburn may have been aware of these machinations, for he quickly offered Hill a deal that Hill initially turned down as being too much to M&StL's advantage. Nevertheless, an agreement finally was concluded by which M&StL would haul coal from at least some of Hill's Iowa properties.[19]

Money for M&StL construction was arranged early in 1881, but work progressed slowly. It was not until December that the line was pushed through to Coaltown—in 1883 to be renamed Angus, honoring R. B. Angus, one of Hill's associates—259 miles from Minneapolis.[20]

Late in November 1881, Hill and Allen Manvel, Manitoba's general manager, were accompanied by E. N. Saunders of Northwest Fuel Company on an inspection trip to Fort Dodge and then boarded a pioneer train to end-of-tracks near Coaltown. What they found at that location was a raw but active village on generally flat terrain at the extreme southwestern corner of Boone County, adjacent to Greene and Dallas counties. Coal had been mined there since the Civil War, mostly for local consumption. The first big mine was sunk by John F. Duncombe of Fort Dodge, but Duncombe subsequently sold out to Climax Coal Company, in which Hill and associates were connected. Hill had other lands in Boone County, which were transferred to Climax Coal, and Manitoba itself held 1,200 acres of coal land plus mining apparatus and 2.5 miles of private rail lines, which collectively could supply 800 tons of coal daily. This production was for Manitoba's own purposes, but Climax and eight other companies in the area sold to M&StL and to coal dealers near and far.[21]

The Iowa extension met the needs of M&StL's equity holders, providing an artery for outbound milled lumber, merchandise, and to a lesser extent flour, as well as a means to deliver grain and coal northbound. But as the wheat belt shifted west and northwest to be replaced by the corn and hog belt, Minneapolis millers had to alter their own buying strategies. So, then, did M&StL need to shift.

The splendid Lake Park Hotel was completed in 1879 and was eventually served by the M&StL's Lake Park Branch.

Early in 1879 the road secured authority to build westward to the south shore of Lake Minnetonka. Although rail service to the area along the north shore had obtained since August 24, 1867, when locals saluted the arrival of a pioneer train on the St. Paul & Pacific route extending toward Willmar and beyond, agitation had surfaced a decade later for additional service to the south shore. For a quarter century wealthy southerners had journeyed by steamboat and more recently by rail to enjoy the sights and especially the cooler summers of Minnesota, and Lake Minnetonka, so close to Minneapolis, stood to capitalize on such seasonal traffic. So, too, did M&StL with its through route to St. Louis via connections.[22]

In January 1880, W. D. Washburn finally announced plans to build to the lake. Others had anticipated as much and made investment decisions accordingly. The splendid Lake Park Hotel, for instance, had been completed in 1879. The local press followed all of

LAKE PARK HOTEL, LAKE MINNETONKA.
On the line of the Minneapolis & St. Louis Railway.

this with great eagerness and enthusiasm, and the public speculated endlessly as to Washburn's purposes beyond the lake. But he kept his own counsel and would say little except that the road looked to the boundary of Dakota Territory as its objective.[23]

Motivations for the move west were much the same as for the extension to Iowa—to establish marketing areas for Minneapolis wholesalers and lumbermen and to claim wheat-bearing territory for the millers—but with differences, too. Iowa offered coal and was rather more established than western Minnesota, but the recent economic panic had been a reminder of opportunities in the American West, and with recovery had come a surge of newcomers from older states and from Europe as well. C&NW, for example,

noted in 1878 that "the new prairies of Minnesota . . . are rapidly becoming productive, and are settling up with an industrious and thrifty people." Timing was an important consideration. The shifting wheat belt was another. Strategic circumstances represented another variable. The big roads—C&NW, CM&StP, Manitoba, and NP—all were about the business of expanding in western Minnesota, and each one had moved into or had stated plans to move into

M&StL tapped Minnetonka Mills in 1881 with its new line pointed westward to Lake Minnetonka and beyond. Minnetonka Mill (center) and other industries fed freight to be billed by the company's agent in the attractive depot at right. Photograph courtesy of the Minnesota Historical Society.

nearby Dakota Territory. M&StL had either to move or to be left out in this race to establish territorial dominion. Finally, during the late 1870s, Minneapolis commercial and business interests developed acute self-confidence, which translated into renewed interest in urban economic imperialism reflected by M&StL's campaigns. "The rapidity with which north and western Minnesota, Dakota and Manitoba are being settled is opening up a large and fertile territory, the inhabitants of which naturally look to Minneapolis for supplies of farm and other machinery, and the entire list of manufactured goods required," observed a confident and optimistic Minneapolis Board of Trade in 1878. Best of all, the Board of Trade boldly asserted, "Minneapolis holds the same relationship to this northwest that Chicago did twenty years ago to the then northwest."[24]

Talk was replaced with action in 1881. Financial arrangements were made for 92 miles of M&StL's "Pacific Extension" and 1.5 miles of Lake Park Branch to serve resorts at Lake Minnetonka. Steel was laid westward from Hopkins, and the new line opened to Excelsior in mid-July. Meanwhile, graders took up their work following engineering stakes to a crossing of CM&StP's Hastings & Dakota at Norwood and then along a wonderfully chosen alignment lying below Hastings & Dakota and above the Minnesota River—a crescent-shaped route through an area certain to provide bountiful movements of wheat and other grains inbound to Minneapolis with a rural customer base sure to demand heavy shipments of lumber, coal, and manufactured goods. So Washburn believed and so M&StL's board agreed. Tracklayers in November reached Winthrop, 69 miles from Minneapolis, where they laid up for the winter. To the west stretched a nearly completed grade into the valley of the Minnesota River; to the rear lay several new communities—Deephaven, Minnetonka Beach, Green Isle, Victoria, Hamburg, Arlington, Gaylord, and Winthrop among them—each tied to Minneapolis by M&StL as the umbilical cord.[25]

By the end of 1881, Minneapolis & St. Louis as an operating entity had been around for a full decade, and while tiny in comparison to the region's giant carriers, was nevertheless a force to be reckoned with. Its 363-mile route structure looked at first blush to be categorically irrational with the 20-mile Taylors Falls Branch stubbing to the northeast and disjointed from the old Minneapolis & Duluth line to White Bear Lake, a single artery southwestward into Iowa, and now the "Pacific Extension" west to Winthrop. But there was a logic to it. The Taylors Falls Branch anticipated further construction in Wisconsin to Superior or Bayfield, maybe both, for a seasonal avenue to the Great Lakes with ample timber stock en route; the line to Albert Lea was a conduit to Burlington, Cedar Rapids & Northern and its crucial links to Chicago and St. Louis gateways; the Iowa route extended the range for Minneapolis lumbermen and merchants while guaranteeing a flow of cereal grains and coal northward; and the new route west promised a nice balance of traffic to and from the Minneapolis hub.[26]

Passenger trains provided for the necessary and important movement of people, baggage, mail, and express, but they also performed a valuable public relations function: passenger service was always the crucial yardstick by which a railroad was measured. Regular passenger listings by M&StL featured the daily *St. Louis Express* with "Pullman Palace Car Sleepers to St. Louis without change" plus mixed runs (freight and passenger) to White Bear Lake and Duluth and to St. Paul & Sioux City at Merriam. Offerings were expanded by late 1880 to include the *Chicago Express*, which represented through service via BCR&N at Albert Lea but also handled cars for Fort Dodge. All trains utilized the St. Paul, Minneapolis & Manitoba depot at Minneapolis, but tickets could also be had from the City Ticket Office at No. 8 Washington Avenue, opposite the splendid Nicollet House. In 1881, round-trip service was added to Excelsior (expanded to six daily turns before year's end) on what was briefly called the Minnetonka Branch, and by the end of the year daily-except-Sunday express and mixed trains were scheduled for the Pacific Division as far as the temporary end-of-tracks at Winthrop. Another train was added to the Iowa route, and both trains were extended to Angus when service began to that place on January 1, 1882.[27]

Of all the railroads serving Minneapolis in 1881, Milwaukee Road clearly dominated the intercity passenger lineup with two

BERTHS IN FREE SLEEPING CAR.

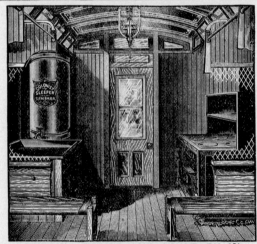

COOKING RANGE AND LAVATORY IN
FREE SLEEPER.

INTERIOR VIEWS OF ST. PAUL, MINNEAPOLIS & MANITOBA

## FREE SLEEPING CARS

FOR FIRST AND SECOND CLASS PASSENGERS, RUNNING
THROUGH WITHOUT CHANGE FROM ST. PAUL AND MINNE-
APOLIS TO GREAT FALLS, HELENA, AND BUTTE, AND THROUGH
WITHOUT CHANGE OR DELAY FROM ST. PAUL AND MINNE-
APOLIS TO WINNIPEG, BRITISH COLUMBIA, AND NORTH
PACIFIC COAST POINTS.

trains daily from Chicago along its river line ("day coaches, smoking cars, and sleepers through to Minneapolis") plus a local between La Crosse and Minneapolis. In addition, CM&StP offered another Chicago–Minneapolis opportunity on the pioneer line through Prairie du Chien and Faribault supplemented by an Austin–Minneapolis local and an Owatonna–Minneapolis accommodation. For its part, Manitoba scheduled two runs through St. Cloud—one to Fargo and the other to St. Vincent (connection with Canadian Pacific to Winnipeg)—as well as two trains on its Willmar line—one to Breckenridge and one to Barnesville. Northern Pacific's entries were one to Fargo and another to end-of-tracks at Glendive, Montana Territory. Omaha/C&NW added to the mix with two runs from Chicago through Madison, Wisconsin, to Minneapolis. And within the city itself, Minneapolis, Lyndale & Minnetonka scheduled fourteen round-trips between downtown and Lake Calhoun and Lake Harriet.[28]

Additional passenger revenues derived from special movements, especially excursions, of which there seemed an endless procession over the next many years. M&StL was particularly aggressive in this regard. Perhaps the grandest excursion of its early days was that hosted by the company itself during mid-July 1878 when "sixty ladies and gentlemen" from St. Louis and "twenty-five businessmen from Cedar Rapids" were delivered to Minneapolis by a special train from Albert Lea pulled by an M&StL locomotive elegantly "dressed with evergreens and national colors." W. D. Washburn freely admitted his purposes in staging the event. He thought there was a lamentable ignorance among leaders of St. Louis "as to this vast and

LEFT: Manitoba featured "Free Sleeping Cars" to its western reaches as a means of attracting permanent settlers.

FACING PAGE: Milwaukee Road favored Minneapolis with two routes eastward: the river line, which dominated, and the pioneer route through Faribault and Austin to Prairie du Chien, Wisconsin. The latter featured through passenger service to Chicago, an Austin–Minneapolis local, and an Owatonna–Minneapolis accommodation. Patrons from or around Fort Snelling could use the pioneer line, boarding trains at the company's depot located just above the Minnesota River bridge. Photograph ca. 1800; courtesy of the Minnesota Historical Society.

beautiful region of the Northwest," which he sought to redress while at the same time showcasing M&StL as "the short and comfortable way to reach" this "magnificent empire." Guests toured Minneapolis, St. Paul, and Lake Minnetonka before going on to Duluth. Upon return to Minneapolis guests were feted to a gala dinner and then reboarded the cars for home. "The party was preeminently a jolly one, enjoyed by all," reported the local press, adding, significantly, that "denizens" of St. Louis had, as Washburn hoped, exclaimed enthusiastically on the wonders of the country they had beheld. One of those "denizens," a reporter from Missouri, was especially taken by what he had seen from his window as the train passed through Iowa

and southern Minnesota. Both states, he contended, were "wealthy and populous, with many thriving cities, towns, and villages" along "with boundless farm country crowned" by "waving wheat and corn fields bathed in yellow light . . . as far as the eye can reach." And, he added in benediction, "Here is the art of God and the art of man commingled."[29]

Washburn and other railroad managers and promoters constantly sought to popularize their respective service areas. There remained great opportunities to be tapped, they sincerely believed. So did thousands of others. As good times followed bad, a veritable flood of persons headed west. For example, one M&StL passenger agent accompanied a special movement of ten coaches, two baggage cars, and forty boxcars bearing eight hundred immigrants from Chicago to Manitoba in mid-October 1881. The train originated on the Chicago, Rock Island & Pacific and moved via BCR&N and M&StL to Minneapolis to be forwarded by StPM&M.[30]

Minnesota railroads throughout this period engaged themselves in a monumental campaign to populate the huge land mass of the northern trans-Mississippi West. It was, of course, self-interest—benign self-interest. Railroads frankly needed hard-working and reliable persons to open and make productive their respective service areas. Major carriers and minor ones, too, established Immigration and Colonization Departments. "Wanted," screamed a Lake Superior & Mississippi poster from 1869, "10,000 Emigrants . . . to Settle on Lands of the Company . . . from Duluth to St. Paul." LS&M promised free transportation for actual settlers "over the completed portion of the railroad" as well as "free quarters in a new and commodious Emigrant House [at Duluth] until they locate themselves." St. Paul & Pacific and successor St. Paul, Minneapolis

**LEFT:** Two boys watch Milwaukee Road's swing span bridge open to let boats on the Minnesota River pass at Fort Snelling. Photograph courtesy of the Minnesota Historical Society.

**FACING PAGE:** Minneapolis, Lyndale & Minnetonka scheduled fourteen trips between downtown and Lake Calhoun and Lake Harriet. Here is the company's Thirty-first Street station. Photograph courtesy of Aaron Isaacs.

& Manitoba were similarly aggressive—the former establishing a Land Department as early as 1862. During the 1860s StP&P distributed thousands of pamphlets in several languages and placed advertising in various publications here and abroad, all with the purpose of attracting permanent residents across western and northwestern Minnesota and eventually beyond. Northern Pacific was no less energized, pointing to abundant opportunities along its line westward from Duluth through Aitkin, Brainerd, and Detroit Lakes and particularly in the Red River valley. "Stretching from the Great Father of Waters to Lake Winnipeg, and from within hearing of the billow beat of blue Superior to the high table-lands of peerless Dakota," wrote one drumbeating NP advocate in describing that road's current and future service area, "it is a region rich and beauteous as ever eye of man, or seraph poised in wondering ruin, beheld."[31]

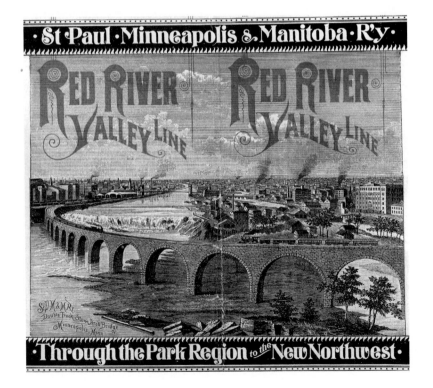

All of it was calculated to put traffic on rails—rails that often emanated from or passed through Minneapolis in a way that would benefit that place as well as the railroad companies themselves. The record of freight carriage by "home road" Minneapolis & St. Louis for the years 1878–80 demonstrated symbiosis among that company, Minneapolis, and territory tributary to Minneapolis served by M&StL. Freight volumes grew as the road expanded and as the shipping public matured in productive capacity. Ton miles increased from 13,841,921 in 1878 to 19,042,053 in 1879; freight revenues rose in the same period from $303,811 to $372,507. In 1880, M&StL's traffic mix included lumber (24.7 percent), grain (21.9 percent), flour (17.5 percent), merchandise (11.2 percent), coal (9.1 percent), livestock (1.7 percent), and assorted other (3.9 percent). M&StL remained the premier carrier of lumber and flour from Minneapolis. In 1878, it handled nearly 49 million board feet of lumber from the mills, although billings slipped to 35 board feet in 1880, nearly all moving south to BCR&N at Albert Lea or to line stations in Minnesota and Iowa. About half of all flour milled in Minneapolis moved out on M&StL rails; in 1878, billings were nearly equal, north and south, to Duluth for transshipment or all-rail to eastern points. (In 1880, M&StL billed 827,713 barrels of flour; CM&StP, 509,617 barrels; Manitoba, 402,823; and Omaha, 298,390. In westbound or southbound lumber, M&StL led with 30,717,000 feet; followed by Manitoba, 11,994,000 feet; and CM&StP, 8,505,000 feet.) Shipments of coal were modest early, with delivery by way of the lakes through Duluth, but with linkage to Iowa after 1877, more cars came from BCR&N than from the north. Volume would jump in 1880 to 34,189 tons (up from 1,830 in 1878) as M&StL's line reached mines in Iowa's Webster County.[32]

LEFT: Manitoba's emphasis on itself as the "Red River Valley Line" and the artist's depiction of that road's prominence at Minneapolis, ca. 1885, implies the categorical symbiosis that existed between the carrier and its vast service territory.

FACING PAGE: Railroads moved prodigious volumes of flour from Minneapolis mills such as Pillsbury's "A." Photograph courtesy of the Hennepin History Museum.

Other freight billings from outlying communities served by M&StL likewise showed the interdependency of Minneapolis and its hinterland. Wheat from noncompetitive points (that is, stations without another railroad) certainly sought Minneapolis as the natural market, but so did oats, barley, and corn. Forest City, on M&StL's line in Iowa, as an example, posted outbound billings of wheat, beans, butter, tallow, hides, live hogs, and empty barrels plus receipts of machinery, merchandise, and building materials. Dressed hogs, eggs, butter, and lard were billed from nearly every station—almost all consigned to Minneapolis. Poultry moved from New Prague and Waterville; apples, from New Richland and Albert Lea; beer, from Jordan; brick, from Chaska; and even ice, from White Bear Lake and Jordan.[33]

# NEW PLAYERS

7

The Minneapolis & St. Louis has been alienated
from state ownership.

MINNESOTA'S STATE RAILROAD COMMISSIONER, 1883

Railroads were, at once, America's first big business and the first modern business enterprises. These twin verities were dramatically magnified in the 1880s—the golden age of railroad expansion in the United States. It was during the same explosive decade that huge interregional systems developed, many of them in the trans-Chicago West.[1]

The breathtaking expansion of route miles and the emergence of giant operations were understandably traumatic. In an earlier era, railroad owners and managers had made alliances and established cartels as means of maintaining at least a semblance of stability. But in the aftermath of the Panic of 1873, railroad managers and then railroad investors and speculators succumbed to instincts of aggression. Overbuilding resulted in increased competition, rate wars, and corporate consolidations. All of it was bound to impact Minneapolis sooner or later.[2]

Considerable trackage was put down for defensive purposes, to fend off interlopers that might have the effrontery to threaten territorial dominion of an established carrier or to preempt potential aggressors in a territory that the same established road presumed to have proprietary rights. "The question whether a railway company has any rights of possession of territory which a rival company is bound to respect has become of unusual interest of late," observed *Railway Age* in September 1880. The view of Illinois Central's William Ackerman was typical of the time: expansion, plainly stated, was "for the purpose of occupying territory and preventing others from building in it." Chicago, Burlington & Quincy's Charles E. Perkins thought similarly and embraced a policy of strategic expansion to prevent invasion of CB&Q territory.[3]

Burlington's policy was replicated by other roads looking westward from Chicago. It was an understandable policy; it was also provocative. A move by Burlington to expand its service area, as an example, was sure to trigger a response by another candidate in that same general region—or in some other area that Burlington might consider its "natural territory," one it thought all others should respect. A move here provoked a move there. This was especially true in critical corridors—Chicago–Council Bluffs, Chicago–Kansas City, Chicago–St. Paul–Minneapolis. Between Chicago and Council Bluffs, for instance, Chicago & North Western, Chicago, Rock Island

& Pacific, and Chicago, Burlington & Quincy had long established primary arteries and a sophisticated pooling arrangement (division of traffic). When Chicago, Milwaukee & St. Paul chose to add its own line in that corridor, reaction to "invasion" was predictable.[4]

Redress was available through defensive construction, of course, but merger or acquisition represented viable alternatives. After all, combinations and amalgamations had been part of the railroad landscape from its earliest days. At one time Milwaukee and North Western had seemed headed for amalgamation; Rock Island and North Western shared many common directors, and John Tracy once had been simultaneously president of both; and in the 1870s CB&Q and Rock Island had explored marriage. It seemed a logical evolution. Burlington's Charles Perkins said as much in 1879: "I have long been of the opinion that sooner or later the railroads of the country would group themselves into systems and that each system would be self-sustaining." And, he added importantly, "any system not self-sustaining would cease to exist and be absorbed by those systems near at hand and strong enough to live alone. . . ."[5]

It was in this increasingly fluid and Darwinian environment that W. D. Washburn charted a course for Minneapolis-based M&StL. Its truncated route structure was simply inadequate. There were so many unrealized aspirations—an independent avenue to Lake Superior through rich pinelands to feed the hungry lumber mills at Minneapolis, as an example. But there was little that Washburn could do. The shooting of President James A. Garfield in July 1881 and his death on September 19 cast a pall. Optimism soured; soberminded investors talked darkly about overexpansion in the railroad industry.[6]

Nevertheless, Washburn enjoyed an important diversion and had a personal investment 19 miles west of Minneapolis at Excelsior, along the south shore of Lake Minnetonka. Even before M&StL rails reached there in 1881, the Hotel St. Louis was in place near

what became the Deephaven station; not far distant at Sunrise Point above Gideon's Bay stood the Lake Park Hotel. The St. Louis Hotel had been erected in 1879 by Charles Gibson of the place's namesake city, and the Lake Park had been put up in the same season. M&StL

SPIRIT KNOB, LAKE MINNETONKA.

Visitors rejoiced at Minnetonka's sparkling blue waters and the handsome resort facilities around the lake—reached best, Washburn immodestly proclaimed, by his *City of St. Louis.*

took a half-interest in the Lake Park, likely at Washburn's behest, and Washburn himself was the initial owner of the $57,000 *City of St. Louis*, a beautiful 150-foot steamer capable of handling a thousand passengers and placed on the lake during the early summer of 1881. The striking side-wheeler met all trains and when not thusly engaged, offered eager vacationers excursions over the lake's broad expanse. Minnetonka became a favored watering spot for southerners, mint-julep-drinking planters and businessmen, their wives, fair southern belles, and their servants, who arrived to enjoy Minnetonka's sparkling blue water and its marvelous sandy beaches as well as splendid social life at the hotels.[7]

None of this was lost on James J. Hill, who quickly committed to a campaign of one-upmanship. A predecessor of St. Paul, Minneapolis & Manitoba had pioneered the area a decade and a half earlier, and in 1882 the Manitoba built a short spur and opened the Hotel Lafayette, one of the largest and finest hotels in the United States—"the Saratoga of the West," some called it. At the same time, Hill took an investment in Lake Minnetonka Navigation, which soon added the *Belle of Minnetonka* to its "fleet." The *Belle* was larger than Washburn's *City*, capable of carrying 2,500 passengers. A lively rivalry surrounded all of this, boats meeting every train and conveying tourists to the several hotels, each one trying to outdo the others in entertainment and splendor. Manitoba, like M&StL, added passenger capacity in season to serve the small towns and summer colonies west of Minneapolis.[8]

W. D. Washburn received pleasure from issuing passes for free transportation on his *City of St. Louis*.

William Drew Washburn had an insatiable "itch" for politics. It struck him again in 1878, just as the economy was turning up, and just when his leadership at M&StL was most needed. He was elected to Congress in that year, took office in 1879, and was reelected in 1880 and 1882, serving until 1885. This seemed a mixed blessing

James J. Hill's response to Washburn's audacity was the Hotel Lafayette—"the Saratoga of the West." Hill also outdid Washburn with the *Belle of Minnetonka,* capable of accommodating 2,500 passengers.

15 MILES FROM MINNEAPOLIS, 25 MILES FROM ST. PAUL.

HOTEL LAFAYETTE,
MINNETONKA BEACH ✛ MINNESOTA.
EUGENE MEHL, Manager.

THE PROPERTY OF THE ST. PAUL, MINNEAPOLIS & MANITOBA RAILWAY COMPANY.

to older brother Cadwallader, who was proud of W. D.'s success in politics but irritated nevertheless, since a contract pledged each one of them to full attention in the flour milling business. Under the circumstances, a frustrated Cadwallader had turned to "outsiders," William Hood Dunwoody for sales and John Crosby—with whom the younger Washburn constantly disagreed—for operations. In 1879, the contract between the two brothers was abrogated, William Drew was dropped, and the flouring company took the name Washburn Crosby, but with Dunwoody as silent if equal partner.

William Drew still held mills of his own, but he gave them little attention, delegating their management, as usual, to others.[9]

Down in the dingy and dusty corporate office of Washburn Crosby at A Mill, gruff and hardworking Cadwallader also had an insatiable "itch," but it was for even more flour production from the company's mills. By 1882, the total capacity of the Washburn plants was 6,000 barrels daily: A Mill, 3,000; B Mill, 1,000; and C Mill, 2,000. For such production a constant and voluminous supply of wheat was required. The wheat culture had continued its shift to the west and northwest, with Iowa and southern Minnesota producing less wheat but more oats and corn. Annual production of wheat in the entire state of Minnesota increased, however, from 30,086,110 bushels in the period 1876–80 to 35,669,540 in the years 1881–85. Most of this flowed to Minneapolis or Duluth and from "line" elevators at country points. These concerns typically featured a chain of trackside grain-handling facilities at outlying locations on a particular railroad or on particular railroads, occasionally with significant storage capacity at key locations, and with common ownership and management. By the mid-1880s, most of the major companies were headquartered in Minneapolis or St. Paul. Along the M&StL, however, a majority of elevators on the line to Albert Lea were owned by local entrepreneurs (six independent dealers at New Prague alone), although S. S. Cargill had facilities at Hartland and Albert Lea. On the line to Morton, in the "new" wheat belt, the story was different, with Minneapolis-based Pacific Elevator Company owning facilities at Green Isle, Arlington, Gaylord, Winthrop, Gibbon, Fairfax, Franklin, and Morton—ten of twenty-two elevators on that route. In aggregate grain storage capacity, elevators along M&StL lines in Minnesota held 585,000 bushels, six times less than the capacity of facilities along Manitoba, NP, or C&NW, and half that of CM&StP.[10]

The year 1882 is generally acknowledged to have marked the beginning of Minneapolis as the premier flour milling center—the world leader in flour production, a record it would hold for a generation. As it turned out, 1882 also would prove to be a pivotal year for the railroad industry in Minnesota and for Minneapolis and M&StL in particular.[11]

As always, the trail to important change was long and complex. During the summer of 1879 had come reports of significant changes in ownership of St. Paul & Duluth, with whom M&StL had a long and usually friendly association. W. D. Washburn had hurried to New York City to investigate. There he learned the awful truth: control of St. Paul & Duluth, of course, had passed to a consortium of persons connected in the affairs of Chicago & North Western, Chicago, Milwaukee & St. Paul, and, curiously, Chicago, Rock

Island & Pacific. This was serious, indeed, for M&StL had a valued alliance with StP&D by trackage rights to gain outlet to the Great Lakes chain as its means of levering rate advantages against the Chicago roads.[12]

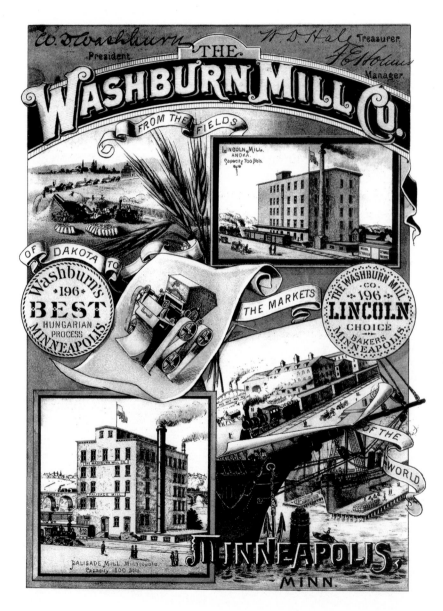

W. D. Washburn still had his own mills, but he delegated their management to others. This advertising poster was created by the *St. Paul Dispatch*; courtesy of the Minnesota Historical Society.

Ownership and management of St. Paul & Duluth were also of critical interest to the cities of Minneapolis and St. Paul and, really, to Minnesota at large; they were not merely the parochial concern of only M&StL and the Minneapolis flour millers. "Minnesota, it is certain, has lost its only competing outlet upon lake navigation," moaned the *St. Paul Pioneer Press*, adding acidly that eastern interests "now held Minnesota in capitalist subjection." Most of the state's citizenry had not been put off by assertions that David Dows and R. P. Flower did not represent North Western (each was on the C&NW board as well as on the boards of CRI&P and newly formed Chicago, St. Paul & Minneapolis & Omaha), and that Jeremiah Milbank and Peter Geddes (both on the board of CM&StP) were not really stand-ins for Milwaukee's Alexander Mitchell and S. S. Merrill. Any doubt soon evaporated. StP&D's President J. P. Ilsley claimed that the Duluth road would run in competition to the Chicago and Milwaukee companies, but when StP&D forthwith raised rates on flour by 14 cents a barrel, there was a general sense that the company, now controlled by a coalition clearly and powerfully connected to eastern interests, was engaged in larceny.[13]

W. D. Washburn was outraged, as was most of the state's press and a majority of Minnesotans, who already brooded about the power of the great railway systems and their owners. "The value of the products of Minnesota are to a greater extent than almost any of the states dependent upon transportation," Washburn had argued earlier in the decade. The problem, he went on, was that railroad transportation was controlled "by a set of sharks and speculators, men who have amassed fortunes not in legitimate business but by a systematic robbery of the people." In Minnesota, he concluded, managers of the Milwaukee Road and Chicago & North Western, "upon which the larger portion of our surplus products are carried to market, have everything their own way." Of course, the matter of ownership and control of St. Paul & Duluth was what earlier had provoked the Washburns into responding with the Taylor's Falls & Lake Superior project, but construction of that road—jointly owned with StP&D—plus operating privileges to Duluth had produced only a mixed blessing.[14]

For M&StL, circumstances only deteriorated. As if to erase all pretense, Alexander Mitchell joined St. Paul & Duluth's board in 1880, as did Milwaukee senior manager William C. Van Horne in 1881. H. H. Porter, large in the affairs of C&NW, also went aboard in 1881. So did James J. Hill and R. B. Angus of St. Paul, Minneapolis & Manitoba, adding an important new twist. In fact, Manitoba as early as 1880 had begun to put significant tonnage on StP&D and in the process had replaced M&StL as the Duluth road's most important connection. On February 26, 1881, banker John S. Kennedy had told Hill that there was a near panic in New York financial circles and suggested that it would be a good time to negotiate with Porter regarding StP&D. Hill took the hint and told Kennedy on April 7, "I have arranged a basis of agreement for the joint control of StP&D with Porter and Merrill." He had indeed.[15]

Cadwallader Washburn had an itch for greater production from the Washburn-Crosby mills. Washburn-Crosby's "A," "B," and "C" mills stood in a row on what is presently South Second Street at Park Avenue. Photograph courtesy of the Minneapolis Public Library, Minneapolis Collection.

It is impossible to overestimate the power and influence of Chicago, Milwaukee & St. Paul across the railroad landscape of Minneapolis and the upper Midwest. The size of the road's freight house in the city was impressive, and Milwaukee's passenger station stood just beyond. Tracks in the foreground were those of M&StL and Minneapolis Eastern; the west-bank milling district is out of sight to the left. The two buildings on the right presently house Mill Place, home of this book's publisher. Photograph courtesy of the Hennepin History Museum.

Hill was protecting Manitoba's flanks, but at the same time he was actively expanding Manitoba's position in and about St. Paul and Minneapolis, forming at the same time an important subsidiary to undertake various improvements in Minneapolis. Elsewhere, growing freight volumes and thriving summer travel to Lake Minnetonka required double-tracking by Manitoba west to Wayzata.[16]

Another major player in the area, Northern Pacific, had both transcontinental and local agendas. Stalled at Bismarck by failure of Cooke & Company and the Panic of 1873, NP had gazed yearningly across the huge domain between its isolated pieces of cross-country route. Minneapolis, it might be recalled, had taken an early and profound interest in Northern Pacific. Indeed, the first issue of the *Minneapolis Tribune*, on May 25, 1867, celebrated the logic of a true transcontinental line from Portland, Maine, to Puget Sound—passing through Minneapolis, of course. The same editorialist pre-

dicted a tremendous flow of business from the West on such a route to Portland's Atlantic tidewater, which, he noted with glee, was one day closer to Liverpool than Boston and two days closer than New York. In any event, westward construction on NP was begun again in 1879. At the same time, however, considerable public sentiment and NP's own management called for NP to look eastward from Duluth for the purpose of reaching Canadian rail at Sault Ste. Marie and/or tentacles of giant trunk roads Pennsylvania and New York Central in northern Michigan. "Such would make Minnesota and Northern Pacific independent of Milwaukee and North Western," gushed the *St. Paul Dispatch*. To that end, NP's President Frederick Billings authorized a survey to the Wisconsin-Michigan boundary in 1880. All of this was attractive in many ways, although some observers, especially in Minneapolis, understandably were concerned because a completed transcontinental line to the north surely would drain business elsewhere. Millers, in particular, worried that wheat would find alternative markets.[17]

In 1881, Henry Villard gained control of NP, vigorously pursued construction in the West, refocused on getting NP into a formidable position in Minneapolis–St. Paul, and put the Wisconsin matter on the back burner. NP earlier had gained access to the Twin Cities by the back door, so to speak, with trackage rights from the west, Sauk Rapids to Minneapolis, over Manitoba, on November 8, 1878, and with its own appendage from Brainerd to Sauk Rapids, NP additionally had through routing to its main line from Duluth into Dakota Territory. It was inadequate. Villard, like his predecessors at NP, was fully alert to the liability of Duluth as NP's eastern terminus and to the growing prominence of St. Paul and Minneapolis—"at once the principal receiving and distributing centers of commerce and industry in the great Northwest," as the company's 1882 annual report noted. "Their growth affords a good measure of that of the region tributary to the Eastern Divisions of the North Pacific."[18]

Villard was ready to move. In 1881, NP committed to an independent line to Minneapolis and St. Paul and then acquired various properties in the two cities for yards, shops, right-of-way, and so on. During the following year NP demanded and got beneficial modifications of its contract with Manitoba that, among other things, allowed NP's use of the new Manitoba passenger station planned for Minneapolis. None of this pleased Manitoba, and in fact the two companies constantly engaged in pulling and hauling at several locations and over several issues. Early in 1882, Manitoba agreed to sell NP its partially completed line between Minneapolis and St. Cloud on the west side of the Mississippi, but the two negotiated further,

and in the end Manitoba rather agreed to sell NP a 43-foot right-of-way adjacent to its east-side line from Minneapolis through Anoka and Elk River to St. Cloud. NP initially planned to gain connection with Chicago, Milwaukee & St. Paul in western Minneapolis and use Milwaukee's line into St. Paul, but that, too, got changed during the fall of 1882 when NP secretly surveyed and then planned construction of its own Minneapolis–St. Paul line. Construction side by side Manitoba all the way from East St. Cloud to St. Paul, about 75 miles, would follow later.[19]

Milwaukee, frustrated in its own earlier attempt to gain the west-bank line to St. Cloud, frustrated again in its attempt to team with Northern Pacific, persisted with its own aggressive campaign to control a giant domain from Milwaukee and Chicago to Missouri River points, including, during the 1880s, Council Bluffs and Kansas City. It poked and prodded generally in southeastern Dakota Territory, throwing out an array of lines. Elsewhere one client reached as far north as Fargo, irritating NP and Manitoba alike. In Minnesota, CM&StP remained the premier road, at least in terms of freight tonnage carried, and was a force to be reckoned with in all instances. "They are bold, determined, and, I think, reckless," said H. H. Porter of Chicago, St. Paul, Minneapolis & Omaha.[20]

The Washburns and M&StL had a love-hate relationship with predecessors of Porter's Omaha, itself formed on May 26, 1880, and into which were poured franchises and assets formerly held by North Wisconsin Railway, West Wisconsin Railway, and St. Paul & Sioux City. The latter road had provided M&StL considerable sustenance by interchange of traffic at Merriam, but West Wisconsin, physically connected to Chicago & North Western at El Roy, Wisconsin, often was seen as a surrogate of Chicago and opposed to the best interests of Minneapolis. The driving force at the two Wisconsin companies and then at Omaha was Henry H. Porter, a native of Maine who had entered railroad service with a predecessor of C&NW and served as a director of that road from 1870 to 1878. Allied with Porter were David Dows and others from New York financial circles, plus, among others, Ransom R. Cable, usually associated with Chicago, Rock Island & Pacific. Indeed, Cable was with Rock Island, a vice president by 1880 and on the board since 1877. For that matter, in 1880, five men on Rock Island's twelve-man board also served on C&NW's board, and five Rock Island board members were simultaneously on Omaha's directory—all of it quite illegal in later days but in 1880 quite typical.[21]

What this meant for Minneapolis and M&StL was not immediately clear. In addition to its strategic line southwest into Iowa and Nebraska, Omaha had two legs in Wisconsin, one extending to C&NW at El Roy and on to Chicago, and the other jutting northeastward from Hudson, east of St. Paul, toward Lake Superior. This latter one was attractive to Minneapolis timber and lumber interests, the Washburns prominent among them, because of the marvelous timber stock it would access. And Omaha confirmed rumors that this line would itself become a wye, with one line continuing to Bayfield, on Lake Superior, and the other bending back to the northwest, heading for Superior City, also on the lake. The second, could it be tapped by an extension of M&StL's Taylors Falls branch, would give the Washburns what they had been looking for: an independent route to Lake Superior and access to a huge supply of timber stock. The matter was much discussed in 1880 as part of a broader package by which M&StL would give Omaha trackage rights into Minneapolis from Merriam in exchange for operating rights over Omaha—if Taylor's Falls & Lake Superior were expanded—from some yet to be selected location into Bayfield. M&StL itself, for good or ill, did not choose to push beyond Taylors Falls, but Omaha's desire to use M&StL from Merriam remained a live if unresolved issue.[22]

Elsewhere, Burlington, Cedar Rapids & Northern since the fall of 1877 had provided M&StL's vital outlet south and east. BCR&N bondholders had taken a substantial part of M&StL's debt, and the two roads had executed a "perpetual contract of unison" regarding traffic. BCR&N maps of the time showed a solid through Minneapolis–St. Louis route via M&StL, BCR&N, with Chicago, Burlington & Quincy from Burlington, Iowa, to Monmouth, Illinois, and then Rockford, Rock Island & St. Louis, and in the *Official Guide*, M&StL schedules were included although subordinated with those

of BCR&N. Yet BCR&N had other alliances, with Chicago & North Western via Cedar Rapids and CB&Q via Burlington, both favoring Chicago over St. Louis. BCR&N, to be sure, had complex and often conflicting loyalties reflected in its directory and in its management. H. H. Porter, who in 1878 sat on the boards at C&NW and Rock Island, also had a seat on BCR&N's board, and Judge John Tracy of Burlington, Iowa—former president of Rock Island and C&NW and a personal friend of CB&Q President Charles E. Perkins—was BCR&N's lawyer and became its president in 1880.[23]

The plot thickened in 1879. By August, *Railroad Gazette* was reporting the lease of BCR&N by Chicago & North Western, a logical notion given BCR&N's alliance with C&NW and the nature of the local road's route structure, which North Western could use as a funnel for Chicago traffic. BCR&N had been, with others, noted *Railroad Gazette*, formed to favor St. Louis, but "the country on its line has insisted on sending its produce to and getting its merchandise from Chicago and the East." Indeed, C&NW did make an offer for BCR&N, an offer that was heartily entertained by the board of directors but in the end rejected in favor of another bid, one by Chicago Rock Island & Pacific and, as it soon turned out, by Chicago, Burlington & Quincy. North Western complained bitterly, arguing that the country above Cedar Rapids was its "natural territory" and urged a partitioning of BCR&N: C&NW to get all BCR&N lines north of Cedar Rapids (the lion's share), and Rock Island the short stub to Burlington plus assorted branches in the area. Rock Island predictably frowned on that design, and the idea of an independent Rock Island presence in CB&Q's namesake city irritated that road. C&NW's petition perished as a result. For Rock Island and Burlington owners and managers, the BCR&N matter was part of a much broader pattern of conciliatory agreements as to territorial domain, and in fact these two prominent roads had seriously considered merger in 1879.[24]

In the end, Rock Island took a lease on the entire BCR&N, but as matters settled out, Rock Island and Burlington were in joint control with CRI&P as the dominant partner. It was a useful arrangement for both roads. BCR&N clearly expanded Rock Island's domain to the northwest, and CB&Q, which earlier had failed in an independent sortie to the northwest, could at least content itself with an established if jointly controlled through route from St. Louis toward Minneapolis–St. Paul. The arrangement would divide territory, insure friendly connections, maintain rate stability, and assure that BCR&N did not fall into unfriendly hands. The *Minneapolis Tribune* celebrated the new arrangement. Rock Island, noted the *Tribune*, "has no other Minneapolis or St. Paul connection, and its entire interests will be at stake in working this up as a new and independent northwestern line . . . a new line from this city to Chicago absolutely independent of the pooled lines, and having no complication in their interest." *Tribune* writers also applauded Rock Island's decision to retain BCR&N's well-respected managers.[25]

Rock Island at the time certainly was respected as a solid, prosperous, and well-managed company; its stock and bonds commanded premium prices. Perhaps its one liability had been inadequate branches to drain traffic from country contiguous to its main lines. Control of BCR&N reflected a more aggressive posture in that regard, and in fact Rock Island was becoming more aggressive in general—mirroring, in great part, the instincts of Ransom Reed Cable. Born in Ohio in 1834, Cable as a young man had moved to Rock Island, Illinois, where he engaged in real estate, coal, and investments businesses before entering the railroad field. By 1870, he was president of Rockford, Rock Island & St. Louis, seven years later he was on CRI&P's board, and in 1880 he was made vice president in charge of operations and sales. He grew impatient with heavy-set and round-faced Hugh Riddle, the road's capable and well-regarded president, whom he would replace in 1883. For his part, Riddle had favored expansion west of the Missouri River in Nebraska and Kansas from Rock Island's core routes to Council Bluffs and Leavenworth; Cable had other thoughts, and these centered on BCR&N and its alignment pointing tantalizingly northwest. BCR&N's main artery connected with M&StL at Albert Lea, but BCR&N also had another line under construction—its "Pacific Division"—that left the main line above Cedar Rapids and angled toward Dakota Territory. Would Cable use this line to make good on the "Pacific" in Rock Island's corporate title? Perhaps. After all, Cable, like most managers of the time, saw the need to defend existing "natural territory," to stake out new service areas, to use expansion as a defensive as well as offensive strategy, and to engage all of this through construction,

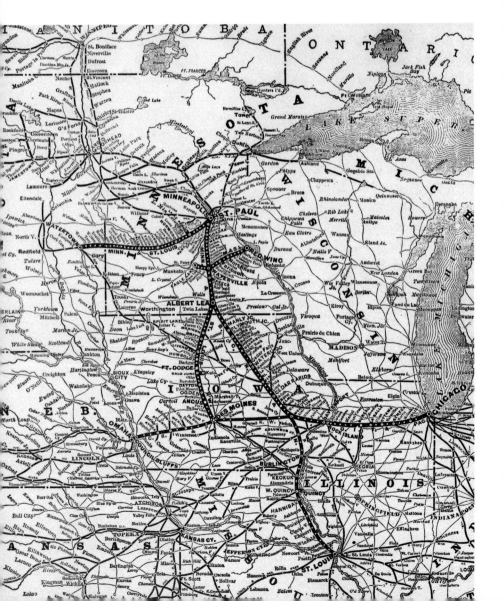

The Albert Lea Route at once demonstrated the symbiotic relation of M&StL, BCR&N, and CRI&P as well as competitive routes in both the Twin Cities–Chicago and Twin Cities–St. Louis corridors.

consolidation, or both. Moreover, he wanted for his road the longest possible haul at the best possible rate. And the timing was right. Although stumbling and remaining a bit nervous following the assassination of President James A. Garfield in the summer of 1881, the economy maintained an essential vibrancy, and investment monies remained available, especially for a "blue chip" like Rock Island.[26]

As Riddle and Cable (increasingly Cable) considered options for expansion, one potential zone of opportunity faded. Rock Island's line southwestward to Fort Leavenworth had failed to produce the revenues expected of it, and in reality, Leavenworth, Atchison, and St. Joseph all began to decline in importance compared to Kansas City. Several on Rock Island's board thus came to favor the Northwest. Among them were Cable, H. H. Porter, David Dows, R. P. Flower, and Benjamin Brewster—each one at that time also on the board of Chicago, St. Paul, Minneapolis & Omaha. Rock Island and CStPM&O touched at only one location, and only indirectly, at Omaha, and if Cable tried to bring CStPM&O into Rock Island's orbit, Chicago & North Western, which held a historic connection with Omaha at El Roy, Wisconsin—and used Omaha under alliance to access Minneapolis–St. Paul traffic—was bound to scream. Merger of CRI&P with C&NW was a possibility, if unlikely, although Porter had been on C&NW's board until recently, and Dows and Flower were still members. Porter, in fact, once had tried to put C&NW under Rock Island's tent, and, of course, John Tracy of BCR&N and former Rock Island president once had been simultaneously president of C&NW. Omaha, in any event, intrigued Cable. And if M&StL could be acquired or leased in conjunction with Omaha, Rock Island would have three prime arteries—southwest, central, northwest—leading from and to Chicago just as William B. Ogden had urged nearly three decades earlier. It also would have a powerful hub in Minneapolis from which to press westward to Pacific tidewater.[27]

It was against this backdrop that the Washburns and their associates who had birthed M&StL and seen it to early adolescence were required to formulate decisions as to the future of the enterprise. In reality, M&StL was caught in the jaws of changed and changing circumstances as the big roads increased in size and power. Where did M&StL fit in? M&StL long had been the favorite of Minneapolis, the local road, locally managed. But compared to Manitoba, NP, C&NW, Milwaukee, Omaha, and now Rock Island, it was not much. Expansion on its own to Lake Superior or even to an Omaha connection in Wisconsin, on to Des Moines or Kansas City, or an extension from Morton to Dakota Territory might be possible but only with a management and directory with a heart for it. That was not the case for M&StL. William Drew Washburn often was absent attending to political aspirations and responsibilities, and brother Cadwallader had wearied of bailing out his brother and of the M&StL project in general. Moreover, he was not well, suffering from Bright's disease.[28]

Cadwallader Washburn had made several trips east, hoping to make a deal with Chicago & North Western, which he knew was intent on getting into the Minneapolis milling district one way or another. John I. Blair, well connected in railroad circles, one heavily invested in C&NW, but who had put his personal weight behind Rock Island in the BCR&N contest, listened carefully to Washburn and pledged to do what he could to dispose of Cadwallader's M&StL stock as well as stock held by several long-term Minneapolis directors. William Drew was appalled and vigorous in dissent, both behind closed doors and in public. By late January 1881, local and trade press alike claimed that C&NW had gathered control of M&StL; William Drew admitted only that C&NW was trying to reach Minneapolis on its own. C&NW at this point, of course, could make no physical connection with M&StL in Minnesota, just as Rock Island could make no physical connection with Omaha's northern lines; however, C&NW could connect variously with M&StL by gathering in Omaha, just as Rock Island could reach Omaha's primary operations by snapping up M&StL. Consequently M&StL and Omaha were simultaneously in play.[29]

The whole issue was confusing. In mid-1879, Cadwallader—who by this time owned slightly fewer shares than William Drew—had given his brother proxy "until revoked by me," but about a year later Cadwallader had reassigned his proxy to W. D. Hale, another long-serving director, and William Drew assigned his proxy to Charles

F. Hatch, a well-respected M&StL officer. But Hatch left M&StL's employ in February 1881 to join Omaha, fueling speculation that C&NW would take both Omaha and M&StL. Nevertheless, William Drew's noisy, powerful, and open broadsides, a groundswell of public opposition to sale of M&StL to a Chicago road, and a bitter personal encounter in New York City between the two brothers over the issue caused Cadwallader to reconsider. In the end, the formerly vigorous but now very weary brother shook his massive head and told C&NW that he would not sell his holdings to that road, but that rather, through eastern bankers and investors, he and several others had agreed to dispose of their stock in another way that would bring "foreign" control to M&StL's board. Out were Cadwallader Washburn, W. D. Hale, R. J. Baldwin, Paris Gibson, John Martin, John S. Pillsbury, and Henry Titus Welles, most of whom had served from the beginning in 1870; in were H. H. Porter, J. F. Withrow, H. R. Bishop, and Benjamin Brewster. Porter and Brewster were on Rock Island and Omaha boards, Brewster was an Omaha director, and Bishop was a lawyer for Rock Island. Which road, if any, now had control of M&StL? It was not clear. On the other hand, it was clear that tired and sick Cadwallader Washburn was no longer a factor at M&StL, and his brother's influence had been tightly curtailed. (Cadwallader suffered a paralyzing stroke in February and would die in May 1882.)[30]

The aggressive Ransom Cable studied and planned. There was much that was attractive about M&StL and the broad potential service area west of Minneapolis. That place in 1880 had a population of 46,887, eclipsing St. Paul (with 41,473) as the state's largest city, and Minneapolis stood as the gateway to a "new" Northwest, a gigantic hinterland stretching all the way to the Rockies and beyond. M&StL was more than a bit player in the commerce and industry of Minneapolis. It remained the premier hauler of flour and lumber, and, Cable noted, BCR&N was M&StL's primary interchange partner, forwarding flour and lumber and receiving, in particular, coal, merchandise, bran, and iron. And business was good. On one day in 1880, one hundred loaded cars jammed the yard at Albert Lea waiting for power to move them. This volume was reflected in earnings

that were increasingly satisfactory. In addition, the road's property in Minneapolis and the prospect of growing coal shipments from Angus, Iowa, made M&StL extremely attractive—to Cable and Rock Island and to others as well.[31]

Certainty gradually emerged from uncertainty. Several more new and "foreign" directors were elected to M&StL's board in October 1881. These included three men from St. Paul—W. R. Merriam, A. B. Stickney, and C. D. W. Young—all of whom had been in one way or another associated with Omaha or its predecessors; also added was Ransom Cable who, like the others, had an Omaha connection as well as a distinct tie with Rock Island. A few months later, however, W. D. Washburn privately suggested to James J. Hill that "it might be desirable for you to have a holding in the stock of our company as there is no possible antagonism between us and so many things in common." Perhaps Washburn had in mind something like the joint control of St. Paul & Duluth, a policy presumably beneficial for all participants. After all, Hill's Manitoba was part of that deal, but Hill did not rise to this bait, and one is left to ponder Washburn's motives. Shortly thereafter, in February 1882, rumors circulated that Northern Pacific wished to acquire M&StL because of M&StL's traffic connections to Rock Island, its ability to tap Iowa coal, and its valuable terminal properties in Minneapolis. The concept was logical, and NP was at the time considering many options in Minneapolis and St. Paul, but Washburn denied the claims. Then, in April a joint announcement was made by M&StL, BCR&N, CRI&P, and CB&Q that an improved through passenger service would be instituted between Minneapolis and St. Louis. Even earlier, Rock Island had begun to advertise Chicago–Minneapolis service over what it trumpeted as "The Albert Lea Route." Furthermore, Rock Island stockholders were told, "a considerable traffic destined to and from Minnesota, Dakota and Manitoba" had begun to move over the "continuous line from Chicago to Minneapolis."[32]

Matters came to a head in May 1882. "Minneapolis & St. Louis has passed through the process which awaits every local road on the American continent," intoned a thoroughly saddened *Minneapolis Tribune* on May 2: "the process of virtual absorption by older, stronger and wealthier corporations controlling great through lines of traffic." The *Tribune*, on the one hand, was referring to a major transfer of stock and management control to "a syndicate of railway managers and capitalists" headed by Cable and Porter. The *Tribune* initially saw Rock Island behind this arrangement, since CRI&P had "sometime since determined to secure a footing in Minneapolis," and M&StL "proved to be the most direct and economical means of accomplishing this end." On the other hand, the newspaper did not understand what Porter's interest was. Others, however, reported that Rock Island also had gained control of Omaha, and that implied a clear motive for Porter's involvement with M&StL. In any event, concluded the *Tribune*, "if Minneapolis & St. Louis must pass out of distinctively local control, it is far better that it pass to the Rock Island people than to either the North Western or the Milwaukee systems."[33]

*Railroad Gazette* maintained that CRI&P and Omaha would manage M&StL for their own interests, and Cable, now president of M&StL, said as much. M&StL would maintain headquarters in Minneapolis and would enjoy an independent management, much like the arrangement with BCR&N. W. D. Washburn stayed on the board and retained his stock in M&StL (for a while as the largest single shareholder), and although he earlier had disposed of his stock, Cadwallader at death still held a heavy investment in M&StL bonds. The community of interests among M&StL, Omaha, and Rock Island was reflected variously. For instance, M&StL stalwarts W. D. Washburn and Henry Titus Welles were elected to Omaha's board as soon as the syndicate took control of M&StL. By late summer, M&StL passenger trains were running into Des Moines (to Rock Island's station) via trackage rights over Des Moines & Fort Dodge from Angus, and effective August 1, 1882, M&StL passenger trains originated and terminated in St. Paul. By late September, contracts were in place facilitating M&StL freight service into Des Moines.[34]

There was much brave talk in Minneapolis and abroad M&StL's service territory as to the impact of "foreign control." But there also was much regret and even anxiety in the wake of the Cable-Porter conquest. "There is no railroad touching this city which is so distinctively a Minneapolis road as the M&StL," the *Tribune* had correctly asserted in 1877. "It had its origins here, and was built by our people, and it belongs to them and will always be run for their benefit." Two years later the *Tribune* continued to heap praise. "The vitality of the Minneapolis & St. Louis is wonderful," said the newspaper during the summer of 1879. Some observers, presumably in St. Paul, had seen the Minneapolis road as a "weakling, soon to be 'gobbled'" and hitched "on as a tail or a side-track to some other line." "But," rejoiced the *Tribune*, "to their astonishment, it continues to grow and wax strong with the rapidity of Jonah's gourd, and now there would seem to be more probability of the Minneapolis & St. Louis providing a veritable Aaron's rod and swallowing the other roads bodily, than of being swallowed by any corporation whatever." That boosteristic prophesy certainly had not come to pass. Instead, as the state's Railroad Commissioner bluntly put it, "the Minneapolis & St. Louis has been alienated from state ownership." Others were plainly bitter, seeing betrayal by the Washburns and their associates who had sold out the M&StL project. "I propose to be loyal to Minneapolis interests, first, last, and all the time," William Drew Washburn had promised nearly a decade earlier. Now those words had a hollow ring for critics who always had seen him as arrogant and presently judged him also as duplicitous. "W. D. Washburn whenever he retired from anything left trouble, as well as maledictions, behind," contended one very uncharitable historian of the flour milling industry. Would that be the case with M&StL?[35]

# DANCING WITH THE GIANTS

8

We propose to fight the war out on this line—
*our share of Minnesota* traffic.

RANSOM R. CABLE, 1882

Ransom R. Cable burst like a comet over the railroad landscape of Minnesota and then the Northwest. He and Rock Island would prove to be agents of precipitous change.

Rock Island in the 1860s and 1870s had been slow in extension of lines—main arteries and feeders alike. Its management had chosen to err on the side of caution. As other roads moved to solidify service areas against "invasion," however, Rock Island was forced to reassess what it saw as its "natural territory." But again Rock Island chose a conservative path. Its alliance with Chicago, Burlington, & Quincy in the Burlington, Cedar Rapids, & Northern matter was an apt application of gaining territory already occupied by an existing road. So was the Cable-Porter plan regarding M&StL. Nevertheless, Rock Island needed to move more expansively—and on its sole account. Hugh Riddle, a perfectly capable manager otherwise, was not the man to perfect a grand strategy.

Cable and associates unveiled for Rock Island's board of directors an aggressive plan to reach the Pacific Coast by a northern route.

Cable reminded that by gathering in BCR&N and M&StL, Rock Island had gained precious and constant sources of traffic, had secured valuable access to Minneapolis–St. Paul, and had significantly extended Rock Island's frontier westward toward tidewater. For example, M&StL's "Pacific Division" already had reached Winthrop, would be extended into the Minnesota River valley at Morton before 1882 was out, and was in position to be pushed on to a junction with BCR&N's "Pacific Division," which in the summer of 1882 would be built northwestward to Lake Park, Iowa, 235 miles northwest of Cedar Rapids, and on a line to intercept an M&StL extension in Dakota. From that point Rock Island could press westward.[1]

Another important variable in Cable's overall strategy was the little remarked Wisconsin, Minnesota, & Pacific Railway (WM&P), which was to be something of a holding and management company for the vast project. WM&P, not to be established until August 13, 1883, would be successor to Minnesota Central and the Cannon River Improvement Company, each with valuable land grants and franchises as well as a 66-mile line of railway finished in 1882 from Waterville, an M&StL station a bit more than halfway to Albert Lea from Minneapolis, eastward through Faribault, Northfield, and Cannon Falls to Red Wing, on the Mississippi River below St. Paul. Franchise rights also permitted construction to the western boundary of the state. A. B. Stickney, already well established in area railroad circles, briefly vice president at M&StL and an important intermediary between Cable and W. D. Washburn in conveying M&StL to Rock Island control, had taken charge of construction, and nobody would be surprised early in 1883 when WM&P was turned over to operation by M&StL as its Cannon Valley Division. Behind all of this, however, were Cable and powerful Rock Island.[2]

In addition to its primary goal of reaching the Pacific by a northern route, Rock Island planners were likely motivated to take advantage of the great "Dakota Boom" that had begun in 1878. Much of Dakota Territory lay within a gigantic province long derisively labeled "The Great American Desert," and in 1869, General William T. Sherman had declared Dakota Territory "barren and worthless . . . as bad as God ever made or anybody can scare up this side of Africa." Six years later General W. B. Hazen had argued that the country was incapable of development. A subordinate, Colonel Alfred Sully, agreed: "The country west of Minnesota, till you reach the Missouri, is decidedly bad: a high, dry, rolling prairie . . . unfit for cultivation, except for a very few detached places along the very few streams." Sully conceded, however, that "the country might do for grazing. . . ." Nevertheless, by 1878 a combination of forces collaborated to propel a surge of settlers into this part of the American West. These forces included economic recovery following the financial Panic of 1873, departure of the grasshopper menace, a renewed determination among many Americans to claim part of the public domain as a birthright, and railroad construction adequate to open a huge chunk of the region.[3]

Chicago, Milwaukee & St. Paul's Hastings & Dakota extension had pioneered the area west of Ortonville, Minnesota, reaching Aberdeen on July 8, 1882, and as if to pointedly declare dominion in that region, immediately put out a 33-mile branch southward to Ashton and a 26-mile branch north to Frederick. Milwaukee even earlier had pressed a veritable system of lines into the southeastern quadrant of the territory and shortly would knit them to the new line at Aberdeen. In between these two portions of Milwaukee's empire lay Chicago & North Western, which had sent its Winona & St. Peter affiliate to Lake Kampeska in 1873, well ahead of demand. To this was added in 1879–80 another major artery through Brookings to Pierre, on the Missouri River, 781 miles from Chicago.[4]

The rush of humanity was soon a torrent with settlers' shacks, infant towns, and even tender cities sprouting variously. Watertown's land office was an especially busy place; a local newspaper reported that 106 immigrant cars had arrived there in the first three months of 1882. Codington County, of which Watertown was the capital, counted 2,156 souls in 1880 but would claim 5,648 by 1885; Brown County, of which Aberdeen was the seat, had 353 citizens in 1880 and would tally 12,241 five years later. New residents, native-born and foreign-born alike, came mostly from nearby states: Iowa, Wisconsin, Minnesota, and Illinois. The agriculturalists among them, a majority, devoted themselves to the wheat culture. Acreage sown to that crop in the future state of South Dakota stood at 720,000 in 1882 but would increase to 2,540,200 in 1884.[5]

Before Cable could afford to look further toward expanding Rock Island's empire into Dakota and beyond, however, he had to consolidate the road's presence in Minneapolis and St. Paul. That presence was hardly welcomed by CM&StP and C&NW, which directly or through surrogates for years had together forcefully represented Chicago. Rock Island's arrival actually reflected a broader shifting and even breakdown of a tacit if watchful interindustry agreement as to "natural territory" shared among Milwaukee, North Western, Rock Island, and Burlington—points of contention being, earlier or later, Council Bluffs–Omaha, Minneapolis–St. Paul, and (except for C&NW) Kansas City. Previous to Rock Island's gaining control

---

FACING PAGE: Sportsmen, perhaps from Minneapolis, were particularly attracted to hunting opportunities along Milwaukee lines in what became the states of North Dakota and South Dakota. Photograph courtesy of the Hennepin History Museum.

of M&StL, Milwaukee and North Western (with participation of an Omaha predecessor) had "pooled" passenger and freight business between Minneapolis–St. Paul and Milwaukee and Chicago. In addition, Milwaukee, North Western (with an Omaha predecessor), St. Paul & Duluth, and M&StL had agreed among themselves as to a division of tonnage in flour and mill stuffs from Minneapolis. This latter arrangement predictably was gauged by the amount of wheat brought to the mills by these roads, that is, the more wheat a road brought in, the more milled product it could expect to take out. Absent from this deal were Manitoba and Northern Pacific, neither of which had lines east or south to carry away flour, but each of which drew on expansive service areas for wheat tonnage producing milled product subject to competitive attack outside the pool agreement. This was the prospective business that caught the eye of Cable and that Milwaukee and North Western were bound to protect.[6]

Cognizant of heavy fixed costs (costs that do not vary with traffic carried) and realizing that even small fluctuations in volume could be dreadfully harmful, managers of railroads with common lines in a single corridor (New York–Chicago, for example) often forged agreements against what they labeled "ruinous competition." In some cases they made elaborate pooling contracts to divide traffic on a pro rata basis adequate to cover fixed costs and more, but as long as roads in the pool had unused capacity, there remained the overwhelming temptation to solicit more than an agreed share at rates covering little more than variable costs. These contracts were fragile, but in general railroaders saw pooling arrangements as legitimate and normal ways to regulate competition. The public was not convinced. Competition long had been viewed as the means to cure "railroad abuses," but railroads, when they did have end-point competition, as Minnesota's Railroad Commissioner observed, had chosen to engage in pooling, secretly setting rates, and dividing the earnings. "The public, instead of receiving the benefits hoped for," he groaned, "have two roads to support, instead of one."[7]

Skirmishing in the area began during the early fall of 1882. Rock Island moved to beef up M&StL's sales force and made provocative noises about being admitted to the Minneapolis pool. Ca-

ble and Porter met with Milwaukee's S. S. Merrill in October and agreed to the pooling of various eastbound freight, but Cable and Porter fussed when Merrill refused to pool "free" wheat (actually flour milled from wheat delivered by Manitoba and NP). Cable said he "did not want war," but pointedly announced that Rock Island intended to "have its full share of both passenger and freight."[8]

Meanwhile, Cable and Porter seemed bent on full amalgamation of Rock Island and Omaha, with M&StL and BCR&N also part of the blend. Rock Island could be tied physically to Omaha through BCR&N and M&StL, and the two already had independent operations into Omaha, Nebraska. Change certainly was in the air. CStPM&O shortly would move into a spacious new general office building in St. Paul and would complete new yards in Minneapolis, and in Wisconsin its construction crews were rushing to finish lines to Superior (reached on November 12) and to Bayfield (not reached until 1883).[9]

Completion of these important twin arteries to Lake Superior plus combination of Rock Island and Omaha under common ownership obviated any further construction by Taylor's Falls & Lake Superior and, for that matter, given M&StL's control by Cable and Porter, any M&StL involvement in that enterprise—one that as late as November 1881 the Washburns had seen as a possible independent outlet to Lake Superior. Indeed, M&StL had operated Taylor's Falls & Lake Superior on its own from December 1, 1881, with trains out of Minneapolis utilizing M&StL's Minneapolis & Duluth track to White Bear Lake, overhead to Wyoming by St. Paul & Duluth, and Taylor's Falls & Lake Superior to the end of the line at Taylors Falls. That stopped on July 31, 1882, when M&StL ceased operation of the branch and also terminated operation over StP&D to Duluth. On the next day StP&D took sole lease of both Taylor's Falls & Lake Superior and, quite surprisingly, M&StL's historic Minneapolis & Duluth as well. The Taylor's Falls operation had been strategically important to M&StL during the Washburn years, of course, but frankly had been marginal. In February 1883, M&StL would sell its half interest in Taylor's Falls & Lake Superior to St. Paul & Duluth.[10]

The relationship between Cable and Porter, between Rock Island and Omaha, and among all of them and M&StL was at best blurred during most of 1882. In the summer the trade press reported that M&StL was "under the control of the Omaha," an understandable conclusion given the collaborative efforts of Cable and Porter and the presence on the Omaha board of W. D. Washburn and Henry T. Welles. Rumors of union were further fanned when M&StL and Omaha entered a lease agreement on September 25 that gave Omaha rights over M&StL from Merriam into Minneapolis; Omaha already had trackage rights over Manitoba from St. Paul to Minneapolis. Together these contracts gave Omaha overhead privileges by which to connect its eastern and western lines right through the Twin Cities and, incidentally, the ability to reach its jointly owned Minneapolis Eastern in the heart of the milling district from both directions. For its part, M&StL gained access to St. Paul over Omaha from Merriam, a doubtful bargain at best.[11]

By late October skirmishing among the Chicago roads escalated to a clash. Cable lowered passenger rates in an effort to establish the

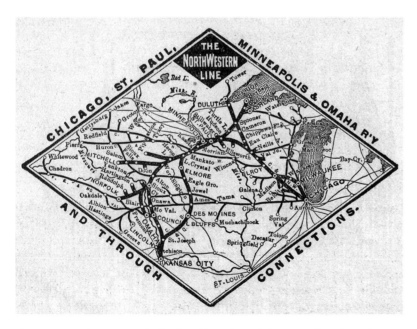

The agreement between Rock Island's Cable and Omaha's Porter allowed Omaha to connect its eastern and western lines right through the Twin Cities.

"Albert Lea Route" on an equal footing with CM&StP and C&NW, while Omaha pondered its own position vis-à-vis C&NW and Cable. The *Minneapolis Tribune* declared that Cable and Rock Island would accept "no less than one-third of the Minneapolis business, if they have to fight until doomsday." Yet, said the *Tribune*, Merrill and Milwaukee "declare that they will see the Rock Island in Hades before they will allow anything like that amount." This was enough to rattle an already skittish stock market, one well-placed New York banker told James J. Hill at Manitoba. The prominent New Yorker also worried that a rate war would lead to even more Granger agitation. His worry and that of others deepened when one-way passenger rates to Chicago slumped to $14.50, to $12.50, then to $5.00, $3.00, $1.00, and finally to $.50. M&StL's offices on Washington Avenue in Minneapolis were flooded on November 14, quickly selling out a five-coach, two-sleeper evening train to Chicago. More importantly, lower rates on flour and mill stuff soon followed.[12]

Charges among contenders provoked counter charges. Asked to explain the current state of affairs, C&NW's Albert Keep blithely replied that the rate war was caused by "intense competition among various companies for business." Rock Island's Cable attacked Milwaukee, which, he charged, wished to deny "the right of the Albert Lea Line to share the traffic furnished to the railroads by the people of Minnesota" and to "drive us from the state by compelling us to do business at rates which to not remunerate." Nevertheless, said Cable, "we propose to fight the war out on this line—*our share of Minnesota traffic*." Omaha's H. H. Porter offered an oblique response, saying that the problem derived from too much speculative construction, presumably by CM&StP. On November 13, however, Porter told Milwaukee's Merrill that he was "ready to have it out now all around, not only in rates and divisions, but territory as well." Milwaukee's Alexander Mitchell said that his road was merely defending itself against assault by Omaha and Rock Island. Cable dug in his heels: Rock Island must have 30 percent of business from Minneapolis and 20 percent from St. Paul.[13]

Then, suddenly, it was over. Managers of warring companies met in New York and on December 13 hammered out a plan by which business from Minneapolis and St. Paul would be divided as follows:

| Minneapolis Traffic | | St. Paul Traffic | |
| --- | --- | --- | --- |
| Milwaukee Road | 37.5 percent | Milwaukee Road | 43 percent |
| C&NW/Omaha | 37 percent | C&NW/Omaha | 43 percent |
| Rock Island/M&StL | 25 percent | Rock Island/M&StL | 14 percent[14] |

As important as was this development, there was even more pressing news from New York. As early as September 1, the *Minneapolis Tribune* had speculated that "Vanderbilt interests" had "gobbled the Omaha line in the interest of the North Western." More importantly, "The question that interests Minneapolis is: Does the 'gobble' also embrace the Minneapolis & St. Louis line, or will the latter go to the Rock Island?" The name Vanderbilt surfaced again among local press reports late in November, and by mid-December Omaha's stock was rising amid broadly scattered rumors of that road's consolidation with C&NW. Rumors proved fact. The rate war

had produced an unintended casualty insofar as Cable's strategic aspirations were concerned. Rock Island's chairman, Hugh Riddle, admitted defeat. "I have no doubt that [William K.] Vanderbilt either has purchased a controlling interest in the Omaha or is acting in this matter for the North Western, which is synonymous." On December 16, 1882, C&NW's Marvin Hughitt replaced H. H. Porter as Omaha's president, and wholesale changes on the board swept out Cable, Porter, and Henry T. Welles among others in favor of William K. and brother Cornelius Vanderbilt plus several others of Vanderbilt or C&NW flavor. Staying, most curiously, was W. D. Washburn.[15]

Additional fallout was not long in appearing. M&StL's position was no longer clouded: the road was clearly in Rock Island's camp. But that camp was diminished after the war. Cable had gambled much, and while Rock Island certainly had made its presence known, it had been forced to settle for only a quarter of eastbound business from Minneapolis. M&StL's General Freight Agent J. A. Hanley affirmed that he and other local managers had expected M&StL to get a full one-third. But, he bravely countered, "25 per cent is very good to start with, though in the course of a year it will be demonstrated that we are entitled to more." Cable had bet on full association with Omaha and with that in mind had signed away M&StL's interest in Taylor's Falls & Lake Superior, given up trackage rights over StP&D to Duluth, and had allowed Omaha entrance to Minneapolis from the west via Merriam. He had gotten for M&StL only access to St. Paul over Omaha. And there was more grief. The rate war had, in fact, inflamed the Granger mentality in

LEFT: Rate wars in the passenger arena often migrated to the freight sector, putting broad smiles on the faces of shippers of flour and mill stuff and deep frowns on railroaders. These workers are near the Galaxy Mill (later Northwestern Consolidated Milling's "A" mill) in the west-bank milling district. Photograph courtesy of the Minneapolis Public Library, Minneapolis Collection.

FACING PAGE: By 1885, M&StL had a substantial engine facility, shop, and yard near Cedar Lake. Map from *A Complete Set of Surveys and Plats of Properties in the City of Minneapolis, Minnesota* (Philadelphia: C. M. Hopkins, 1885); courtesy of the Minneapolis Public Library.

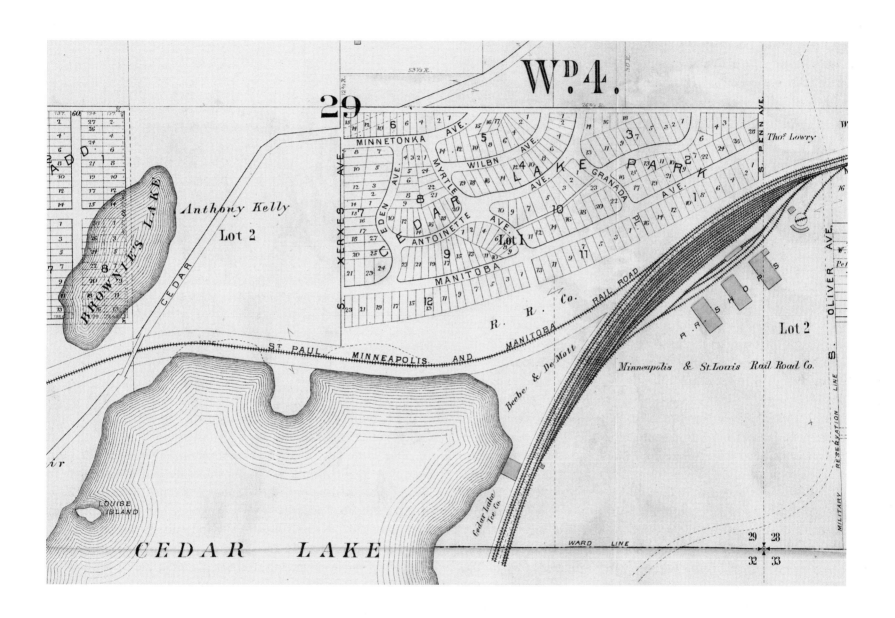

W<sup>D</sup> 4.

29

BROWNIE'S LAKE

ADD. 1

Anthony Kelly

Lot 2

MINNETONKA AVE.

WILBN AVE.

MYRTLE AVE.

CEDAR AVE.

ANTOINETTE AVE.

MANITOBA

LAKE PARK

GRANADA AVE.

Lot 1

S. XERXES AVE.

EDEN AVE.

S. PENN AVE.

Thos Lowry

St. Paul Minneapolis and Manitoba Rail Road

R. R. Co.

Beebe & De Mott

Minneapolis & St. Louis Rail Road Co.

Lot 2

R. R. SHOPS

S. OLIVER AVE.

MILITARY RESERVATION LINE

Cedar Lake Ice Co.

WARD LINE

29 | 28
32 | 33

LOUISE ISLAND

CEDAR LAKE

opposition to railroads and those who owned and managed them. "The distinctive life of the Omaha is now blotted out and it is henceforth merged into the hands of the North Western, the control of which is in the hands of strangers," wailed Minnesota's Railroad Commissioner. "Whether the Vanderbilt invasion of the northwestern empire is to wholly subordinate us to the uses of earlier systems and to the Vanderbilt methods, or that we are to be granted sufficient autonomy to guard our interests, remains for experience to determine," he glumly concluded.[16]

Winter seemed to have a calming effect. "The unprecedented dullness in local railroad circles continues," complained the *Minneapolis Tribune* on March 30, 1883. Compared to bizarre machinations of the recent war, matters now certainly were more relaxed. Cable and M&StL were conspicuous only by quiet. In fact, M&StL's meager contribution to regional news in 1883 was construction of a twelve-stall roundhouse at Cedar Lake.[17]

But there were salient developments elsewhere, and 1883 proved to be as news rich as 1882, with the spotlight shining brightly on Northern Pacific, which after years of fits and starts, finally made good on its northern transcontinental entitlement. Under the forceful leadership of German-born Henry Villard, NP construction crews struggled toward each other in Montana Territory; by late summer the tall, blue-eyed Villard was able to throw out his chest in anticipation of a gala celebration to mark completion of the line. Prominent guests from Europe and across the United States were put aboard special trains on the East Coast and whisked westward to Chicago and—some of them using the Albert Lea Route—to St. Paul. President Chester A. Arthur, on his way back to Washington from Yellowstone Park, joined the entourage, which used the Hotel Lafayette on Lake Minnetonka as its headquarters during the stay. Then early on the morning of September 5, these happy excursionists reboarded special trains for additional festivities at Fargo, Bismarck, Billings, Livingston, and Helena before reaching a scenic if remote location west of Garrison—appropriately labeled Gold Creek—where, on September 8, the final spike was driven. The Great Lakes were connected to Pacific tidewater; Duluth, Superior,

Manitoba's passenger station in Minneapolis often was called Union Station, perhaps because technically it was owned and operated by a Manitoba subsidiary, Minneapolis Union, but more likely because the facility over time was used by many other roads including Omaha, Northern Pacific, St. Paul & Duluth, and M&StL. Only portions of the new facility on Hennepin Avenue and High Street were available in 1884; the main part would not be in use until April 25, 1885. Photograph courtesy of the Minnesota Historical Society.

St. Paul, and Minneapolis were united with Portland and Tacoma. In between lay a gigantic 2,000-mile hinterland.[18]

That hinterland might be expected to produce eastbound tonnage that M&StL could profitably wheel beyond Minneapolis or, like wheat, could be milled and moved as flour to destination by M&StL. Potential synergies were apparent, and not surprisingly M&StL looked to NP as a possible ally and waited expectantly to see how that road developed its service area, to see how financial swings affected its management and strategic planning, and to see how NP would physically configure itself in Minneapolis and St. Paul. Villard predictably had put full energy against completion of NP's main line in Montana, if to the detriment of other projects. Grading on NP's line adjacent to Manitoba from East St. Cloud to Minneapolis consequently did not begin until September 1883 but would be completed by year's end, and work on a fine bridge over the Mississippi River upstream above the milling district was well along. When completed, NP would have its own line into Minneapolis from the west with trackage rights over Manitoba into St. Paul.[19]

In getting to and from St. Paul, NP trains would pass over Manitoba's great Stone Arch Bridge, finished late in 1883 but used little until April 1884, and then mostly for freight. Soon, however, NP passenger trains as well as those of owner Manitoba, Omaha, St. Paul & Duluth, and M&StL would use that bridge and also Minneapolis Union's (Manitoba's) new passenger station at the foot of Hennepin Avenue—this effective September 1, 1884. Actually, only portions of the new facility were fully prepared—the main part would not be in use until April 25, 1885—but Manitoba's old depot, at Washington and Fifth Street was abandoned.[20]

Late in 1883, a new—and from M&StL's point of view, patently ironic—variable burst onto the local railroad scene when the Minneapolis, Sault Ste. Marie & Atlantic Railway was organized under the laws of Wisconsin. Strategic purposes were implied in its very name: to link Minneapolis with Atlantic ports via Sault Ste. Marie,

bypassing Chicago in the process. It all sounded so familiar. The specific idea had been broached as early as 1873 in a speech by Israel Washburn, the notion had percolated in the minds of others who associated the concept with purposes of Northern Pacific, and it had finally taken root when "a number of prominent citizens" of Minneapolis were summoned to the office of William Drew Washburn, whose mixed genius and boyish enthusiasms quickly won them to this daring enterprise. Included in the directorate were Washburn, J. K. Sidle, Henry T. Welles, John Martin, and W. W. Eastman—every one incorporators of M&StL in another age—as well as W. D. Hale, C. A. Pillsbury, and Charles Martin, all of whom had been members of M&StL's board at one time or another. Even at that very moment Washburn was on the board at M&StL and at Omaha; the idea of conflict of interest was not yet mature.[21]

---

BELOW LEFT AND RIGHT: The two tracks on the far left of the left photograph were those of M&StL headed to and from the west-bank milling district. The remaining tracks were owned by Minneapolis Union (Manitoba) and connected its passenger station with the Stone Arch Bridge (in right photograph). Photograph on left courtesy of the Minnesota Historical Society. Photograph on right courtesy of the Hennepin History Museum.

The "Washburn Road" (that, too, sounded familiar), or "Soo Line," as it became popularly known, elbowed out M&StL, now under Rock Island domination, as the favorite local road but, like M&StL at birth and later, Soo was strapped for cash and the road would not gain its Sault Ste. Marie goal until 1887. Meanwhile, however, in 1884 a satellite, also a "millers' enterprise," the Minneapolis & Pacific, was to be organized for the purpose of building west from Minneapolis. Taken together, these predecessors of Minneapolis, St. Paul & Sault Ste. Marie were designed to bring wheat into Minneapolis and take flour from it—at the expense Duluth, on the one hand, and Chicago, on the other—all very much like the original purposes of M&StL and led by the same cast of characters. "The importance to this section, and especially to Minneapolis, of this enterprise can hardly be overestimated," observed the *Minneapolis Tribune*. Déjà vu. Nevertheless, Soo, if a latecomer, would have to be reckoned with locally and, as it developed, in the grand scheme of railroad strategy as well.[22]

Railroad construction in the United States had continued apace in 1881 and 1882, before turning down to the level of 1880 in 1883. For its part, *Railroad Gazette* worried that too much capacity had been added too quickly and warned that "work could not be continued at this rate without bringing on financial disaster." Bankers, too, were worried, brooding about the anarchy of rate wars and "blackmail lines." They chided railroad leaders, reminding that steady revenues were required to cover fixed costs from bonds marketed in New York and elsewhere. In truth the national economy was contracting, and investors, fearing a bloodletting the result of too much railroad construction, tightened purse strings. For his part, Cable shrugged and observed that neither Rock Island nor its associates and surrogates had played much of a part in the great construction boom. Perhaps Rock Island's purpose had been to catch its breath after taking control of M&StL and after the tumultuous rate war, or maybe it was licking its wounds after losing Omaha to C&NW.[23]

Peace among the giants was tenuous, however, and Cable would not sulk endlessly. Late in 1883, he declared Rock Island's intention of withdrawing from Northwest Traffic Association (pool). That announcement plus an assortment of additional grievances was adequate to set off an unseemly squabble between Cable and William K.

LEFT: Minneapolis, St. Paul & Sault Ste. Marie promised to be a prominent player in the railway affairs of Minneapolis. Attesting to that reality was the Soo Line boxcar in this view, awaiting a load at the Anchor Mill. Photograph courtesy of the Hennepin History Museum.

FACING PAGE: Soo Line would headquarter in Minneapolis and place its Shoreham heavy shops and principal yard there, too. Photograph by C. P. Gibson; courtesy of the Minnesota Historical Society.

Vanderbilt, successor to the fabulous Cornelius Vanderbilt fortune, a man well established in his own right among railroad moguls, and the very being who had snapped Omaha from Porter and Cable late in 1882. Vanderbilt, in reality, was committed to infiltrate Rock Island's board, to obliterate Cable, to change Rock Island's strategic compass, and possibly even to grab control of the entire enterprise. Cable, however, was equally determined that Vanderbilt would succeed in none of this.[24]

Financial circles, recalling the recent battle for Omaha and knowing the personalities involved, were hardly surprised at this fight for control of CRI&P. Vanderbilt was known to be the largest single holder of Rock Island stock—valued at about $1.4 million or approximately one-fortieth of all Rock Island shares. What he wanted, said Vanderbilt, was two seats on CRI&P's board—seats awarded to Albert Keep and Marvin Hughitt, president and vice president, respectively, of Chicago & North Western, and each man also a member of C&NW's board. Foul, cried Cable, who pointed out that Vanderbilt also owned about $20 million in C&NW's stock and was very well represented on that company's board. Vanderbilt was characteristically direct in explaining: "I wanted to choose who should represent the North Western and myself, and not let an opposing interest, Cable and Porter, run the Rock Island." Cable was equally blunt: "As I do not manage the property to keep Vanderbilt's interests, I cannot expect his approval, and he is welcome to his criticism." Both sides blustered as they simultaneously built alliances in preparation for a nasty proxy fight in June 1884. The vote resulted in a crushing defeat for Vanderbilt. Indeed, Rock Island shareholders, typically conservative investors well accustomed to Rock Island's long tradition of cushy dividends, backed Cable by an amazing 85 percent majority.[25]

Aside from personal animosities, which were palpable, Vanderbilt was trying to crush Rock Island's instinct for survival through expansion. In 1882, C&NW had made another pass at BCR&N, and Vanderbilt and C&NW management had been greatly put out when Cable picked up M&StL and with Porter sought Omaha. They had been further agitated when Cable sought (but failed to get) full stock ownership of M&StL late in 1883. One Vanderbilt associate snarled that Porter and Cable were "probably two of the least popular railroad managers in the Northwest" and ridiculed "the speculative Directors" of Rock Island, who, he predicted, would "probably try to force upon" CRI&P "the Minneapolis & St. Louis Railroad Company—a miserable and comparatively worthless property." The acerbic quality of his rhetoric belied reality: Cable and Rock Island (now with BCR&N and M&StL) had frightened and thoroughly aroused Vanderbilt and C&NW. With good reason, they thought. C&NW (now with Omaha) earlier had been "violated" by M&StL's "invasion" of "natural territory" in Minnesota at Merriam and Waseca, and in Iowa at Luverne and Ogden. BCR&N was, if anything, even more of an irritant, challenging C&NW right in Cedar Rapids and throughout much of Iowa and Dakota where C&NW surrogates had built, were building, or were planning expansion. And Vanderbilt knew that Cable was adamant that Rock Island should "receive its share of the traffic to and from all territory tributary to its system. . . ." To put a fine point on it, said Cable, "It might be well" for Mr. Vanderbilt "to become reconciled with our arrangements for like advantages for competition with the North Western and the Milwaukee in northern Iowa, Minnesota, and Dakota." He had thrown down the gauntlet.[26]

But Cable continued to move cautiously, treading carefully, probably because of the severe national recession that took hold in 1883 and would not yield to recovery until 1886. Investors and most railroad managers—including Cable—believed in general that the country's rail net had expanded too far compared to demand and that more mileage at the moment would waste capital. To that rule was an exception, however, an exception that even the skeptical *Railroad Gazette* acknowledged. "There is one very encouraging feature in the situation, and that is the rapid settlement of the new lands in Northwest recently made accessible by railroads." Indeed, the "Dakota Boom" continued, slowed to be sure, but was not yet exhausted. Cable could justify expansion there, to stake out territory, to share in a growing traffic from a region not yet saturated with lines, and to position Rock Island for its planned drive to the Pacific.[27]

Rock Island strategists gathered information, pondered data; they would have to be well prepared for questions when Cable sought funding in a cautious financial market. Emigration, they found, continued strong. Thirteen trans-Atlantic steamers dropped 7,891 emigrants at New York's Castle Garden during the first week of May 1884; in the last week of that month, eleven vessels brought another 6,198. Most of these persons were from northern and western Europe, and many were destined for the upper Midwest. On March 27, for example, M&StL had handled 150 emigrants into Minneapolis—persons destined for new homes along the Northern Pacific; a few days later, Manitoba ticketed 200 emigrants to various points north and west of Minneapolis. Not to be outdone, Milwaukee actively and successfully solicited newcomers for settlement along its line west from Minneapolis into Dakota. Growth at C&NW locations to the south was equally impressive. Beadle County, with Huron as its capital, and traversed by North Western's line to the Missouri River, held 1,290 persons in 1880, but over 10,000 would claim residence there a half decade later. The growth of Codington County and Watertown, on the original C&NW penetration of Dakota, was similarly impressive. The land office at Watertown was second busiest in the entire territory for 1881–82, and during the first seven months of 1882, 400 immigrant cars had reached Watertown. The population of Codington would escalate from 2,156 in 1880 to 5,648 in 1885. For that matter, the number of residents in the future state of South Dakota would shoot up from 97,734 in 1880 to 262,515 by mid-decade, and in the same period the number of farms would grow by 270 percent—13,414 to 49,656. In 1882, the number of acres "filed on" totaled 4.3 million, but that figure had grown to 7.3 million in 1883, and ballooned to a startling 11 million in 1884.[28]

The "boom mentality" in Dakota was not matched nationally and certainly was not reflected in financial centers, where gloom precluded issuance of large blocks of securities necessary for major construction. Cable put transcontinental plans on hold, but he scoured endlessly for funding to take Rock Island clients into Dakota. The boom there was still on, he told potential investors, and

demand on the public domain continued. Moreover, he pointed out, the eastern reaches of the territory represented an extension of the prairies of Iowa and Minnesota, dotted with lakes and groves, and traversed by numerous streams—in other words, very much like productive country they were already familiar with. The soil in eastern Dakota was immensely fertile, and the average annual rainfall approximated 24 inches. Heavy traffic westbound would include lumber, coal, and manufactured and consumer goods of all kinds; eastbound tonnage in live stock, corn, and cereal grains—especially wheat—could be expected. Indeed, wheat production was especially promising; farmers in Brown County around Aberdeen had reported 25 to 40 bushel per acre yields in 1882. In addition, any extension of M&StL beyond the Minnesota River valley would be heartily applauded by Minneapolis flour manufacturers, whose mills had insatiable appetites and increasingly were burdened by competition at Duluth.[29]

Cable remained conservative and constrained; he moved by indirection. After an M&StL board meeting in October 1883, the press reported that "the company at present prefer to say nothing relative to an extension of their road into the country of the Red River valley." But on November 30, articles of incorporation for Cedar Rapids, Iowa Falls, & Northwestern, a BCR&N subsidiary in charge of constructing and operating that company's "Pacific Division," were altered to allow further movement in Iowa, Minnesota, and Dakota Territory. At about the same time, articles pertaining to Wisconsin, Minnesota & Pacific were changed to give that enterprise rights to build by "a most feasible route in the direction of the Great Bend of the Missouri River." Plans jelled during the winter of 1883–84. WM&P surveyors studied the country west of Waterville on the stub from Red Wing, and local press reports promised track work "as soon as this work is completed." Cable settled on another plan, however, one that used WM&P's general authority for expansion but hitched it to M&StL's existing line west from Hopkins into the Minnesota River valley. In that way WM&P could leapfrog ahead, leaving a gap between Waterville and a connection with M&StL's Pacific Division at some yet unidentified location that could be filled

later. On April 1, 1884, Rock Island purchased all of WM&P's securities, stocks and bonds alike, and advanced monies to that road for construction of an extension from the M&StL line at Morton "to some point on the Northern Pacific, probably Jamestown, Dakota," opined *Railway Age*. On the same date, BCR&N sold bonds adequate to push a new line of road from Lake Park in northwestern Iowa, in a "northwesterly direction, to the city of Bismarck."[30]

This news was not received kindly by owners and managers of NP and Manitoba and, in truth, represented a revocation of what Cable had promised earlier. "We will make some extension either from the Minneapolis & St. Louis, or Burlington, Cedar Rapids & Northern in a westerly or northwesterly direction in the territory now occupied by the North Western and Milwaukee roads," he had confided to Manitoba's James J. Hill on May 14, 1883. But, he went on, "we have no intention of going north of points already held by them, knowing very well," he said, "that the Northern Pacific and your company are disposed to give our interest at St. Paul and Minneapolis a full share of business from the territory covered by your respective lines." In other words, Cable had pledged not to transgress into the service areas of NP and Manitoba west of Minneapolis if each maintained favorable traffic relations in the Twin Cities. Failing that, Cable implied retaliation. What explained the move now? Perhaps Hill or NP managers had irritated Cable, but more likely he was pursuing his own instincts in pressing on toward the Pacific.[31]

Construction on M&StL began west of Morton in the early spring of 1884. C&NW threatened retaliation by lengthening a branch northwestward from Redwood Falls across the WM&P survey "to prevent encroachment on its territory," but it did not do so. WM&P surveyors soon located a line out of the river bottoms onto the rich, undulating prairie, for 70 miles following the northwestward angle of the Minnesota River but diverging from it gradually before turning abruptly west to cross the boundary of Dakota Territory and

Manitoba had extensive operations in Dakota Territory and would not look kindly on Ransom Cable's westward aspirations for Rock Island and M&StL.

dropping into the broad drainage basin of the Big Sioux and James rivers. By early May it was clear that Cable had selected Watertown as an intermediate destination with confluence of WM&P and BCR&N. The latter, meanwhile, had chosen a route from Lake Park, Iowa, that crossed the extreme southwest corner of Minnesota and then continued along the west side of Coteaux des Prairie northward in the fertile valley of the Big Sioux River through Dakota's easternmost counties before angling northwest to Watertown.[32]

As WM&P and BCR&N construction crews labored through the summer of 1884, Cable's lieutenants considered plans by which the two companies would "build jointly to Bismarck," a distance of about 225 miles from Watertown. C. F. Hatch, president of WM&P, and C. J. Ives, president of BCR&N, pointed out that when completed a year hence, the route to Bismarck would "secure a large traffic" benefiting Chicago via BCR&N and CRI&P as well as Minneapolis via WM&P and M&StL. Meanwhile, by early fall, WM&P announced plans to fill the gap between Waterville and M&StL's Pacific Division at Gaylord. These assertions set off a predictable wave of rumors, among them that Cable's real goal was to build a line parallel with Manitoba to Winnipeg, and—most expansively— that Rock Island, "the most vigorous and aggressive corporation in the Northwest" was out to "scoop" Milwaukee and Manitoba alike by gathering in the new or planned Washburn roads east and west of Minneapolis and, not so incidentally according to one observer, furnishing "healthy competition where it will be needed."[33]

Elsewhere, facts and not rumors marked progress toward Watertown. Tracklayers for WM&P and BCR&N, in spirited rivalry, pressed toward that mutual destination. BCR&N rail went down at the rate of 2 miles per day; track layers were north of Pipestone by early August and near Elkton at month's end. WM&P, however, won the race; its rails were put down in Watertown on October 27, a few days before BCR&N arrived. M&StL initiated passenger service from Minneapolis on November 1.[34]

The *Minneapolis Tribune* called Rock Island's twin thrusts to the northwest "a significant event in railroad circles" since until now that part of Dakota Territory had been the province of C&NW and Milwaukee. And the *Tribune* looked forward to 1885 when "a new road will be pushed on toward Bismarck, and the upper territory of the Northern Pacific Railroad will be invaded by the redoubtable Rock Island." Surveyors had problems in the hill country east of the James River, but before winter closed in, they found a favorable route with easy grades leading toward Bismarck.[35]

# 9

# FALLING RATES AND ENCROACHMENT

M&StL penetrates "the very heart of the agricultural paradise of the Continent" where "the civilization, wealth and culture of American farm life are seen at their best"—"a land like that which gladdened the prophetic vision of Moses, 'flowing with milk and honey.'"

CRI&P, 1886

M&StL's life under the great protective shield of Ransom Cable and Rock Island during the remainder of the 1880s proved a mixed blessing—much like the relationship of a younger sibling with a "big brother." There were times when M&StL was sheltered and nurtured by the arrangement; there were times when the road suffered from inattention and from an inability to act unilaterally on its own merit. In any event, it was often heady business being an integral part of CRI&P's well-known and well-respected railroad empire.[1]

Samuel F. Boyd, in charge of passenger sales at M&StL, missed no opportunity to ballyhoo "the celebrated Albert Lea Route," while his counterpart at Rock Island, E. St. John, likewise pumped "the direct and favorite line . . . to the watering places, summer resorts . . . and hunting and fishing grounds of Iowa and Minnesota." More-

over, they trumpeted, the Albert Lea Route was "the most desirable path to the rich wheat fields and pastoral lands of interior Dakota," and, reminded Rock Island, "parties seeking homes in the Northwest" should know that "fine farm land" was "still for sale" in Minnesota and beyond. "Wheat raising in these sections has been demonstrated to be a sure means of getting wealth," but, cautioned CRI&P, "as every year adds to the scarcity of unoccupied lands and their value, we advise going at once." Boyd promised "close connections" in Minneapolis to "all points North and Northwest."[2]

In addition to trademark service to and from Chicago and St. Louis, M&StL likewise offered options west and southwest. In 1883, one passenger and one mixed train daily worked the line to and from Morton; service extended to Watertown a year later. M&StL's

"Des Moines Air Line," however, received more attention, providing, as it did, "the only direct line to Central Iowa Points" as well as access to Rock Island in Des Moines for connections to Omaha and from there to "all points in Missouri, Kansas, Texas" and, indeed, "all points in the South and Southwest." Two trains daily ran as far as Fort Dodge, only one beyond to Des Moines.[3]

In all cases, Minneapolis and St. Paul were center stage from M&StL's perspective. By 1883, about 100 passenger trains moved in and out of Minneapolis each day; even more, 155, served St. Paul. During the Washburn years, St. Paul had played second fiddle in M&StL's strategy, but Cable thought Rock Island's empire incomplete without service to Minnesota's capital city—"giant young chief of the North, marching with seven-league stride in the van of progress," as Mark Twain described it in *Life on the Mississippi*. St. Paul was, without question, vastly important in commerce, jobbing, government, and transportation. Cable was right to seek avenue to St. Paul, gained it with the Omaha contract (a modest advantage in carriage of freight), and initially wedged access to St. Paul Union Depot for passenger trains over Manitoba. Located at the foot of Sibley Street, hard by the public levee on the Mississippi, that facility had opened in August 1881; two years later it saw an average of 14,000 patrons daily and handled about 119 tons of mail weekly.[4]

Rock Island enthusiastically advertised tourist attractions such as Lake Minnetonka—"The Queen of Northern Lakes"—on M&StL. Four daily trains from Minneapolis served Excelsior and Lake Park. As added inducement, "Pullman Palace Sleeping Cars" from Chicago were run through in season to Lake Minnetonka. "This arrangement enables passengers to reach any one of three points on Lake Minnetonka, viz. Hotel St. Louis, Solberg's Point and Excelsior, without change of cars or other inconvenience," pointed out Rock Island. As always there was spirited competition among the major resorts. Hotel St. Louis—"Three stories high . . . running water and gas throughout the house"—had accommodations for 500 guests and rates of $15.00 to $21.00 per week, "liberal arrangements made for children and servants." Lake Park offered "large and airy" rooms to comfortably accommodate 350 guests, who could enjoy "full brass band and orchestra discourses enlivening music during the day and in the evening." Never to be outdone, Hotel Lafayette, "the finest summer resort hotel on the American continent," had rooming accommodations for 1,200 guests, who gladly paid $3.00 to $5.00 per day for the privilege.[5]

Demand grew for passenger service as M&StL expanded its domain and as population increased throughout the growing service

LEFT: Freight paid most of the bills, and M&StL's focus was on the Minneapolis milling district. This view looks west at what is now the West River Road side of the Mill City Museum. The Crown Roller Mill can be seen in the distance. Photograph courtesy of the Minneapolis Public Library, Minneapolis Collection.

FACING PAGE: The fuel-starved Northwest had an understandable need to import coal—and lots of it—delivered usually in open-top cars such as those on the right, which have been spotted for unloading in an alley of the city's manufacturing area. A significant percentage of coal arrived in Minneapolis from pits in Iowa, and even more from eastern points by way of Duluth. Photograph courtesy of the Minnesota Historical Society.

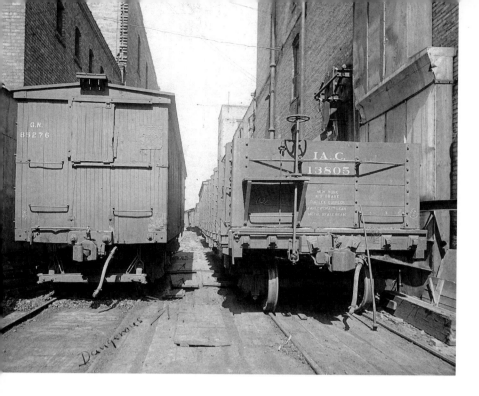

area. In 1881, 145,510 passengers boarded M&StL's cars, traveling an average of 34.9 miles and generating $131,335 in revenue. In 1889, however, 510,569 passengers traveled only an average of 25.5 miles and paid $384,029 for the privilege.[6]

Freight, as always, brought in the greatest revenue. Loadings increased predictably with expanded mileage, with favored linkage to BCR&N and CRI&P, with growing population in the service area, and when Cable "bought" tonnage through rate wars. Ton miles jumped from 19 million in 1880 to 110 million in 1886.[7]

Cable's focus on the Twin Cities during the first half of the 1880s coupled with M&StL's historic position in Minneapolis was reflected statistically. In 1884, M&StL handled 44,264 loads in and out of Minneapolis, was the clear leader in lumber billed out of the city (40 percent), and led all roads in delivery of coal (140,377 tons). Two years later, M&StL hauled 26,926 cars into Minneapolis (18.6 percent), stood fourth behind Manitoba, Milwaukee, and Omaha in delivery of wheat, third in tonnage of flour taken from the mills (14.5 percent), second behind Milwaukee in delivery of merchandise (26.0 percent), and first in coal (30.0 percent).[8]

Ransom Cable was president of M&StL from late 1882 until 1888, but early in 1883, Cable placed a talented and trusted friend in charge of local operations, retaining ultimate control from Chicago. William H. Truesdale, late of employ by Omaha, was the man chosen as assistant to the president of M&StL—"evidence of Cable's good judgement," declared the *Minneapolis Tribune*. Born at Youngstown, Ohio, on December 1, 1851, Truesdale had moved west with his family to Rock Island, Illinois, where he received a common school education before gaining employment as a clerk for the Rockford, Rock Island & St. Louis Railroad. Cable met him there and nurtured his career. Indeed, shortly after arriving in Minneapolis, Truesdale was named vice president.[9]

Though talented and respected, Truesdale would be thoroughly tested at M&StL. The road was no longer the local favorite but was perceived rather indistinctly as a Minneapolis-headquartered concern, yes, but an arm of Rock Island, one of the Chicago trunk roads. Important local shippers shifted allegiances absent the powerful Washburn influence, and despite the fact that he remained on M&StL's board, W. D. Washburn himself took only a dispassionate view of routing traffic from the Minneapolis mills. "You or Joe should say to the M&StL people that we expect the same drawback on our shipments by that line as are accorded other parties," he told W. D. Hale in 1883. Even more annoying was the decision in 1884 among several millers (including Charles J. Martin, C. H. Pettit, J. K. Sidle, and Charles A. Pillsbury—all former M&StL directors) to form the Minneapolis Western Railway, a switching and transfer company, to serve mills and manufacturing plants on the west bank of the Mississippi right under M&StL's nose. There was no doubt that Minneapolis Western was favorably inclined toward James J. Hill and the increasingly powerful Manitoba. In fact Manitoba had

FOLLOWING SPREAD: The west-bank milling district offered railroads a traffic bonanza. At lower left is Milwaukee Road's passenger station and freight houses. Map from *A Complete Set of Surveys and Plats of Properties in the City of Minneapolis, Minnesota* (Philadelphia: C. M. Hopkins, 1885); courtesy of the Minneapolis Public Library.

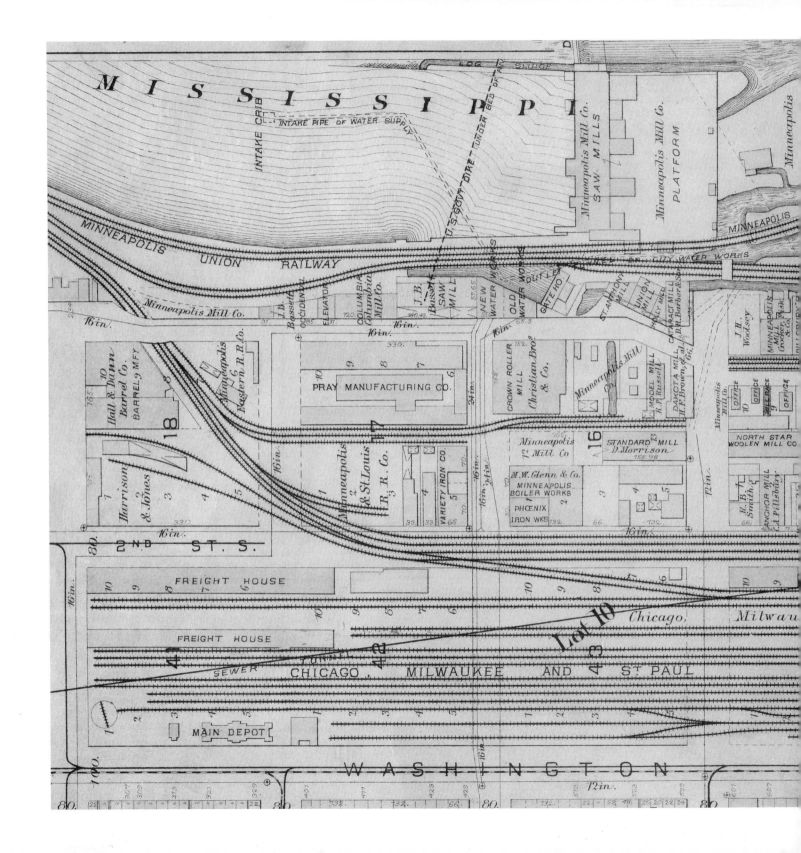

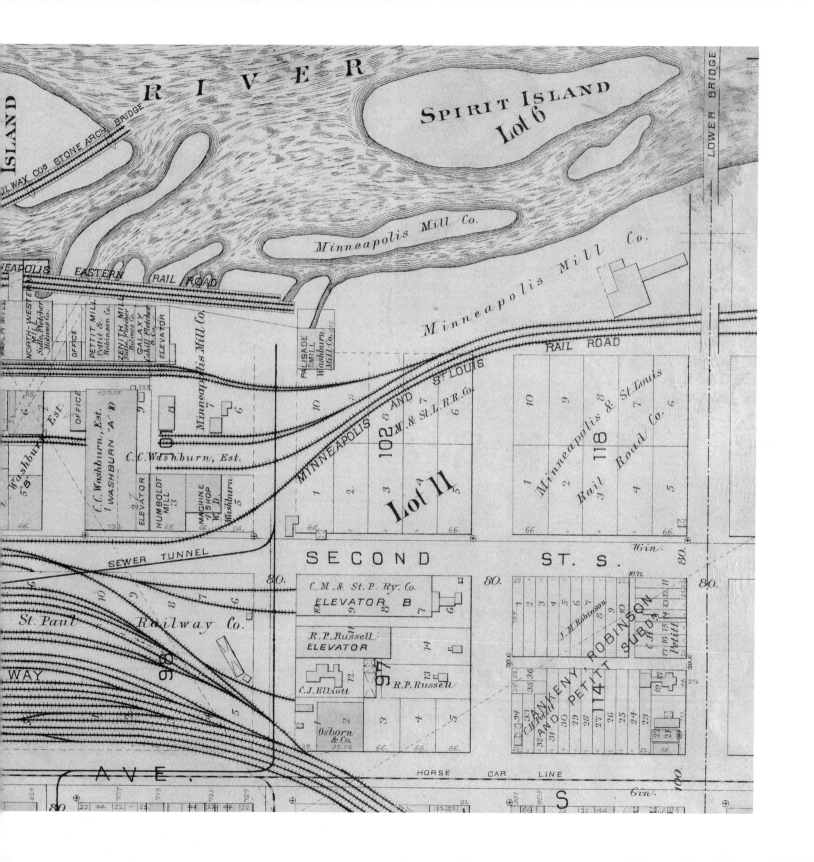

advanced funds adequate for construction of the new pike. And, of course, Minneapolis Eastern, a jointly held stooge of Milwaukee and Omaha, likewise had a prominent presence in this traffic-rich district of Minneapolis.[10]

M&StL and Manitoba seemed endlessly locked in a variety of contentious issues in and about Minneapolis. Irksome and expensive litigation over the legitimacy of leases that M&StL had entered into with Manitoba predecessor St. Paul & Pacific, and between city authorities and M&StL, Manitoba, and NP over the closing of grade crossings lasted most of the decade. For M&StL's Truesdale, it was as much a matter of principle as it was of defending M&StL's prior rights in the heart of town. And, believed Truesdale, James J. Hill in several instances had not acted honorably toward M&StL. Tensions mounted, and in the summer of 1885 M&StL stopped running trains to and from St. Paul over Manitoba.[11]

Periodic cooperation did occur, however. In 1883, M&StL became a full partner in newly created Minnesota Transfer Company, a substantial and neutral operation located midway between Minneapolis and St. Paul. Owned by and for the benefit of M&StL, Manitoba, Milwaukee, Omaha, and NP, Minnesota Transfer provided for interchange of cars as well as less-than-carload (LCL) freight, owning trackage, stockyards, warehouses, and platforms for those purposes. In 1886, M&StL moved about 11.5 percent of LCL passing through Minnesota Transfer, standing fifth in volume among the owners. Two years later, Minnesota Transfer would employ 250 men and handle 2.36 million pounds of LCL and 380,978 head of livestock. Local industry quickly sprouted up at the edges of the yard, and a whole community grew up nearby.[12]

Minnesota Transfer became a substantial operation owned by the several roads serving Minneapolis and St. Paul with principal operations located about midway between the two great cities. Photograph courtesy of the Minnesota Historical Society.

Cooperation at Minnesota Transfer was dictated by mutual advantage, but tensions mounted during the middle to late 1880s as the giants vented their instincts for aggression, as more competitors appeared, and as all comers eagerly sought business in a capricious economy that ebbed and flowed. An economic downturn that began in 1882 reached a trough in May 1885 when an upswing in the business cycle began and was quickly reflected by an increase in railroad stock prices and renewed expansion of lines. Much of new construction was on behalf of strong, established companies—usually as feeders—but there were important bursts of energy by newcomers as well. This pattern was patently manifest in the upper Midwest and involved several roads.[13]

One of these was Wisconsin Central. It began service into St. Paul and Minneapolis on January 20, 1885, with a diagonal route from near Milwaukee through Fond du Lac and Stevens Point. Wisconsin Central also had a branch to Ashland, on Lake Superior, and in 1886 would complete its own line into Chicago. In this way Wisconsin Central gave the Twin Cities four outlets to Lake Superior (StP&D, Omaha to Superior and to Bayfield, and WC) as well as a new line to Chicago.[14]

Another enterprise on the scene was Minnesota & Northwestern, brainchild of the redoubtable Alpheus B. Stickney, former M&StL officer and builder of the Cannon Valley route from Waterville to Red Wing—a man who well knew the area railroad scene and a most interesting and complex character. Stickney's concern began at St. Paul, where he directed its affairs from offices in the Metropolitan Opera Building, and stretched southward, roughly parallel to the east of Milwaukee's pioneer line, converging at and passing through Austin to Lyle, on the Iowa border, 109 miles. At Lyle, Minnesota & Northwestern made connection with Illinois Central, owner of a stub route up the Cedar River valley from near Waterloo, Iowa, and a junction there with its important Chicago–Sioux City line. This set off a fusillade of rumors that Stickney was merely a puppet for Illinois Central—a logical notion, since that road long had been expected to penetrate Minnesota—but IC's President James C. Clarke said that in his view there were already too many roads in

Wisconsin Central (shown here departing Great Northern's Minneapolis depot) carded two daily trips between Chicago and Minneapolis. Photograph courtesy of the Minnesota Historical Society.

the Chicago–Minneapolis–St. Paul corridor, and consequently, his company had no intention of creating an alliance with Minnesota & Northwestern. So Stickney's road persisted southwestward into Iowa, to Manly, and connection there with hard-luck Central Iowa Railway. That, too, set off speculation as to Stickney's strategic intent—speculation that accelerated later when he served simultaneously as president of both roads. Most likely Stickney was playing all angles to benefit his road, securing access to Chicago via Illinois Central, gaining a doglegged route to St. Louis using Central Iowa and others, and recruiting coal traffic for the fuel-starved Northwest from mines in southern Iowa.[15]

Stickney's road, like Wisconsin Central, considerably upset the status quo. "This questionable multiplication of railroad lines between Chicago and St. Paul is injurious to us," said Manitoba's

Henry D. Minot, "because such of them as find themselves starving, may feel the necessity of getting at the breast of this country, where the milk flows: that is, into the region which the Manitoba company now drains." James J. Hill put a considerably different face on it in reporting to Manitoba shareholders: "The increased competition thus introduced by new roads in the Chicago-St. Paul corridor cannot but benefit the whole Northwest, by improving and cheapening its communication with the central and eastern parts of the country." Privately, however, Hill and Minot both fumed at the temerity of the Stickney's of the world, saving particular venom for Stickney's announced plans to branch northward to Duluth (an idea never

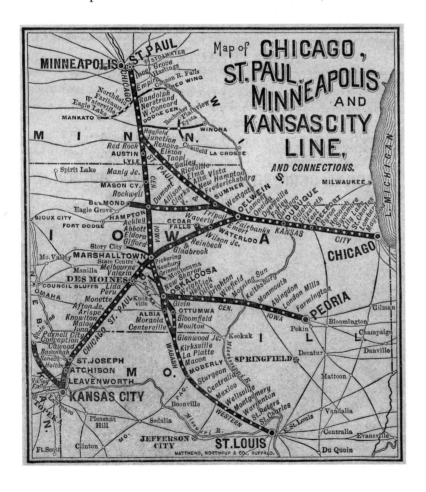

consummated). In any event, Minnesota & Northwestern expanded elsewhere, initiated independent operation to Chicago on August 1, 1887, eventually evolved into Chicago Great Western, and ultimately carved out additional gateways at Kansas City and Omaha as well as the Twin Cities and Chicago.[16]

Rising economic tides likewise lifted fortunes of the "Washburn roads." By late 1884, Minneapolis, Sault Ste. Marie & Atlantic operated with rights over Omaha from St. Paul to Turtle Lake, Wisconsin, thence by its own line to Bruce, 128 miles, far from its Sault Ste. Marie goal, but the intervening distance would be completed before the end of 1887. "We have had to fight our way inch by inch," declared Washburn when the final spike was in, "but we are here to stay." Progress northwestward by Minneapolis & Pacific, also delayed, began in 1886; two years later track extended to Lidgerwood, Dakota Territory, 218 miles from Minneapolis, passing through and opening prime wheat lands. This development totally unnerved Hill at Manitoba, a man who "had a bitter feeling toward Mr. Washburn" anyway and who now saw Manitoba bracketed by Washburn's line ("the shortest haul to Minneapolis") and Northern Pacific ("the shortest haul to Duluth"). Hill—and others, too—had ample reason to worry. Washburn late in 1886 signed an agreement with Canadian Pacific Railway to bridge the St. Mary's River at Sault Ste. Marie, facilitating a connection there for traffic to and from the Atlantic seaboard and beyond. The "Washburn Roads" would be consolidated in 1888, emerging as Minneapolis, St. Paul & Sault Ste. Marie (Soo Line).[17]

Proper, prudent, and prosperous Chicago, Burlington & Quincy was hardly disinterested in any of this, for it, too, long had coveted a wholly owned line to St. Paul and Minneapolis, had blundered in an earlier attempt, and was less than enthusiastic about joint ownership of any kind—Burlington, Cedar Rapids & Northern, in

**LEFT:** Chicago, St. Paul & Kansas City, successor to Minnesota & Northwestern, was the brainchild of the redoubtable Alpheus B. Stickney and upset the status quo.

**FACING PAGE:** The "Washburn Roads" would emerge as Soo Line—an everlasting irritant to James J. Hill.

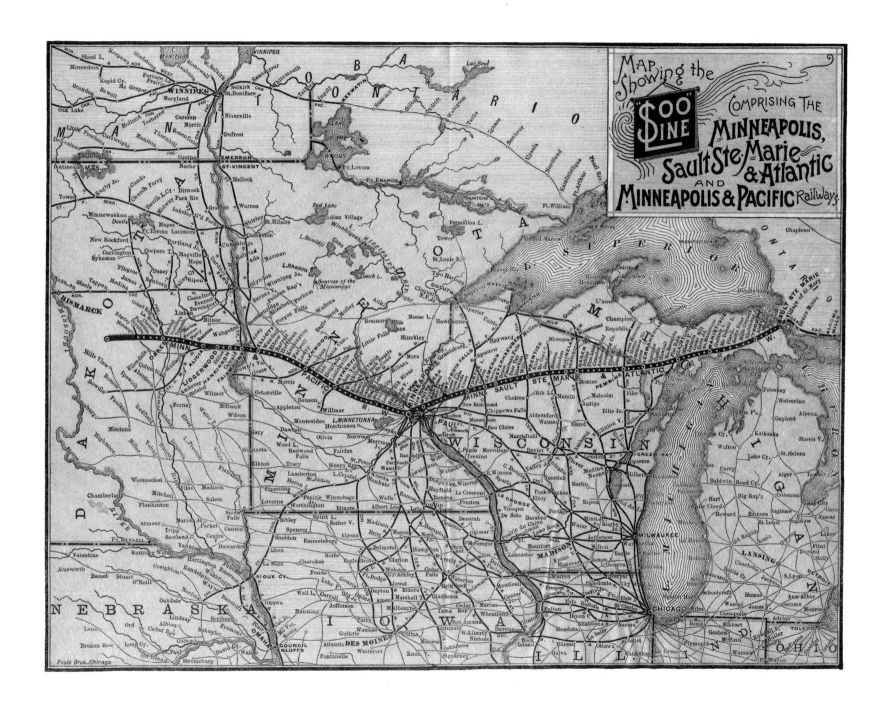

MAP Showing the "SOO" LINE COMPRISING THE MINNEAPOLIS, Sault Ste. Marie & Atlantic AND MINNEAPOLIS & PACIFIC Railways

particular, since that arrangement clearly favored Rock Island over Burlington. By early 1883, CB&Q had quietly run surveys up the east side of the Mississippi in Illinois and Wisconsin, had seen to incorporation of a puppet company—Chicago, Burlington & Northern (CB&N), adequate in rights to cover the enterprise—and had levered Manitoba into property concessions in the Twin Cities that were advantageous. For that matter, principal owners of CB&Q bought an interest in Manitoba, and certain owners of Manitoba bought a block of Chicago, Burlington & Northern; this provoked speculation that CB&Q was about to absorb Manitoba, reports hotly denied by James J. Hill. Yet Hill had been courting Bostonians in control of CB&Q, talking to them of alliances that would benefit both Burlington and Manitoba. From Hill's point of view, such agreements would help defend Manitoba from incursions and encroachments from or by CM&StP and CRI&P. Boston money certainly was welcomed by Manitoba in any event. CB&N track work was completed during the summer of 1886, freight service began on August 23, passenger offerings October 31.[18]

Burlington's arrival in St. Paul and Minneapolis met mixed reviews. The Chambers of Commerce of the two cities were predictably pleased, as was much of the area press, certain shippers, Manitoba, and to some extent, NP. River interests, nearly on their knees already, took no celebration, and neither did rail carriers in—or those scurrying to complete lines in—the now very cluttered Chicago–Minneapolis corridor. Wall Street was aghast, as was the influential *Commercial & Financial Chronicle,* which charged that CB&Q was building "outside of its own territory" and "deliberately sowing the seeds of war." Indeed, said its irate editor, "the building of the new line is not to be commended, but to be condemned, and very strongly condemned." But CB&Q was a carefully managed concern, not prone to speculation, and as the great carriers ranged themselves into "systems," Burlington had seen itself disadvantaged by not having a Twin Cities gateway. There was more. CB&Q could bring Illinois coal and Chicago merchandise and manufactured goods, taking away flour and lumber while at the same time acting as a conduit for traffic to and from Manitoba and NP, neither of

which had lines east of St. Paul. Yes, CB&Q would ruffle feathers and worse, but President Charles E. Perkins reasoned that CB&Q would have trouble with rivals Milwaukee, North Western, and Rock Island "whether we go there or not." Furthermore, Perkins's thrust up the east bank of the Mississippi was consistent with long-term policy at CB&Q. As early as 1871, President James F. Joy had argued that it was not "possible to avoid competition," that it would become "more and more intense," and that the successful road would be "compelled to rely upon the advantages of location and route . . . and upon the volume of business and the economy with which it may be done, for profits."[19]

Problems were not long in surfacing. "Chicago, Burlington & Northern, if it can secure sufficient tonnage, will be able to do business profitably at lower rates than have ever obtained between Chicago and St. Paul," predicted Manitoba's Henry D. Minot in referring to the new road's handsome profile. "It will probably be Mr. Touzalin's [CB&N's president] policy to fight [for all the business] that he can get," he added. To do that, Touzalin would have to cut rates, irritating other roads, and provoking retaliation near at hand or elsewhere to the great annoyance of parent CB&Q. That is exactly what happened. CM&StP blustered about an extension to Kansas City and then proceeded to make good on that threat, in the meanwhile sparking a passenger rate war for Chicago–Twin Cities business, a war that quickly spread elsewhere.[20]

This entire scenario perplexed Rock Island and thoroughly vexed M&StL. The press fully expected and generally predicted that Cable's wrath would be vented variously. In far-off Boston, the *Transcript* claimed "an abundance of room in the great Northwest for thousands of miles of new railways" and asserted that Rock Island, through BCR&N and M&StL, "have on foot three extensions in Dakota." The *Commercial & Financial Chronicle* thought similarly, contending that "Rock Island we may rest assured would not fail to use its Minneapolis & St. Louis and Burlington, Cedar Rapids & Northern to advantage . . . in pressing Manitoba in different parts of its territory." Early in 1886, the *Chicago Tribune* argued that M&StL had acquired right-of-way from Minneapolis northwestward to Anoka and shortly would survey a new line up to Duluth. At the same time, Rock Island unveiled a new campaign advertising advantages of Dakota "for young men of active health and brains," who no longer had to "stay in the over-crowded, slow-moving Eastern communities" and compete there with "the accumulated capital of ages." Rather, persons of "push" could take advantage of the marvelous opportunities presented in the West, in Dakota, where, promised Rock Island, the "citizenship" was already "enriched with some of the best blood that flows in American veins." To put its money where its advertising was, Rock Island announced plans for a 32-mile BCR&N branch to Sioux Falls from that road's line to Watertown, completed later in the year. "Rock Island is striking out in all directions," exclaimed a banker close to Manitoba, "and I am well advised have Bismarck in view as one of their objective points, and I believe they will soon be there!"[21]

Bismarck, however, was a community pioneered by Northern Pacific, and Cable's great concern and irritation was not with that road but rather with Manitoba, especially given its tangible support for CB&Q's Chicago, Burlington & Northern as well as tiny Minneapolis Western. It was not lost on Cable that Manitoba was becoming the region's premier wheat carrier—important in itself but magnified by pooling arrangements giving carriers pro rata tonnage in flour based on inbound deliveries of wheat to Minneapolis. Manitoba was not a party to these arrangements since it had no eastbound avenue. Flour milled from wheat hauled in by Manitoba was hotly competitive, but because of Manitoba's close relationship with Burlington, nobody doubted that Hill would do whatever he could to influence routing by way of Chicago, Burlington & Northern. NP also delivered "free" wheat to Minneapolis, but not nearly the volume as Manitoba, and NP did not have the same cozy association with Burlington. Yet, NP and M&StL shared at least a mixed history of cooperation.

Cable and principal Rock Island shareholders studied their maps. A line from Watertown to Bismarck plus a branch to Duluth from Minneapolis would provide connections with Northern Pacific at these two places in addition to Minneapolis. Such a prospect brightened eyes severally, and for that matter, during much of

1885–86 the prospect of complete amalgamation of Rock Island and Northern Pacific was a particularly tantalizing rumor. Cable's instincts always had been to expand Rock Island's domain by gaining control of existing properties, and potential synergies of CRI&P with NP were startling. NP could extend Rock Island's dominion to Pacific tidewater in a single stroke, while Rock Island could provide NP the important link to New York–Chicago trunk roads; in a general way, raw materials could roll eastward from NP, while Rock Island could wheel finished goods for NP's huge service kingdom. Meanwhile, M&StL stock traded upward on advice that Rock Island would take formal lease of it as part of an overall expansion package. Cable, on an inspection trip over Northern Pacific, said there was "nothing in the yarns of consolidating M&StL, or the purchase of Northern Pacific by Rock Island." But the mere fact that he *was* on an inspection trip over NP gave credibility to the story. Moreover, said Cable juicily, he now regarded NP "more favorably than ever before." Perhaps, he told *Railway Age* in the most provocative way, eastern directors and shareholders of CRI&P were purchasing NP securities in order to protect their own interests in Rock Island. M&StL, of course, was integral in any amalgamation, and its relations with NP were cordial. M&StL eagerly solicited colonists in central Iowa for NP's service area in northern Dakota, and in 1883, when NP wanted to favor a special party with transportation, William Truesdale agreed on behalf of the Albert Lea Route to provide a special train from Chicago to St. Paul, taking "great pleasure in making it complimentary to the NP." And when NP sought concessions in Minneapolis from M&StL, Cable expressed "his willingness to allow you [NP] the joint use of our facilities.[22]

Rumor in 1886 was reinforced by physical examples. Effective July 1, 1884, NP had begun to operate over its new line adjacent to Manitoba from East St. Cloud to Minneapolis, using Manitoba to reach St. Paul, but a year later contractors began work on NP's own line between those cities, one that required a tunnel in St. Paul and another bridge over the Mississippi at Minneapolis plus use of M&StL through the milling district. Having fussed with Manitoba over access to St. Paul, among other irritants, M&StL in 1885–86 turned to a most indirect and hardly satisfactory route from Minneapolis to St. Paul: using the Cannon Valley from Waterville to Randolph, then Stickney's Minnesota & Northwestern to the capital city. It was an awful arrangement. NP, however, was agreeable to M&StL's use of its new line when completed in March 1886. This prospect thoroughly inflamed Manitoba's Hill, who had tried to get NP into partnership for a six-track thoroughfare between the cities, and, curiously, most NP trains did continue to use Manitoba trackage under contract. Neither was Hill amused at the possibility of a new and rival passenger station in Minneapolis employed by NP, M&StL, Minnesota & Northwestern, St. Paul & Duluth, and maybe even Milwaukee. Nothing ever came of it, but the arrogant and domineering Hill had managed to rub several interests the wrong way; the depot idea was a manifestation of that irritation.[23]

Yet Hill and Manitoba were juggernauts, growing yearly in power and influence. Hill was adamant in protection of Manitoba's "natural territory," but he never saw contradiction or inconsistency

BELOW AND FACING PAGE: Northern Pacific would complete a second bridge at Minneapolis to facilitate its own trains as well as those of M&StL (and eventually others) through the west-side milling district, in the process providing an important new thoroughfare between Minneapolis and St. Paul. Beneath the bridge was a portion of Bohemian Flats, a community populated mostly by those whose breadwinners worked in the mills and factories nearby or for the railroads that served them. The F. D. Noerenberg Brewery can be seen in both views on the far side of the river just upstream from the bridge. Photograph below by Emil Hilgarde; courtesy of the Minnesota Historical Society. Photograph on facing page courtesy of the Minneapolis Public Library, Minneapolis Collection.

in raiding others. Using St. Cloud as a fulcrum, Manitoba built or acquired various lines during the middle to late 1880s that reached southwestward to Sioux Falls and Sioux City as well as to Aberdeen, Watertown, and Huron—areas already well staked out by the Chicago roads and angering them considerably. Hill's motivation was to draw traffic, especially wheat, to Duluth and to a lesser extent to Minneapolis. Lake-bound business could be taken through St. Cloud to Hinckley and interchanged there with St. Paul & Duluth, which Manitoba interests held jointly with Milwaukee and Omaha. But that control agreement was abrogated in 1885, and Hill soon committed a Manitoba surrogate to a new line from Hinckley to Superior and Duluth, an appendage that would be completed in 1888, fully operational the next year, and complemented by a fleet of steamships—disguised as an entity separate from Manitoba—plying

the Great Lakes. Hill, of course, was motivated to protect Manitoba through expansion and by preempting others, such as NP, which in 1887 threatened to build a "double track low grade railroad from St. Paul to Superior and Duluth" connecting there "with a new line of large steel steamers upon the lakes."[24]

In 1886, Rock Island promoted the "Favorite Albert Lea Route" with gusto, bragging that "its astonishing success and well earned popularity" were "attributable solely to superior management and the excellence of accommodation provided for transportation of both passengers and freight." Furthermore, said Rock Island, "this combination of different lines" penetrated "the very heart of the agricultural paradise of the Continent" where "the civilization, wealth and culture of American farm life are seen at their best"—"a land like that which gladdened the prophetic vision of Moses, 'flowing

with milk and honey.'" Rock Island would continue to advertise the Albert Lea Route and its productive countryside over the next several years, but not again with the same intensity or purpose. "I think the Rock Island has seen its best days," Hill told a member of Manitoba's board during the summer of 1886, "and will not go to Bismarck." Furthermore, Hill speculated, "Its M&StL was not a financial success for that company whatever it might have been for the individuals" who had acquired M&StL securities—"Flowers, Cable, Brewster and possibly Bishop."[25]

Hill had it right. Cable and Rock Island lost interest accordingly, in fact throwing in the towel on its attempt to reach the Pacific by northwest passage. The reasons likely were several, but two stand out: competition and strategic checkmate. Rivalry for the crucial Chicago–Twin Cities business had been intense after Rock Island cobbled together the Albert Lea Route but increased maddeningly with Wisconsin Central, Minnesota & Northwestern, and Chicago, Burlington & Northern in the fray. With the long-mile route (532 miles versus 407 for Omaha-C&NW, the shortest) among several options, Rock Island's margins were thinner than others. In 1886, M&StL was first among carriers delivering coal to Minneapolis, second in delivering merchandise, fourth in wheat, first in hauling away lumber, third in flour billings, and handled nearly 20 percent of all cars into the city. Two years later the numbers were much less impressive. In 1888, M&StL remained number one in lumber, dropped to third in merchandise, retained fourth place in wheat, dropped to fourth place in coal, but plummeted to seventh place in flour, and handled a mere 8.7 percent of all inbound cars. (Car count also was down precipitously, from 25,926 in 1886 to only 14,526 in 1888.) Drawing business away from M&StL were Omaha and St. Paul & Duluth, handling greater consignments of waterborne coal from Duluth, and newcomers Soo Line and Chicago, Burlington & Northern, both of which cut rates to gain premier status as flour carriers. Indeed, M&StL would carry a tiny 2.2 percent of Minneapolis flour when the decade ended.[26]

## Carload Freight Delivered to Minneapolis, 1889

| | |
|---|---|
| Chicago, Burlington & Northern | 6,384 |
| Chicago, Milwaukee & St. Paul | 32,273 |
| Chicago, St. Paul & Kansas City | 7,340 |
| Chicago, St. Paul, Minneapolis & Omaha | 25,726 |
| Eastern Minnesota | 1,529 |
| Minneapolis & St. Louis | 17,277 |
| Northern Pacific | 9,504 |
| St. Paul & Duluth | 8,245 |
| St. Paul, Minneapolis & Manitoba | 40,101 |
| Soo Line | 11,155 |
| Total | 162,472 |

## Carload Freight Shipped from Minneapolis, 1889

| | |
|---|---|
| Chicago, Burlington & Northern | 9,778 |
| Chicago, Milwaukee & St. Paul | 38,438 |
| Chicago, St. Paul & Kansas City | 11,075 |
| Chicago, St. Paul, Minneapolis & Omaha | 21,716 |
| Eastern Minnesota | 5,878 |
| Minneapolis & St. Louis | 13,359 |
| Northern Pacific | 7,722 |
| St. Paul & Duluth | 9,054 |
| St. Paul, Minneapolis & Manitoba | 17,656 |
| Soo Line | 11,783 |
| Wisconsin Central | 2,601 |
| Total | 149,060 |

FACING PAGE: Ransom Cable and Rock Island could not expect to gain much traffic from Pillsbury's "A" Mill and other shippers on the east bank, where Manitoba dominated. Photograph courtesy of the Hennepin History Museum.

FOLLOWING SPREAD: St. Paul, Minneapolis & Manitoba dominated the east-bank industrial district. Map from *A Complete Set of Surveys and Plats of Properties in the City of Minneapolis, Minnesota* (Philadelphia: C. M. Hopkins, 1885); courtesy of the Minneapolis Public Library.

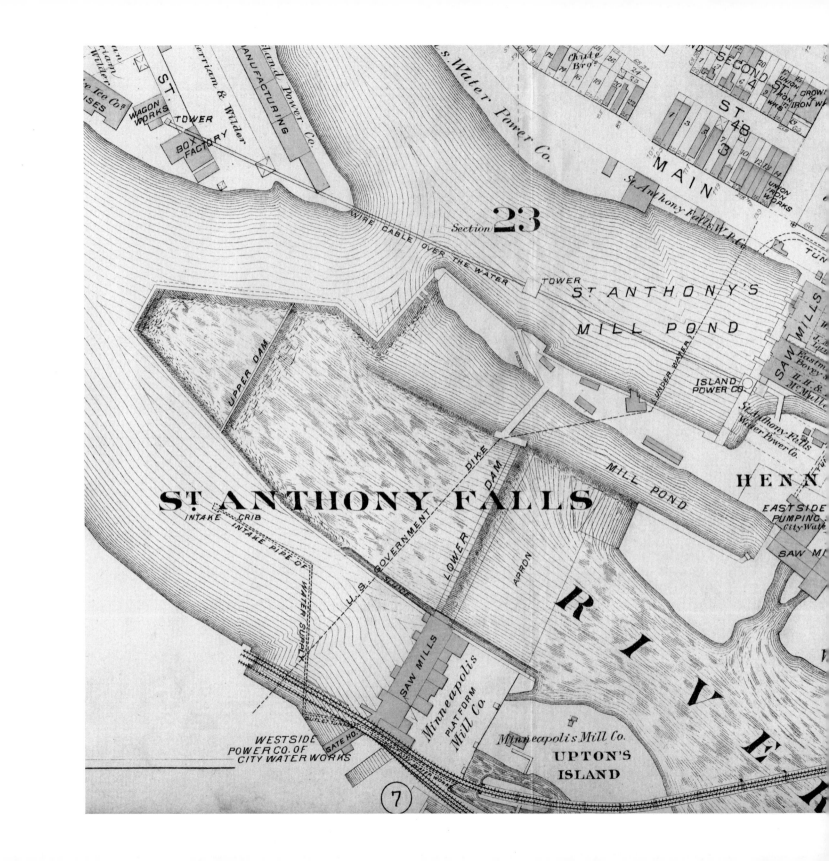

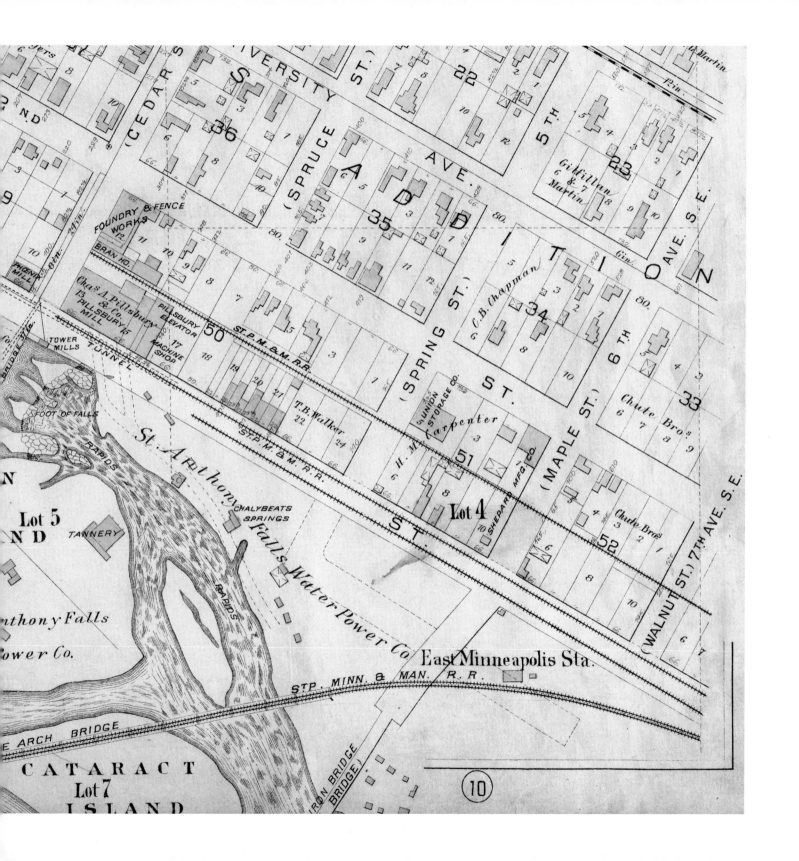

CEDAR S.

(UNIVERSITY ST.)

SPRUCE

AVE.

22

5TH

AVE. S.E.

36

35

ADDITION

23

Gilfillan
Martin

34

C.B.Chapman

(SPRING ST.)

6TH

33

Chute Bros

FOUNDRY & FENCE WORKS

BRAN HO.

PHENIX MILL

Chas A. Pillsbury & Co.
PILLSBURY MILL

PILLSBURY ELEVATOR

MACHINE SHOP

TOWER MILLS

TUNNEL

50

ST. P. M. & M. R. R.

ST.

MAPLE ST.

Union Storage Co.

Carpenter

51

H. M.

SHEPARD MFG CO.

52

Chute Bros

WALNUT ST.) 7TH AVE. S.E.

FOOT OF FALLS

RAPIDS

St. Anthony Falls Water Power Co.

CHALYBEATE SPRINGS

RAPIDS

Lot 5
LAND

TANNERY

Lot 4

Anthony Falls
Power Co.

East Minneapolis Sta.

ST. P. MINN. & MAN. R. R.

ARCH BRIDGE

(IRON BRIDGE)

CATARACT
Lot 7
ISLAND

10

Rock Island also lost out in the strategic race, M&StL checkmated at Minneapolis and M&StL/BCR&N together at the lonely Watertown outpost, while Wisconsin, Minnesota & Pacific only crawled westward from Waterville a few miles to Eagle Lake, although the company puffed that it would move on to Mankato and New Ulm shortly—the prospective destination on M&StL's Pacific Division at Gaylord already on the scrapheap. Cable had failed to move quickly in 1882 and 1883, had moved inadequately in 1884 and not at all in 1885, and by 1886 Rock Island's options in the entire region were tightly circumscribed. Beyond Watertown, C&NW drove a line northward through Aberdeen to meet a Northern Pacific branch from Jamestown to Oakes. Manitoba was infesting much of Dakota Territory including lines to Watertown and Aberdeen, and the Washburn Road sealed other options.[27]

The respected *Commercial & Financial Chronicle* and several others in the investment community frowned on Rock Island's performance. The company's record for 1885, as an example, was hardly stellar, with both gross revenue and net less than in the year previous, and surplus above the usual dividend less than any in the previous thirteen years. What explained such dreary news? Competition and encroachment, a microcosm of which had been seen in Minneapolis and environs. Other roads had carved off slices of Rock Island's domain elsewhere, and rates applied over the entire system had plummeted—passenger fares per mile from 2.97¢ in 1877–78 to 2.42¢ in 1885–86, freight per ton mile from 1.56¢ in 1877–78 to 1.07¢ in 1885–86. Among Rock Island's commodity groups, flour and wheat were hardest hit, mirroring in large part the road's unwillingness to meet lowered rates from Minneapolis. More frightening, however, was CRI&P's failure to hold or increase merchandise traffic, *down* 7.4 percent in 1885–86 from 1882–83. None of this could be adequately explained by crop failure, national economic distress (although clearly a factor), or lack of population growth in Rock Island's service area. Falling rates tightly coupled with encroachment better explained the problem.[28]

Cable's strong preference for expansion was always through acquisition or control of established roads such as BCR&N and M&StL, but while Rock Island earlier had explored merger with C&NW, Burlington, and more recently NP, nothing came from these high-stakes adventures, and smaller candidates were few and reluctant. Meanwhile, Burlington had reached Denver and was known to be considering further expansion to Salt Lake, perhaps beyond. C&NW had several hundred miles of line west of the Missouri River and was understood to have even more expansion in mind. Milwaukee rail by 1888 would touch the Missouri River at three locations: Chamberlain, Council Bluffs, and Kansas City. Even Illinois Central was a player at Sioux City and by now Sioux Falls; rumors urged that IC soon would extend to the Black Hills. Others had stolen the march on Rock Island, and Cable also had to worry about being frozen out of grand alliances then much talked about—Atchison, Topeka & Santa Fe with Baltimore & Ohio, Chicago & North Western with New York Central, and Burlington and Pennsylvania in combination with Manitoba.[29]

Cable saw no choice but expand Rock Island—through construction. Burlington's Charles Perkins had anticipated as much in 1883 and was pleased that Cable became preoccupied with the Albert Lea Route because then he would "be less likely to break out elsewhere, and the Rock Island must break out somewhere." And break out it did, in 1888, with a breathtaking program that took CRI&P from the Missouri River at St. Joseph to Colorado Springs (trackage rights to Denver from Limon), to far southwestern Kansas at Liberal, to El Reno, Indian Territory, in 1888–89 and down to Fort Worth in 1893. Rock Island never would make good on the Pacific in its corporate namesake, but early in the next century it would link up with Southern Pacific to create the Golden State Route, and it would also extend all the way southward to Houston. Nevertheless, in the "March of the Four Armies," as *Railway Age* once phrased it, Rock Island proved the weakest and least able compared to C&NW, Milwaukee, and Burlington.[30]

FACING PAGE: By the mid-1880s the railroad landscape of Minneapolis took mature form. Other contestants such as Soo Line would appear later. Map courtesy of the Minneapolis Public Library.

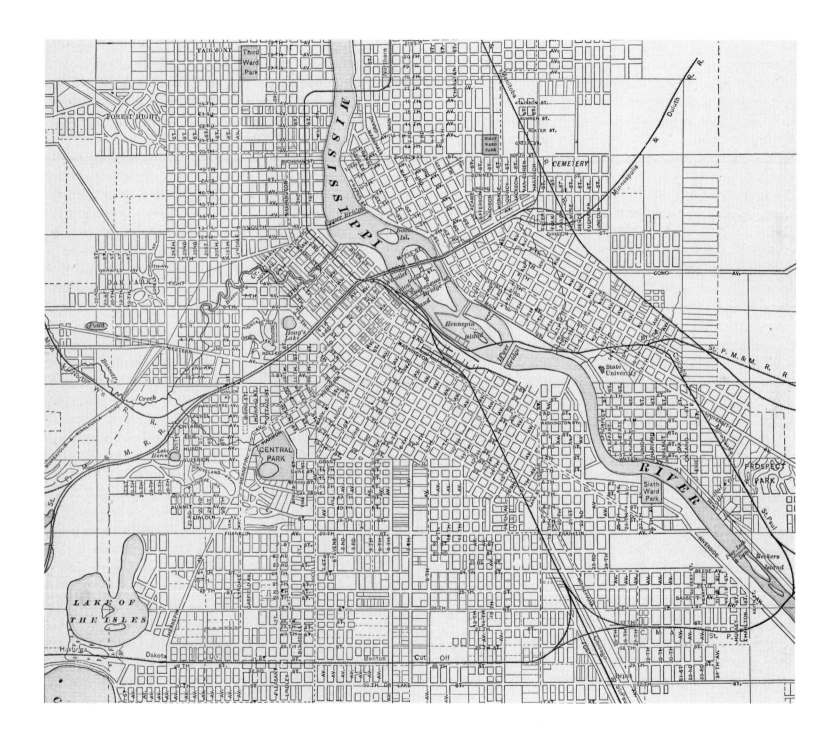

M&StL's William H. Truesdale's morale must have sunk as he saw Rock Island's interest in the Albert Lea Route slacken. There were other problems. Indeed, one matter that Truesdale and virtually all other railroad managers brooded about was government regulation, public support for which had ebbed and flowed for nearly three decades but in the late 1880s flowed with a vengeance. The carriers had been bitterly disappointed in 1877 when the Supreme Court upheld state regulation in the *Munn v Illinois* case. "I have always found in dealings with legislatures that you cannot reason with them," complained financier John Stewart Kennedy, who likely reflected the views of most investors and railroad officials. The same twin groups likely concurred with the *Milwaukee Sentinel* regarding agrarian discontents: "There is one thing Mr. Barnum has never had on exhibition," claimed the *Sentinel*, "and that is a granger who wasn't a kicker." Farmers and businessmen in rural areas complained often about rail rates, but tariffs actually had gone down, drastically and demonstratively, the result of competition and other factors. The record of powerful CM&StP was typical; in 1865 Milwaukee had charged an average of 4.11¢ per ton mile, but in 1887, only 1.09¢. Facts aside, many Americans had come to fear and despise railroads as giant corporations, seeing in them perversion of private enterprise embodying liberty, freedom, and individualism. Critics also saw railroad leaders as flaunting riches and selfishly increasing their own private power and fortune. They further equated the practice of basing rates on "all that traffic will bear" with outright gouging. Not so, said Burlington's C. E. Perkins, who asserted that only the market determined rates and "that the only fair and reasonable price is all you can get without losing trade . . . ," and, he growled, charging what the traffic will bear did imply discrimination—*for* some and *against* others. "It is principle, not of extortion," affirmed an economist, "but of equitable concession to the weaker members of the community."[31]

The debate heightened. In 1885, Minnesota replaced its office of Railroad Commissioner with a three-member Railroad and Warehouse Commission in response "to the growing indifference and intolerance of railway managers to complaints," two years later add-

ing greatly to that body's power by giving it rate-making authority. And the railroads had yet another headache; on April 5, 1887, the Interstate Commerce Act took effect, placing the federal government squarely in the regulatory arena. Its consequences could only be guessed at.[32]

By coincidence, the Great Dakota Boom came to an end just as federal regulation of the rails began. Several factors converged, among them an economic contraction that began late in 1886, the virtual disappearance of free land, trouble between the federal government and various tribes of Indians, slowed railroad construction in the area, and devastating drought that dragged into the next decade. The hardest hit areas in what soon would become South Dakota were west of Watertown, between the James and Missouri rivers; if Ransom Cable had any lingering ideas of expanding to the northwest, they were quashed by increasingly dreary reports from that region.[33]

William H. Truesdale, now M&StL's president, must have slumped deeply in his chair at the company's thinly appointed offices in Boston Block at Hennepin Avenue and Third Street. There simply was no good news as 1887 ended; the new year promised little relief. Before Christmas 1887, the hearty, bluff Truesdale had been forced to tell Cable that M&StL could not pay interest on bonds due in January. It was an awful humiliation, and the usually unflappable and judicious Truesdale took out his frustration on Minnesota Railroad Commissioners, whom he accused of ruining "the business of this railroad." The state's regulatory authority was increasingly cavalier and worthy of scorn, true, but Truesdale's blast was off the mark in explaining M&StL's embarrassment. In addition to regulatory woes, M&StL suffered greatly from an inadequate route structure, from intense competition not only in Minneapolis but at many locations (Chaska and Waseca, as examples) where traffic could be bled off by one of the stronger roads (short hauling M&StL in the process), from inability to meet low rates offered by others on critical tonnage during most of 1887, from absentee principal owners no longer vigorous in support. On May 26, 1888, the large, handsome Truesdale straightened his back, drew in a deep breath, gritted his teeth, and bluntly told M&StL bondholders that during the first five months of the year "net earnings fell short of the interest on the company's bonded indebtedness." Monies due on June 1 could not be paid out of earnings. Shortly thereafter a demand for payment was made by certain holders, the road demurred, foreclosure followed, M&StL fled to protection of the courts, and Truesdale was named receiver.[34]

# ADRIFT

10

Sale of Minneapolis & St. Louis must be regarded as a good thing for this city and the Northwest, as it indicates that the road will remain independent and a competitive factor in transportation.

MINNEAPOLIS TRIBUNE, OCTOBER 12, 1894

William Haynes Truesdale was one of the most able managers M&StL ever had. Bright, sagacious, and a born leader, Truesdale was well on his way to a distinguished career in the railroad industry. But at M&StL his considerable talent was constantly under test. No longer the local favorite in its home city, merely a part of the "Great Rock Island Route," M&StL was rather viewed as a poor stepchild of one of the oft-despised Chicago roads. Moreover, its principal owners were distant and distracted. Truesdale and M&StL usually had to fend for themselves. Growing government regulation was a constant vexation as were periodic rate wars in which M&StL was the universal loser; if it went with the crowd, it lost money on traffic gained or retained, and if it did not go along, traffic assuredly went elsewhere. At particular risk was M&StL's powerful position in the Minneapolis milling district, where stronger roads increased pressure and from which location the lumber industry was making a precipitous exit. And Truesdale was acutely perplexed by the "extremely slow and tedious" nature of "foreclosure proceedings." It was as frustrating as it was irritating.

Some of Truesdale's perturbation may have been reserved for Ransom Cable's attention to Rock Island interests elsewhere, although he said nothing in that regard for public consumption. For his part, the vigorously frank Cable indeed was preoccupied with integrating and prospering Rock Island's new lines west and southwest of the Missouri River, paid scant attention to M&StL, and plainly had given up on a "northwest passage." To be fair, however, "The Albert Lea Route" was still advertised as a fully coordinated effort by Rock Island in combination with BCR&N and M&StL. Early in 1890, furthermore, a trainload of Rock Island passenger agents—making a systemwide swing—arrived in Minneapolis from Watertown on M&StL, gaily toured that city and St. Paul, and departed for Chicago via Albert Lea. And a few months later Cable himself brought Rock Island's entire board of directors and other prominent shareholders on a trip from Chicago to Minneapolis over M&StL that returned by way of Des Moines.[1]

Such trips fueled local speculation that Rock Island or Rock Island principals would acquire an even larger holding in M&StL and

perhaps embrace a plan for "eventual absorption of the St. Louis road itself," according to one area source. There also was speculation in Minneapolis that Cable and friends would acquire lonely St. Paul & Duluth—all of it certainly logical from a strategic point of view and also perfectly consistent with Cable's original preference for expansion through acquisition and not construction.[2]

Nevertheless, Rock Island's late flurry of building in the West, coupled with persistent and costly rate wars and growing regulatory pressures had combined to sharply diminish its options. In fact, improvements to Rock Island properties had dwindled since 1881, and surplus by 1887 was minuscule. Dividends were trimmed accordingly, and while Rock Island was long considered one of the safest investments traded on the New York stock exchange, investors had come to worry about the company's prospects. One New York analyst who eagerly jumped into the fray contended that Rock Island's financial condition was truly deplorable and resulted plainly from convergence of four crucial factors: "overbuilding, granger laws, communistic railroad commissions, and the everlasting, foolhardy rate cutting by general managers."[3]

Aside from the New Yorker's caustic assertion as to communistic railroad commissions, he was right on target. Government regulatory powers did increase as more and more Americans found comfort in assailing laissez-faire economics. The breadth and rapidity of change abroad the American landscape during the late nineteenth century was breathtaking and exhilarating, but it also was confusing and frightening as old and familiar conventions were swept aside to be replaced by a more complex economic and political universe. Uncertainty was the desperate handmaiden of change, and most Americans came to see "capitalists" and/or "industrialists"

---

FACING PAGE: In 1890 Ransom Cable brought Rock Island's entire board of directors to Minneapolis. They must have been impressed with the city's robust industrial base, including the gigantic Washburn mills. The mills and trestle in this photograph stood at the present location of Mill Ruins Park, where the foundations of the mills and steel girders from the trestle may be seen. Photograph courtesy of the Minnesota Historical Society.

as primary agents of those frightening and revolutionary alterations in the very warp and woof of American life. In much of the land—certainly in Minnesota—farmers and their kin in small communities ranked those who owned and operated railroads among chief enemies of their best interests. "The railroad system, as at present managed, is a system of spoliation and robbery . . . absorbing the substance of the people in the interest of the millionaires," declared the People's Party of Nebraska in 1890. Sectional tension also was part of the equation. "The East has placed its hands on the throat of the West," snarled one agitated writer in Kansas. "The eastern capitalist," reasoned many agrarians, was responsible for exorbitant rail rates that produced unseemly dividends for shareholders, and, they cried further, railroad property was undervalued for tax purposes but overvalued when it came to rate making. In sum, they concluded, railroads were nothing less than rapacious monsters, a notion nicely encapsulated in this ditty:

"Near the track of a railway newly laid,
A farmer leaned on his earth-worn spade;
While his taxes were high and his crops but thin,
The charge for freight played the deuce with him;
So he growled a growl at the train's sharp din—
I'll gather you in; I'll gather you in!"

"I have borne you long, and here I vow
Your railroads to best, some way, or how;
I will get up a law, by the great horned owl!
To cut down your profits and make you howl;
And but little or nothing, I'll ship from bin
Of hoarding corn, till I've gathered you in!"[4]

Minnesota had responded early by enacting a state regulatory agency predicated on the assumption that railroads were bilking the public. The Grange faded after a flourish in the 1870s but was supplanted by other grassroots organizations in the 1880s coalescing in the next decade as the People's Party or Populists. More stringent regulation of railroads was at the core of this movement and was reflected not only in the Interstate Commerce Act of 1887 but in greatly increased regulatory powers for state railroad commissions. Industry leaders and allied groups were quick to complain. New legislation imposed "additional vexatious restrictions" on rail carriers that would prove "detrimental to the North West," predicted the St.

Paul Chamber of Commerce, which urged a hands-off approach that would "leave the railroads of this country to compete for the business offered to them upon such basis as other business is done." Charles E. Perkins of CB&Q complained of "serious reverses" for his company in 1888, largely because railroads had lost "the right to pool" under the Interstate Commerce law. William Truesdale bluntly asserted that M&StL was bankrupt solely "because of the existing rates in" Minnesota, and he joined a squadron of other railroad managers in denouncing a proposal to establish a flat "two cents per mile" tariff on passenger trade. Members of the Minnesota Railway Employees Club likewise complained that their livelihoods were threatened by overzealous railroad commissioners whose "interference" with the carriers was so extensive that some companies—among them M&StL, Omaha, Manitoba, and St. Paul & Duluth—were curtailing pay and laying off workers. And, thundered Ransom Cable at Rock Island, "the practical working of the" Interstate Commerce Act "was unexpectedly hurtful of jobbing and manufacturing centers which had theretofore thriven under the old conditions."[5]

Railroad managers had good reason to grouse about well-intentioned but heavy-handed regulation. Yet they undercut credibility early through failure in their own pooling arrangements and then by a parade of rollercoaster rate wars that thoroughly unsettled customers. Indeed, said Chicago, St. Paul & Kansas City (CStP&KC) in 1890, "the war of rates has been fierce and continuous throughout the year." And those wars were inevitably counterproductive, impairing the financial viability of roads like M&StL but also most western companies, whose earnings dropped and whose dividends declined. One problem fed another. Rate instability alarmed politicians, who

Many Americans during the late nineteenth century came to fear and loathe the "capitalists" and "industrialists," but from them came money to improve and make more productive the country's industrial base, including mills and factories in the west-bank milling district. A plank road and elevated tracks serving the mills eventually covered the canal. This view from 1885 looks southeast along what is now the wooden plank section of West River Road. Photograph by Henry R. Farr; courtesy of the Minnesota Historical Society.

then sought more regulation; more rate wars and more government intervention frightened financial institutions, which then tightened credit. Soo Line often led rate wars in the Minneapolis district, especially in the carriage of flour, with Milwaukee, CStP&KC, Wisconsin Central, and CB&N following suit. Omaha and M&StL were occasional players. Freight rates in the vital Chicago–Minneapolis corridor were demoralized for the entire period 1887–89, dropping nearly 40 percent at one point in 1888. First-class passenger fares likewise suffered frequent gyrations—M&StL usually meeting rates, not setting them, and periodically holding fast when all other roads lowered theirs. Wars over passenger rates provoked active coverage by the press and endless comment by politicians, but vacillating freight charges had a more dramatic impact on income ledgers of all roads.[6]

Haulage of lumber remained an essential component of M&StL's traffic mix, but it always was subject to competitive attack and

Soo Line often led rate wars in the Minneapolis district, and its expansion in and about the city during the late 1880s and into the next decade promised to make it an even more prominent contestant. Considerable work was necessary to add capacity at this location north of the Great Northern station in 1892. Photograph courtesy of the Minnesota Historical Society.

machinations of government rate makers. The road's curiously configured route structure actually favored the movement of lumber out of Minneapolis as the market for Minnesota white pine shifted south and west when Michigan's supply diminished. M&StL proved favorably located to serve the needs of Iowa and, by connections, those of Nebraska and Kansas as well. The road also profited from new marketing techniques reflected in "line yards"—several retail yards located at individual stations operating under common ownership and management. As Minneapolis became "lumber emporium of the Northwest," it also became headquarters for millers and for many line yard companies. On M&StL, C. A. Smith Lumber and J. N. Queal Company were pioneers—the latter, for instance,

Roads like A. B. Stickney's CStP&KC had to be innovative and aggressive to survive.

with yards on the Watertown line at Hanley Falls, Clarkfield, Dawson, and Madison. It was to these locations and others that M&StL wheeled car after car of lumber spewing from the Minneapolis mills. Indeed, it hauled more lumber out of Minneapolis in the years 1888, 1890, and 1891 than any other carrier, despite the fact that by now most mills were "off line," in the northern part of the city.[7]

The story of flour and wheat volume was less satisfactory as M&StL's relative position among Twin Cities' carriers floated downward even as the prominence of Minneapolis as a great wheat exchange and flour milling center went up. In 1888, M&StL delivered 4.9 percent of the wheat received in Minneapolis, but during one particular week of the year the percentage of flour billed out on M&StL was a minuscule 0.5. The reasons for M&StL's awful slippage from premier status were many and included the continuous shift of the wheat culture to the northwest and away from its lines, loss of support from the Washburn interests, ruinous rate wars brought on for the most part by new contenders, rail-water movement of export flour via Duluth and East Coast ports by more favorable routes, and Rock Island's preoccupation otherwise. M&StL remained a bit player even in 1891, when a bumper 58-million-bushel harvest required the court to grant Truesdale's request for two hundred new boxcars to help move wheat to the hungry mills. Truesdale, however, saw no reason to throw in the towel. M&StL retained extremely valuable access and egress in the west-bank milling district, Minnesota stood first in production of wheat, nearly 90 percent of milling capacity at St. Anthony Falls now was held by only four companies (Pillsbury and Washburn-Crosby the top two), and the decade of the 1890s would prove profitable for millers who would respond by doubling capacity. Furthermore, permanence and stability in the trade were implied by the eleven-story Flour Exchange in downtown Minneapolis, construction of which began in 1892.[8]

To protect and enhance its valuable properties in the milling district, M&StL had seen to incorporation of Railway Transfer Company of the City of Minneapolis (Railway Transfer), a wholly owned subsidiary, on March 31, 1883. Railway Transfer was authorized to buy, lease, construct, and operate a system of transfer tracks

"between the different lines of railroad and the mills and factories within Minneapolis." To this end, M&StL leased Railway Transfer up to twenty-five tracks with four leads including two main tracks—about 12 track miles in all. M&StL and NP used the main tracks as part of their joint operation between Minneapolis and St. Paul.[9]

M&StL's alliance with Northern Pacific did nothing to better the feelings of James J. Hill and the increasingly powerful Great Northern (GN, successor to St. Paul, Minneapolis & Manitoba). Neither did it enhance relations with powerful millers, since NP held a surprisingly modest rank in delivery of wheat to Minneapolis and carried little flour anyway. GN, by comparison, usually stood first in delivery of wheat and was a strong ally of Chicago, Burlington & Northern, an energetic contender in competition for flour billings. GN, of course, had a muscular presence in the east-bank milling area, and on the west bank, since 1884, had entry through Minne-

Local timber was scarce by the 1890s, and although logs still came down the Mississippi to the falls, more found delivery by rail from northern points in the state. The Akeley Lumber Company was one of several mills supplying lucrative traffic for the city's railroads. Photograph courtesy of the Minnesota Historical Society.

apolis Western, organized by several local personalities and millers (most of whom once had been prominent in M&StL affairs) but in fact a surrogate of Hill and company. Initial operation was homely at best, cars moved by cable and not locomotives, and delivery was through M&StL since Minneapolis Western had no physical connection to GN or any road other than M&StL. But in 1889 several shippers proposed a more expansive operation—Millers Transfer Company—which, if perfected, would handle all switching in the district and into which would be poured Minneapolis Western, Minneapolis Eastern (owned jointly by Milwaukee and Omaha), and, they hoped, M&StL's Railway Transfer. One miller denied that this was a "Manitoba [GN] scheme," but it was, with Sam Hill, James J. Hill's son-in-law and president of Minneapolis Trust Company, laboring diligently behind the scene. There was a fly in the ointment, however—William Drew Washburn, until recently president of Soo Line, now U.S. senator, still on the boards of Soo and M&StL, and, as always, deeply involved in flour milling, lumber, and real estate. Devious and perpetually arrogant, Washburn—Sam Hill believed— would try to promote "a terminal company" of his own preference or, in league with M&StL, buy up properties in the district in a way that would alienate others. In the end, however, nothing came of Millers Transfer, in large part because M&StL placed an exorbitant price on Railway Transfer to discourage others; GN responded by purchasing all outstanding shares of Minneapolis Western. Then,

in 1892, James J. Hill cemented a lifelong alliance with William H. Dunwoody, at the time chief stockholder of Washburn-Crosby, and built a bridge downstream from GN's famous stone-arch structure to make direct connection to the previously disjointed properties.

---

BELOW AND FACING PAGE: In 1892, James J. Hill cemented a lifelong alliance with William H. Dunwoody, at the time chief stockholder of Washburn-Crosby, and built a steel bridge (on the left, pictured below) just downstream from the famous Stone Arch Bridge. That gave Minneapolis Western, a Great Northern puppet, full access to the west-bank mills, eroding M&StL's once dominant position. The bridge on the right in the photograph below is the Tenth Avenue wagon bridge. On the east bank beneath the bridge was a small neighborhood known as the East Side Flats, similar to the better-known Bohemian Flats just downstream and across the river, shown here in 1890 in the photograph on facing page. Photograph below courtesy of the Hennepin History Museum. Photograph on facing page courtesy of the Minnesota Historical Society.

Eventually GN's Minneapolis Western had fourteen stub tracks by which to serve west-bank mills, further curtailing M&StL's once dominant position. Not surprisingly, GN became favored by Washburn-Crosby to move much of its export flour via the Head of the Lakes and GN's own Northern Steamship Company.[10]

M&StL and the City of Minneapolis were at the same time involved in a bitter legal contest that likewise involved GN and its Manitoba predecessor. Part of the issue reflected the historic rela-

tionship between the city and its railroads, part the historical relationship between M&StL and GN's predecessors, and part Hill's determination to flex muscles in Minneapolis. In 1871 and in 1874, a GN predecessor had given M&StL perpetual rights to build and operate a line on its land leading to and from downtown Minneapolis—that is, between what became M&StL's Cedar Lake Yard and its Lower Yard (Railway Transfer) in the milling district. Those agreements were in subsequent periodic dispute, especially during the

early and mid-1880s when Northern Pacific negotiated to and then did enter Minneapolis. Matters became feverish when NP formed an alliance with M&StL to move trains jointly between Minneapolis and St. Paul with NP utilizing M&StL's Railway Transfer as the essential link between its otherwise disconnected properties. Hill was not slow in responding, ordering M&StL to vacate its historic location between Cedar Lake and the city, then to cross twelve sets of tracks, and occupy a new avenue parallel with but on the opposite side of the original. Should M&StL accede, the crossover would require a long, dangerous, and time consuming process with Hill's dispatchers controlling the operation. Truesdale would have none of it, and the two companies headed for the courts.[11]

Meanwhile, as Minneapolis grew, and as street railways and public roadways proliferated, its city government enforced a long tradition of demanding that all expense of crossings, underpasses, and bridges be borne by railroad companies. The issue came to a head when the city demanded that M&StL construct "underways" at three locations. Truesdale, as receiver of the company, decided

that M&StL would share those costs, but that the city also should shoulder part of the burden. Hill of GN jumped in to side with the city, a decision Truesdale saw as opportunistic at best and duplicitous at worst. Truesdale's long frown was justified, but GN quickly was involved in the case in its own right because the city demanded that it, too, lower tracks and provide underpasses in the same area. Truesdale dug in his heels, telling the Minneapolis Board of Trade on May 1, 1889, that Hill's real purpose in what had become a joint problem regarding the "crossings" issue *and* the city's demand for "underways," was to sever M&StL's aorta between terminal properties (Cedar Lake and Lower Yard) and to keep the road forever in

As Minneapolis grew, the city demanded that M&StL construct "underways" beneath city roadways at three locations. M&StL's William H. Truesdale objected, but eventually the expense was shared with other roads, who all benefited from a corridor unimpeded by grade crossings. Some of these tracks are still in use and lead from Northeast Minneapolis via Nicollet Island. Photograph courtesy of the Minnesota Historical Society.

bankruptcy. The *Minneapolis Tribune* initially thought Truesdale's determination to refuse arbitration was merely a "mistake," but soon turned on him with a vengeance—laying M&StL's current financial woes solely to the "ruinous war with the city which called it [M&StL] into existence." The road was "practically worthless without a fair Minneapolis patronage," warned the *Tribune*, and in "a contest between a bankrupt corporation and a great city," it sanctimoniously concluded, "the chances are decidedly in favor of the latter."[12]

Matters ground slowly to resolution. GN's Hill quietly involved himself with certain M&StL bondholders, who were already nervous about the company's condition. The *Minneapolis Tribune*, once its most determined supporter, continued to lambaste M&StL, calling it "mulish, clearly in the wrong," an ingrate "indifferent to public interests," and "without a supporter or sympathizer in the whole world." Truesdale and company attorneys hunkered down and absorbed the abuse. They were not wrong to brood about Hill's intentions for he was a determined fighter with a well-stocked arsenal at his disposal. And the stakes were high. M&StL's position in the milling district, while reduced in importance by competitive incursions, was still impressive and, for the company's survival, absolutely essential. Moreover, Truesdale understood that Hill's purpose was, if not actually to evict M&StL from this crucial corridor, at least to restrict it to a narrow channel controlled tightly by GN from which no spurs could emanate to current or potential customers and from which M&StL would be divorced from connection to NP's freight yard in Minneapolis (thereby nullifying the joint operation by NP from St. Paul via M&StL to those same facilities). A compromise was crafted, finally, during the summer of 1890, when Judge A. H. Young brought all parties together. GN and M&StL agreed to shoulder heavy expense in demolition, excavation, bridgework, and new trackage, but in the end they both saved burdensome legal expenses and put in place useful improvements such as new passenger and freight facilities for M&StL along a highly trafficked, multitrack corridor unfettered by irritating grade crossings. M&StL retained its historic alignment (avoiding the awkward crossovers) and got exclusive use of one main track and joint use of two other

By 1890, Minneapolis was increasingly important in the production of linseed oil. Archer-Daniels owned one of the primary plants. Photograph courtesy of the Minneapolis Public Library, Minneapolis Collection.

main tracks to guarantee the integrity of an independent avenue to and from Lower Yard in the milling district as well as to its many customers along the route. Omaha and NP breathed easier, too, for Omaha used M&StL to reach its Sioux City line at Merriam, and NP, of course, utilized M&StL as a bridge between disconnected pieces of its lines in Minneapolis.[13]

One reason Truesdale fought so tenaciously in the "crossings" case was that M&StL had little capital for improvements, and in any event, all expenditures were overseen by the court. He was not parsimonious, just cautious. A new freight house at Third Street and Fourth Avenue and a new passenger station at Washington Avenue came as the result of settlement in the protracted litigation, and a modest overflow freight yard was authorized at nearby Kenwood. Truesdale also obtained permission from the court to replace the wooden machine shop at Cedar Lake—"a dangerous fire trap"—with "a substantial building of stone, brick, and iron." In addition, the physical plant of the road was enhanced with strengthened bridges, ballast, and more telegraph capacity. And to alleviate congestion, to serve a growing body of local shippers, and to upgrade commuter operations to and from Lake Minnetonka, the receiver gained permission to double track 5 miles between Kenwood and Hopkins, a task completed in July 1892.[14]

Much of M&StL's available capital was expended in and about Minneapolis, seat of its management and clearly the most important single location in production of tonnage and revenue through local customers and connections. By 1890, the city claimed 164,738 residents—ahead of St. Paul, with a population of 133,156. Minneapolis had become the country's largest primary wheat market; it still produced monumental stacks of milled lumber and was increasingly important in production of linseed oil, farm machinery, and other manufactured goods. St. Paul, by comparison, was the state capital, a center of transportation, an established manufac-

turing city, and a vastly important jobbing center. "The traveling men of St. Paul are to be found in every part of a huge expanse from western Wisconsin to the Pacific coast and well into Iowa and Nebraska," claimed an enthusiastic Chamber of Commerce. Small wonder that M&StL—and Rock Island through it—had wanted a presence there. In 1888, an average of 221 trains moved in and out of St. Paul Union Depot, and the city received 158,892 carloads of freight while dispatching 93,006 cars.[15]

M&StL managers recognized danger in being too tightly wedded to the Twin Cities, however, and increasingly looked to the country tributary to its lines to supply a larger portion of resources. M&StL's three-state service area—Minneapolis and St. Paul to the contrary—remained much as it had been: rural and agricultural. In 1893, M&StL's system percentages for grain and merchandise were 22 and 6.5; for neighboring Chicago Great Western and Milwaukee Road, they were 28.8 and 8.9, and 22.5 and 9.0, respectively. For the "Granger Roads," as Midwestern carriers came to be called, changing the numbers in any appreciable way was problematic. M&StL station agents like those of other roads were made to submit regular reports during the crop year as to local conditions regarding wheat, corn, oats, flax, barley, rye, potatoes, and hay. Reports of blight, rust, hot winds, heavy rains, and early frost drew frowns just as news of positive growing conditions and bumper crops brought smiles. As early as 1890, Truesdale told stockholders that "only in the development and up-building of its local traffic can this road . . . hope to earn even a moderate return upon the capital invested in it." He would "encourage by all reasonable means the establishment of local industry"—mills, creameries, brickyards, grain elevators, and the like. These might be remote from Minneapolis, but they could be as close as St. Louis Park, established in 1886 as a railroad suburb and named after "the St. Louis Road," as M&StL often was called. Certainly this was the

Manufacturing plants in and about Minneapolis spewed forth a growing array of products for the American farmer. Arrived on this day in 1890 at St. Paul & Duluth's Center City depot (on the Taylors Falls Branch) were steam tractors, wagons, and a threshing machine—all reflecting agriculture's rush to mechanization. Photograph courtesy of the Minnesota Historical Society.

case for Hopkins, where several industries and supply houses flourished by the 1890s. Among them was Minneapolis Threshing machine, predecessor of Minneapolis-Moline.[16]

But M&StL, for better or for ill, was tied irrevocably to agriculture, celebrating, as in 1891, when good crops and high markets allowed farmers to pay off debt and make improvements, "erecting new houses, barns, fences, etc." and "adding machinery, blooded stock and articles of consumption . . . never equaled before in a like period." Moreover, said M&StL management to company owners, "the country through which the road passes is showered with all of Nature's blessings . . . good soil, water, and diversified crops" with a "population that is thrifty and takes advantage of natural conditions." Puffy rhetoric, yes, but not far from the mark in describing M&StL's rich and productive domain—a domain worth expanding if possible, one clearly coveted by others, one well worth protecting, one constantly

and fervently prized by Minneapolis manufacturers and commercial leaders as an important part of the city's broad hinterland.[17]

M&StL's interest in traffic via Duluth, historic but nearly moribund during the mid-1880s, rekindled as M&StL and St. Paul & Duluth together attempted to blunt the growing influence of James J. Hill throughout the region and to drain off some of Omaha's impressive lake business via Duluth or Washburn, Wisconsin. At stake were prodigious volumes of coal, cement, and merchandise inbound; grain, flour, and lumber outbound. In 1888, M&StL agreed to provide StP&D terminal facilities in Minneapolis (Lower Yard) on an

Chicago, Milwaukee & St. Paul was a 5,700-mile giant, and Minneapolis was crucial to its fortunes. The road's prominence and prosperity were implied in this view of the downtown Minneapolis passenger depot and freight yards. Photograph courtesy of the Minnesota Historical Society.

annual rental basis giving M&StL much needed cash and a friendly connection northward once more. For the years 1890–94, M&StL stood either first or second among several carriers interchanging freight with StP&D.[18]

There was, of course, a constant swirl of activity involving the larger roads. Albert Keep retired from the presidency at Chicago & North Western to be followed by equally impressive Marvin Hughitt, while Roswell Miller rose to the top at CM&StP when Alexander Mitchell died in 1887 (S. S. Merrill had died three years earlier). Suave and genial, Miller would preside over a highly respected 5,700-mile operation that continued to prosper. Miller took a conservative view as to expanding Milwaukee's huge machine, but he did tweak M&StL in 1889 by building a 16-mile appendage to Lake Minnetonka, ending M&StL's monopoly on the south shores, wounding its ego, and eroding its short-haul passenger business to and from the resorts. Meanwhile, the "Washburn roads," Soo Line, by 1894 stretched west to Portal, North Dakota, and east to Sault Ste. Marie, Michigan, with Minneapolis as the fulcrum. At each extremity, Portal and Sault Ste. Marie, Soo linked with Canadian Pacific—not incidental connections, as it turned out. In January 1890, W. D. Washburn asked James J. Hill in confidence as to the prospect of amalgamating Great Northern and Canadian Pacific. "I hope to see these great properties operated as one system," said Washburn breezily. Given the massive egos of Hill at GN and William Van Horne at Canadian Pacific, that was a most unlikely prospect, and Washburn's comment was suspect. In any event, Great Northern finished its own line to Pacific tidewater in 1893 and immediately plunged into deadly competition for transcontinental business with both Northern Pacific and Canadian Pacific. For his part, Van Horne retaliated in anticipation of Hill's move west in mid-1890 by swallowing up Duluth, South Shore & Atlantic and by guaranteeing interest on Soo Line's debt and then by taking a majority of its equity. Soo thereafter was a nominally independent Minneapolis-based concern, but Montreal called its major shots. And Soo was forever a thorn in Hill's throat.[19]

Hill's name was associated with other real or imagined changes on the railroad landscape of the upper Midwest. In 1889, rumors again had combination of Hill's road with Burlington and then absorbing Chicago, Burlington & Northern—the "Western Pirate," as labeled by Wall Street for its predilection to rate wars—to perfect control of "over 8,000 miles of good paying road." A year later other observers predicted that Great Northern would instead acquire Chicago Great Western (née Chicago, St. Paul & Kansas City), a rumor repeated during the next year along with an equally bogus claim that Hill would gain control of Soo Line.[20]

One bit of quite correct information that the press did not pick up on was Hill's quiet attempt in 1888 and 1889 to acquire M&StL. Just as that road headed into the dungeon of receivership, Hill wrote to banker John S. Kennedy in New York, saying, "I think we can probably make some arrangement that will give us control of the reorganization of the company without the necessity on our part of paying out much money." Hill was particularly covetous of M&StL's Minneapolis properties, observing that "next to our own they are the largest and most valuable in that city." Indeed, said Hill, M&StL "is almost invaluable to us as it would give us permanent control of all the valuable terminals in Minneapolis except those of" Milwaukee Road. Hill also wanted leverage in the hotly contested "crossings case." To those ends, Hill ordered the company treasurer to begin buying M&StL debt and equity "to be covered up in the account of 'Bills Receivable,'" in a way that would prevent "anyone examining the books to know what it was." Truesdale learned early to be wary of the wily Hill; he had ample reason.[21]

Handsome, capable, and well-liked, Truesdale had been the unanimous choice of creditors to manage their affairs, and he discharged the receiver's duties with skill. "None of the diverse interests have made any complaint regarding his management policy," observed one Minneapolis newspaper in 1891. But the man of "exceptional ability," as the *Minneapolis Tribune* said of him, must have been antsy. M&StL had to expand. But where? And how? Geographically, options were few—farther into Iowa or beyond Watertown in what by now had become the state of South Dakota. Yet there is no evidence that Truesdale made efforts to push beyond Angus to Des Moines, to Council Bluffs, or anywhere else in the

Hawkeye State. And while Watertown presented itself as a "marvelous city" and railroad hub (M&StL, BCR&N, C&NW, and GN), the bloom was off the "great Dakota boom." In any event, dreams of broadening M&StL's reach in any way were dashed irrevocably by onset of the terrible Panic of 1893.[22]

The national economy had been vibrant in the late 1880s, and *Bradstreet's* in April 1891 reported that Wall Street was "in a fairly healthy condition." But the economy softened during the summer of 1891, and international investors increasingly shied away from American securities, especially railroads. This plus growing political hostility toward the industry at large slowed expansion of the national network in 1891 and 1892. Developments moved in train. Residential construction slumped, immigration dropped, weak and overextended banks stumbled, financial failures increased, and the stock market plunged. In 1893 alone, owners of one-sixth of American rail mileage entered bankruptcy. Additional misery followed in 1894 with massive strikes in the soft coal and railroad industries and crop failures in many parts of the country. Unemployed numbered in the thousands and often were uprooted; tramps commandeered trains with regularity. Freight ton miles bottomed out in January 1894, but recovery would prove halting and awkward.[23]

The problem of bankruptcy among railroads grew exponentially during the Panic of 1893. In 1888, when M&StL was cast into receivership, only 22 of the country's roads aggregating 3,270 miles of line found themselves so embarrassed. In 1892, 36 roads owning 10,508 miles of line were in the courts, but in 1893-94, 112 companies with 36,365 miles of line found themselves on the dreary list of unfortunates. By mid-1894, about 25 percent of the nation's entire rail mileage was operated by insolvent companies. But operate they did, for railroads—as quasi-public service entities—had to run even as they went through receivership, reorganization, and rehabilitation, a period of two or three years on average. Yet it was inevitably a bumpy path, for earlier federal bankruptcy laws had been repealed, and they did not pertain to large corporations like railroads anyway. Despite the absence of an authoritative body of law, courts over time developed rules to deal with financial failures: the assignment of a

M&StL's talented William H. Truesdale often had to scrimp and connive to find funds adequate to perform routine betterments such as ditching (to improve drainage) just outside the city near Hopkins. Photograph ca. 1890; courtesy of the Minnesota Historical Society.

receiver, provisions for protective committees representing various classes of securities, processes for reorganization, and finally foreclosure sale. The process involved much pulling and hauling among the protective committees and ultimate disappearance of old obligations plus the old company itself, establishment of a new company and new capital structure, and dismissal of the receiver.[24]

In times that were flush, railroad managers looked to bankers for capital to extend lines or make improvements; in hard times the same managers looked to bankers for means to reorganize and rehabilitate the property. Yet this came at considerable cost—not just capital, but also managerial prerogative, for bankers tended to frown on expansion and reckless competition, favoring instead cooperation and community of interest. Bondholders likewise blanched since bankers typically wished to trim a company's fixed costs so that payments could be made even in lean years, and shareholders inevitably shuddered because in reorganization they usually suffered the most, often losing everything. Successful reorganization, when it finally came, usually meant that fixed costs tilted downward, and creditors were forced to exchange old bonds for new ones paying lower interest rates, and that the debt to equity ratio was adjusted, not just to juggle stocks for bonds but, in fact, to reduce total capitalization.[25]

"There is no competition so mischievous as that of a bankrupt road with no dividends or coupons to pay," J. M. Forbes of CB&Q had groused in 1879. However accurate Forbes's assessment in general, it did not apply to M&StL, which never had the muscle itself nor the impetus from Rock Island to do more than maintain stability during its long season of receivership. M&StL was not "ruined" by overzealous state regulation as Truesdale once had shrilly complained (although well-intentioned but wrongheaded regulation hardly helped), nor was it grossly overcapitalized, poorly managed, or badly maintained. It simply generated too little compensatory traffic in a highly competitive region; its margins were predictably thin.[26]

Reorganization rocked along at a painfully slow pace. "But little progress seems yet to have been made in adjusting the affairs of the road by means of an amicable reorganization," Truesdale sorrowfully complained in 1891. Finally there was movement. In 1892, Frederic C. Olcott, president of Central Trust Company, had taken the lead in establishment of a stockholder protection committee including himself and four other prominent New Yorkers: William A. Read, August Belmont, William L. Bull, and J. Kennedy Tod. Olcott and Central Trust were close to Hill and Great Northern, and rumors quickly flew again that Hill would find a way to grab M&StL—something, incidentally, that Northern Pacific's senior management privately believed to be imminent. "I beg to say that neither our company, nor anybody connected with it, that I know of, has any interest in the Minneapolis & St. Louis," Hill told Truesdale when challenged on the matter. That was hardly the case. In any event, change was afoot. In October 1892, Read, Belmont, Bull, Tod, and another but rather more obscure New Yorker, Edwin Hawley, replaced a like number of Minneapolitans on M&StL's board. The change was not cosmetic. Rock Island maps presently showed

M&StL as a friendly connection, not as an integral part of CRI&P as in the past. Wall Street insiders still believed, however, that Rock Island expected "to buy the Minneapolis & St. Louis Road at forced sale for a low figure," which, most likely, had been Rock Island's intent from the beginning.[27]

On June 6, 1894, Rock Island held its annual meeting in Chicago, where William H. Truesdale was named third vice president of the company. Reorganization of M&StL was at hand, and Rock Island was confident of the outcome since that road and its friends owned a substantial chunk of M&StL bonds, and bondholders, not stockholders, usually came out ahead in such proceedings.

Ransom Cable and Rock Island had lost M&StL and a presence in Minneapolis and St. Paul.

Truesdale could at once be a senior manager at Rock Island and head of M&StL. It did not work out that way. Henry Siebert, on behalf of CRI&P, had rolled the dice in 1888 with the view of forcing M&StL fully into Rock Island's web. But the dice failed Siebert and Rock Island. Stockholders and the New York syndicate composed of August Belmont & Co., J. Kennedy Tod & Co., and Vermlye & Co., which had grown out of Olcott's protective creation, levered itself into ultimate control, and Rock Island—not the power it had been less than a decade ago—came up short. When the sheriff's sale was held in Minneapolis on October 11, 1894, Ransom Cable and Truesdale were on hand to represent CRI&P, but they were there only to assure that the sale would bring in enough to pay the bonds held by Rock Island and friends, not to make competing bids. In the end, $5,010,000 was adequate to win the property.[28]

The new Minneapolis & St. Louis *Railroad* assumed the rights and properties of the Minneapolis & St. Louis *Railway* of Minnesota and Iowa. Officers of the new company included William L. Bull, president; Edwin Hawley, vice president; Richard B. Hartshorne, treasurer; Joseph Gaskell, secretary; William Strauss, general counsel; and A. L. Mohler, general manager. Gaskell and Mohler, the latter recently arrived from GN, were holdovers and the only ones from Minneapolis; the rest were New Yorkers, as was the entire board of directors. Gone was Truesdale, who went to Rock Island and then to Delaware, Lackawanna & Western, where he finished his distinguished career.[29]

The *Minneapolis Tribune*, which long had followed M&StL's fortunes, thought sale to New Yorkers "must be regarded as a good thing for this city and the Northwest, as it indicates that the road will remain independent and a competitive factor in transportation." Curiously, the *Tribune* said nothing of the categoric absence of Minneapolis influence on the board. Even William Drew Washburn had been vanquished, ending a tenure begun in 1870. Clearly M&StL had passed over the threshold into a new era.[30]

But what did that era hold for the company? What were the intentions of the new owners? Ransom Cable and those of Rock Island persuasion might pay lip service to "friendly relations," but losing Minneapolis and St. Paul as endpoints in the highly competitive domain of the Chicago roads clearly disadvantaged CRI&P against Burlington, Milwaukee, and North Western. The loss must have smarted. How would Rock Island finally respond? Furthermore, railroad systems were either growing through or disappearing by consolidation. By the 1890s the greatest systems were the largest enterprises not only in this country but in the world, and no governmental unit in the United States equaled, for example, employment by the Pennsylvania Railroad—110,000 workers in 1891, compared to 39,000 in the military and 95,000 in the Post Office. What did all of this mean for M&StL? What did it mean for Minneapolis?[31]

# THREE CENTS PER MILE

# 11

The country through which this road passes is showered
with all of Nature's blessings. Good soil, good water
and diversified crops, briefly emphasize this statement,
while the population is thrifty and takes advantage
of natural conditions.

WILLIAM L. BULL TO M&STL STOCKHOLDERS, 1895

For persons living in the Minneapolis & St. Louis service area during the mid-1890s there was nervousness as to purposes and intentions of the road's new owners and management. Every member of
the directorate was from New York, as was William L. Bull, president, and Edwin Hawley, vice president. Albert L. Mohler, already
a seasoned and respected railroader and destined to be president
of Union Pacific some years later, remained as general manager;
Joseph Gaskell of Minneapolis, secretary and treasurer since 1883,
and William Crooks, chief engineer and long associated with Minnesota railroads, each provided links to the past and a sense of con-
tinuity. Yet concerns were understandable. Union Pacific's Charles F.
Adams Jr. complained that William Bull was part of "a Wall Street
gang," and indeed, Bull and Hawley—like fellow directors W. A.

Read, J. Kennedy Tod, and August Belmont—were New York bankers or financiers.[1]

Nevertheless, leading elements of Minneapolis were unguarded
in their glee at M&StL's refound independence and reminded ener-
getically that the road had been born primarily as an adjunct to the
business interests of the city and as protection against tyranny of
the Chicago roads. The recent Rock Island association had not been
greatly beneficial to Minneapolis, they thought. Now, happy to say,
M&StL was "no longer a branch of a great system swayed by Chicago influence but an independent corporation free from domination
of any road and dedicated to this city and the towns along its line
of track, which in helping to build up," predicted the *Minneapolis
Tribune*, "will in return make increased business for the road." To be

sure, Minneapolis interests again embraced M&StL as a vehicle of economic imperialism—a device to expand hinterland, especially in southern Minnesota and northern Iowa, rich in potential but hotly contested by Chicago-based carriers. For its part, M&StL was both a willing and aggressive player on behalf of Minneapolis, hosting promotional excursions for merchants and others from the disputed area, improving freight and passenger service, and working closely with the city's milling, hardware, grocery, drug, clothing, and agricultural machinery constituents. At the same time, M&StL sought alliance with grain dealers to make Minneapolis a serious market for corn and oats, which could be stored in elevators over the winter and dispatched eastward via Soo Line/Canadian Pacific or by water from Duluth/Superior. The idea was freighted with symbiosis and

was as simple as it was historic—providing M&StL with loads in both directions, lumber and merchandise outbound, corn and oats inbound—and reflected, in the process, the concept that merchandise would be ordered from locations where grain was marketed. The idea also reflected the continuing swing from wheat production to corn and hogs in southern Minnesota and in all of Iowa—a reality that F. H. Peavey, "the Napoleon of the elevator business," and other

M&StL was a willing and aggressive player on behalf of Minneapolis. It eagerly sought freight billings from Washburn, Northwestern Consolidated, and other companies in the west-bank milling district. The M&StL cars on this trestle were moved about using a system of cables and pulleys, which can be seen on the end of the trestle. Photograph courtesy of the Hennepin History Museum.

grain dealers wanted to capitalize on with a newly independent and energized M&StL.[2]

The Panic of 1893 continued to lock much of the country in its vicious grip. As the depression deepened and as unemployment increased in 1893 and 1894, the so-called Coxey's Army roamed the West. Although railroads were one of its targets, Minneapolis and its carriers were not greatly violated. The American Railroad Union and Pullman strikes of 1894 were another matter, in both instances shutting down much of the local railroad scene, if briefly. And neither was the level of tension and grief as dramatic locally as in other places around the country. Tragedy did strike not very far away, however, with devastating fires around Hinckley, northeast of Minneapolis, about halfway to Duluth, on St. Paul & Duluth and Eastern Railroad of Minnesota, where the inferno of September 3, 1894, destroyed lumber and mills and snuffed out the lives of perhaps five hundred persons. More would have perished except for the courage of railroaders who gathered up terrorized residents just ahead of flames.[3]

The Panic of 1893 notwithstanding, Minnesota's population increased even in the face of hard times with gains registered in every county, Hennepin (Minneapolis) leading with a 19 percent gain over the decade. This provoked the *Minneapolis Tribune* into a spate of spirited boosterism that sounded very much like that of a quarter century earlier. Said the *Tribune*:

> There is no state in the Union that offers so many attractions and even allurements to immigrants. With a matchless soil, a superb climate, a health-giving and invigorating atmosphere with abounding wealth of timber and minerals, with three great commercial cities, and with facilities for manufacturing unsurpassed by any state in the Union, our state offers more comfort and more varieties of employment, more opportunities for acquiring wealth, than any other section of equal area on this continent. It is the Empire State of the Northwest—Imperial Minnesota.[4]

Despite hyperbole, there was truth in what the writer said. Indeed, much of Minnesota's soil, especially in the southern third of the state and in the west, proved marvelously productive for tillers of the soil. And many of those same farmers were embracing crop rotation and diversification of crops as means to avoid soil exhaustion and dependency on a single commodity. Of course, Minnesota remained the country's leading producer of wheat, but increasingly farmers were turning to oats, corn, hay, barley, rye, flax, potatoes, and alfalfa. The latter crop reflected one dimension of the "new agriculture," dairying, with attendant establishment of creameries. Yet another shift to diversification was reflected in livestock numbers—cattle, sheep, and especially hogs, which, in turn, resulted in establishment of the nearby St. Paul Union Stockyards in 1887, itself attracting Swift & Company, a major meat packer, which opened a nearby facility a decade later.[5]

Expansion and changes on the agricultural landscape in Minnesota and Iowa, and more slowly in the Dakotas, were part of a broader national pattern. During the period 1870–1900, the number of farms, the number of acres in production, and the total farm population all doubled, as did the production of wheat and corn. Cattle and swine numbers nearly tripled with numbers so impressive that one observer claimed the Midwest was nothing less than "corn, cattle, and contentment."[6]

Agricultural diversification bespoke several changes, among them the ongoing shift in the wheat culture to be replaced by the corn and hog culture and the extension of the St. Paul but, more importantly, the Minneapolis hinterland, which protruded eastward over perhaps one-third of Wisconsin, included the top portion of Iowa, encapsulated most of South Dakota, engrossed all of North Dakota, and extended over about half of Montana. Railroads, of course, had been and continued to be the mechanism responsible for this vast expansion of empire. Yet St. Paul had been the early leader. Several important roads—Great Northern, Northern Pacific, Chicago Great Western, St. Paul & Duluth, and Omaha—were headquartered there, and even mighty Chicago, Milwaukee & St. Paul throughout this period was popularly known as the "St. Paul

VIEW OF VESTIBULE OF OUR PULLMAN SLEEPING CARS.

## GOOD LANDS IN MINNESOTA

The best farm lands to be found in the state are along the line of the Minneapolis & St. Louis Railroad. Purchase a ticket to Marietta, Madison or Dawson, in Lac Qui Parle County, Minnesota, and convince yourself that less than thirty bushels of wheat per acre is a small crop. Other cereals, including corn, in proportion. Crop failures unknown.

For rates and particulars call on nearest agent of the M. & St. L. R. R. or address A. B. CUTTS, G. P. & T. A., M. & St. L. R. R., Minneapolis, Minn.

Road." The city of St. Paul had ample reason to puff out its chest and did so with regularity. This little ditty by Judge C. E. Flandrau is representative:

'Twas said "all roads do lead to Rome;"
Today we bring that saying home;
There is not a railroad, great or small,
But has its center in Saint Paul.

M&StL and Soo Line, with headquarters in Minneapolis, would have disputed this, and Minneapolis more than St. Paul stood to gain as Twin Cities influence stretched west and northwest—a vast domain that railroads continued to promote with vigorous colonization efforts. Minneapolis flour merchants heartily applauded, eager as they were for an even greater supply of wheat for their voracious mills. The city's wholesalers similarly approved and encouraged, knowing, as they did, that the filling in of the hinterland automatically spurred demand for the myriad of items farmers required and the city provided: oil, candles, soap, pots, stoves, harness, wagons, engines, machinery, and a full array of foodstuffs including coffee, tea, crackers, vinegar, spices, cheese and other essentials such as beer, whiskey, and wine.[7]

Railroads stood to gain from all of this; small wonder they poured great effort into recruiting and holding a hearty and productive constituency for their service regions. "The Best Homes for 10,000,000 people now available for occupancy in Minnesota, North Dakota, Montana, Northern Idaho, Washington and Oregon—the new and prosperous Northern Pacific Country with its great natural resources," boasted NP during the 1880s. The same road touted Duluth, "The Zenith City of the Unsalted Sea," pointing to marvelous opportunities in and about that place. NP publicists were merely warming up. "Land for the Landless, Homes for the Homeless," was that road's message during the 1890s in advertising

An expanded productive population to the west could only benefit Minneapolis.

"cheap farm lands on long time and easy payment in Central Minnesota." NP likewise sought more settlers for the "rich and fertile Red River Valley," where land was available "at prices ranging from $4 to $10 per acre." For its part, Great Northern pointed out that there existed "a large amount of government land along our line in Dakota and Montana, which is available for settlement." Moreover, said GN, its lines reached "many new towns which afford opportunities for the establishment of business enterprises of all kinds. The country abounds in pure water, an abundance of fuel, and timber along the streams." Like other roads, CM&StP offered a wide variety of free publications. "Plain Facts about Dakota: Its Fertile Lands, Its Wonderful Crops and Its Inexhaustible Resources" was one such pamphlet among a blizzard of others. CM&StP reported that over 4,000 immigrants passed through its Minneapolis depot in 1888; a similar number utilized a specially arranged room for them at the nearby Manitoba station. During the year 1882, 57,059 emigrants rolled up 16,682,996 passenger miles on St. Paul, Minneapolis & Manitoba alone.[8]

There were other equally significant changes abroad the land during the same period of 1870–1900. The value of farm products more than doubled over that thirty-year span, but the value of manufactured products quadrupled, and in 1890 the total value of manufactured goods was greater than the total value of agricultural products. Moreover, while the rural population doubled, the urban population tripled. The rise of urban industry and the division of labor coupled with sophisticated rail transport increased demand for agricultural production, while increased income in the hinterland meant additional marketing potential for industry.

The ornery and stubborn Panic of 1893 put a predictable damper on travel. The country's railroads carried 594 million passengers in 1893, but only 541 million a year later, and 489 million in 1897

All railroads engaged in a vigorous game of one-upmanship; competition was intense. For a while Northern Pacific had control of Wisconsin Central, together featuring through sleepers between Chicago and the West Coast via St. Paul and Minneapolis.

before recovery. Similar patterns obtained locally. CM&StP, the most prominent of Minneapolis railroads, saw its systemwide passenger numbers drop from 8.3 million in 1893 to 7.1 million in 1897. NP also reported a sharp decline: 2.7 million passengers in 1893, only 1.0 million in 1897. Omaha, Chicago, St. Paul & Kansas City, and Great Northern suffered only modest losses, however. Ticket sales at M&StL actually went up, from 494,000 in 1893 to 571,000 four years later.[9]

The Panic certainly did not stop the carriers in their incessant one-upmanship in trying to lure customers to the cars. "Entire train lighted by gas," enthused Chicago & North Western in pointing to its (with Omaha) service to Milwaukee and Chicago—"Elegant Day Coaches, Luxurious Smoking Compartment Sleepers and Dining Cars, the Finest in the World on All Trains." CM&StP countered with "Solid Electric Lighted Vestibule Trains" to dominate in the Chicago–Minneapolis corridor. Chicago, St. Paul & Kansas City promised "Through Coaches and Pullman Vestibuled Compartment Sleeping Cars." Wisconsin Central handled Northern Pacific's West Coast cars to and from Chicago, and Chicago, Burlington & Northern (after 1890 fully a part of CB&Q, which had taken 98.3 percent of its capital stock) advertised "through coaches and sleepers" to both Chicago and St. Louis. So did M&StL in concert with Burlington, Cedar Rapids & Northern, CRI&P, and CB&Q. M&StL claimed that its dining service was "not surpassed by the finest hotels in the land"—"all meals are served at 75 cents each." St. Paul & Duluth scheduled three round-trips to Duluth, one to Taylors Falls, and five to Stillwater. M&StL offered the only direct linkage to Des Moines (connection via CRI&P to Denver); Great Northern tapped Duluth with roundabout service via Elk River and Milaca; CStP&KC provided a direct path to Kansas City and put two daily trains on that route; and Milwaukee Road, in addition to service on its major east thoroughfare down the river, carded two through trains to Chicago on its pioneer line via Faribault, providing also an Austin local. Omaha advertised two daily options to Sioux City (connections on to Council Bluffs/Omaha) plus a Mankato local as well as two trips northeastward to Bayfield and Superior each day.

Soo Line, with trains east to Sault Ste. Marie, promised "Superb Dining and Sleeping Cars" in addition to "Day Coaches with Porter in Charge"—"Every Modern Convenience or Appliance for Comfort and Safety of Passengers." Soo also provided a round-trip out to Oakes, North Dakota, and a Paynesville local. Milwaukee placed one train on its line west to Aberdeen (and a Milbank local); M&StL offered a through train to Watertown, South Dakota (and two Waconia locals); Great Northern rattled out to Hutchinson with one daily turn. Northern Pacific had a lock on Puget Sound business until Great Northern completed its line to Pacific tidewater in 1893. NP's *Pacific Mail* consisted of "Vestibuled Pullman Palace Car, Pullman Tourist Sleeping Car, Free Colonist Sleeping Cars, Diner" and first- and second-class "Day Coaches." That train and another gave NP double daily service to Portland and Seattle, supplemented by another heavy train composed of two segments—one section going up to Winnipeg, Manitoba, and the other proceeding on to Jamestown, North Dakota. A Brainerd local also was part of the mix. Great Northern put two trains westward on its line through St. Cloud with another set dispatched through Willmar, splitting there, one section heading for Sioux City, Iowa, and the other to Winnipeg, each one featuring "Palace Buffet Sleeping Cars."[10]

Special trains and special car movements were routine. So were excursion promotions. All carriers were active in this, but none more so than M&StL—focusing quite predictably on Minneapolis. M&StL teamed with the Minnesota Experimental Farm during December 1893 in sending a delegation westward over the Watertown line to hold "farmer institutes" at Fairfax, Echo, and Clarkfield among other places, and three years later it used three trains to bring farmers from stations on that line to visit the state's Experimental Farm at St. Anthony Park. Eager excursionists from St. Paul and Minneapolis headed for the State Saeagerfest at Jordan in 1889, and in the same year three hundred foresters from Albert Lea took the cars to Minneapolis. Almost two thousand persons in three trains from the line above Fort Dodge, Iowa, arrived in Minneapolis for a jolly day of sightseeing during August 1895, and a few days later another train originating at Madison brought a large group from western Minnesota for a Sunday outing. The list was nearly endless. Some travelers came to shop—at Donaldson's Glass Block Store, which in 1895 announced a "Leather Goods Sale" after M&StL delivered a carload of it on February 28—while others came for social events or dramatic, athletic, or musical performances. A decade earlier large numbers of Freemasons and Knights Templars attended the laying of the cornerstone at the Minneapolis Exposition Building, and in 1899 a surge of patriotism motivated a throng to entrain for the Twin Cities to see President William McKinley greet the Thirteenth Minnesota Regiment on its return from the Philippines.[11]

The Chicago World's Columbian Exposition of 1893—the "White City" as it came to be known—provided a chance to visit that bustling and brawny city but also through the exposition to see "ancient Rome and Greece" as well as "marvels of the modern

In 1898, CM&StP charged passengers $13.50 for a one-way ticket from Chicago to Minneapolis. Some of those patrons reached the Mill City aboard trains like this one, nearly home, working along the company's pioneer line above the Fort Snelling bridge, now the popular Minnehaha Trail. *Minneapolis Journal* photograph; courtesy of the Minnesota Historical Society.

world." Frederick Law Olmsted, dean of American town and park planners, laid out the fair. The Electric Building, Transportation Exhibit, Horticultural Hall, plus the world's first Ferris Wheel and the Duryea brothers' automobile were among great attractions. All carriers working the Chicago–Minneapolis corridor promoted the event, and all were rewarded by volumes that taxed capacity. In addition to regularly scheduled movements, Chicago carriers during one four-day block in October delivered seven hundred extra sleeping cars filled with customers anxious to see the sights and stay in wooden hotels that had sprung up like mushrooms near the fair. CB&Q, as a representative example, saw its passenger revenue soar by 43 percent in October, mostly attributable to the Chicago fair.[12]

M&StL and others continued to look to Lake Minnetonka for important if mostly seasonal passenger traffic. Competition at that place always was part of the equation. Manitoba (and then Great Northern) had a profound presence at the north end of the lake, and its Lafayette was clearly the most impressive of the many hotels. James J. Hill had a special affection for the area; here he had secured wood for his fuel business in early St. Paul, and here he had purchased a small farm. By 1880, he engaged an architect to study hotels in the East, and out of it came the splendid Lafayette managed by an experienced hand from New York City's famous Hotel Brevoort on Fifth Avenue. Opened in 1882, the Lafayette was enlarged the next year to accommodate nine hundred guests. Often

**LEFT AND BELOW:** Patrons boarding Milwaukee Road trains at the Fort Snelling stop had to descend a lengthy stairway from near the post commander's quarters (which at the time of this view had a mansard roof). The Austin local called regularly. Photograph on left courtesy of the Minneapolis Public Library, Minneapolis Collection. Photograph below from the Aaron Isaacs collection.

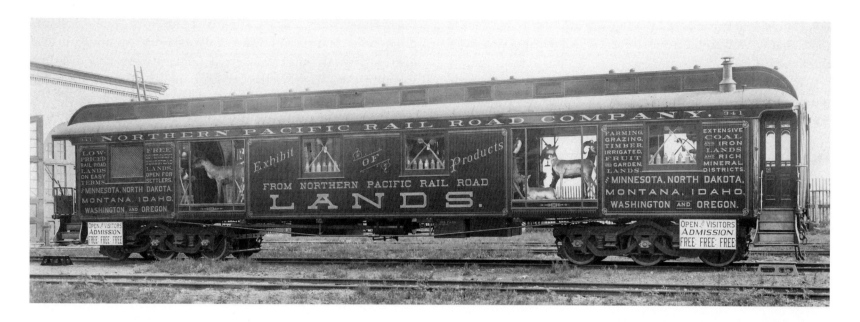

called "Saratoga of the West," it certainly was one of the largest and finest summer hotels in the world. Business was brisk in season. On July 5, 1886, as an example, Hill's Manitoba carried six thousand persons to the resorts on hourly trains. Rail competition only increased when Milwaukee Road arrived on the south shore, and an electric line soon was on the scene. Nevertheless, M&StL was a major player at this famous watering place throughout the 1890s, carrying trainloads of patrons who looked forward to refreshing days of bathing, boating, fishing, and sailing or to extended stays at Lake Park Hotel, set among an impressive stand of oak, maple, and elm, with a twenty-two-horse stable, roller-skating rink, billiard parlor, bar, and dance pavilion only a few steps from M&StL's Tonka Bay depot and telegraph office. M&StL held a one-half interest in the

**ABOVE AND RIGHT:** Northern Pacific dispatched two cars for exhibition at the 1893 World's Columbian Exposition at Chicago. Inside and available to an eager public, said NP, was "a large collection of diversified products, symmetrically arranged, showing the rich natural resources" of Minnesota and of "the Northwestern States." Photographs courtesy of Burlington Northern Santa Fe.

hotel but had no financial stake in the *City of St. Louis*, the fine old vessel that W. D. Washburn once owned, which remained in service through 1898.[13]

Attractions at Minnetonka were many and varied; so, too, were the people who came to visit. Croquet and tennis lured some, others admired boat races, and still others anticipated performances by the Lyceum Company, which "occupied the boards" at the Lake Park theater. The younger set looked forward to "hops" at the St. Louis Hotel, while oldsters admired Lake Park's "grand ball and promenade concert" with Danz's full orchestra" promising to "furnish music for the most fastidious." And there was yet another timeless attraction. "They say the number of pretty girls at Minnetonka this season is unprecedented," gushed one Minneapolis newspaperman in 1890. "The hotels swarm with them, and at the hops their elegant costumes are the cynosures of all eyes," he concluded with a nearly audible sigh. All of this created a great demand for transportation, to which M&StL responded by scheduling (in addition to regular through runs for Winthrop and Watertown) four trains in each direction for the 1889 season, eight in 1896, and five in 1900. (GN ran six in 1889, Milwaukee operated six in 1900.) Furthermore, M&StL ran a nearly endless stream of special excursions to Excel-

Chicago, Milwaukee & St. Paul was the interloper in the Lake Minnetonka trade, but its station facilities at Deephaven suggested that it would be a powerful player. Lake vessels met all Milwaukee trains at the substantial platform in the foreground. Photograph from the Aaron Isaacs collection.

sior and Lake Park—for the Railroad Porters Association, United Typothetae, Minneapolis Engine Company No. 7, Ancient Order of Hibernians, Scandinavian Church of Christ, Mt. Zion Hebrew, Knights Templars, and Gustavus Adolphus Society to mention but a few. M&StL also involved itself in an interesting "reverse commute" in 1895 when it arranged to handle passengers from Minnetonka to Minneapolis for a lecture at the Metropolitan Opera House by the popular Mark Twain.[14]

Several groups in 1895 required special trains. Fully 1,200 persons attended a picnic and series of athletic contests hosted by the Ancient Order of Hibernians and Daughters of Erin, and at the end of summer entire trains were required for the Modern Woodmen of America's annual log-rolling contest and picnic at Tonka Bay. Then there was the excursion and charter trip on the *City of St. Louis* for the Concatenated Order of Hoo Hoo. Made up of lumbermen and railroad managers, this organization required an initiation fee of $9.99, annual dues of 99¢, restricted its membership to 9,999, and met at 9:09 P.M. on the ninth day of the ninth month of the year with the black cat (nine lives) as its official symbol. Surely Hoo Hoo Day on the M&StL was one to be remembered.[15]

Not nearly as important as Minnetonka but still significant in M&StL's passenger calculations was Lake Waconia, about 13 miles west of Excelsior, which competed for tourist dollars as best it could. For years the masthead of the *Waconia Patriot* declared Waconia to be "Paradise of the Northwest," and the attractions of Lake Waconia and amusements at Coney Island were worthy indeed. From late May into September, passengers in large numbers unloaded at the Waconia depot or at Coney Island, 1.7 miles east, and headed for picnic grounds, baseball games, or theatrical performances, or rented rowboats, went fishing, or merely lounged. The steamer *Niagara* met trains and conveyed passengers to hotels. M&StL advertised special runs to "Coney Island of the West" and conducted thither a stream of groups—the grocery clerks of St. Paul, Murphy Temperance Society, Chaska Literary Society, People's Party of Carver County (with Ignatius Donnelly as speaker), and United Order of Horseshoers among them.[16]

M&StL predictably focused on traffic moving between that road's outlying stations and Minneapolis and St. Paul; this matter, in turn, was wrapped up in station facilities at the road's two primary locations. A contract had been entered into with Northern Pacific back in 1883 by which joint operation was pledged between Minneapolis and St. Paul as soon as NP completed its "A Line," 9.5 miles, most of the intervening distance. This was not accomplished until 1886, however, and on February 8, M&StL began use of the joint line with freight service into NP's Seventh Street facility in St. Paul. Passenger operation was delayed briefly, though, since M&StL had been ejected from St. Paul Union Depot—likely reflecting the powerful hand of James J. Hill and his antagonism toward NP and M&StL. Meanwhile, NP arranged temporary passenger accommodations in the basement of its general office building nearby. M&StL soon leased property from NP and established its own depot at Broadway and the foot of Fourth Street, about four blocks from Union Depot. In Minneapolis, however, GN was obligated to provide M&StL with a passenger depot adjoining the Washington Avenue bridge as part of the finally concluded crossings case. Cass Gilbert, the eminent architect, was consulted but there is no evidence of his considerable talent in the extremely modest and barely functional product, which, both M&StL and GN expected, would suffice for only a few years until M&StL made other arrangements. The city ticket office at Washington and Hennepin was much more impressive than M&StL's shabby depot.[17]

A curious sidebar to the M&StL-NP contract of 1883 gave M&StL rights to provide passenger service for intermediate stops between Minneapolis and St. Paul. NP duly constructed "first class standard passenger stations" at University Avenue, Prospect Park, St. Anthony Park, Hamline, Warrendale, Como Avenue, and Rice

---

FOLLOWING SPREAD: Lake Minnetonka was served by several railroads, including Great Northern, M&StL, and Milwaukee Road. Lake steamers met all trains for the lake's famous hotels. Map from *Plat of Minneapolis and St. Louis Park* (Minneapolis: Minneapolis Land and Investment Company, ca. 1891–93); courtesy of the Minneapolis Public Library.

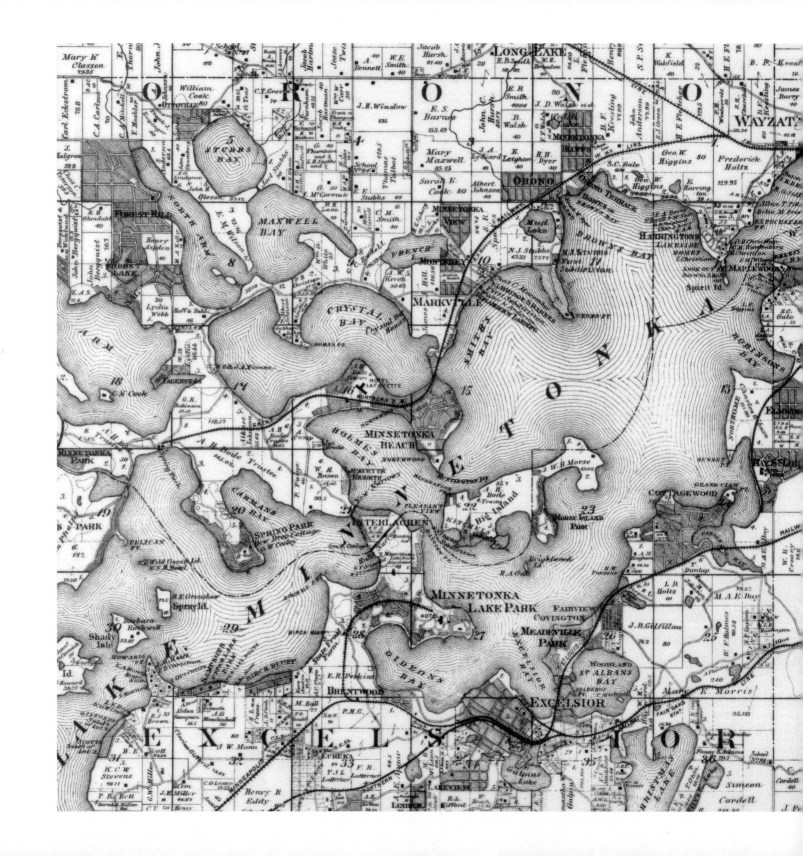

MINNETONKA

ARLINGTON HEIGHTS

PALESTINE

MINNETONKA STA.
ST. ALBANS STA.

WEST MINNEAPOLIS

HOPKINS

MENDELSSOHN

Crane Lake
Hannan Lake
Shady Oak Lake
Shell Lake
Gray's Bay

Josephine Rodner
Elias Frick
Mary E. Ottaway
Mary Haley
R. M. Woodville
James Ryan
G. O. Lamb
G. W. Lamb
Schiebe
Benj. Frost
Thos Halloran
Pat Collins
M. Luby

Dennis Doley
J. J. Larkin
C. E. Lamb
Michael Ryan
Wm. Ryan
Fred Glassing
C. E. Lamb
Isaac Bernheimer
David Luby
Albion Bressel
Fred Keller Jr.
Francis X. Crepeau
Dennis Halloran

Martin Doyle
O. P. McGenty
T. F. Rooney
John J. Larkin
F. S. McDonald
Fred Glassing
John Wetzel
L. F. Menage
C. J. Bartelson
Patk Halloran

T. F. Andrews
Dennis McGenty
C. M. Tuttle
K. Daley
William Dobson
S. A. Quale
Dora S. Makowski
Simon Mayes
W. C. Pickering
W. J. Byrnes
R. N. Jordan
John Christy
Eugene Haley
John Harmon
Michael Hannan

Ellen McGawn
James McGenty
Donald McGenty
School No. 105
H. Lawrence
Mary Q. Doyle
S. G. Noyes
David Corbett
E. F. Rode
J. R. Hofflin
Michael Carr
D. M. Gilmore
Mary M. Bruce
Larkin

Edward E. Santo
C. E. Brown
L. D. Brock
R. Aylor
A. N. Jordan
E. J. Allen
W. & N. S. Smith
W. S. Fraser
T. J. Higlin
Eliza Murphy
J. R. Hofflin
Minnehaha
W. A. Mitchell
W. A. Edwards
Hanora Larkin

Susan A. Brown
Geo. Biggle
R. W. Barton
S. H. & N. S. Smith
N. S. Smith
Shell Lake
F. R. Allen
F. P. Clough
Daniel Larkin

Henry Ogin
C. J. Alger
Paul Miller
S. H. & N. S. Smith
J. E. S.
Olivia Burns
Ignaz Souba
Anna Souba
Kenny Souba
A. H. Nelson
Geo. H. Burns
Amelia P. Burns
Jennie G. Hofflin

C. I. Olson
W. Hebe
Frank Miller
Paul Miller
G. B. Shepherd
A. A. Perkins
B. E. Dow
C. L. Gadlt
N. Hampton
O. F. Sackison
Bates
H. S. Garfield

John M. Chastek
Frank Kinsel
Frank Picha
Alois Zrask
F. Zabalka
John Kokesh
L. W. Kokesh
Isaac Bernheimer
G. A. Austin
Isaac Bernheimer
Wm. Wilson
J. R. Jackson
C. R. W. Bland
Henry W. Dominic
Frank Bren
J. H. Empenger
J. R. Hofflin
John E. Empenger
John Copley

Joseph Kinsel
Joseph Kinsel
Joseph Svec
Susan A. Brown
Wm. Dunton
J. Makowsky Jr.
A. Makowsky
J. Makowsky
E. C. Cooke
E. C. Cooke
Hennepin Co. Poor Farm
H. A. C. Thompson

John Miller
Nellie M. McGrath
Frank Dworak
Frank Kwetensky
School
J. Popelka
Frank Kinsel
J. Makowsky Jr.
Frank Bren
Shady Oak Lake
H. Baston
B. A. Dunsmoor
J. Smetance
L. F. Menage

W. C. Thorn
I. Wadd
Isaac Westbach
Frank Picha
Wm. Dworak
Jos. Schmeider
Isaac Bernheimer
John Makowsky
W. P. Doxtad
J. Petrak
John Felix
Vanderoon & Holmes
E. & J. Smetance
Joseph Makowsky
Thomas Kyte

J. K. & R. D. McQuaid
E. Huber
I. Stodold
Frank Picha
E. Curtis
John M. Chastek
J. Makowsky
John Dworak
Cath. Church Cemetery
Joseph Bren
F. J. Bren
John Kyte

Frank Brakel
John Picha
E. A. Curtis
J. E. Kuchera
John Dworak
Wm. McCague
Jos. L. Miller
Chas. Newer
Chas. Berens
J. E. Pavelka

Street, but there were no similar stations constructed by M&StL on its tiny portion of the Minneapolis–St. Paul thoroughfare. M&StL began commuter service during the early spring of 1886 with hourly runs, but by 1888 trimmed to eight daily turns plus five daily through trains in each direction. During State Fair season each summer, however, M&StL ran trains on ten-minute headways to accommodate that demand. M&StL shared such business with Manitoba, and indeed, the railroads built four tracks to a commodious "Union Depot" near the center of the grounds.[18]

M&StL was hardly the first to involve itself with commuter business in and about the Twin Cities. St. Paul & Pacific, almost as early as it opened the state's railroad era in 1862 between St. Paul and St. Anthony, introduced three daily turns between those points—mixed trains hauling freight and passengers but in effect a commuter operation. Demand was good, and StP&P quickly adver-

tised a seven-day-per-week schedule. This, however, had the unintended consequence of activating both the local pulpit and the local press in denouncing Sunday trains as "a reckless thrust at the cause of good morals in the community." That storm blew over when other forces observed that Sunday trains provided "a benefit for the working people." By 1867 St. Paul & Pacific was running six trains daily, charging 2.5¢ per mile for commutation tickets. CM&StP's early long-mile route between St. Paul and Minneapolis was not much competition for StP&P and its Manitoba successor, but in 1880 after completion of its "Short Line"—"the only double track in the state"—that pattern changed abruptly. In the next year CM&StP offered thirty-minute runs each hour in each direction between 6:00 A.M. and 8:00 P.M.; intermediate stops were made at Short Line Junction, Union Park, and Chestnut Street. Manitoba, in turn, matched that level of service, and, in fact, increased demand and intense rivalry between Manitoba and Milwaukee served to drive up the number of scheduled runs. Manitoba added capacity by installing a four-track thoroughfare between the two cities (two tracks for passenger trains, two tracks for freight); in 1883, it offered twenty daily turns. Five years later Milwaukee Road dispatched an amazing sixty-two daily passenger trains (including through trains) between Minneapolis and St. Paul, and Manitoba ran commuter trains every thirty minutes over its "great four-track lines." Manitoba also operated a year-round Wayzata accommodation (up to seven daily turns in season), and M&StL served the south shore of Lake Minnetonka with two Waconia accommodations plus four commuter runs to Lake Park. *Railroad Gazette* admiringly observed that the collective suburban service of Twin Cities railroads was without parallel outside of Boston.[19]

Yet neither Manitoba nor Milwaukee nor M&StL was making any profit in this capital-intensive and highly visible public service. And as if to throw salt into that wound, the *Minneapolis Tribune* in 1889 joined other forces in denouncing the "injustice of a 50 cent round trip fare" (2.5¢ per mile) and demanded a 35¢ tariff (1.42¢ per mile). A political move soon was afoot to legislate such low commuter rates. This angered railroad managers including Milwaukee's Roscoe Miller, who said his company was not making ends meet now,

announcing further that Milwaukee "as it alone is concerned, would gladly discontinue . . . the trains." Another important variable was the bicycle craze of the 1890s and, more importantly, the expansion of streetcar lines including one completed in 1890 that reached from Hennepin Avenue in Minneapolis to downtown St. Paul. Increased frequency of streetcars and very attractive fares (20¢ per round trip, 1¢ per mile) quickly drew traffic from the steam railroads; in fact, revenue passengers on the Twin Cities Rapid Transit would double

in the period 1899-1903. Milwaukee responded by cutting Minneapolis–St. Paul commuter service to thirty-two trains and then sixteen while lowering the rate to 25¢ per round trip. But there was no profit in it. Milwaukee threw in the towel in 1893, Great Northern about the same time. M&StL already had done so effective October 1, 1892.[20]

One authority has argued that no invention from the time of the Civil War to World War I had more impact on the American city "than the visible and noisy streetcar and tracks that snaked down broad avenues into undeveloped land." To be sure, the streetcar accelerated the suburbanization process ushered in by steam rail-

roads. In Minneapolis, the earliest impulse came in 1873 from a consortium of local leaders that greatly resembled M&StL's board of directors—W. D. Washburn, W. W. McNair, R. J. Mendenhall, et al.—who formed the Minneapolis Street Railway. The enterprise failed, but another, taking the same name, dating from 1875 and eventually headed by Thomas Lowry, succeeded with horse-drawn cars. Electrification began in 1889 over a 115-mile system (restyled

Members of the Minneapolis Commercial Club joined with soldiers in cheery celebration at the opening of the Fort Snelling car line in 1905. Photograph courtesy of the Minneapolis Public Library, Minneapolis Collection.

Twin Cities Rapid Transit Company) that was described by one admirer as capable of transporting "passengers from the furthermost limits of Minneapolis to the outermost limits of St. Paul, for the pittance of ten cents."[21]

Despite the drubbing that the Twin Cities steam roads had taken in the commuter business, passenger operations remained an extremely important part of the railroad enterprise. For Manitoba in 1882, passenger revenue (tickets, mail, express, baggage) produced 26.2 percent of the total; at M&StL in 1897, passenger service yielded 25.8 percent of company revenue. But carriers in Minnesota properly complained about state-mandated 3¢ (per mile) fares, which failed to recognize varying levels of financial strength among the state's railroads, did not consider variable costs between high-volume main lines and low-density branches, and failed to recognize greatly increased costs of operation over time. (St. Paul & Pacific had charged 2.5¢ per mile back in 1862.) In any event, for the year 1898, 3¢ per mile was the rate charged for rail passenger travel within the state of Minnesota. The following is a brief selection of one-way fares charged by roads emanating from Minneapolis to outstate destinations.

| Road | Destination | Fare |
| --- | --- | --- |
| CB&N | Dayton's Bluff | $0.35 |
| CGW | Austin | $5.70 |
| CM&StP | Winona | $3.40 |
| Eastern RR Minn | Duluth | $4.30 |
| GN | Moorhead | $7.24 |
| M&StL | Dawson | $4.86 |
| NP | Hawley | $6.83 |
| Omaha | Worthington | $5.15 |
| StP&D | Taylors Falls | $1.35 |
| Soo Line | Glenwood | $3.90 |

NP in 1898 charged $60 for a ticket to Portland, Oregon; CM&StP received $11.50 for a fare to Chicago; GN asked $38.00 to reach Great Falls, Montana; and CGW pocketed $12.50 for a trip to Kansas City.[22]

As recovery followed in the aftermath of the awful Panic of 1893 and as the decade wound down, Minneapolitans wondered as to Minneapolis & St. Louis, the old favorite, the local road. Its New York owners still had given no signal as to their long-term intentions. M&StL started somewhere of importance but went to no place in particular. Its tiny route structure could not support independence, and as the Panic of 1893 ended, the giants again awakened to imperial conquest. Would the New Yorkers merely gussy up M&StL for marriage? Would they milk the property for all it was worth and then throw the carcass to jackals? Would they expand M&StL as a means of goading the giants into bidding for the pesky smaller road? Or would they chart a strategic course designed for long-term independence? Whatever the cards in that hand, they would be played by Edwin Hawley, named president of the road in 1897.

Edwin Hawley's life was reminiscent of the popular Horatio Alger stories contemporary with his own time. Referred to as "the little Harriman" during the early twentieth century, Hawley's beginnings were nevertheless humble. Born in 1850 at Chatham, New York, he left home at age seventeen and headed for New York City. He took the first job offered—as messenger boy for Erie Railroad. Hawley moved subsequently to Ohio & Mississippi and in 1870 to Chicago, Rock Island & Pacific as clerk and contracting agent. His personal characteristics took hard form: he worked, he watched, he studied, he learned, he kept silent. And he invested, buying railroad stock that he considered undervalued.[23]

Luck was with him at Rock Island, where he came to the attention of those in charge of the California Fast Freight Line, which controlled considerable Pacific freight business and to which company Hawley moved next. At California Fast Freight he met Collis P. Huntington of "Big Four" and Southern Pacific (SP) fame. Huntington liked what he saw in Hawley, saying to him, "You ought to be working for me. You know how to keep your mouth shut." Indeed, Hawley soon found employment at SP, turning down an important position at the headquarters in San Francisco but assuming responsibilities at New York as general eastern agent and then, in 1890, as assistant general traffic manager. His reputation grew steadily. SP's respected J. C. Stubbs called Hawley "able, assiduous, and agreeable," adding importantly, "he leads while seeming to follow." The *New York Times* applauded Hawley, saying he was "recognized as one of the brightest and most competent railroad men in the city." Internally and to a few outside SP, Hawley was known also as one of Huntington's chief aids and confidants. Even fewer, perhaps only Huntington himself, knew that Hawley was doggedly pursuing his own ends—saving every penny he could, even salvaging mutilated postage stamps from correspondence, and investing in SP and other rail stocks.[24]

Hawley seemed a riddle. One newspaperman said Hawley was an interesting man because he was directly opposite in habits and manners compared to those persons usually considered engaging. For instance, he talked little. A reporter once asked him for an interview, but Hawley said that talking was distasteful to him, and that he hated any attempt to make him do so. Another writer said Hawley was one of a "vanishing race of silent men," and friend Bernard M. Baruch recalled that Hawley "was one of the few men I knew who had a natural poker face. It was pale and cameolike, and when he talked he hardly opened his lips." Another observer said "his smooth face" was "immobile and unemotional" and when he talked it was "in a low, even voice . . . almost in monosyllables." Hawley tended to be a loner, seeking and giving little counsel. Not that he was without friends. Indeed, by the mid-1890s Hawley spent nearly every Saturday afternoon and evening at the Hoffman House at Broadway and 25th Street, playing poker with some of the city's best-known personalities.[25]

Hawley's closed-mouth style, his reticence to seek limelight, and the absence of surviving diaries or papers combine to irritating mystery regarding his intentions early and late. Thus there is no record of how he fell in with William Bull and others during M&StL's reorganization. Perhaps it was M&StL's stock that young Mr. Hawley "bought cheap" and then held. In any event, Hawley's was a rising star among those in the railroad industry as well as on Wall Street. Despite his position as vice president and then president at M&StL, Hawley remained connected in New York with Southern Pacific and was one of its significant shareholders.[26]

M&StL during these years was as much a conundrum for Minneapolitans as this man Edwin Hawley who controlled it. Hawley rarely appeared on the property, and he always eschewed publicity—for himself and the railroad alike. What *were* his intentions for M&StL? It was a vexing question for local leaders. A few observers thought they had a clue when congressman and future Minnesota governor John Lind and others from the enterprising community of New Ulm met with M&StL representatives about a "plug line" down from Winthrop, on M&StL's South Dakota route, to the capital of Brown County. There followed incorporation of the Minneapolis, New Ulm & Southwestern Railroad with a board of directors reflecting New Ulm's milling and brewing industries. M&StL said the New Ulm road would be "operated independently," but in fact M&StL purchased all of its bonds and in 1899 would purchase the road outright. In any event, Lind's dream was realized on July 4, 1896, when New Ulm residents celebrated the arrival of two special trains over the newly completed line—one train from Minneapolis and St. Paul and the other from nearby Winthrop. An important question remained: What was implied by the word "Southwestern" in Minneapolis, New Ulm & Southwestern? *Railroad Gazette* suggested a tantalizing possibility. M&StL, it said, would extend the New Ulm line "to connect with roads to the Missouri River."[27]

Meanwhile, the unsettling Panic of 1893—bringing with it a loss of confidence in the federal government's financial stability, widespread unemployment, massive labor unrest, and strong Populist prescriptions—was giving way to recovery and optimism. "A splendid little war" with Spain in 1898 vented a surge of patriotism and planted the United States very firmly among the world's imperial powers. M&StL started the Twelfth Minnesota Infantry Volunteers on its trek to Camp George H. Thomas in Georgia; in October 1899, a reception committee from Minneapolis and St. Paul met the returning Thirteenth Minnesota Infantry at Fargo. Days later President William McKinley arrived in the Twin Cities by special train to review the troops. The sweet smile of prosperity finally shone brightly on the North Star State. And the era of heroic entrepreneurship was in full flower. The most immediate stellar example was James J. Hill, the "Empire Builder," from nearby St. Paul. But Edwin Hawley also was increasingly recognized as a member of that class.[28]

Hawley had an unusually keen intellect and an active imagination, but he was in no sense an educated man. He was scarcely five feet in height, a compact "well groomed . . . little, gray-eyed man" one writer noted, who found work his chief pleasure. An associate remembered him as frugal, "a string saver," always investing, with an innate capacity to make money. These were characteristics that Collis P. Huntington had found marvelously attractive. The two men were increasingly close; Hawley bought more SP stock, and Huntington followed Hawley's advice and bought M&StL. Then, late in 1900, Huntington died suddenly, and for a while Hawley was in control of SP through his own stock and by influence he had with the Huntington heirs. A debate quickly raged as to what the heirs should do with their SP holdings—whether they should sell to Speyer & Company, SP's financial agent, or to Kuhn, Loeb, and Edward H. Harriman as agents for Union Pacific. Hawley soon pledged his own shares to Harriman and openly urged sale of the estate's stock to UP. It was done. Harriman rewarded Hawley with a seat on SP's board of directors, and in the process Hawley's name was presented to a much wider audience.[29]

Meanwhile, Hawley responded to growing national self-confidence by studying means to expand M&StL's dominion and carve out a broader strategic niche. Late in 1898 or very early in 1899 he decided to lengthen the New Ulm stub southwestward, keeping his own counsel as to the ultimate destination and exact route, but three routes were considered over a 35-mile swath leading generally toward Council Bluffs, Iowa. Hawley continued his tight-lipped approach, but M&StL's general manager announced that "we shall eventually reach Omaha, but probably not this year."[30]

Hawley's motivations were at once tactical and strategic. M&StL needed more traffic, originated locally or handled "overhead" as an

The Fifteenth Minnesota Infantry Regiment departs for action in 1898. Photograph courtesy of the Minneapolis Public Library, Minneapolis Collection.

intermediate carrier. Line expansion into new territory would accomplish the former, and pushing into Council Bluffs and/or Omaha to meet Union Pacific and others might satisfy the latter. The line would pass through glaciated plains typified by deposited drifts or windblown loess soils—beautiful for agriculture. Iowa in the 1890s dominated in corn and hog production as well as in cattle and horses, and prosperity in that state was real, if uneven. Timber was scarce, found only along creek and river bottoms, but so much the better for M&StL, which could wheel vast supplies of lumber from Minneapolis. The new route also had sure appeal for Minneapolis wholesale merchants as well as manufacturers of everything from agricultural implements to oil-based paint.[31]

Construction started at each end of the extension—southward from New Ulm in Minnesota and northward from Storm Lake in Iowa. Meanwhile, the Iowa & Minnesota Land & Townsite Company, with offices in the prestigious Lumber Exchange at Minneapolis, set off campaigns to launch several new communities. The pattern was the same at each new location. The townsite company secured a block of land and, as M&StL's "Omaha Extension" was nearing completion, held "a special town lot sale." The one at Ormsby, Minnesota, on October 24, 1899, was typical. Located 12 miles south of St. James and 20 miles north of Sherburn "in one of the finest agricultural districts in southern Minnesota . . . Ormsby has a splendid opening for all classes of business," announced the townsite company. "We want live, energetic, wide-awake businessmen to locate in this town where a prosperous future is assured." The surrounding

area, the company continued, was settled by "fore-handed" farmers, "about equally divided among Germans, Scandinavians, and Americans"—"well out of debt and in a position to pay for what they purchase."[32]

On August 19, 1900, the entire southwestern extension to Storm Lake, Iowa, was open for business. The line gave birth to fourteen new villages and punched a surge of adrenaline into the seven existing communities. Every new town was fleshing out. Hanska, Minnesota, for instance, sprouted a dozen businesses including Torgrimson & Synsteby, which handled seeders, drills, harrows, and other machinery eagerly acquired by farmers from the surrounding countryside. Yet however rapid the growth at these new locations, the townsite company still had plenty of property to dispose of; another round of auctions was scheduled to correspond with opening of the "new Omaha extension." Investors, said the townsite

Monterey was one of fourteen new townsites spawned on M&StL's Southwestern. Business there was good—a matter for celebration in Minneapolis, for Monterey reflected an expanding hinterland for the Mill City.

company, "can and will double their money on every lot they buy inside six months." Moreover, the surrounding countryside was rich—" immense crops this year and crop failures never known."[33]

Train service was an instant hit. On June 1, 1900, M&StL instituted double daily passenger service between Minneapolis and Estherville, Iowa, with one of those sets extended to Storm Lake on August 19. Freight schedules included a daily local in each direction. M&StL's passenger department quickly instituted fishermen's excursions to Minnetonka and half-fares to the Minnesota State Fair. A $2.50 round-trip rate to Minneapolis on Sunday, June 17, emptied Monterey, Minnesota, and filled the train. Two months later M&StL hosted a special train for Minneapolis jobbers, stopping at each station for the Minneapolitans to see and be seen in a calculated campaign to demonstrate a powerful symbiotic relationship between the Mill City and this part of its broad hinterland.[34]

As these denizens from Minneapolis headed home, they likely speculated as to Hawley's next move. Surely, they believed, he would make good on the "Omaha extension" in the next year. The territory southwest of Storm Lake would be competitive with Omaha, of course, and it already was with Chicago, but if Hawley pressed on, M&StL would have a short-mile route from Minneapolis. Chicago, St. Paul, Minneapolis & Omaha was long in place in that corridor, A. B. Stickney's Chicago Great Western was known to have intentions of an entry there, and if M&StL pressed on, Minneapolis customers would have three options. Competition, these Minneapolis jobbers must have noted with glee, would be intense among the carriers. And Hawley might even push M&StL on to Kansas City, giving Stickney's CGW a run for its money on such traffic. For that matter, Hawley might have still other imperial aspirations. But if he did not, others—particularly Great Northern, Northern Pacific, Soo Line, and Milwaukee Road—certainly could be counted on to continue campaigns to flesh out their systems in ways surely beneficial to Minneapolis. As M&StL cars rumbled back toward Hennepin County, these ebullient ambassadors of the city must have concluded that the growth and development of their fair community in the last half of the nineteenth century was but a puny prelude to what the future held. Railroads had made Minneapolis what it was; railroads would make it all it could be.

# RUMORS AND REALITY 12

Combination is . . . nothing more than the endeavor
to secure the largest possible amount of tonnage and
transport it with the least expenditure of money.

COLLIS P. HUNTINGTON, 1891

America was patently vibrant at the turn of the century. Average per capita income led all other nations, and the country enjoyed virtually full employment. Census takers counted 75,994,575 persons and determined that the national center of population was a bit southeast of Columbus, Indiana. Minnesota was home for 2,805,346. Railroads, the country's first big business, remained dominant with 195,526 miles of track—6,942 in Minnesota—and railroad assets made up about $14.5 billion of the nation's $90 billion estimated total wealth. Only agriculture exceeded railroads in the amount of invested capital and in the value of annual business.[1]

Although increasingly under attack, apostles of laissez-faire economic theory and practitioners of social Darwinism continued to advocate unbridled competition across an unregulated environment. In 1901 was established United States Steel Company, America's first billion-dollar corporation. Nevertheless, this remained the age of railways—an age in which the industry was dominated more and more by large carriers. During the 1860s and 1870s, Pennsylvania Railroad (PRR) and then to a lesser extent New York Central and Baltimore & Ohio modeled the practice of lease or control to create giant systems. By 1874, Pennsylvania Railroad alone claimed more miles of line than could be found in any nation of the world other than Great Britain or France. A decade later PRR operated 7,950 miles of line, was capitalized at $842 million, and employed 110,000 persons. (By comparison, the entire U.S. military establishment numbered 39,492 personnel, and in 1893 the gross national debt of $997 million was only about $155 million more than PRR's capitalization.) In the immediate area, several roads in 1893 ranked among the nation's largest business concerns.[2]

| Company | Miles of Line | Capitalization |
| --- | --- | --- |
| Chicago & North Western | 7,955 | $314 million |
| Chicago, Burlington & Quincy | 6,533 | $274 million |
| Chicago, Milwaukee & St. Paul | 6,128 | $225 million |
| Northern Pacific (including Wisconsin Central) | 5,216 | $370 million |
| Great Northern | 3,682 | $147 million |

All of these important regional roads were even stronger at the turn of the century. "The business of the past year has been exceptionally good," rejoiced President Charles S. Mellen at NP in 1900. "The operating results have shown satisfactory improvement over the preceding year." NP was impressive, owning 656 locomotives and 23,975 freight cars, handling in that year 7,121,655 revenue tons, and earning $26,048,673 by operating trains over a system of 5,005 miles. Great Northern was even more impressive, earning $28,910,789 in gross revenue by handling 11,529,601 tons over 5,202 route miles with 505 locomotives and 22,934 freight cars. Minneapolis-based Soo Line was hardly a bit player with 6,752 freight cars and 97 locomotives, which shouldered 3,102,244 revenue tons over 1,278 route miles to earn $5,151 million in gross revenue. And it was a source of local pride that Thomas Lowry served as Soo's president; the directory listed John Martin, William D. Washburn, John S. Pillsbury, and Charles H. Pettit—all long seasoned in Minneapolis rail affairs.[3]

All of this played out against a changed and changing landscape. A burst of combinations in the railroad field followed the Spanish-American War. Within two years at least 40,000 miles of railroad were transferred to companies owning other lines. Of course the pattern was hardly new; consolidations, joint ownerships, and mergers were, and long had been, as elemental to American railroading as ties and spikes. What was new—and frightening to a growing body of citizens—was the speed and magnitude of recent developments by which consolidation resulted in gigantic chunks of the national

BELOW LEFT AND RIGHT: Elegant downtown ticket offices spoke to the prominence of great carriers during the age of railways. Chicago & North Western's Omaha client was typical, its Minneapolis entry positioned fashionably on Nicollet Avenue. Photographs courtesy of the Minnesota Historical Society.

FACING PAGE: This 1895 Rand, McNally & Company map of the "main portion" of Minneapolis shows the city's rail arteries and helps pinpoint most of downtown's passenger and freight facilities. Map courtesy of the Minneapolis Public Library.

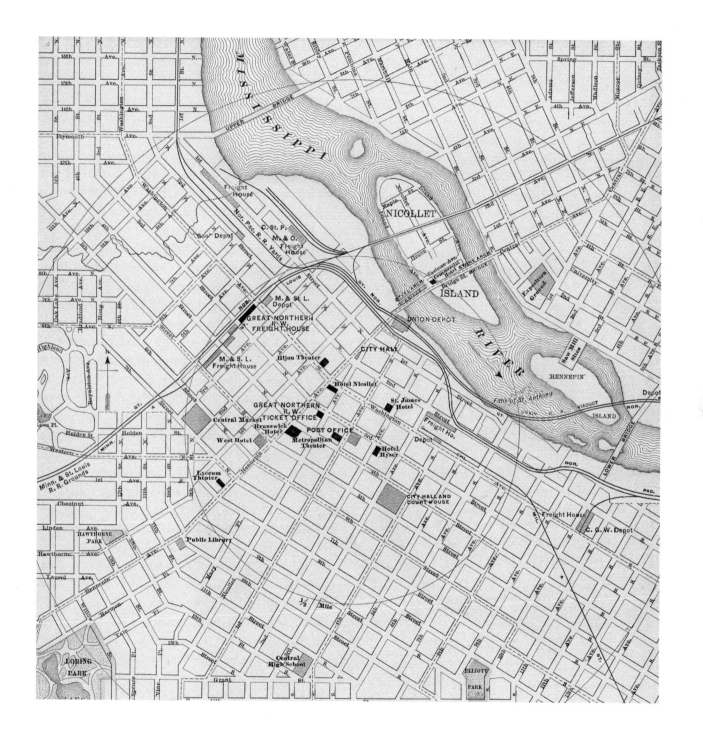

network held by particular syndicates—Vanderbilt, Gould, Hill-Morgan, Belmont and Harriman-Kuhn, Loeb as examples. The late C. P. Huntington, like most railroad leaders of his time, had seen this movement as "the natural tendency of railroad corporations toward unification of interests." To public nervousness he shrugged and said consolidation was nothing more than "the endeavor to secure the largest possible amount of tonnage and transport it with the least expenditure of money."[4]

Other railroad leaders shrugged similarly. "I have long been of the opinion that sooner or later the railroads of the country would

In what seemed a natural progression, Northern Pacific had taken lease of Wisconsin Central to gain access to Chicago.

group themselves into systems," CB&Q's Charles E. Perkins had written in 1879, "and that each system would be self-sustaining, or in other words that any system not self-sustaining would cease to exist and be absorbed by those systems near at hand and strong enough to live alone." If James H. Hill from nearby St. Paul had been privy to Perkins's thoughts he certainly would have nodded in agreement. Indeed, Hill had done all he could to assure that Great Northern would be one of the "self-sustaining systems . . . strong enough to live alone." Hill had no such feelings for arch rival Northern Pacific. When that road tumbled into receivership on August 15, 1893, Hill saw a golden opportunity to get control—to delimit its territory, to cancel any of its rate-making advantage, and to nullify NP's high-cost lease of Wisconsin Central (which had given NP access to Chicago). The powerful banking house of J. P. Morgan & Company had a huge stake in the Northern Pacific enterprise and in 1895 looked kindly on a community of interests agreement that gave Great Northern a majority on NP's board of directors and gave every indication of a first step toward eventual amalgamation of these two roads. That prospect, however, had the effect of triggering active opposition in every state of each road's service territory from Wisconsin to Washington, especially in always hypersensitive and politically volatile Minnesota. Suit was brought, and in 1896 the courts ruled that, under Minnesota law, the proposed Hill-Morgan joint arrangement on parallel and competing lines was illegal.[5]

Meanwhile, Hill and Morgan were designing otherwise. NP was reorganized in 1896, controlled by a voting trust fashioned by J. P. Morgan, with Hill and associates soon taking a substantial block of the company's shares. Then Hill and Morgan went shopping for an outlet from Minneapolis and St. Paul to Chicago. Morgan favored blue chip Milwaukee Road, but he could not bring about an acquisition. Hill tried to purchase Chicago, Burlington & Northern, CB&Q's route in the Chicago–Twin Cities corridor, but that attempt foundered too. Then Hill approached Charles E. Perkins with a proposition to acquire the entire CB&Q package. Burlington, of course, would provide both Great Northern and Northern Pacific direct connection with powerful trunk roads of the East at Chicago, would give outlet for lumber and other commodities from GN and NP throughout CB&Q's broad territory, and would funnel southern Illinois coal to the fuel-starved Northwest. For that matter, marvelously maintained and hugely profitable CB&Q was an investment plum in and of itself. Hill and Morgan understood and appreciated all of it.

Edward H. Harriman of Union Pacific was similarly enamored of Burlington and, in fact, as early as 1899 had begun to court Perkins. Burlington would provide UP with a prime entry to Chicago from Omaha, would obviate any Burlington threat west of Denver and elsewhere, would put UP head to head with Hill in the Twin Cities, and was a sparkling stand-alone treasure. In the end, however, CB&Q went to Hill-Morgan for $200 per share in cash and bonds of GN and NP. By mid-May 1900, Hill-Morgan had locked up 91 percent of CB&Q's stock, rising to 97 percent in November. Ownership was divided equally between NP and GN.[6]

Meanwhile, Harriman's influence expanded dramatically when he gathered in the Southern Pacific colossus. But Hill-Morgan in the driver's seat at CB&Q posed a profound threat to Harriman's empire. Harriman determined to attack by indirection—by purchase of NP equities. Kuhn, Loeb & Company, acting on Harriman's behalf, began to buy NP stock on the open market, soon driving the price of both common and preferred to over $100. Harriman's plan was audacious—seeking control of CB&Q by securing a majority of NP's stock. He nearly succeeded. NP common eventually reached $1,000 per share, precipitating a short-lived but dramatic panic in May 1901, but Hill-Morgan retained control, barely. A compromise in this high-stakes contest resulted in formation of Northern Securities, a holding company, chartered in New Jersey, capitalized at $400,000,000, which exchanged its stock for that of NP and GN. Harriman, by virtue of his huge investment in NP, held a strong stake in Northern Securities, and his hand-picked directors would protect the welfare of Union Pacific–Southern Pacific, but Hill-Morgan owned a controlling interest, and Hill would be president.[7]

Activation of Northern Securities proceeded as planned. The company accepted Northern Pacific shares at the rate of $115 each,

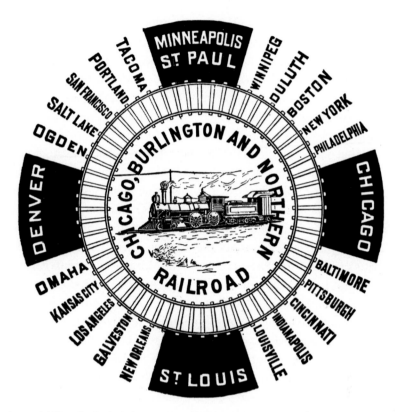

James J. Hill earlier had tried to acquire Chicago, Burlington & Northern but in the end purchased the parent, CB&Q, to be shared in equal portions by Great Northern and Northern Pacific.

those of GN at $180 each. On November 18, 1901, Harriman and his supporters sold all their NP stock to Northern Securities, and on January 1, 1902, NP retired its preferred stock in such a way as to maintain for Hill-Morgan its previous proportion of NP common. By March 1902 Northern Securities held about 96 percent of NP's authorized capital stock and about 76 percent of GN's.[8]

By that time the state of Minnesota and the federal government had challenged the validity of the holding company. The attorney general of Minnesota brought suit in a U.S. Circuit Court on the charge of violating state statutes. Meanwhile, the Interstate Commerce Commission (ICC) was expressing concern over "community of interest" combinations, and at the direction of President Theodore Roosevelt, Attorney General Philander C. Knox in Washington was giving his opinion that Northern Securities contravened the Sherman Antitrust Act of 1890. Consequently, on March 10, 1902, Knox initiated action in the U.S. Circuit Court in St. Paul against GN, NP, Northern Securities, and associated individuals. Both cases ultimately reached the Supreme Court. In *Minnesota v. Northern Securities* that court remanded the case to state courts because the circuit court should not have accepted jurisdiction. In the federal suit, the Supreme Court upheld Knox's argument that it was not necessary to prove that competition between GN and NP had been suppressed but that "the offense which the law forbids is the obtaining of the power." By a five-to-four vote the justices ruled that Northern Securities violated the Sherman Act. Hill-Morgan-Harriman had no choice but to dismantle the Northern Securities holding company.[9]

All of this had local importance, of course, and the impact—both immediate and long-term—had dramatic consequences. The case clearly demonstrated anger at and fear of big business at the grassroots level and put in bold relief the aspirations of President Theodore Roosevelt to make his mark as the "trust buster." Laissez-faire was in retreat, "progressivism" was in flower.[10]

Northern Securities machinations sent a shudder through the entire rail industry as well as the nation's financial institutions, but railroad expansion and consolidation continued, if nervously. In far-off New York City, Edwin Hawley and friends gained stock control of Iowa Central Railway, a hard-luck orphan road to the south where predecessors had played various parts in M&StL thinking from the beginning. Hawley became president of Iowa Central on June 20, 1900; associates who were on M&StL's board of directors took a majority position on Iowa Central's board at the same time. M&StL and Iowa Central main lines were separated by only 17 miles, Northwood, Iowa, to Albert Lea, but rails owned in portions by M&StL and Burlington, Cedar Rapids & Northern spanned that distance and were an integral part of the "Albert Lea Route," which provided through routing between Minneapolis and Chicago and Minneapolis and St. Louis in an old arrangement among M&StL,

BCR&N, CRI&P, and CB&Q. Iowa Central began its own operation into Albert Lea on July 1, 1901, giving the Hawley roads a 488-mile route from Minneapolis to Peoria, Illinois.[11]

Hawley's linkage of M&StL with Iowa Central was only one part of a very large shift that would see the "Albert Lea Route" sundered as giants jockeyed for advantage in the region. One of those giants was Harriman controlled—not Union Pacific, but Illinois Central. A nearly constant swirl of reports in 1897 through 1901 had that company taking control of M&StL. Prosecution of M&StL's Southwestern extension in 1899–1900 fueled some of this because IC at the same time was hurrying toward Omaha with a new artery from near Fort Dodge. M&StL's Southwestern tapped IC's existing Sioux City line at Storm Lake, and if lengthened, it could be made to connect with IC's Omaha route. Moreover, shortly after that route entered service in January 1900, M&StL and IC initiated a through Minneapolis-to-Omaha passenger schedule via Fort Dodge.[12]

BCR&N, too, was active. By late 1899 it was clear that with prodding and financial backing from Chicago, Rock Island & Pacific, BCR&N was about to launch itself directly into the Minneapolis market. Company surveyors were in the field north of Albert Lea before the year was out.[13]

But the spotlight shifted again to Illinois Central, which in 1899 announced intentions to bend a little-used branch from near Waterloo, Iowa, to Lyle, Minnesota, on the Iowa border just south of Austin, to the northwest: "to Albert Lea . . . there to meet the Minneapolis & St. Louis Railroad." The job was done in 1900, with IC yarding with M&StL in Albert Lea and dispatching its first passenger train from that place on December 3.[14]

M&StL now met Illinois Central at three locations: Albert Lea, Fort Dodge, and Storm Lake with the prospect of another at Denison. Iowa Central met IC at Peoria (Illinois), Ackley (Iowa), and Albert Lea. This added fuel to speculation that M&StL and maybe Iowa Central soon would pass to IC. Strategic advantages were obvious. M&StL could provide access to Minneapolis and St. Paul from the east (Chicago–Waterloo–Albert Lea) and from the west (Omaha–Fort Dodge–Albert Lea), while the Southwestern presented opportunities to and from Sioux City. In the end, Harriman opted not to take advantage of this opportunity, but M&StL and IC remained active partners at Fort Dodge, and IC stood ready for similar arrangements at Albert Lea.[15]

As these negotiations between M&StL and IC rolled forward, BCR&N pressed northward. It reached Owatonna, 33 miles north of Albert Lea, in 1900, and then moved on to Faribault; with 75 miles of construction and 46 miles of trackage rights, BCR&N would have its own route to St. Paul and Minneapolis. But the entire scene was played out against the backdrop of startling changes at Rock Island that in 1901 swept out much of the historic power structure and replaced it with one of dubious fame—the Reid-Moore syndicate. The new order was reflected locally on June 1, 1902, when CRI&P leased BCR&N; in the next year it would acquire virtually all BCR&N equity. So BCR&N disappeared, and the "Albert Lea Route" consortium among M&StL, BCR&N, CRI&P, and CB&Q was undone. Rock Island initiated passenger service to Minneapolis on November 2, 1902; freight service commenced on January 25, 1903.[16]

Rock Island was the last major player to enter the Minneapolis–St. Paul rail scene, and Rock Island did not add mileage elsewhere that had any direct bearing on the Twin Cities. But others continued to flesh out their systems, generally in ways that were pleasing and even celebrated by local manufacturing, processing, wholesale, retail, and financial forces. Northern Pacific added 225 miles of feeders across North Dakota during the first decade of the new century, and a satellite, Minnesota & International, added 118 miles to perfect a line from Brainerd to International Falls in northern Minnesota. Great Northern and clients in the same decade put down 460 miles of new line in North Dakota, 103 miles in South Dakota, and 158 miles in Minnesota—mostly in northern Minnesota to serve the iron mining industry. Omaha laid a paltry 25 miles of line in southwestern Minnesota. Chicago & North Western likewise added 133 miles, mostly in southern Minnesota, and another 295 miles in South Dakota—virtually all of it tributary to Chicago, however.[17]

Hometown Soo Line busied itself in the state with an important leg from Glenwood to Emerson (connecting with Canadian

Soo Line outgrew its original six-story headquarters and chose to construct a new building at Fifth and Marquette in downtown Minneapolis, which it occupied in 1915. Its size was much greater than an earlier management had thought necessary. Photograph by Charles J. Hibbard; courtesy of the Minnesota Historical Society.

Pacific for Winnipeg). "80 lb. steel rails, gravel ballast, new trains," boasted Soo. Another important artery protruded westward from near Thief River Falls across the fertile Red River valley to a junction with Soo's existing line running northwestward to another Canadian Pacific connection at Portal, North Dakota. This line, said Soo, "runs through the largest and richest wheat producing belt on earth." And while "the entire territory covered is uniform, well improved and populated," there nevertheless remained opportunity in the twenty-two new towns to be established—indeed, said Soo's townsite agent, "exceptional opportunities to those desiring business locations." Elsewhere Soo promised a branch through "the finest of all grazing lands" to "the land of Nod"—a new town northwest of Bismarck, North Dakota. Soo also announced plans to drive a diagonal line northeastward from Brooten, Minnesota, to Duluth. This one did not bring smiles to Minneapolis interests, for it offered western wheat producers an option of delivery to the Twin Ports. Indeed, Soo delivered the first train of grain over this line to Duluth on September 10, 1909. On a happier local note, Soo actively expanded its presence in Minneapolis by adding yard and shop facilities and by erecting a "six-story fire proof office building" downtown.[18]

Of all area railroads, none was more enthusiastic in venting its instincts for expansion than Chicago, Milwaukee & St. Paul. That road spiked down 129 new miles of line in southern Minnesota during the 1900s, another 131 miles in North Dakota, and a whopping 478 in South Dakota. A significant portion of this was to complete Milwaukee's line all the way to Puget Sound—completed on May 19, 1909, with the final spike being driven near Garrison, Montana.[19]

Curiously, relatively obscure Minneapolis & St. Louis also had a fling with "Pacific" fever, reflecting Edwin Hawley's growing influence in railroad circles. Before that, however, a syndicate composed of Hawley and associates in 1902 acquired Colorado & Southern, which itself held a majority interest in Forth Worth & Denver City. At almost the same time Hawley joined with John W. Gates in a pool that briefly controlled Louisville & Nashville; these important holdings in L&N were sold only a few months later at an immense profit.[20]

Hawley was hitting his stride. He needed new worlds to conquer. At Minneapolis, M&StL managers urged him to look west, to drive that road's existing line to Watertown, South Dakota, on to the Missouri River, and perhaps beyond. South Dakota, they noted, was getting back on its feet after the devastating "Dakota bust." The state had only 4.19 miles of railroad per 100 square miles of territory and only 72.7 miles of line per 10,000 inhabitants. There was room for expansion—for people and railroads alike. At the same time, emigration to the United States was surging, and Americans and foreigners alike continued to covet land and to embrace farming as an occupation and a way of life; indeed, in 1900, 42 percent of the country's population lived on farms. Moreover, agriculture was in one of its rare periods of prosperity—further driving thirst for land. During the years 1898–1903, inclusive, 88.5 million acres of the public domain passed to private ownership. The demand was insatiable but would be met, at least in part, as the federal government redefined Indian policy to provide smaller reservations, thus freeing up more land for white settlement. M&StL managers were alert to all of it. Minneapolis, and to a lesser extent St. Paul, claimed a huge hinterland—Minnesota, the Dakotas, much of northern Iowa, and most of Montana. An M&StL expanded westward surely would yield a treasure trove of grain for the great terminal elevators and mills at Minneapolis, while area-milled lumber and manufactured items plus all nature of goods from the city's wholesalers would flow outbound.[21]

Hawley gave the nod to go ahead. Construction started in 1906. Track workers passed Conde in October, hurrying on northwestward over the James River a bit more than half way to Aberdeen, then through that place to Leola, arriving there before Christmas. Meanwhile, other crews pressed west of Conde, were held up by winter, and did not drop rails in place to the Missouri River at LeBeau until September 1, 1907. Behind lay 228 miles of new railroad serving what one M&StL representative labeled "The New Empire." That "empire" called for farmers and townsfolk alike. M&StL turned to Thomas A. Way and his Dakota Townsite Company to meet the need. Way's approach was as simple as it was effective. He studied the territory contiguous to the new lines, calculated the potential farm population and its capacity to support a town, and then determined to sell no more lots than the hinterlands justified. "We have excellent crops, rich farmers, good land, everybody making money, country settling up rapidly," exclaimed the irrepressible Way. "A new town was opened on the line 'every week,'" said Way; five of them would "have 1,000 people at once." He was especially interested in recruiting parties that would build and operate hotels, livery barns, cafés, billiard halls, general stores, implement houses, hardware stores, and feed and flour mills. In Way's wake sprouted no fewer than sixteen new or renewed and very eager communities westward from Watertown.[22]

M&StL managers noted seventy livestock shippers strung out over the new lines, but most of these were piddling accounts compared to a handful of very large customers at LeBeau. Indeed, the catalyst for LeBeau's brief glory years clearly was the cattle trade—two-year-olds inbound and "double-wintered" animals outbound for slaughter. Many of these were billed to Chicago, where Nelson Morris, Philip D. Armour, Gustavus F. Swift, A. A. Libby, and John Cudahy had established themselves among the titans of meat packing. Others were bound for St. Paul Union Stockyards and/or the Swift plant nearby.[23]

By 1909, M&StL managers had a clarified picture as to business development along the South Dakota extensions. There were 680 identifiable potential freight customers or about 2.97 freight accounts per mile of road west of Watertown. Aberdeen led with 199; Nahon had the fewest, 2. Setting Aberdeen aside, the average was 17.2 accounts per station. Shippers of grain, seed, and hay dominated, followed closely by coal and wood dealers (often as part of grain elevators and/or lumber yards). Grocery, dry goods, and general merchandise accounts were followed by building materials and then a long list of miscellaneous. Minneapolis-based lumber companies earlier had placed numerous line yards on M&StL's Hopkins-to-Watertown route, but these were conspicuously absent west of Watertown. In their absence appeared line yards owned by smaller companies or independent yards that dotted tracksides in

Minneapolis business interests understandably celebrated M&StL's westward instincts.

many of the new towns. Grain elevators, of course, were omnipresent. Most were locally owned and operated, but Minneapolis-based Great Western, Pacific, and Security companies had line elevators at several stations; Pacific Elevator, in fact, had fifteen facilities along M&StL's extensions. It was a pattern typical of the time. Cargill ran a string of forty-one elevators along Milwaukee's line across southern Minnesota between La Crescent and Pipestone, another forty-

Opening of the Cheyenne Reservation in 1909 promised expanded opportunity for agriculturalists, who would feed increased produce to Minneapolis and receive from Minneapolis all nature of consumer goods.

one on Great Northern lines west of Minneapolis into the Red River valley, and another seventy-five in the Dakotas. That was small potatoes compared to the Peavey empire, which at the turn of the century had controlled 435 country elevators in the upper-Midwest.[24]

What of M&StL's "Pacific" aspirations? During the summer of 1909, locating engineers set stakes to the west, and piling and other materials littered the waterfront at LeBeau awaiting crews to drive a bridge over the Missouri River. "This paper stated several weeks ago that bridge work would be in full blast at this point before the snow flies," exulted the *LeBeau Phenix*. Its editor could not contain himself. Surely, he concluded, M&StL meant to go all the way to the Pacific, with branches, incidentally, to the Black Hills, Wyoming, and elsewhere. It was not to be. Milwaukee Road had sprinted ahead with its own line to Pacific tidewater and, as if to block off M&StL forever, spiked down rails from its new line to the coast just west of Mobridge to Trail City, one route turning west from that place to Isabel, and the other proceeding south over the Moreau River and then west to Faith—essentially preempting M&StL.[25]

M&StL's campaign to recruit a productive populace for its expanded territory was distinctive but hardly unique. Northern Pacific worked closely with Hamburg-American, North German Lloyd Line as well as independent emigration agents to recruit foreign movement to its still lightly populated service region, especially central North Dakota. NP promised prospective settlers that they could stay in tourist cars until they could provide homes for themselves. Great Northern reminded that "the thriving towns along its new extensions" offered "exceptional opportunities for young men, men of energy, men of moderate means, and men of capital. There are abundant openings for merchants, manufacturers, mechanics, professional men and *every man willing to work*." Milwaukee was particularly expansive in soliciting settlement in South Dakota. "It is an important fact that the Chicago, Milwaukee & St. Paul Railway has tributary to its railway the very best and most reliable farming section in the United States. Nowhere are crops more certain and markets more accessible. In no section are there better educational advantages, greater social opportunities, or more healthful climatic conditions."

Milwaukee pointed especially to its 50-mile branch from Eureka, South Dakota, to Linton, North Dakota, but also advertised commercial opportunities at the new towns of Wanamingo, Elko, and Lonsdale on recently opened lines in Minnesota. *Railroad Gazette* reported that three thousand farmers, mostly Dunkards from Indiana, Ohio, Michigan, Pennsylvania, and Virginia, passed through Chicago during the first week of April 1900 en route to North Dakota. Great Northern in the same year noted with pleasure that "the immigration wave for that season exceeded in the results anything in the history of the company." GN estimated that 35,000 persons "who largely came with their household effects" had taken up settlement along GN lines in that one year alone. Two years later James J. Hill told GN shareholders that the "large movement of people to the Northwest during the past few years . . . still continues without abatement . . . and has resulted in the settlement of a base area of vacant lands adjacent to the company's line." Hill noted in particular that "during this period more than 5,000,000 acres of Government land in the northern part of North Dakota has been taken under the Homestead Act." The campaign would continue. Great Northern, Rock Island, Northern Pacific all retained immigration agents, and M&StL and Soo Line both sported townsite agents.[26]

This station scene from Bottineau, in north-central North Dakota on a Great Northern branch, implies the powerful symbiotic relationship between Minneapolis and its broad hinterland. Grain elevators in the background hold a bounty of wheat for the mills, while draymen in the foreground daily delivered consumer and durable goods from Minneapolis wholesalers and manufacturers. Orders for those goods likely went east by mail aboard a Railway Post Office car or by wire from the depot telegraph office; items arrived by express or LCL in boxcars such as that spotted on the house track behind the depot. The wheat was billed to millers from that same depot office.

Perhaps some of those going west to take up residence rode one of the growing number of "name" trains serving Minneapolis. NP's premier entry was the *North Coast Limited,* which, as one authority observed, would "consistently rank among the finest trains in North America." Introduced on April 20, 1900, between the Twin Cities and Seattle–Tacoma–Portland, it required an investment of $800,000 to acquire ten eight-car train sets. Each train consisted of one each mail car, baggage car, second-class coach and smoking car, first-class coach, tourist sleeper, standard sleeper, and observation car exclusively for lounging and recreation. It was, NP management told stockholders, "an unqualified success." Great Northern's belated response was the *Oriental Limited,* placed in service in December 1905 and designed to link up with periodic sailings of its mammoth "new twin-screw steamships *Minnesota* and *Dakota*" between Seattle and Yokohama and other Pacific Rim ports. Relative latecomer Milwaukee Road would not enter name trains on its new Pacific extension until May 11, 1911, when its *Olympian* would be unveiled.[27]

Milwaukee Road's *Pioneer Limited,* dating from 1898, was a favorite in the overnight trade between Chicago and Minneapolis.

**BELOW:** Northern Pacific attached an elegant observation car to its famous *North Coast Limited.*

**RIGHT:** Northern Pacific, like other major railroads serving Minneapolis, operated a line of fine sleeping cars on its major long-distance and overnight trains. The interior of this car reflects its typical elegance. Photograph courtesy of the Minnesota Historical Society.

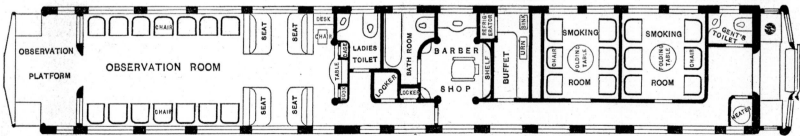

The *Pioneer* in 1904 left Chicago at 6:30 P.M. and arrived in Minneapolis at 8:00 A.M. the next day; return departure was at 10:25 P.M. with arrival in Chicago at 10:25 A.M. *Pioneer*, Milwaukee proudly announced, was completely "electric-lighted" and was composed of "compartment car, standard sleepers, buffet library smoker, 'free reclining chair car,' and coaches." Diners were available between Chicago and Milwaukee in both directions. Chicago & North Western (with Omaha) countered with its splendid *North Western Limited*—"The most comfortable, convenient, unique, and beautiful train ever placed in service between Chicago, Milwaukee, Minneapolis and St.

Paul"—completely reequipped in 1905. Wisconsin Central, Chicago Great Western, Chicago, Burlington & Quincy, and Chicago, Rock Island & Pacific also had candidates in that highly competitive and very busy corridor.[28]

So, too, was Minneapolis & St. Louis a participant, initially teamed with BCR&N and CRI&P; but when that ended, M&StL turned to alliance with Illinois Central at Albert Lea. Out of its shabby station at Washington and Fourth Avenue North on November 2, 1902, strutted M&StL's shiny *North Star Limited*—a "luxurious train" that would "challenge comparison" with elegant new cars, "all broad vestibuled and built to Pullman's latest and best models," including two sleepers (one standard and one compartment) plus a chair car and buffet-library for Chicago (diner on IC to and from Chicago). The *North Star* also contained a sleeper and coach for St.

BELOW: Milwaukee Road's passenger station on Washington Avenue always bustled with activity, whether individual passengers or groups entraining or detraining at all hours of the day and night. Photograph by Charles J. Hibbard; courtesy of the Minnesota Historical Society.

RIGHT: In this view looking east from Milwaukee's passenger terminal at least four passenger trains can be seen. To the left and in the distance are Milwaukee's downtown freight tracks and part of the west-bank milling district; to the right is Washington Avenue (note the streetcar). Photograph courtesy of the Minnesota Historical Society.

Louis in association with Iowa Central at Albert Lea and Wabash at Albia, Iowa (diner on Wabash in and out of St. Louis). Competition to that place was not as intense as Chicago, but M&StL–Iowa Central–Wabash did have to contend with CB&Q's direct route as well as a CRI&P-CB&Q combination via Burlington, Iowa.[29]

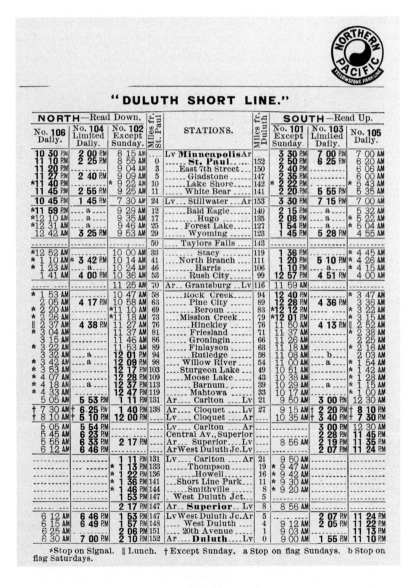

Elsewhere, Great Northern, Northern Pacific, Omaha, and eventually Soo Line tilted for advantage between Minneapolis and Duluth, and GN and Soo were rivals to Winnipeg. GN's *Winnipeg Limited*—"solid vestibules, steam heated, acetylene lighted equipment—Palace Sleeping Cars, Day Coach and Smoking Cars, and Diner"—made the 458-mile overnight run in fourteen hours and fifteen minutes. Chicago Great Western contested with CStPM&O to Omaha, but its *Southwestern Limited* to Kansas City was without rival, as was M&StL–Iowa Central to Peoria, but M&StL was challenged by Omaha-C&NW to Des Moines.[30]

Passenger representatives from every road were ever alert to any chance of increasing boardings. The St. Louis Fair of 1904 proved an especially inviting opportunity. Of all Minneapolis roads, M&StL was the most enterprising in that endeavor. Its *North Star* was no more than launched in November 1902 when M&StL's Anson B. Cutts began a vigorous awareness campaign, pointing out that the St. Louis fair would be twice as large as Chicago's splendid Columbia Exposition in 1893, and that *North Star* patrons could get "a full view of the grounds and buildings" from the cars. He was right. Among St. Louis railroads, Wabash was most actively associated with the fair; its line was adjacent to the grounds, and it built a special if temporary station just outside the gates. When the extravaganza finally opened, Wabash ran a fleet of shuttle trains to and from Union Station downtown, and in the end, Wabash handled more fair passengers than any other single road. M&StL offered round-trip excursion fares for only $12.98 from Minneapolis and nearby stations. The cars bulged with persons anxious to see

LEFT: Northern Pacific had to cope with Great Northern, Omaha, and eventually Soo Line in hot competition between Minneapolis and Duluth. Its Duluth Short Line promised three trains daily with a branch to Taylors Falls.

FACING PAGE: Chicago Great Western's property holdings and operating rights in and about Minneapolis changed often. For a while, CGW passenger trains utilized Northern Pacific's "A" Line and bridge over the Mississippi River near the University of Minnesota campus. Photograph by Charles J. Hibbard; courtesy of the Minnesota Historical Society.

Minnesota's "Butter Exhibit" and other marvelous sights. A delegation from St. Louis was in Minneapolis during the fall of 1904, reminding that the exposition soon would close and urging a late dash to enjoy the spectacle. Cutts lowered the tariff to $10; that brought the desired response. On November 14, as an example, two hundred additional passengers boarded the *North Star*, requiring more sleepers and coaches than usually assigned.[31]

For M&StL's Cutts the St. Louis fair was a dramatic opportunity to put patrons on that road's passenger cars, but in his fertile mind there was a constant flow of lesser opportunities. During the 1890s, he had inaugurated the company's marvelously successful "popular excursions," patterned to move people to any number of events and programs at almost any place on the system. Other carriers admittedly engaged in the same practice, but from about 1890 to 1917, no road in the upper Midwest was more energetic or effective in this regard. Half-rate fares were made for the Republican State Convention in Minneapolis and for the Minnesota State Fair. Early in the

fall of 1900, nearly five hundred Iowans from Storm Lake, Rembrandt, Sioux Rapids, and Spencer boarded a Minneapolis-bound special—school suspended so that teachers and students alike could enjoy the "educational experience." Another special train handled Minnesotans to the Democratic National Convention at Kansas City in 1900—rail fare plus $6.00 in sleepers "including two nights on the track at Kansas City." During the next year five carloads of excursionists from stations on the Southwestern and from west of Winthrop were forwarded to Duluth through St. Paul, and in 1903 eager partisans flocked to cars on the Watertown line when President Theodore Roosevelt visited Minneapolis.[32]

Jordan, on M&StL's main line 24 miles south of Hopkins, became a premier destination for excursionists from the Twin Cities, especially after Schultz & Hilgers improved its dance pavilion and park across from the brewery. The Ironmolders gathering in August 1902 drew about a thousand persons; "both hotels had their hands full waiting on the hungry," reported the local newspaper. A few weeks later, 580 tickets were sold to Herman Sons, who came to enjoy the Jordan Cornet Band, a waltzing contest, and athletic events including a tug of war and boy's shoe race. In 1903, two trains were required to bring the St. Paul Eagles, two more for the Meat Cutters' Union. Later on four hundred persons appeared for the Minneapolis & Jordan Brewers' Union Picnic, and two thousand enjoyed Cigar Makers' festivities.[33]

Cutts was constantly alert to opportunities for "popular excursions," but he counted on regular patronage aboard M&StL's scheduled trains. Every Wednesday, for example, M&StL dispatched a sixteen-section tourist car from the Twin Cities to Los Angeles "via the Santa Fe route"; another car departed on Thursdays using "the Scenic Line through Colorado and Salt Lake." Tickets: "$32.90 and through berth rate of only $6." Others were equally aggressive in this regard. Three years later CGW every Tuesday started a tourist car from Minneapolis to San Francisco (via Omaha, Colorado Springs, Pueblo, and Salt Lake City), and on the same day of each week Rock Island launched a "personally conducted" tourist car to Los Angeles (via Santa Rosa and El Paso).[34]

Passenger revenues were a crucial element of railroad fortunes. A trim Northern Pacific 4-6-0 heads a passenger train over the Stone Arch Bridge in this view from 1900. Photograph courtesy of Burlington Northern Santa Fe.

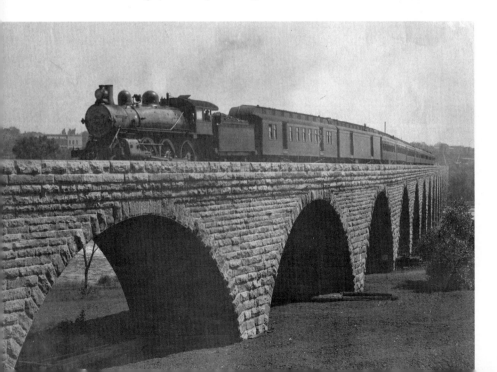

Passenger business was, without doubt, a crucial element of rail-road fortunes at the time. Passenger revenue (tickets, mail, express, baggage) made up 25.2 percent of all at NP for 1900, 21.6 percent at GN, and 21.3 at Soo. Passenger revenues for M&StL during the 1890s represented about 35 percent of all, but in 1905 spiked to an astonishing 51.6 percent. Giant Milwaukee Road in 1909 earned 21.3 percent of its revenue from the passenger trade. However impressive, passenger carriage obviously was less important than freight to the profit and loss statement of any railroad.[35]

For companies serving Minneapolis, products of agriculture always loomed large in freight billings. Wheat—elemental to the flouring business—predictably ranked high in the tonnage rankings of all roads. Just as predictably, Great Northern and Milwaukee Road, each with an expansive network of grain-gathering branches in the wheat-producing districts west and northwest, led in delivery of wheat to the Minneapolis mills. In 1902, as an example, railroads delivered a staggering 88.7 million bushels.[36]

By the turn of the century Minneapolis was the country's un-disputed flour milling center, output increasing from 9.349 million barrels for the 1892–93 crop year to 16.505 million barrels in 1902–3.

Much of this was for export—4.7 million barrels of it in 1900, fully one-quarter of all flour shipped from the United States for that year. Among Minneapolis millers, Washburn-Crosby and Pillsbury were the two that dominated; Washburn-Crosby's Gold Medal Flour and Pillsbury's Best were internationally known and respected. Washburn-Crosby bought or leased other Minneapolis plants dur-ing the 1890s, but it also established another milling site at Great Falls, and built, bought, or leased plants in Louisville, St. Louis, and Buffalo. Pillsbury followed a similar pattern of expansion.[37]

Lumber, always a staple in the traffic mix of Minneapolis rail-roads, still flowed in prodigious volume from mills now located primarily north of St. Anthony Falls in Minneapolis. Local millers produced 307.1 million board feet in 1896, 493.0 million board feet

LEFT: The coach yard upstream from Great Northern's Minneapolis depot was a busy place where cars were cleaned, restocked, and made ready for the next run. Photo-graph courtesy of the Minnesota Historical Society.

ABOVE: Mill stuff and flour poured from plants on both sides of the Mississippi—a most pleasant reality for the city's railways. M&StL's trackage penetrated Washburn's "A" Mill, where cars from several roads were loaded. Photograph courtesy of the Min-nesota Historical Society.

in 1899, to become the leading lumber market in the world, and 465.2 million board feet in 1902. Most of this was construction material—lumber, shingles, and lath—and most of it headed for traditional marketing areas west of the Mississippi River, but as production waned in Wisconsin and Michigan, billings also went east. Area demand remained high, much of it supplied at the retail level by line yards; in 1907, no fewer than fifty line yard companies had corporate headquarters in Minneapolis. During the late 1890s and into the next century CM&StP, CStPM&O, and M&StL led in Minneapolis billings.[38]

There were no surprises in terms of tonnage and revenue by commodity during the 1890s and into the decade following. Grain and lumber produced hefty percentages for all railroads serving Minneapolis, often followed by flour, coal, cement, and merchandise. Information on shipments to and from outlying stations is elusive and anecdotal, but Minneapolis, which did not tire in its claim to the greatest jobbing, manufacturing, and wholesale center in the "whole Northwest," clearly received or dispensed everything from school suits, waistcoats, shoes, and fall hats to pickled lambs' tongues, ginger ale, and Colorado peaches and Muscatine melons from Iowa in season. In general, rural stations were most reliant on agricultural produce for outbound tonnage, while building materials and general merchandise typified inbound lading.[39]

LEFT: Logs came from as far away as Leech Lake to keep the Minneapolis lumber millers alive. Photograph courtesy of the Minneapolis Public Library, Minneapolis Collection.

ABOVE: Shipments in wood products (mostly lumber, shingles, and laths but increasingly treated and untreated poles from several plants in northern Minneapolis) remained strong. Photograph courtesy of the Minnesota Historical Society.

FACING PAGE: Grain produced heavy tonnage for most Minneapolis railroads during the 1890s and 1900s. Terminal grain-handling facilities, such as Republic Elevator served by Northern Pacific at Twenty-ninth Avenue and Main Street Northeast, were found around the city. Photograph by Sweet; courtesy of the Minnesota Historical Society.

CAMERA WORK BY SWEET MPLS.

REPUBLIC ELEVATOR COMPANY.

# SHIFTING WINDS

13

On your week-end trips, take advantage of our low rates;
one fare plus 25 cents for the round trip on sale each day Friday
and Saturday for trains each Sunday morning. Rates apply
between all stations on the Minneapolis & St. Louis Railroad.

M&StL FLYER ADVERTISING MINNEAPOLIS

The United States underwent significant growth during the first decade of the twentieth century. The national population expanded from 76 million to 92 million—half of the increase represented by newly arrived immigrants—and the center of population shifted westward to near Bloomington, Indiana. Minnesota grew nicely, from 1.75 to 2.75 million. And Minneapolis swelled to 301,408 by 1910. Except for a significant downturn in 1907 that lasted into 1908, the economy was vibrant; capital investment grew by 76 percent during the decade, and unemployment was negligible. The national outlook was generally optimistic, the average citizen had faith in government as a proper medium for challenging social problems, and the time became known as the "Progressive Era."[1]

It remained the age of railways—celebrated by some, condemned by others. At issue were private power and public responsibility. What were the responsibilities of investor-owned railroads to the broad public, especially in an era of near modal monopoly? Public sensibilities were moving rapidly away from a laissez-faire approach in an increasingly unsettled political environment with the result that railroad leaders were chary about making substantial financial investments to plant and equipment. What explained this new circumstance? The shift from a rural and agrarian society to one that was urban and industrial only accelerated in the new century. And the pace and degree of this change unnerved many Americans, frightened more, and radicalized some. Nebraska's Senator William Vincent Allen likely spoke for most western agrarians when he argued that it was the "fixed purpose of the East" to transfer the wealth of the West from the "pockets of those who produce it to the pockets of those who have had no hand in its production. . . ." Indeed, fumed Allen, "the East has placed its hands on the throat of the West. . . ." Allen and those who thought like him pointed accusingly to the East as the area of growing metropolises, of huge industrial complexes, of teaming slums, of vice and corruption. In the East, by the way, were many owners of the mighty railroads and the powerful manufacturers; in the East lived the rich and strong—the Vanderbilts, the Goulds, the Rockefellers, the Carnegies, the Mellons, and their like. These feelings were intense, and they were predictably reflected in political reaction and legislative action. Agrarians were amply reinforced by the "non-urban middle class," especially small-town businessmen who had a palpable fear of an urban industrial America with its billion-dollar corporations, its aggressive mail-order houses, its greedy and narrow-eyed bankers, and, of course, it rapacious railroads.[2]

Grangers and others earlier had brought about state regulation of railroads and in 1887 the Interstate Commerce Act. Railroad managers and investors thought it all a bad dream, one that would surely go away. "It is said that bad laws, when they are seen to be so, are usually repealed," Charles E. Perkins had cautiously

Railways in Minneapolis set the tempo of the time during the steamcar civilization. The city's industrial zone along the west bank of the Mississippi teemed with activity, all of it tied tightly to rails as part of the nation's cardiovascular system. These tracks led northward (past what is now the Mill Place office building) and under the First Street bridge to Great Northern's passenger station.

reassured CB&Q shareholders back in 1888; "perhaps the evil of too much regulation by law will in time cure itself," he concluded with only a hint of optimism. Perkins likely reflected the thinking of most railroad managers. He was greatly irritated at public meddling in private affairs; in addition, he simply could not fathom government intrusion when rates demonstrably had been going down—the result of competition. Neither did Perkins nor other railroad leaders have respect for their antagonists. In 1895, one Minnesota state senator—a well-known populist and "anti-monopolist"—had the audacity to write a letter on official "Senate Chamber" stationery

requesting "transportation" by M&StL for two of his constituents. M&StL's A. L. Mohler fussed and fumed but bent to political expediency, noting that the letter came from a "member of the Senate, and I think under the circumstance it would be best to issue it [free tickets]." Five years later Milwaukee's highly agitated A. J. Earling declined a request for $400 from those who wished support for the national convention of the People's Party. "I am not in favor of making contributions for gatherings of this kind," he told a fellow railroad president in a model of understatement.[3]

But the anti-monopolists, the populists, and then the Progressives would not go away. "Corporations engaged in interstate commerce should be regulated if they are found to exercise a license working to the public injury," thundered President Theodore Roosevelt. After all, he continued, "great corporations exist only because they are created and safeguarded by our institutions; and it is therefore our right and duty to see that they work in harmony with

Milwaukee Road's venerable Minneapolis depot (on left) was razed after a new facility was opened nearby on Washington Avenue at Third Street (on right). Would massive expenditures such as these be justified in a changed and changing environment? Photograph on left by Edward A. Bromley; courtesy of the Minnesota Historical Society. Photograph on right courtesy of the Minneapolis Public Library, Minneapolis Collection.

these institutions." Roosevelt's message resonated mightily with the average citizen who, whatever the true merits of the matter, nevertheless demanded more and more "hands-on" government, that is, regulation. Railroads were the easiest target. They continued to hold a near modal monopoly. They touched everybody in one way or another. Teeth were added to ICC's statutory authority. The Elkins Act of 1903 stiffened penalties against rebating, and the Hepburn Act of 1906 gave ICC authority to set "just and reasonable" maximum rates as well as legal power to check railroad books. The Mann-Elkins Act of 1910 further empowered ICC in the matter of establishing reasonable rates and, strange to say, placed on carriers—not the government—responsibility for demonstrating the reasonableness of proposed rates.[4]

In the aggregate, the federal government now had power to establish de facto price ceilings with no convenient or expeditious way for railroads to respond to escalating costs. They remained capital and labor intensive, captive to huge fixed plants, and now found themselves tied by law to a governmental bureaucracy that would establish maximum rates; at the same time railroads were subject to market forces in determining costs of labor, material, fuel, equipment, bank loans, and all other necessities of business. In sum, railroads could not pass on their increasing costs except after lengthy bureaucratic procedures subject to political whim or pressure.[5]

Additional anti-railroad public policy was manifest at the state level to reflect populist and then progressive instincts. On the far left stood those advocating government ownership and operation of transportation and communication devices, but many more Americans wanted only government control of rates plus regulation of working hours and conditions. Railroad attorneys made the case that such laws would deprive owners of property without due process of law, rebelling in part against powerful state railroad commissions such as those in Minnesota that had assumed authority to fix maximum rates on intrastate traffic.[6]

In 1906, Minnesota reduced intrastate rates for merchandise freight, and on May 1, 1907, moved to institute a maximum 2¢ per mile rate on intrastate passenger fares. Other reductions followed on freight tariffs—grain, coal, lumber, livestock, and other commodities—to show the political muscle of rural and small town constituencies. At Northern Pacific, influential shareholders demanded that company managers not cave in, but citing "legal penalties, both against officers and against the corporation," these demands were refused. NP's Howard Elliott did, however, attempt to get Minnesota's other major railroads together for a frontal assault, but Milwaukee and then North Western dropped out "and after that several others." Suits were brought by individual shareholders against some of the state's railroads demanding that they not accede to unwarranted governmental intrusion, and a temporary injunction forbade the state's attorney general from enforcing the rates. He did so anyway and in 1908 was rebuked by the U.S. Supreme Court. Nevertheless, the issue remained alive, working its way through the judicial process and would not be resolved until 1913.[7]

In the end, the court did *not* rule on the reasonableness of these intrastate rates—a matter that universally irritated railroad managers and owners early and late. Nationwide, they pointed out, ton miles increased by 9.4 percent in 1910 over 1907, but freight revenues grew by only 3.7 percent, and payrolls jumped by over 6 percent. CGW's respected A. B. Stickney cogently remarked that to carry this impressive growth in tonnage the railroads had "been compelled to invest in additional equipment and enlarged facilities, enormous amounts, the interest on which . . . consumed the largest part . . . of per mile net earnings." Rates, he said most emphatically, were "already so low that it is impossible to get capital to invest in new railroad enterprises." Indeed, observers in the financial community blamed legislation unfriendly to business for the Panic of 1907. The Hepburn Act of 1906, they pointed out, was especially onerous since it made rate increases so very difficult to obtain. That kicked in a multiplier. Railroads found themselves with trimmed profits, which made investors skittish about railroad stocks; this, in turn, deprived the carriers of huge sums necessary to improve and expand plant. NP's Howard Elliott forcefully contended that Minnesota's 2¢ per mile passenger rate resulted in profits inadequate to "pay expenses, taxes, interest and a dividend . . . and at the same time . . . provide investment in improved . . . trains and stations which all of us would like to have."[8]

The handicapping nature of the Minnesota law was particularly deleterious for smaller roads such as Minneapolis & St. Louis. Inadequate rates had forced M&StL to abandon a proper standard of maintenance; without higher tariffs the road would continue on a "downward slide of condition," the road's general manager told the Interstate Commerce Commission in 1910. A year later M&StL's president reminded shareholders that "the trend of railroad rates has constantly been toward a lower level—the result of competition, increased operating efficiencies the consequences of modern equipment," and an ever improving "science of railroading." He thought it more than ironic that "while operating costs during the past ten years have been steadily increasing, rates of transportation have been gradually decreasing," to wit he offered the following examples from M&StL's experience: [9]

|  | 1900 | 1910 |
| --- | --- | --- |
| Average rate passenger mile | 2.019¢ | 1.884¢ |
| Average rate ton mile | 1.145¢ | 1.050¢ |
| Taxes | $107,932 | $225,278 |

Freight volumes went up impressively, especially during the second half of the century's first decade, although freight revenue failed to keep up on a percentage basis. Grain continued to dominate for most Minneapolis railroads, and wheat led. Minnesota in 1899 had been foremost among wheat producing states, but by 1909 North Dakota assumed the lead as the wheat culture continued its northwesterly march. The shift in the kind of crops grown was reflected in Lac qui Parle County, in far west-central Minnesota, where wheat production in 1910 was only 53 percent of what it had been in 1900.

---

Wheat moved in great volume to Minneapolis, much of it arriving in single car lots from small stations such as Crooks, South Dakota, on a Great Northern branch near Sioux Falls.

During the same time, however, production of oats doubled, and the corn harvest increased by about 60 percent. Despite these alterations, wheat, as always, moved to Minneapolis in great volume—Milwaukee Road, Great Northern, Soo Line, Omaha, and M&StL usually the leaders in delivery. Coal arrived from pits in Iowa and Illinois, and increasingly from Duluth and Superior, where it had been landed by lake vessels from Illinois and elsewhere.[10]

Lumber remained greatly in demand, but shipping patterns were changing as production at the Minneapolis mills slumped. In 1902, not one mill worked to capacity, owing to a "lack of logs," and as the supply of raw material eroded, companies long established in Minnesota looked southward to East Texas or westward to other great timberlands. James J. Hill told Great Northern shareholders in 1901 that "the timber of Michigan, Wisconsin, and Minnesota will soon be gone. The forests of the state of Washington must hereafter, to an increasing extent, supply the demand for lumber in the prairie states of the Middle West." GN tapped many of those reserves, NP even more. In 1902, NP billed 40,890 carloads of Pacific Coast lumber, up from 29,155 cars the year earlier. After 1905, Minneapolis

was no longer the nation's sawmill center, although at least fifty line yard companies maintained headquarters in the city. Carriers also noted a decline in cordwood shipments to Minneapolis markets as nearby timber stands were exhausted and as customers turned to alternative fuels.[11]

Livestock tonnage exploded during the first decade of the twentieth century, some of it pausing at Minnesota Transfer only for feed, water, and rest before passing on—cattle to Iowa, for example, to be fattened on corn or to Chicago slaughterhouses. Other animals, cattle and swine, were destined for the Union Stockyards at South St. Paul. Promoted by the tall, red-bearded Alpheus B. Stickney and others, Union Stockyards had moved from Minnesota Transfer to its new location in 1887. Ten years later 757,229 animals (cattle, hogs, sheep, horses) passed through its gates. Two years later the number was 980,183, and its management said that 100,000 beefs, 1,000,000 hogs, and 500,000 sheep would be required in 1900 to satisfy trade. By 1916, St. Paul Union Stockyards would rank fifth among the nation's livestock markets. Northern Pacific, Milwaukee, Great Northern, and M&StL usually led in carloads of western cattle delivered to the yards.[12]

As farmers continued their diversification of crops, as they more fully embraced the market economy, and as they pushed westward to practice extensive farming, they also more fully embraced mechanization. Regional offices of McCormick Harvesting Machine Company were established all over the country in the 1880s and 1890s. One of these was at Minneapolis, where machines from the manufacturing plant were assembled and distributed to franchise dealers in the field. McCormick in 1902 merged with Deering & Company to form International Harvester, which turned out a full line of agricultural implements—plows, harrows, seeders, and so on. Others followed suit. One of these, Minneapolis Threshing Machine Company, with a substantial operation at Hopkins, advertised "complete steam threshing outfits." Railroads, of course, provided requisite transportation.[13]

LEFT: A Minneapolis–St. Paul car passes the Lumber Exchange Building (home for important line yard companies) on Hennepin Avenue in 1900. Photograph by Sweet; courtesy of the Minnesota Historical Society.

FACING PAGE: Minneapolis Threshing Machine Company could be counted on to provide prodigious shipments of farm equipment, including entire trainloads such as this one about to depart over the Omaha. Photograph courtesy of the Hennepin History Museum.

Minneapolis became an impressive manufacturing center for items necessary in mechanized agriculture. Railroads eagerly delivered both raw materials and finished goods.

Beer, a beverage central to tastes and traditions of many who settled the upper Midwest, predictably took an important position in the traffic mix of Minneapolis railroads. The city itself was home to major brewers—Gluek Brewing and Minneapolis Brewing among them—but important firms in St. Louis and Milwaukee also found a market locally. So did smaller brewers at Jordan and New Ulm among others. Each one required barley and hops as well as bottles, barrels, and crates, and each one, depending on the size of operation, shipped by the carload, by the barrel, or in case lots to individual customers or to company-owned warehouses or cold storage facilities and then on to retail distribution.[14]

Some of this beer likely was cooled by "natural ice," harvested variously from lakes and streams. During the early twentieth century ice shippers were found at many outlying locations, and most of these forwarded natural ice as opposed to "artificial" (manufactured) ice. Railroads themselves were major customers, moving ice

Locally produced beer was shipped in carloads, by the barrel, and even in case lots to thirsty individuals. Grain Belt is the proud Minneapolis label on several cases unloaded from a Milwaukee Road baggage car at an outlying station. Photograph courtesy of the Minnesota Historical Society.

to central locations for the resupply of refrigerator cars, but greater volumes went for domestic consumption. Lake Riley, between Eden Prairie and Chaska, supplied appreciable tonnage, but Lake Waconia near the community of its namesake, likely provided more. Much of it went to Cedar Lake Ice Company, which had a huge warehouse covering nearly an acre adjacent to the Cedar Lake yards of Great Northern and M&StL. Sawdust, otherwise a little valued by-product of lumber mills, provided packing necessary to see ice through the warm summer months.[15]

Not to be forgotten was a bewildering array of lading billed in less-than-carload-lots (LCL) that moved to and from the city's railroad freight houses: Milwaukee's, being the largest, fronting on Third Avenue South, M&StL's between Third and Fifth Streets North, Great Northern's nearby, and Northern Pacific's a bit to the west. In these could be found everything from caskets to corsets—agricultural implements, furniture, nails, musical instruments, groceries, pumps, cigars, drugs, harness, dry goods, windmills, sewing machines, engines, confectionery, soft drinks, paint, oils, wallpaper,

Ice was harvested in season and stored or shipped for railroad or commercial use. Here is Cedar Lake, near M&StL's Kenwood station. Photograph courtesy of the Minneapolis Public Library, Minneapolis Collection.

desks, brushes, brooms, gloves, shades, molding, washtubs, mirrors, glass, lanterns, linoleum, pitchforks, chain, rope, and much more. Inbound cars from near and far were unloaded, items for local customers given to draymen for delivery, goods for other destination mixed with those of Minneapolis shippers and loaded into cars destined for larger cities—Chicago, St. Louis, Kansas City, and so on—or into "line cars" or "peddler cars" appropriate to serve smaller communities in the state such as Benson, Cambridge, Delhi, New York Mills, and Wabasha, as examples.

Passenger business was similarly strong, but there were changes, particularly pertaining to commuter operation west to Lake Minnetonka. The attractions there remained the same as always: miles of shoreline with clean, sandy beaches and sparkling blue water that invited boating, sailing, fishing, and bathing. Yes, bathing, not swimming, for this era yet reflected Victorian morality when "Milady's attire for bathing included heavy stockings, a parasol, mittens, and a full skirt." The great hotels at Lake Minnetonka were gone or in decline, however. Seasonal "cottagers" were more evident, and the area was increasingly suburban with permanent residents.

The decline and demise of the elegant Hotel Lafayette provided a case in point. James J. Hill at Great Northern recognized the hotel's public relations value, but he kept an unemotional eye on the "bottom line." Results for 1892 were hardly satisfactory—"Not encouraging from any point of view," the hotel's crestfallen manager admitted to Hill at the end of the season. Indeed, expenses exceeded

LEFT: Minneapolis railroads hauled huge volumes of LCL freight, much of it billed to or consigned from the City Market area of the city. Photograph by Sweet; courtesy of the Minnesota Historical Society.

ABOVE: A large percentage of LCL tonnage to and from the Minneapolis area flowed through CM&StP's freight house on Third Avenue near the passenger depot. In the background to the left beyond Milwaukee's freight house are tracks of Minneapolis Eastern and M&StL as well as the gigantic west-side milling district. Photograph courtesy of the Minneapolis Public Library, Minneapolis Collection.

revenue by $14,598.52, and that, Hill groused, was "no improvement on former years." Moreover, concluded the hotel manager, "It is no exaggeration to say that to satisfy the public and at the same time make a favorable financial exhibit is a problem hard to solve." The famous Hotel Lafayette burned in 1897, and Hill likely felt relieved, although he did not immediately rule out the possibility of rebuilding on that location. By 1899, though, his mind was fixed on the matter. "The lake business has never paid any profit," he said in response to one inquiry. He was more expansive a bit later. "This summer business is not as advantageous to a steam railway as is generally supposed. . . . In dollars and cents, it does not amount to as much as a very small station in the country." In the end, Hill declared, "We do not intend to build a hotel at Minnetonka."[16]

Minneapolis & St. Louis took a more optimistic approach—at least in the short run. Its service—six local trains to Minnetonka points during the summer of 1900 to meet seasonal demand, and two trains to Excelsior (plus through runs to the west) during the winter of 1904 to handle volumes not affected by seasonal swings—reflected as much. Fares were reasonable: 50¢ one way, or $9.00 for a fifty-ride ticket. And during the first five years of the new century M&StL spent lavishly to make its facilities at Minnetonka points

attractive and efficient. In 1902, for example, a new pavilion, sidewalks, and "arc" lighting were authorized at Tonka Bay. And the depot was painted. M&StL, as it had for years, scheduled extra trains to accommodate demand on the Fourth of July in 1907. "Large, roomy cars, and seats for all," promised the Passenger Department. But the bloom was off. The great steamers were gone from the lake, replaced by smaller craft. Gone, too, of course, was the Lafayette as well as the Hotel St. Louis. M&StL carried the Lake Park Hotel on its books with a value of $17,869, but the enterprise typically turned in net losses. Early in the new century it was disposed of to Thomas Lowry, the Twin Cities streetcar magnate, who earlier had taken a half-interest in the place, and who would continue to operate it through 1911. For that matter, Lowry pushed his streetcar network to Lake Minnetonka in 1906, and on October 1, 1907, M&StL threw in the towel, leasing its 1.4-mile Tonka Bay branch to the Minneapolis & St. Paul Suburban Railroad, which electrified

James J. Hill gave up on the hotel business at Lake Minnetonka, but steamboats continued to call at Great Northern's Wayzata station, and the railroad continued to run accommodation trains to that location. Photograph by Sweet; courtesy of the Minnesota Historical Society.

the line, giving it access to Wildhurst and the Lake Park Hotel. Milwaukee Road, which as recently as 1900 had scheduled six round-trips daily between Minneapolis and Lake Minnetonka, pulled out about the same time.[17]

M&StL's Anson B. Cutts, in charge of passenger sales, was likely saddened by what had come to pass at Lake Minnetonka, but he was undaunted. Cutts was ingenious in promoting popular excursions (much to the chagrin of the Western Passenger Association, whose other members in 1907 wanted to kill them) and in soliciting all sorts of special movements. The "Popular Excursion" of October 13, 1906, to Minneapolis and St. Paul from Des Moines and intermediate stations up M&StL's line to Fort Dodge was typical. Round-trip coach fares from Des Moines, $4.50; "double berth accommodating two people" in tourist sleeping cars an additional dollar. What to do in the Twin Cities? Visit area lakes or Minnehaha Falls, "see the largest flour mills in the world," tour the state capitol in St. Paul ("erected at a cost of over $4,000,000"), or head to the many theaters. The weary conductor on one crowded extra train from Watertown, South Dakota, in October 1906 turned in 1,013 excursion tickets purchased at stations on that line. Another of Cutts's favorites focused on civic responsibility. "Visit the Legislature" was his routine admonition whenever solons were in session. The annual Minnesota State Fair was also an attractive target. Other special movements were innumerable and included the usual stream of groups heading from the Twin Cities to Waconia. These included seven hundred rambunctious (locals thought them riotous) *Minneapolis Journal* newsboys in 1907 and presumably more decorous Brown & Bigelow salesmen in 1911. Jordan's Schultz & Hilgers Park near the brewery remained a popular destination for excursion groups, in the summer of 1907 drawing the Blacksmiths of Minneapolis, the German Benevolent Societies, and the Colored Elks of Minneapolis among others. A growing prohibitionist sentiment stalking the countryside forced the Sunday closing of Jordan's several saloons, which threw a damper on Sunday excursions, but many groups circumvented do-gooders by scheduling Saturday outings. And extra coaches were added to regular trains when the State University of Iowa played Minnesota in football at Minneapolis.[18]

Among the region's railroad leaders, none cast a longer shadow than James J. Hill—the "Colossus of the Railroad World," as one admirer put it, or the "Empire Builder," as he was popularly known. Hill's accomplishments at Great Northern were undisputed. Nor were in question his indefatigable efforts to improve all sorts of conditions throughout GN's wide territory. Never shy of limelight, Hill was active in political matters (usually behind the scenes) and in any matter bearing on the railroad business. After the death of Edward H. Harriman in 1909, he was arguably the best-known and most widely regarded spokesman for the entire industry. Not surprisingly, myths grew up around the man. Perhaps the most prominent misnomer was that Hill, like a commissar, ruled the affairs of Great Northern and Northern Pacific alike. The joint ownership of Chicago, Burlington & Quincy by GN and NP encouraged that myth as did later joint ownership of Spokane, Portland & Seattle. But after dissolution of Northern Securities, those who owned its stock were issued shares of GN and NP—shares that, in time, were sold in a way that diluted control of NP by Hill and his allies. Certainly by 1910 there was a pronounced cooling in relations between the two St. Paul-based giants—they were thereafter friendly enemies or hostile friends. Nevertheless, the myth lived on that GN, NP, CB&Q, and SP&S were the "Hill Lines." In 1910, NP's domain stretched over 5,814 route miles, and the road tallied gross revenue of $67,820,014 by hauling 18,268,998 tons of freight and 9,639,994 passengers. NP in the same year was about the important business of implementing a huge capital program in Minneapolis—a thirty-stall roundhouse and yard for two thousand cars at Northtown. A year later GN was adding twenty-eight tracks at its Cedar Lake Yard in Minneapolis and received $60,974,996 in total revenue by moving 23,070,655 tons of freight and 8,362,189 passengers over its 7,295-mile domain.[19]

James J. Hill was hardly the only railroad man of the area with national import. A neighbor of Hill's on St. Paul's prestigious Summit Avenue, Alpheus B. Stickney, was best known for fathering what became Chicago Great Western and for his important involvement in sponsoring St. Paul Union Stockyards. But unlike his friend Hill, Stickney consistently and fervently backed government regulations of railroads, promoting his view in book form (*The Railway Problem*, 1891) and otherwise. Another important area railroad personality, Howard Elliott, Northern Pacific's long-serving president, held a great respect for Stickney but sided most assuredly with Hill

James J. Hill's accomplishments at Great Northern were undisputed, as were his efforts to improve conditions throughout the railroad's service area. His son Louis W. Hill is at right, ca. 1911.

on the matter of government regulation. Indeed, Elliott eagerly took the point position for the industry in the Minnesota Rate Case. And there were other important distinctions among the three. While Hill and Stickney represented the now rapidly disappearing era of heroic entrepreneurship, Elliott reflected the age of the professional manager.[20]

Although hardly a member of the local leadership set, Edwin Hawley at M&StL certainly could not be ignored. Hawley was not a professional manager. He more resembled the mold of Hill and Stickney, but unlike them he was also a financier. His trips to Minneapolis on behalf of Minneapolis & St. Louis were surprisingly few, and when he came to see the property, he eschewed opportunity to meet employees, influential public figures, and even important shippers. He was not being aloof; he simply wished to be in the shadows. But he was not disinterested. In 1907, he and a consortium of others gathered control of Chicago & Alton (Alton) and Toledo, St. Louis & Western (Clover Leaf), which, with M&StL and Iowa Central, were commonly referred to as "Hawley Roads." Two years later Hawley and crew disposed of Colorado & Southern to Chicago, Burlington & Quincy at a most handsome profit and then picked up splendid Chesapeake & Ohio, which itself quickly procured a derelict property that it used to gain independent entry to Chicago from the east as well as a direct link to Alton and Clover Leaf (Alton touched Iowa Central at Peoria, Clover Leaf at East St. Louis). A few months later Hawley and friends took control of Missouri, Kansas & Texas, with which Clover Leaf and Alton made head-to-head connection at St. Louis and with which Alton connected at Kansas City. "I buy a railroad just as an individual buys a piece of real estate," Hawley told a writer from the *Saturday Evening Post*. But there was a logic to it. Hawley's curious collection of companies, when taken together, reached from the Great Lakes at Chicago and Toledo to the Gulf of Mexico at Galveston. After Edward Harriman died, *American Magazine* labeled Hawley "the little Harriman" and wondered if he would become the country's new "railroad king." And business and community leaders at Minneapolis wondered what role Minneapolis & St. Louis might play in Hawley's future strategic aspirations.[21]

# THE STRUGGLING GIANT

14

There was a little man
    Had a wooden leg;
Hadn't any money,
    Didn't want to beg.

So he took four spools,
    And an old tin can,
Called it jitney
    And the blamed thing ran.

*THE INDEPENDENT* (1915)

The new decade, the second of the twentieth century, seemed auspicious enough. The national economy was strong, the Dow Jones Industrial Average remained steady, and emigration to the United States continued apace. The Victrola and the vacuum sweeper were part of the domestic landscape, as were hamburgers and hot dogs. Arizona and New Mexico soon would complete the "continental 48 states," and national politics provided both entertainment and excitement. In 1912 the electorate would put Woodrow Wilson in the White House, the first victorious Democrat since Grover Cleveland. And the railroad industry remained dominant across the broad landscape of America.[1]

Not all news was good, sad to say. The country, and indeed the world, was stunned in April 1912 when the British liner *Titanic* went down in the Atlantic, and with it perished persons with real plans (or plans that some sources imagined them to have) for railroad expansion in the United States and Canada.[2]

The loss of wealthy persons on the *Titanic* who were sympathetic to railroad investment was only one element of a growing damper that afflicted the industry. Often well-intentioned but just as often wrongheaded government intervention was another. The Interstate Commerce Act of 1887 actually changed tariffs very little during the decade following. Rather, market forces controlled, and they clearly drove rates downward. Causes for this drop included disorganization within the industry, vigorous competition among the carriers, and the Panic of 1893. Nationwide, the average revenue ton mile slipped from .941 cent in 1890 to .742 cent in 1899. That fact escaped notice of most reformers, who saw only evil in railroads when they sought order out of chaos with traffic-association agreements, and such practices were outlawed by the Supreme Court in the Trans-Mississippi cases of 1897. Additional regulation, intemperately enforced, followed during the Progressive movement as did vicious attacks on mergers. Indeed, the Northern Securities decision so thoroughly discouraged consolidation that the matter would not be quickly revived.[3]

Strengthening competition, Progressives and President Theodore Roosevelt believed, was simply inadequate; they insisted on further expansion of the national railway network *in addition* to further regulation. That feeling among reformers intensified as railroads, caught in a price squeeze the result of increased costs of operation, gradually raised rates after 1900. More restrictive legislation followed in the form of the Elkins Act of 1902 and the Hepburn Act of 1906. Congress was unrelenting. Next came the Mann-Elkins Act of 1910, which revitalized the long- and short-haul clause of the Interstate Commerce Act and empowered the ICC to suspend proposed changes in rates pending investigation as to "reasonableness." And Mann-Elkins also allowed the commission to suspend new rates for up to ten months, with the burden on the carriers to demonstrate "reasonableness." The Panama Canal Act of 1912 gave the ICC jurisdiction over joint rail and water transportation and prohibited railroads from owning coastwise vessels using the canal. A year later came the Railroad Valuation Act, which required the ICC to place a value on all railroad property—the financial history of each line, original cost of it, the replacement cost, depreciation, present value—so that the commission might one day establish rates based on the "real value" of a company's property. The assumption, of course, was that railroads were full of "watered stock" and thus overcapitalized. (The Valuation Bureau would spend twenty years and a public fortune to determine that, with few exceptions, railroads were not overcapitalized, that dividends were not being paid on watered stock, and that railroads were not making excessive returns on investment.) Matters only worsened. The Pujo Committee of the House of Representatives produced a report in 1913 that brooded over the concentration of banking power; two years later another government study warned that America's basic industries were in the clutches of a small number of wealthy and powerful financiers.[4]

All of it reflected the prevailing mood of the Progressive Era. Unfortunately, however, cumulative government involvement put a distinct chill on investors, who increasingly shied away from railroad issues with the result that railroads had to pay more for capital. This in turn caused a growing malnutrition among the nation's railroads and, much worse, as historian Albro Martin has amply demonstrated, drove the spirit of enterprise from the railroad sector. Simultaneous if conflicting demands for increased and faster service along with better equipment, higher compensation for labor, and cheaper rates for transportation were a marvelous prescription for railroad disaster. On the West Coast came a blast from Southern Pacific's venerable Julius Kruttschnitt: "Demagogues and well intentioned though unenlightened reformers," he snorted, together were responsible for the passage of "many unreasonable laws . . . which serve no public good and which add unnecessarily to the cost of operation." William Sproule, another SP executive, tried to put a better face on it. "The era of regulation has definitely arrived," he ruefully admitted; "the principle of regulation is accepted." But, Sproule argued, "the question of what is good in regulation and what is bad in regulation remains debatable." Railroad managers at Minneapolis and across the land would have nodded in agreement.[5]

Close at hand, M&StL's Newman Erb in 1914 estimated that heavy-handed government regulation since 1906 had wiped out $6 billion in the market value of railroad securities. "There is a tendency by both the National and State Governments . . . to press further upon the railroads lower freight and passenger rates and increased expenditures," Erb complained. "This tendency, with the unrestful condition of labor, is retarding the prosperity of the country's transportation systems and must more or less affect their ability to keep pace with the development of the country, and respond effectively to the demands which are ever to be made upon them for new extensions, additional equipment and further improvement in service."[6]

Equity holders and railroad leaders alike chafed at the new environment of private ownership and government control. Labor militancy added another sulfurous element. "No business can be conducted to best results if its managers are prevented from deciding what they will pay for material . . . and what they will receive for its product," M&StL's T. P. Shonts complained in 1911. "Labor organizations seek to control the cost of railroad operations and government officials determine income derived from operations," growled Shonts as he threw up his hands in utter exasperation. And labor's power certainly was growing. The Adamson Act of 1916, as an example, came about when four operating craft brotherhoods demanded federal legislation mandating the eight-hour day, and to prevent a threatened nationwide strike, Congress and President Woodrow Wilson bent to labor's demand. That stunning success emboldened other labor groups to take advantage of liberal support in the nation's capital at a time of growing manpower shortage. Industrial wage disputes had entered politics.[7]

Competition among railroads, naysayers notwithstanding, became acute. Nowhere was this more evident than in business flowing to and from the Pacific Northwest after Milwaukee Road pressed itself all the way to Puget Sound to contest for Chicago–Tacoma/Seattle traffic against already entrenched CB&Q-NP, CB&Q-GN, Soo-CP, and C&NW-UP (central overland route). Milwaukee's entry immediately diluted business volume and had particular impact on Northern Pacific, whose line most closely paralleled the newcomer. After Milwaukee established double daily passenger service between Chicago and Puget Sound via Minneapolis in 1911, NP dolefully admitted that the new trains "naturally took a very considerable proportion of . . . business . . . from Northern Pacific, not only the long-haul through business, but . . . also . . . much intermediate business handled heretofore by the company." In fact, Milwaukee's decision to enter the transcontinental field proved debatable—not only in terms of its own welfare but in terms of the industry at large. One authority would call this former bluest of blue chips "the ulcer of the Northwest."[8]

There were other problems. Opening of the Panama Canal in 1914 had a very clear and deleterious impact on all cross-continent rail business. NP early tried to put a happy face on it, arguing that the "bulk of traffic moving into and out of the ports on either ocean starts from or is destined for, the country's great interior, which the Panama Canal can never reach," acknowledging, however, that "Atlantic and Pacific Coasts will certainly be brought closer together by the canal, and some exchanges of commodities between them can hereafter be effected at smaller cost than heretofore." NP's position was a mixture of caution and defense: "To holders of stock of the transcontinental railways, and especially to the holders of those railways running from the Great Lakes across the northernmost tier of states, to the Pacific Coast, the most important question is, the probable effect of the new route upon traffic of these lines." NP, as it turned out, was overly sanguine. The canal forced rail rates even further downward and caused transcontinental roads to rely more on short-haul and less compensatory traffic. Newcomer Milwaukee Road, likely more than all the others, felt the Panama Canal trauma most severely.[9]

The near modal monopoly that railroads had enjoyed for more than a half century was even more severely eroded by a new transportation technology—the motor vehicle. Indeed, only a few visionaries perceived the astonishing impact that the "horseless carriage" would have on the life and times of the American people—and on the nation's railways. Before the turn of the century, Thompson Wagon Company, Minneapolis Jarless Spring Carriage Company, and Minnesota Carriage & Sleigh were among established area manufacturers of traps, broughams, family carriages, sleighs, and cutters that crowded city streets. Indeed, the local scene was typical of the time. Elsewhere, however, Charles and Frank Duryea, Massachusetts bicycle and toolmakers, in 1892 cobbled together a contraption that was the first gasoline-powered automobile built in the United States. Eight years later found four thousand motor vehicles across the country; but the automobile was merely a high-priced toy, often denounced as the "devil wagon."[10]

Randsom Olds in Detroit nevertheless had gathered up $350,000 in capital to create the first quantity-production plant, and one contemporary observer declared that "potentially . . . [the automobile's] . . . utility is unlimited." After all, he said, "the automobile solves the

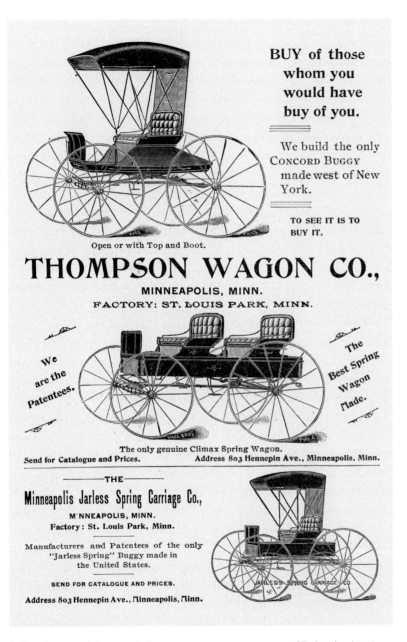

Before the turn of the twentieth century, area newspapers were filled with advertisements featuring locally manufactured carriages and coaches. Small wonder, then, that horse-drawn vehicles clogged city streets.

problem of a portable power adapted to the needs of personal and commercial transportation without the supplementary inconvenience and expense of oats thrice daily, or the limitations of steel tracks and prescribed routes of travel." Another chipped in: "The train is a service. A motor car is a servant."[11]

Nonsense, responded one student in the authoritative *Engineering Magazine* for 1902. "That the automobile has a great future I do not deny," he wrote, but "its chief mission is to change city streets from manure yards to clean thoroughfares." He scoffed at those who contended that "this light locomotive running upon macadam is going to make great inroads on the business of the railways." On the contrary, he predicted, "the automobile, instead of being a menace to the railway, will be a feeder to it." The automobile, he concluded, could not "reach high efficiency on stone roads. It can for pleasure, but not for business."[12]

Most railroaders were at first bemused or supportive of the intruder. Indeed, it became nearly an article of faith among senior managers that a direct and measurable relationship connected the condition of roads and streets and the volume of rail traffic. They asserted that good roads would encourage emigration, help farmers diversify their operations, and in these and other ways benefit railroad prosperity. NP's Howard Elliott, as an example, applauded Minnesota's "progressive policy about good roads," especially in northern reaches of the state, where, he urged, roads should be put down "before the settler comes in." Other forces were more emphatic, lobbying for intercity arteries, Mankato to Minneapolis by way of Faribault as one model. Railroaders may have cringed at that notion, but as early as 1900 many of them were in support of the "good roads movement." Chicago & North Western, Great Northern, and Illinois Central were especially active.[13]

America's love affair with the automobile became quickly pronounced. The number of automobiles registered in the United States jumped to 77,988 in 1905, and a year later a Packard arrived in New York City after a fifty-two-day trek from San Francisco. When M&StL's A. B. Cutts in 1902 took a delegation of local newspapermen to Chicago to show off that road's resplendent *North Star*

*Limited*, the group was met by Illinois Central representatives, who loaded the visitors into automobiles for a tour of the city. Neither Cutts nor the journalists uttered as much as a peep of astonishment as to the use of autos instead of horse-drawn carriages, the motor vehicle already being a routine fixture in their minds. "The Maxwell Touring Car is the aristocrat of moderate priced automobiles"—"not a luxury" advised A. F. Chase, the Minneapolis Maxwell dealer. At $1,450 it was "the greatest value on the market." But Walter G. Benz, another auto dealer in the city, disputed that contention, offering instead "the 1,250.00 Jackson"—"absolutely the strongest two-cylinder built." Northwest Automobile Company, still another vendor, touted Ford Runabouts, Model R without top, for $750, and promised prompt delivery on orders. Northwest in 1907 claimed to have 250 of these vehicles "in customers' hands in the immediate vicinity." Henry Ford would present his famous Model T in 1908, and a year later Ford would produce 19,051 of these "universal cars," priced nominally at $850 per copy. All of it would be reflected locally. Minneapolis in 1907 counted 9,210 horses and 655 autos, new and used motor vehicles were advertised in the classified sections of the city's newspapers, and editors already were clucking over the "lethal speed mania" that had resulted in accidents "claiming its regular quota of victims." And the auto craze was hardly restricted to metropolitan areas like Minneapolis. M&StL, for instance, in 1909 numbered 190 vehicle dealers outside Minneapolis in its mostly rural four-state service area.[14]

Auto fever only increased in its expanse and in its intensity. The *Minneapolis Journal* in 1911 featured an automobile section in its Sunday editions; large advertisements by local dealers were routine. Winton Motor Car Company promoted the Winton Six as "the first self-cranking motor," Ranger Auto guaranteed for life the "Rutenber Motor" in Nyberg autos that it sold, and Northwest Automobile sported Fords at prices from $590 to $900—Model T Touring Cars now down to $690. Elsewhere, $750 would fetch a Hupmobile Runabout, $1,450 an Oakland Model 40 Victoria (top and windshield extra). On the high end, Locomobile "Enclosed Sixes with Ten Inch Upholstery" required $5,500 to $6,250.[15]

Motor wagons—trucks—also were available in several makes and models. Robinson-Loomis sold trucks ("any size required") and contended that the question of quick, inexpensive delivery of payload was solved by the Detroit Motor Wagon with "stake body" and solid rubber tires. It was, said the local dealer, "a snappy, powerful, dependable commercial truck—built 'from the ground up' for one purpose—BUSINESS. Not a 'made-over' touring car constructed from obsolete parts." Price: $670. Northwest KisselKar, however, boasted a full line of KisselKar trucks including thirty-horsepower "light delivery" for $1,750 or a fifty-horsepower "five-ton" at $4,500. Moreover, "the combination of KisselKar standards of manufacturing and construction with a SERVICE contract extending for a period of 1 to 5 years, giving trucks nightly inspection and attention, insures KisselKar owners of efficiency at minimum cost." Initially nothing more than a sidebar to the production of automobiles, the motor truck by 1910 "was standing on its own basis," and as the *Minneapolis Journal* pointed out, was "applicable to the hauling and delivery of every line of business." Already in the Northeast, one firm, Interstate Express, dispatched a four-ton truck daily to haul "express business" between Salem, Massachusetts, and Portsmouth, New Hampshire. And the operator was "making a good living."[16]

A cartoon titled "The First One" in the *Minneapolis Journal* for February 18, 1912, showed a "horseless carriage" coughing down a dirt street cluttered with horses, wagons, barking dogs, and itinerant gawkers, one of whom volunteered to another: "I tell you Jedge, they hain't good fer nuthin' but show purposes." Naysayers like this one remained, true, but the same issue of the *Journal* was crammed with a forty-page supplement celebrating the Annual Automobile Show to be held at the Armory and Auditorium. Open for seven days, "mornings, afternoons and evenings," and including "band concerts, vocalists, and features without number," the focus, nevertheless, very clearly was on the seventy-four makes of automobiles and trucks on display. The Pence Automobile Company alone paid freight bills of $212,000 to bring two hundred rail cars (four fifty-car special trains) of Buicks for the show (Rock Island and Omaha shared in delivery). In the end, dealers inked

$2 million in sales contracts for automobiles alone, mostly in "low-priced cars."[17]

In 1912, 20,000 automobiles were registered in Minnesota; five years later the total would be 180,400. Agitation was keen for a system of intrastate and even interstate roads—Des Moines to Minneapolis, as an example. Not surprisingly, agitation moved public policy. The Federal Highway Act of 1916 obliged all states to establish highway departments, and the Federal Bureau of Public Roads was mandated to cooperate with state agencies in the design and implementation of a coordinated system of highways.[18]

Railroad owners and managers by now were properly perplexed. "There seems to be no limit on the touring range of the automobile," Chicago Great Western's Samuel M. Felton confessed. Moreover, just as the automobile was eroding short-haul passenger traffic, the truck was eating into short-haul and less-than-carload freight. "The radius of motor truck delivery is now well over 30 miles," Felton sighed, "and every mile of improved road the railroads help lay adds to its length and efficiency." Oh yes, Felton might have added, a tiny jitney operation had begun in Minnesota's iron ore country—the earliest predecessor of Greyhound.[19]

There was no gainsaying the impact of motor vehicles on the fortunes of the nation's railways, especially in the passenger-carrying trade. Northern Pacific's passenger count dipped in 1912, prompting senior management to explain to shareholders that there was "little doubt but that the growing use of the automobile has had its effect on the volume of passenger business. The latest figures for registration of automobiles show that . . . there are about one for ever 115 people, and in the states served by your company, one

automobile for about every 90 people. This results in considerable decrease in short travel on the railroad. . . ." Milwaukee Road and Rock Island both experienced similar dips in 1911, Great Northern and Burlington in 1915, Minneapolis & St. Louis and Chicago Great Western in 1916, Soo in 1917. Chicago & North Western and its Omaha surrogate both reported sluggish numbers in the second decade of the century. C&NW, CB&Q, CGW, CRI&P, GN, M&StL, and NP experienced upward bumps in 1919–20, the result of the war, but CM&StP, CStPM&O, and Soo did not. Of all roads serving Minneapolis, CM&StP—in many ways the city's most important carrier—turned in the dreariest numbers for the decade. Despite completing its lengthy appendage to Puget Sound and fleshing out otherwise, Milwaukee saw its boardings drop in 1911 and 1912, turn up slightly in 1913 through 1916, drop again in 1917–18—and continue downward. There would be occasional deviations from this depressing norm over the next years, but the trend seen locally was reflective of the industry nationally, and it would not change. Americans—of whom there were greater numbers each year—preferred

FACING PAGE: Only dreamy-eyed futurists might have contemplated that motor wagons—trucks—soon would contend for shipments like these farm implements moving by rail from the local Minneapolis Steel and Machinery plant to distant destinations. Photograph courtesy of the Minnesota Historical Society.

RIGHT: Short-haul passengers congregating on the platform of Soo Line's suburban Lake Sarah station between Loretto and Rockford were especially susceptible to traveling by automobile rather than rail. Photograph courtesy of the Minnesota Historical Society.

highway transportation, particularly for local needs, over rail. Annual traffic statistics told the tale.[20]

None of this implied, however, that railroad companies fled the field. Indeed, passenger operations remained a central ingredient of American rail operations despite such gloom. And long-haul business especially in sleepers and parlor cars continued to grow. In 1915, gross passenger revenues at Rock Island contributed a full 31 percent of all, 27 percent at Great Northern, and 26 percent at Northern Pacific. Minneapolis passenger terminals remained vibrant—the heart of the city, pumping passengers, mail, and express into the nation's steel rail cardiovascular system. And the beat of that powerful heart continued to set the tempo of life in Minneapolis. When storms delayed the arrival of traveling troupes, for example, Minneapolis burlesque theaters adjusted by staying open later and by substituting "moving pictures" (film delivered earlier by rail).[21]

There would be modest variations over time, but by 1916 nearly all passenger trains of the major roads entering and leaving the city used Milwaukee's stately stub-end station on Third Avenue South or Great Northern's through-track facility on Hennepin Avenue. Milwaukee shared with Rock Island and Soo Line, and GN was host to trains from Burlington, Omaha, Great Western, North Western, and eventually M&StL in addition to its own. Milwaukee's edifice dated from 1898, but GN's was new, opened on January 22, 1914, costing $1.9 million, designed to handle 20,000 passengers daily, featuring 11,540 square feet of waiting area with seating for 240 persons, eleven ticket windows, eighteen telephone booths, a dining room, a barbershop, a newsstand, and even a small infirmary. By the summer of 1916, 174 intercity trains started from, passed through, or terminated at Minneapolis. Per below, the list was impressive.[22] Note that all train numbers are matched by the same number of trains in reverse route, and the numbers in bold are for trains that start or terminate in St. Paul.

| Road | Number of Trains | Destination(s) |
| --- | --- | --- |
| C&NW | 5 | Chicago, Milwaukee, Minneapolis Chicago, Madison, Minneapolis (includes *North Coast Limited* for NP) |
| CB&Q | 3 | Chicago, Minneapolis (includes one West Coast train for GN, one for NP) |
| | 2 | St. Louis, Savannah, Minneapolis |
| CGW | 2 | Chicago, Minneapolis |
| | 2 | Kansas City, Minneapolis |
| | 2 | Omaha, Minneapolis |
| | 1 | Mantorville, Minneapolis |
| | 2 | McIntire, Rochester, Minneapolis |
| CM&StP | 6 | Chicago, Milwaukee, Minneapolis (includes two through trains for Seattle/Tacoma) |
| | 1 | La Crosse, Minneapolis |
| | 1 | Chicago, Dubuque, Austin, Minneapolis |
| | 1 | Calmar, Minneapolis |
| | 1 | Austin, Minneapolis |
| | 1 | Wells, Mankato, Minneapolis |
| | 1 | Deer Lodge, Minneapolis |
| | 2 | Seattle, Tacoma, Minneapolis |
| | 1 | Aberdeen, Minneapolis |
| CRI&P | 1 | Chicago, Minneapolis |
| | 2 | St. Louis, Burlington, Minneapolis (with CB&Q) |
| | 3 | Kansas City, Minneapolis |

| | | |
|---|---|---|
| CStPM&O | 3 | Omaha, Minneapolis |
| | 1 | Sioux City, Minneapolis |
| | 1 | Ellsworth, Minneapolis |
| | 1 | Stillwater, Minneapolis |
| | 2 | Duluth, Ashland, Minneapolis |
| | 1 | Spooner, Minneapolis |
| GN | 1 | Winnipeg, Minneapolis |
| | 1 | Seattle, Minneapolis via St. Cloud |
| | 1 | Melrose, Minneapolis |
| | 1 | Minot, Minneapolis |
| | 1 | Fargo, Minneapolis |
| | 1 | Seattle, Minneapolis via Willmar |
| | 1 | Grand Forks, Willmar, Minneapolis |
| | 1 | Fargo, Willmar, Minneapolis |
| | 1 | Willmar, Minneapolis |
| | 2 | Hutchinson, Minneapolis |
| | 3 | Duluth, Minneapolis |
| | 1 | Sandstone, Minneapolis via Milaca and Anoka |
| M&StL | 2 | Aberdeen, Minneapolis |
| | 1 | New Ulm, Minneapolis |
| | 1 | Peoria, Minneapolis |
| | 1 | St. Louis, Minneapolis via Albia and Wabash |
| | 1 | Des Moines, Minneapolis |
| NP | 2 | Seattle, Tacoma, Minneapolis |
| | 1 | Glendive, Minneapolis |
| | 1 | Fargo, Minneapolis |
| | 1 | Winnipeg, Minneapolis |
| | 1 | International Falls, Minneapolis |
| | 1 | Taylors Falls, Minneapolis |
| | 3 | Duluth, Minneapolis |
| | 1 | White Bear Lake, Minneapolis |

| | | |
|---|---|---|
| Soo Line | **2** | Portal, Minneapolis |
| | **1** | Thief River Falls, Minneapolis |
| | **1** | Winnipeg, Minneapolis |
| | **1** | Chicago, Minneapolis |
| | 1 | Sault Ste. Marie, Minneapolis |
| | 1 | Pembina, Minneapolis |

Some on the above list were upscale name trains proudly showing the flag of the host road. "The passenger service of a railroad is indication, so to speak, of the aristocracy of the line," said one thoughtful observer. Most senior managers agreed. CGW's *Nebraska Limited* was that road's pride and joy between Minneapolis and Omaha, but it had hot competition from CStPM&O's *Omaha-Kansas City Limited*. Competition was, in fact, intense in every corridor. To Duluth, as an example, NP's *Lake Superior Limited* had to contend with GN's *Gopher State Express*, Omaha's *Twilight Limited*, and Soo's ascetically named *Night Train*, plus lesser lights operated by the same companies. Burlington touted its "Mississippi River Scenic Line—Where Nature Smiles Three Hundred Miles" between Minneapolis and Chicago, but Milwaukee's *Pioneer Limited* ignored scenery and continued to dominate overnight business in a passageway ripe with rivalry. CGW remained a contender to Kansas City and Des Moines, but Rock Island's recently completed "short line" gave it advantage to both cities. Those two roads and others, too, had fashionably located city ticket offices on Nicollet Avenue where urban patrons could browse through timetables and promotional materials or gaze at posters proclaiming a particular road's superiority in equipment or service. Several companies prided themselves in onboard dining opportunities. "Special table d'hote service—75¢ luncheon, 75¢ dinner . . . are to be had on all of Great Northern's

FOLLOWING SPREAD: Great Northern's new, broad-shouldered station opened for business in 1914. The approach from above the station was an intricate maze of tracks serving multiple railroads. Photograph on right courtesy of the Minnesota Historical Society.

Milwaukee Road's facility included space for the Travelers' Aid Society, which addressed a range of passenger concerns and problems with thoughtfulness and consideration. Photograph courtesy of the Minnesota Historical Society.

**ABOVE:** Unheralded and working behind the scenes, carmen, coach cleaners, and laundry workers were absolutely essential to make a railroad's intricate passenger operation functional. These Minneapolis-based Pullman employees worked cars assigned to Milwaukee and Rock Island trains. Photograph courtesy of the Hennepin History Museum.

**FACING PAGE:** Milwaukee Road's pride and joy in the highly competitive Chicago–Twin Cities passenger trade was its famous *Pioneer Limited,* due in from the east at 7:50 A.M. Passengers, mail, and express unloaded, a switch engine would then drag the consist to the coach yard, where cars would be inspected, cleaned, restocked, and made ready for the return trip to Chicago at 8:00 P.M. Note the growing congestion on nearby Washington Avenue. Photograph courtesy of the Minneapolis Public Library, Minneapolis Collection.

dining cars"—and these meals included "a choice of soup, a choice of one order of meat, fish or entrée, a choice of two vegetables, a choice of dessert, coffee or tea, and bread and butter," boasted GN. Others were less specific. "Burlington East—Rare Travel Treat. Try 'em on any of our Chicago Limited trains," suggested CB&Q. Burlington also added a touch of class by providing roses for dining cars from a company greenhouse at Aurora, Illinois.[23]

Of all roads serving Minneapolis, however, none had a finer reputation for "famously good food" than Northern Pacific. Indeed, NP was a pioneer in feeding passengers en route—as early as 1883 claiming to be the only transcontinental road "running dining cars of any description." NP supplied its own eggs, milk, and cream from a company-owned farm and stocked its cars with bread, cakes, pies, and French pastry from its own bakery. NP likewise featured food items from its service territory: huge baking potatoes from Idaho, apples from Washington, prunes from Oregon, trout (in season) from Rocky Mountain streams, poultry from North Dakota, dairy

products from Minnesota, and Royal Chinook salmon, saltwater clams, and oysters from the Pacific Coast. Dining on NP's renowned *North Coast Limited* was especially elegant. Moreover, passengers could indulge themselves in tantalizing scenery. "Runs through the Heart of Wonderland," said NP of its feature train on a route styled "The Scenic Highway through the Land of Fortune." To be sure, NP's line in Montana, Idaho, and Washington afforded passengers

spectacular sights. And NP saw to it that the *North Coast*'s equipment matched that splendor. "Electric lighted trains composed of modern Pullman Drawing Room and Compartment Standard Sleeping Cars, Pullman Tourist Sleep Cars (leather-upholstered, 16-section, smoking room), Observation Library Car (with barber and bath), Dining Car and Coaches," boasted a proud NP. In 1911 NP made arrangements with Chicago & North Western to handle the train in and out of Chicago, and on the other end of the route, passengers at Portland could avail themselves of the *S. S. Northern Pacific*, "The Palace of the Pacific," to gain San Francisco.[24]

Northern Pacific was hardly without rivals in the Great Lakes–to–Puget Sound trade. Great Northern's contender was the *Oriental Limited*, and GN took particular pride in reminding that "tickets routed Great Northern means tickets via Glacier National Park" for, indeed, its line did skirt the base of that handsome panorama. "It is no exaggeration to state that the *Oriental Limited* is the fulfillment of inventive genius in train equipment," argued an immodest GN. Dining cars reproduced the atmosphere of an English pub—overhead beams, leather-covered chairs, and "overhead cathedral globes." Like NP, GN contracted to get the *Oriental* in and out of Chicago (for GN over CB&Q), and like NP, GN offered water carriage to destinations beyond West Coast terminals—in GN's case to Japan and China by its cavernous steamships *Minnesota* and *Dakota*.[25]

Latecomer Milwaukee Road in the Puget Sound sweepstakes was not to be denied. It entered the fray with two "All-Steel Transcontinental Trains Daily Over the Short Line between Chicago and Seattle." Of these, Milwaukee's *Olympian* was premier—"Fit for the Gods," argued the road with unabashed enthusiasm. Indeed, *Olympian*'s equipment was furnished on the interior with expensive carved hardwoods; each car was electric-lighted with Mazda lamps. "The West has never had a train approaching in excellence," asserted Milwaukee. And its cuisine rivaled that of NP.[26]

**BELOW LEFT AND RIGHT:** Northern Pacific supplied its own eggs, milk, and cream from a company-owned farm and stocked its dining cars with bread, cakes, pies, and French pastry from its own bakery. It likewise featured food items from its broad service area, especially huge baked potatoes from Idaho.

Observation cars assigned to Great Northern's flagship *Oriental Limited* oozed opulence.

That did not end the list of contestants to the Northwest. After Soo Line tucked Wisconsin Central under its corporate belt to gain Chicago access, it teamed with Canadian Pacific to challenge NP, GN, and Milwaukee with a slower, longer route through the spectacular Canadian Rockies to Vancouver, British Columbia (to Seattle by Canadian Pacific Steamship). Soo's *Pacific Coast Express* was extravagantly appointed as was the custom for such trains. Sleeping cars were slightly larger than standard Pullmans; "no expense has been spared in making these sleepers perfect," claimed Soo. "Safety and Courtesy included with your Ticket," promised the Minneapolis-based carrier. "All cars vacuum cleaned."[27]

"Mobile hotels [passenger trains handling sleeping cars] dart across the country in a stream of light at aeroplane speed on a nonstop schedule," wrote one euphoric observer of the railroad scene in 1915. Perhaps he was thinking of Milwaukee's high-stepping *Pioneer Limited* up from Chicago with a train of heavily laden sleeping cars, or Burlington's *Minnesota Limited*, a similar train hustling the same highly prized overnight business. In any event, sleeping cars in the second decade of the twentieth century were ubiquitous. In 1900, the Pullman Company had 3,006 cars (including diners) in its service, employed 9,308 persons in this branch of its business, and handled 7.1 million patrons, who traveled 274,006,488 miles aboard its equipment. These Pullman cars operated under contract with individual railroads and constituted majority, but some roads—Canadian Pacific, Milwaukee, and Great Northern among them—owned and operated their own cars. Nevertheless, "The World's Greatest Hotel" was an apt description of Pullman.[28]

What was Pullman's customer base? Aboard what one writer called the "narrow precincts of the sleeper" were "city-wise 'traveling men,'" as well as the uninitiated, who often felt compelled to read etiquette books before boarding so that they might be aware of protocols: what clothes to wear, what cosmetics to bring, how to direct the porter, and how to be directed by the porter. One Englishman considered travel by Pullman in the United States an "absolute civilizer [encouraging] social amenities, aesthetic tastes and refinement of life." For men traveling by Pullman, likely the largest constituency, morning brought a solemn ritual in the washroom: shaving, brushing teeth, dressing—no privacy, however.[29]

Minneapolis in 1915 was, of course, an integral element of Pullman's national sleeping car network, in some cases serving as an intermediate stop on through runs, in other instances a place where car lines started or ended. CStPM&O dispatched a Pullman sleeper to Kansas City via Omaha and CB&Q; Rock Island and CB&Q each forwarded cars to Peoria; and Milwaukee, North Western, Great Western, Rock Island, Soo Line, and M&StL (with Illinois Central) all offered overnight service from Minneapolis to Chicago in that constantly frenetic corridor. NP, GN, and Soo each boasted sleepers on night trains to and from Duluth; Rock Island and Great Western

**BELOW LEFT AND RIGHT:** Sleeping cars on Great Northern's *Oriental Limited* were a blend of Pullman and company owned. Photographs courtesy of Burlington Northern Santa Fe.

both ran Minneapolis–Kansas City sleepers; CGW and CStPM&O carried cars to Omaha; M&StL (with Wabash), Rock Island (with CB&Q), and CB&Q all handled cars to St. Louis; GN and Soo vied for overnight business to Winnipeg; and CGW, M&StL, and CRI&P sent cars to Des Moines. Other car lines included:[30]

| Omaha/C&NW | Minneapolis–Milwaukee, Wisconsin |
| Omaha | Minneapolis–Sioux City, Iowa |
| | Minneapolis–Mitchell, South Dakota |
| | Minneapolis–Huron, South Dakota |
| | Minneapolis–Redfield, South Dakota |
| CM&StP | Minneapolis–Milwaukee, Wisconsin |
| | Minneapolis–Aberdeen, South Dakota |
| M&StL | Minneapolis–Aberdeen, South Dakota |
| | Minneapolis–Fort Dodge, Iowa |
| NP | St. Paul-Minneapolis–Bemidji, Minnesota |
| | St. Paul-Minneapolis–International Falls, Minnesota |
| | St. Paul-Minneapolis–Jamestown, North Dakota |
| | St. Paul-Minneapolis–Fargo, North Dakota |
| Soo Line | Minneapolis–Montreal, Quebec (with Canadian Pacific) |
| | Minneapolis–Harvey, North Dakota |
| | Minneapolis–Oakes, North Dakota |

Pullmans mixed with sleepers owned by Great Northern on the 2,262-mile run of the *Oriental Limited* from Chicago through Minneapolis to Portland (CB&Q, GN, SP&S), and that train or other of GN trains also carried individually assigned sleepers to Seattle, Spokane, Butte, Minot, Crookston, Grand Forks, Fargo, Aberdeen, and Yankton. NP's through trains from Chicago likewise handled Portland and Seattle cars as well as one to Gardiner, Montana (Yellowstone Park), and Soo joined with Canadian Pacific to move sleepers through Minneapolis to Seattle and Vancouver from Chicago. For its part, Milwaukee provided long-distance cars from Chicago to Seattle, Tacoma, and Portland (with Union Pacific).[31]

Fortunately for railroad companies, demand for long-distance travel continued to increase even as local business waned. And not surprisingly, the carriers did all they could to encourage it. "Passengers at Minneapolis and Duluth may occupy sleeping cars at 8:00 P.M. and remain there until 9:00 A.M.," promised Soo Line. "Tourist Sleeping Car, leather upholstered, with range and smoking-room" was a proud feature of Northern Pacific's *North Coast Limited*. Railroads predictably relied on a regular flow of business travelers to fill the cars, but they also targeted discretionary travelers with endless enticing advertising in Minneapolis newspapers. "No Minnesota Business Man or Woman Can Afford to Go Without a Vacation," admonished Rock Island. "Try Colorado this summer and via Rock Island's *Rocky Mountain Limited*—Daily to Denver, Colorado Springs, and Pueblo" (connection from Minneapolis at Des Moines). Burlington promoted interline "Excursion Fares for Summer Vacation to New York, Boston, and Other Eastern Resorts from Minneapolis via Burlington's Famous Mississippi River Scenic Line and Chicago," and in 1912 it teamed with Illinois Central for a special train to New Orleans and the steamer *Atenas* for seven days in Panama. "Ample time to visit New Orleans and the South. $135 round trip, including ten days meals and berths on steamer." Chicago Great Western ("Emphasize the 'Great'") also promoted vacation fares to points near and far. "Eastern Circle Tours—Go One Way, Return Another," urged CGW. "Variety is the rule in Great Western tours." Northern Pacific contended that "The Best Fishing and Shooting Grounds in Minnesota" were reached by its lines. "Spend your vacation at one of these places—in hotel, cottage, or tent—fishing, boating, bathing, canoeing, etc.," suggested NP. But that road also urged travel in season to Yellowstone National Park ("America's only Geyserland and our largest National Playground") convenient to NP. After it electrified 440 miles of transcontinental line over the Belt, Rocky, and Bitterroot Mountains ("no smoke, no cinders, just smooth, clean travel on trains traditional for excellence of their service"), Chicago, Milwaukee & St. Paul reminded that "the glories of Puget Sound Country and Rainier National Park await you at journey's end." During hot and sultry Minneapolis summers, Great Northern shrewdly confirmed that "snowballing" in the passes of Glacier Park was "a midsummer sport." Glacier Park, said GN, "has the Alpine Grandeur of Switzerland—on a far *bigger* scale"—all reached most conveniently by its trains. "Modern hotels, Alpine chalets, Tepee camps. Vacation $1 to $5 per day." Soo Line understandably focused its advertising on Canadian Rocky Mountain resorts at Banff, Lake Louise, Glacier, and Field, but it also urged Minneapolitans not to "forget the hundreds of nearby summer resorts only a few hours away on its lines."[32]

Glacier National Park was a favorite advertising target for Great Northern, which served the park directly. "You can freshen up there," said GN.

Excursions and special trains to and from Minneapolis remained in vogue, although not the staple of the past, reflecting, no doubt, inroads made by the automobile. Minneapolis & St. Louis, with a highly restricted route structure that yielded few long hauls and one especially vulnerable to vehicular competition, continued to lead in excursion activity. The irrepressible Anson B. Cutts remained in charge of M&StL's passenger service. In 1913 he thanked local agents for their good efforts in the year previous but wondered, "Don't you think we can do a little better in 1913?" It was vintage Cutts. He was, as always, at his best in promoting special movements and special trains. In 1913, M&StL arranged special movements for the Methodist General Conference Committee to its Minneapolis convention, and the St. Olaf College choir to the Twin Cities for concerts. One of the more unusual excursions in 1914 required special trains from that road's several Iowa branches bound for Minneapolis—rates extraordinarily attractive, $4.00 from points on the Newton Branch, for example. Another dollar purchased double bedroom space one way in Pullman tourist cars. Rates from Iowa stations had been equally attractive in 1913 for a special train taking football fans to Minneapolis for a contest between the University of North Dakota and the University of Minnesota. And several sections were required in 1916 to move the First Regiment of the Minnesota National Guard to active duty along the Mexican border.[33]

Not likely found on excursion or special trains but ubiquitous in "dusting the cushions" on locals and limiteds alike was the traveling salesman, "drummer," or "knight of the grip." Most were in the employ of manufacturers or wholesale houses whose businesses had expanded with the railroad; their number nationally increased by a factor of six between 1880 and 1920. Minneapolis and St. Paul together put five thousand "knights of the grip" on the road in 1915. The drummer was usually a "live wire" who seemed to know the latest slang, the latest song, the newest dance, was attired in the latest style of dress, and was known as a ladies' man. He was also a link to the great outside world—a man who "knew the territory," as Meredith Willson put it in the *Music Man*. Minneapolis drummers usually crafted circular itineraries designed to get them home by the weekend. By working westbound on M&StL, for example, a salesman could make calls at hamlets such as Young America, Green Isle, Echo, Wood Lake, and Hanley Falls, catching Great Northern to Granite Falls, and then moving eastward on Milwaukee to make calls at Sacred Heart, Bird Island, and Brownton before arriving home on Friday evening or Saturday morning.[34]

The railroad was centerpiece for any drummer. He left from and arrived back at large urban terminals, he detrained and reboarded at country depots, his sample trunks were unloaded from the train's baggage car and drayed to display rooms at a town's small hotel or directly to local merchants, drayed back to the depot where the salesman rebilled them, wired his orders to headquarters, bought a ticket, and moved on to his next destination—a routine practiced to great efficiency.[35]

The goods ordered by a small-town merchant through the traveling salesman may soon have arrived at the local depot by express—Adams Express, Wells Fargo, or another depending on the road and its express contract. Distilled spirits, wine, and even beer in small lots were among a profusion of items handled by express companies during this time. Magazines such as the *Saturday Evening Post* in bulk, precious metals, specie or paper money, dressed game and fowl in season, Coca Cola syrup in cases, fresh fruits and vegetables, baked goods, cheese, milk, cream, cut flowers, and even race horses in carload lots were expedited by passenger trains. Newspapers were yet another

Echo, west of Minneapolis on M&StL, was one of innumerable stations called on by "knights of the grip" throughout the Minneapolis hinterland during the age of railways.

# MONITOR

## PRESS DRILLS, HOE DRILLS
### AND SEEDERS.....

The Manufacturers are in touch with the West—know what it wants and can
supply promptly the most successful Press Drills, Hoe Drills and
Seeders made. **Send for Catalogue and Prices.**

These Machines excel in lightness of draft and perfect work, and are
manufactured in all desirable sizes.

*THE MONITOR PIPE FRAME PRESS DRILL HAS AUTOMATIC TRANSFER
OF PRESSURE. CLOSED HEEL SHOES, THAT DO NOT LOSE ANY
OF THE ADVANTAGES THE OPEN HEEL MAY HAVE.
THE SHOES AND ROLLERS ARE INDEPENDENT. PRESSURE COVERING
ROLLERS CAN BE SUBSTITUTED FOR COVERING CHAINS.*

The Monitor can put seed in hard packed soil where no other Shoe Drill can.
Perfect Grass Seed Sowers are sent as an attachment. The Monitor is absolutely the best, and Manufactured within your own State.

## Monitor Manufacturing Co., MINNEAPOLIS, MINNESOTA.

Monitor Manufacturing likely was one of the many Minneapolis firms employing
traveling salesmen to canvass the territory hustling orders.

example—the *Minneapolis Journal, Minneapolis Tribune*, and others dispatched in bulk to outlying communities in every direction.[36]

Among the very best of express company customers were mail-order houses, Montgomery Ward, the first of them beginning in 1872,
and then the even more aggressive Sears, Roebuck & Company, which
began business in 1887. Its catalog—"the silent salesman"—presented
everything from accordions to windmills, boric acid to yarn.[37]

If railroads provided the conduit for delivery of goods from
Sears, Roebuck and other firms large and small, they also provided
the means to order from them. Urgent matters might go by telegraph, but the vast majority of messages were letters and cards handled by the U.S. Post Office Department, which in turn contracted
with railroads to haul the mail. Railway Post Office (RPO) car routes
provided en route sorting of mails on nearly all lines operated by

The Railway Mail Service was an intricate, efficient, and reliable means of moving
the country's mail. En route sorting aboard Railway Post Office cars such as this one
attached to a Milwaukee Road passenger train was a central ingredient. The clerk
in the far background is sorting newspapers; others worked letter mail. Photograph
courtesy of the Minnesota Historical Society.

railroad companies serving Minneapolis and were part of an extremely intricate and very efficient national web that connected major metropolitan hubs with every village and hamlet—and after full implementation of Rural Free Delivery, begun late in 1896 and gradually accomplished, every nook and cranny of the country. RPO cars attached to passenger trains heading into or leaving from Minneapolis stations fed or received first-class (letter) mail and second-class (individually addressed magazines and newspapers) to or from "all lines diverging." RPO cars were assigned to specific passenger trains of every railroad with lines between Minneapolis

and Chicago, but Milwaukee Road's Chicago & Minneapolis (RPO designation identified head-out and terminal points, not railroads) dominated. Mail was shared when two or more roads served common points, Minneapolis–Des Moines, for instance, where M&StL, CRI&P, CGW, and Omaha/C&NW all vied for business. To the west, depending on the year, NP or GN handled the bulk of mails to Puget Sound. Mails for Canada typically moved west to Canadian RPO routes (GN and Soo to Noyes, Minnesota, NP to Pembina, North Dakota, or Soo to Portal, North Dakota), and east via Chicago and Detroit or by Soo Line to Sault Ste. Marie. St. Paul was a much larger mail hub than Minneapolis, and more RPO lines started and ended there, but Minneapolis was extremely important, with cars heading out on or coming in to terminate on rails of CGW, CRI&P, M&StL, Omaha, and Soo and occasionally even GN, Milwaukee, and NP.[38]

Express companies routinely handled live animals, including race horses, but Dan Patch had his own car eagerly provided by the Omaha. Photograph courtesy of the Hennepin History Museum.

# Mixed Blessings

The demand for the service of transportation is at all times a derivative of the contemporaneous output of general industry. Only to the extent that things are being produced and consumed, are being bought and sold, is there an effective demand for their transport.

*The Nation, June 22, 1932*

The United States was greatly changed during the five decades following its Civil War. At the end of that awful conflict there was no transcontinental railway; by the end of the century there were multiple options, and the nation's rail net was fully integrated. In 1860 whale oil was the chief illuminant, and it was in scarce supply; kerosene was its replacement, and by 1879 Standard Oil held 95 percent of American refining capacity and controlled the bulk of the world market in refined petroleum. In 1867 total domestic production of steel was a paltry 2,600 tons; in 1901 United States Steel became the country's first billion-dollar corporation. Tinkers/entrepreneurs Thomas Edison and George Westinghouse perfected reasonably priced lightbulbs, transformers, and generating stations to usher in the era of applied electricity, and by 1900 the telephone was in general use throughout the business community. After the census of 1890, government bureaucrats determined that there was no longer a definable frontier line across the country's broad landscape—the promise of manifest destiny delivered, the continent conquered.

Dramatic surges in immigration—8,795,386 in the ten-year period 1901–10 alone—coupled with increased native birth rates drove the national population to 91,972,266 in 1910, up from 75,994,575 in 1900. The number of Italians living in New York City in 1890 exceeded the population of Naples; Chicago's population in 1900 was 1.7 million, three-quarters foreign born. America's transformation from a society and economy rural and agricultural to one increasingly urban and industrial was astonishing in its rapidity. In 1870 Great Britain produced one-third of the world's finished goods; by 1900 that had dropped to one-fifth—the United States and Germany challenging, and this in the face of increased annual British production. And in 1898 the United States declared itself to imperialism with the concomitant need to defend its empire with a powerful navy.[1]

Railroads—agents of profound change across the broad national fabric—now found themselves increasingly subjects of change. The steamcar civilization, the age of railways, was passing. So was the era of heroic entrepreneurship. John D. Rockefeller no longer was

active in management of Standard Oil, and Andrew Carnegie was gone from steel. Among railroad titans, death claimed Edward H. Harriman in 1909, and James J. Hill—the renown "Empire Builder"—in 1916. Gone, too, was William Drew Washburn, a man active in local railroad matters since the 1860s. "He was always in the forefront with those laboring for the material prosperity and moral uplift of the State and City in which he made his home," declared fellow directors of Soo Line upon his death in July 1912. And those directing the affairs of Minneapolis & St. Louis had been shocked on February 1 of that year when they learned of the sudden death of Edwin Hawley.[2]

Hill before his death had handed over primary responsibility for management at Great Northern, and Washburn long since had done the same at Soo, but Hawley was thought to have expansive plans for M&StL and other roads under his umbrella. M&StL had been the city's early favorite, the home road, but its record over the years had been mixed. Small wonder Minneapolis cheered when rumors swirled as to Hawley's plans for expansion. What of those plans following his death? In 1911, Hawley had announced merger of M&StL with Iowa Central to give the Minneapolis road a 488-mile main line to Peoria, Illinois (amalgamation accomplished in 1912), and New York news tickers bristled with reports that M&StL then would build northward to the international boundary to connection with a Canadian road, and southward to St. Louis and thus make truth of "Minneapolis and St. Louis." Withal, Hawley would have, taken with his Missouri, Kansas & Texas at St. Louis, a system stretching all the way from Canada to the Gulf of Mexico. But Hawley's unexpected death put an end to these and other plans. M&StL lurched into an uncertain future.[3]

Others were more successful in bucking a growing hesitation among financial institutions toward railroad investment. Soo Line

continued to perfect terminal facilities in the Twin Cities, added auxiliary lines to the north and west, and through a complicated arrangement in 1908 took control of Wisconsin Central to give it entrance to Milwaukee and Chicago and at the same time make possible, with Canadian Pacific, passenger operation from Chicago through Minneapolis to Vancouver and other points on the North Pacific Coast. Great Northern continued fleshing out its domain in Minnesota and the Dakotas during the first decade of the new century, and 233 miles in North Dakota during the next decade. Northern Pacific was equally active in putting down track tributary in some way to Minneapolis—333 miles in North Dakota during the years 1910–20.[4]

Of all railways serving Minneapolis, Chicago, Milwaukee & St. Paul was the most aggressive in expansion. CM&StP's construction during the initial decade of the century was an amazing 738 miles in Minnesota and the Dakotas (some of it as part of the Pacific line), and another 299 miles in the Dakotas in the ten years following. Close at hand, Milwaukee Road in the years 1912–16 also was engaged in a monumental project to carve a nearly 3-mile channel for its route west out of Minneapolis paralleling 29th Street. This required excavation by steam shovel for a cut averaging 22 feet in depth—crossed by thirty-seven municipal streets on reinforced concrete bridges. Waste was removed by twenty-five-car work trains to Bass Lake Yard, used as fill to enlarge Milwaukee's important receiving yard for western grain. About five hundred men were employed on the Minneapolis project alone.[5]

CM&StP gave permanent employment to an even larger force at its substantial South Minneapolis shops. In 1881, the company had acquired some seventy acres of land upon which to erect facilities valued at $250,000 and, the Minneapolis Board of Trade proudly announced, "giving employment to 1,500 mechanics." Nearby stood a twenty-four-stall roundhouse—eventually expanded to forty-six stalls—and employing another four hundred men. Still other persons found jobs at Milwaukee's freight houses or fruit house, in train or engine service, as telegraphers, dispatchers, track laborers, clerks, helpers, coach cleaners, porters, mail handlers, ticket agents,

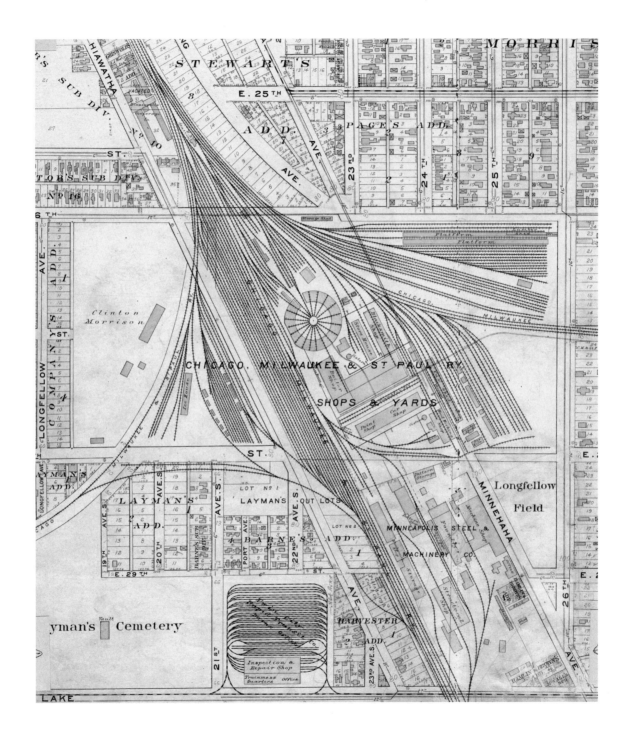

salesmen, managers, or the myriad of other tasks required by railroads at the time.[6]

Minnesota did not succumb to the electric traction or interurban fever that swept Iowa, Illinois, Indiana, and other states, although there were occasional symptoms. The grandiose Minneapolis, Kansas City & Gulf Electric Railway got a lot of attention early in the century with its proposed "double-tracked" route from Minneapolis to Galveston, but it predictably failed to birth. The Mesaba Electric Railway enjoyed brief life with service between Hibbing and Gilbert, as did St. Paul Southern between Inver Grove and Hastings. More durable was Minneapolis, Anoka & Cuyuna Range, which in 1913 linked Anoka with Minneapolis; when it electrified in 1915, cars ran into downtown over streetcar rail. Better known was the Minneapolis, St. Paul, Rochester & Dubuque Electric Traction Company—"The Dan Patch Electric Railroad"—which promoter M. W. Savage (owner of the famous race horse) in 1911 postured as "the great People's Railroad." Dan Patch was never electrified, however, and never got beyond Northfield, 45 miles south of Minneapolis. (It did forge a 10-mile branch that protruded from 54th Street through Bloomington to Auto Club.) Savage actively solicited passenger business—offering fifty-four-coupon commutation books at a one-third reduction compared to regular one-way fares. The road eventually evolved into Minneapolis, Northfield & Southern. Elsewhere, W. L. and E. D. Luce spawned the Electric Short Line Railway, which pushed west from Minneapolis in 1914–15 to Winstead

FACING PAGE: Milwaukee Road's huge south Minneapolis repair and service complex employed hundreds of people. Map from *Atlas of Minneapolis, Hennepin County, Minnesota* (Minneapolis: Minneapolis Real Estate Board, 1914); courtesy of the Minneapolis Public Library.

BELOW: Milwaukee Road in the years 1912–16 was engaged in a monumental project to carve a nearly 3-mile channel parallel to Twenty-ninth Street for its route west out of Minneapolis. Today this corridor has found new use as the Midtown Greenway, a bicycle and pedestrian trail connecting the chain of lakes with the Mississippi River. Photograph by Charles J. Hibbard; courtesy of the Minnesota Historical Society.

RIGHT: Nels Anderson was one of several hundred people employed by Milwaukee Road at its impressive shop and terminal properties near Lake and Hiawatha. Photograph courtesy of the Hennepin History Museum.

and Hutchinson. The "Luce Line" shared facilities with "Dan Patch" at Seventh Street and Third Avenue North. It was neither electrified nor profitable, evolving into Minnesota Western and later extending modestly to Clara City and Gluek.[7]

"Booming" is the word that characterized traffic on Twin Cities Rapid Transit, which carried 39.6 million revenue passengers in 1897, 146.9 million in 1910. By 1914 the company operated 412 miles of route serving a territory "16 miles north and south—48 miles east and west" from Stillwater and White Bear Lake on the east through St. Paul and Minneapolis to Deephaven, Excelsior, and Tonka Bay on the west. The firm also operated "streetcar boats" (painted yellow like the trolleys) that called at Deephaven, Excelsior, and Wildhurst docks on schedules coordinated with cars to and from Minneapolis. Weekday excursions in season "including a trolley ride and trip on

famous Lake Minnetonka all for 75 cents from Minneapolis," promised the company. "Take the family—make a day of it." For that matter, it reminded, "Chartered cars and steamboats for private picnic parties."[8]

Some of those persons riding the city's streetcars were in town for a few hours or a few days before heading north or west to seek new residence. "There are big opportunities waiting for you in the Great Northwest," counseled Great Northern in 1912—"chances to build up an independent home on the farms and in the towns and cities of a new and growing country, chances to bring up your children in a land where they can grow and prepare without breaking home ties and find their chances." For its part, Minneapolis & St. Louis continued to promote development along its lines in South Dakota. "The

---

**RIGHT:** Dan Patch was never electrified and never got beyond Northfield, but it had staying power, eventually emerging as Minneapolis, Northfield & Southern.

**BELOW:** Twin Cities Rapid Transit streetcars met the Dan Patch at a station near Nicollet Avenue and Fifty-fourth Street. The company's delivery trucks also met the trains at that location to provide expeditious multi-modal express and freight service. Photograph from the collection of Aaron Isaacs.

farmers of this territory have grown rich," said M&StL. "They have proved the character of the soil, they are all rich and contented." Every road offered free literature of one type or another. Milwaukee Road prepared a pamphlet detailing how homesteads might be acquired, the location of land offices, the cost of homesteading, and hints of value to prospective settlers. "The City Man on a Farm" was one of the many folders provided by Rock Island; "How to Manage a Farm" was another. "Emigrants' Moveables" rates were offered by most roads. "One man will be passed one way with one or more cars of settlers goods, provided the car contains horses, mules, cattle, hogs or sheep," promised Chicago, Burlington & Quincy. "No return pass given."[9]

Northern Pacific was particularly aggressive in colonization efforts. Its immigration agent reported 19,810 requests for information in a twelve-month period from 1910 into 1911, and he distributed 181,940 pieces of promotional literature during the same time. NP worked diligently with large groups and small alike. It took pleasure, as an example, in courting the Augustana Swedish Lutheran Synod in 1914 when that body declared itself to an enthusiastic colonization plan of its own to acquire large tracts of land in Minnesota and the Dakotas for the purpose of "establishing Swedish communities

ABOVE: Minneapolis, Anoka & Cuyuna Range in 1913 linked Anoka with Minneapolis, electrified its operation two years later, and ran frequent cars, to the delight of local patrons. Photograph courtesy of Aaron Isaacs.

BELOW: The Luce Line was functional, if hardly elegant. The company's yards were near Second Avenue North and Bassett's Creek. Much of the company's present right of way is currently the Luce Line State Trail, a popular recreational trail in the western suburbs of Minneapolis. Photograph from the collection of Aaron Isaacs.

thereon and build churches as centers of each community." A year earlier NP handled 684 "immigrant outfits" to points on its lines in Minnesota, up from 466 in 1912, and the company rejoiced when 363 movements occurred in only the first three months of 1914. But Great Northern moved an even greater number of outfits to communities on its Minnesota lines in 1914, a source of acute vexation at NP, which consoled itself modestly by noting GN's greater mileage in the state and by observing that "Great Northern had more men working immigration than we have had." Two years later GN dryly reported that "the coming of settlers into the territory adjacent to this Company has continued, principally into Minnesota, North Dakota, and Montana." M&StL in the same year announced that "revenue from South Dakota homeseeker travel amounted to approximately $18,000 for the year."[10]

It was not simply adequate to populate a road's service territory, railroad managers understood. Persons going into tributary lands needed to be productive—in that way generating traffic essential for a company's financial health. Carriers thus continued to embrace a plethora of programs to enhance that productivity. Self-interest, to be sure, benign self-interest, railroaders recognizing the very tight symbiotic relationship between the road and its service area. If customers suffered financial malady, so did the carriers; if customers prospered, so did the carriers. "I represent a business which is closely associated with the best development of agriculture and is much interested in doing all it can in reason to promote that great business," said NP's Howard Elliott in 1912. NP, he said, was dedicated to "the development and use of the land, of which much that should yield today a comfortable income and offer a healthful life to settlers is still unused, and much of which, sad to say, is unwisely and inefficiently used." James J. Hill at Great Northern concurred. In an address at the 1906 Minnesota State Fair, Hill admonished that the first step in guaranteeing the nation's future was "to realize our dependence on the cultivation of the soil," to rotate crops and to enrich the soil in ways that would provide "food for multitudes." Railroads were active on several fronts. Soo Line gave subscriptions to *Hoard's Dairyman* to selected farmers along its routes; Soo, Omaha, and C&NW provided "Land Clearing Trains" with stump-pulling machines and dynamite to show how cutover land could be made ready for the plow; GN gave cash awards for good farming technique in each congressional district of Minnesota and the Dakotas; NP and GN sponsored demonstration plots to study agricultural potential; GN promoted scientific methods of raising sheep; and Soo, GN, and NP contributed money to provide agricultural agents for individual counties. NP's "Better Farming Special" of 1910 was especially memorable, drawing about 20,000 persons in North Dakota alone. "Davenport, Lisbon, Maddock, Turtle Lake, Goodrich, and McHenry . . . greeted the train with such throngs that the utmost capacity of the train itself and of the lecturers was taxed," reported *The Farmer: A Journal of Agriculture* in a glowing tribute.[11]

Just as it was necessary for railroads to protect and nurture their rural and agrarian constituents, so, too, was it essential to look to the welfare of urban customers. What railroads hoped for, of course, was prosperity in both sectors—loads in both directions, wheat, for example, inbound to Minneapolis, and flour outbound, or lumber outbound and wheat inbound. The deterioration of the local lumber milling industry put a crimp in that calculus, however. After a slump in the mid-1890s, Minneapolis hit her stride again, and in 1899 exceeded all previous production records to establish itself as the leading lumber market of the world. All carriers profited therefrom to

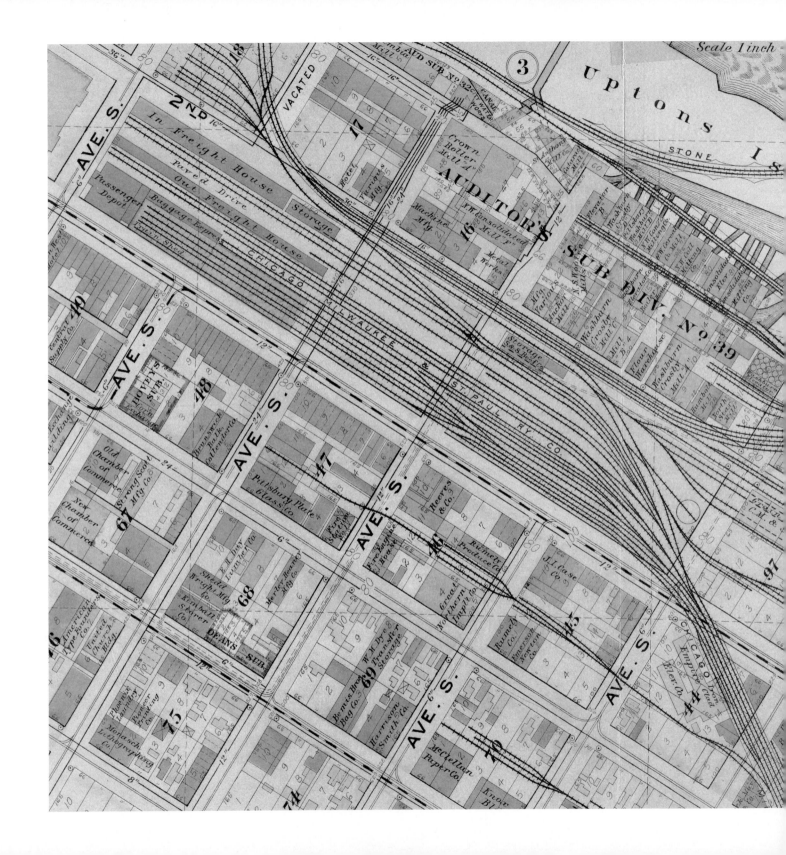

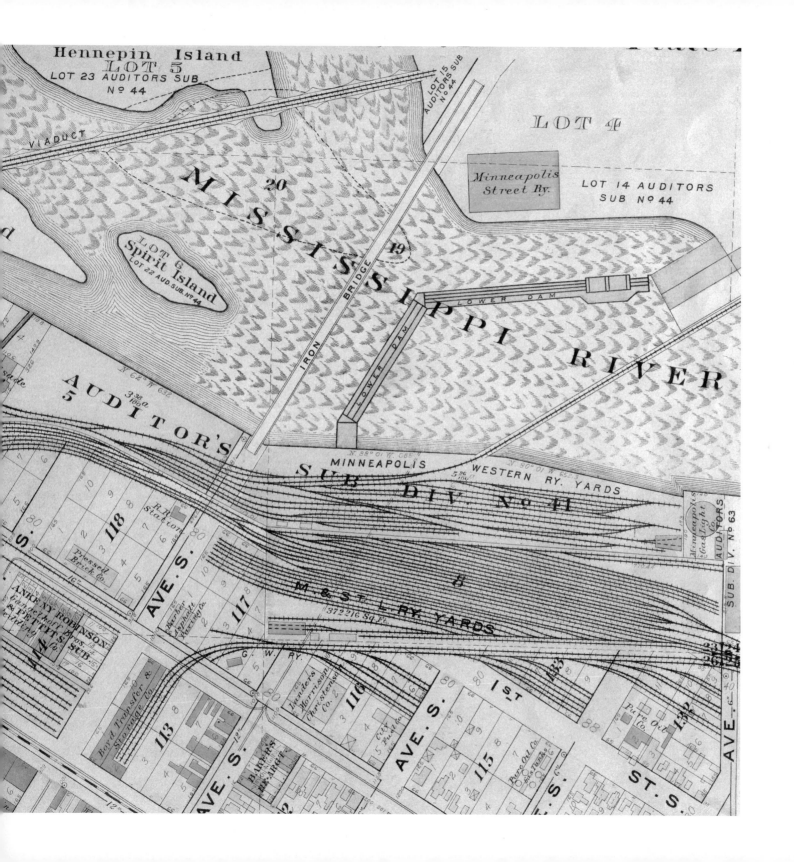

Hennepin Island
LOT 5
LOT 23 AUDITORS SUB
Nº 44

VIADUCT

LOT 15
AUDITORS SUB
Nº 44

LOT 4

Minneapolis
Street Ry.

LOT 14 AUDITORS
SUB Nº 44

MISSISSIPPI RIVER

20

LOT 6
Spirit Island
LOT 22 AUD SUB. Nº 44

19

IRON BRIDGE

LOWER DAM

LOWER DAM

LOWER DAM

AUDITOR'S 5

3 38/100 a

N 62° W 632

MINNEAPOLIS

N 88° 01 W 685

N 80° 01 W 652

WESTERN RY. YARDS

SUB DIV. Nº H

5 96/100

Minneapolis
Gas Light
Co.

AUDITORS

SUB. DIV. Nº 63

R.H.
Station

118

Plessell
Brick Co.

80

16"

AVE. S.

Barber
Asphalt
Paving Co.

10

117

8

M. & St.L RY. YARDS

372.216 SQ.FT.

S.

ANKENY ROBINSON
& PETTIT'S SUB.

Wachendorff
Bros.
Building

G. W. RY.

Boyd Transfer &
Storage Co.

113

Sanders
Morrison
Christensen
Co. 2

110

3

City
Pud Co

AVE. S.

1 ST

ave

Pure Oil
Co.

115

Pure Oil Co.
Oil Tanks Co.

AVE. S.

ST. S.

BLACK'S
MARKET

AVE. S.

ST. S.

one extent or another. In 1889, M&StL had been the city's premier carrier of outbound milled lumber; in 1900 Milwaukee led and was followed in order by Omaha, M&StL, CB&Q, and CGW. But production from the city's sawmills ebbed in 1902 and plummeted thereafter, not for lack of demand but for lack of logs as available timber was cut. Mill after mill closed as pine gave out. The last one in Minneapolis shuttered its operations in 1919, and the last great mill in the state would cease production a decade later. Lumber remained a staple of rail traffic, of course, but increasingly it derived from the Pacific Northwest and then from southern forests.[12]

In 1900, Minneapolis sawmills produced 398,970,000 feet of lumber, laths, and shingles, most of it to be hauled away by the city's railroads—valuable tonnage difficult to replace. Fortunately, however, the establishment of several large linseed oil mills partially offset loss of lumber traffic. Receipts of flaxseed (often called linseed) in 1889 had been a mere 526,000 bushels, but in 1900, 5,993,410 bushels were delivered to the city, primarily by Milwaukee Road, NP, M&StL, Soo, and CGW. Outbound linseed oil, oil cake, and paint

provided 1,489,785 tons of value-added freight billings in the same year. By 1920, Minneapolis would be the world's premier center for the manufacture of flaxseed products with major mills within the city and at St. Anthony Park.[13]

In the important production of flour and millstuffs, the years 1909–20 saw Minneapolis mills at their height, peak output being reached in 1916 when they turned out 18.5 million barrels, perhaps

---

BELOW LEFT: The years 1909–20 saw Minneapolis flour mills (including these west-side properties at their peak) as very good news for the city's rail carriers. Photograph courtesy of the Minnesota Historical Society.

BELOW RIGHT: Beyond Great Northern's famous Stone Arch Bridge stood the impressive east-bank industrial district, where Pillsbury was a particularly powerful participant. Photograph courtesy of the Minnesota Historical Society.

FACING PAGE: This spectacular view from 1912 looks over Milwaukee Road's train shed to take in the muscular industrial districts on both sides of the Mississippi River. The whole place hummed with feverish activity night and day every week of the year. Photograph by Sweet; courtesy of the Minnesota Historical Society.

one-sixth of all domestic volume. As always, railways provided the essential transportation link between producing areas near and far, on the one hand, and primary consuming areas near and far, on the other. In 1900, for example, railroads delivered to Minneapolis 3,312,320 bushels of wheat—CM&StP leading, followed in order by GN, Omaha, M&StL, and Soo Line. This volume was nearly three times that delivered to Duluth, not quite twice that delivered to Chicago, and far more than could be processed immediately at the mills. Much was stored at grain elevators located in and about the

city, these having an aggregate capacity of 29,625,000 bushels (not counting mill storage capacity). In that same year of 1900, Soo Line led all roads in the movement of flour from the city, trailed in order by CM&StP, CGW, Omaha, and GN. Ranked in order for delivery of wheat a decade later were GN, CM&StP, Soo, Omaha, and M&StL, but curious alterations were seen in the order of roads carrying away the flour: Soo (with lease of Wisconsin Central now under its belt) dominated, followed by CB&Q, CM&StP, GN, and CGW.[14]

In 1920, Minneapolis millers (Washburn-Crosby, Pillsbury, Northwestern, and eight others) had a daily capacity of 99,860 barrels of flour and eagerly consumed most of the 112,366,000 bushels of wheat delivered directly to the mills or sent to storage. As always, those roads with great range and gathering capacity to the west and northwest—Great Northern, Chicago, Milwaukee & St.

Minneapolis & St. Louis once held a near monopoly in the west-bank milling area, but by the turn of the century had to share that plum with several other roads. This view from 1911 looks down on the current site of the Guthrie Theater and the Mill City Museum. Photograph courtesy of the Minnesota Historical Society.

Paul, Northern Pacific, and Omaha—delivered the bulk, but in 1920 there was much greater equality among the top eight contenders for flour and millstuffs billings than ten years previous. After 1920, however, local flour production slumped, several factors combining in explanation. Favorable milling-in-transit rates long had worked in favor of Minneapolis, but pressure from other milling centers around the country forced the Interstate Commerce Commission to broaden those advantages to Chicago, Milwaukee, Kansas City, and other places. Additional factors included the rise of Buffalo as a milling center, inadequate supplies of high-grade wheat in some seasons, competition from southern Minnesota millers, a decline in per capita consumption of wheat flour, and a shift away from home baking to commercial baking.[15]

Managers and owners of railroads serving Minneapolis and, in fact, all railroads around the country could not ignore accumulating clouds across the horizon. Advocates of more and better public highways were no longer simply interested in providing opportunities for tinkerers and the rich and famous to entertain themselves with newfangled pleasure vehicles. Railroaders were curiously squeezed between growing public impulses to promote tax-supported highways sure to enhance modal competition and other public impulses to shackle railroads in their ability to compete. Equity holders and managers alike chafed at the depressing environment of private ownership of railroads but government control of them. The courts recognized the legal principle that government-set rates should not deny a fair return on investment, but railroads rarely succeeded in sustaining that right. The Minnesota Rate Case—long in litigation—illustrated the point; the Supreme Court ultimately upheld the State of Minnesota against Great Northern, Northern Pacific, and others. Moreover, the Interstate Commerce Commission, now greatly strengthened, had become at once prosecutor, judge, and jury—paradoxically often proclaiming policy that was harmful to the industry it was designed to regulate, but also in many instances to the very consumers it presumed to protect. Even Charles Francis Adams, himself a pioneer advocate of railroad regulation and a person who had much to do with the origin of the Massachusetts Railroad Commission, in 1914 felt compelled to speak out against the ICC. "Here is the largest investment and active business in the country," he said to President Woodrow Wilson in referring to the railroad industry, "and those managing it control neither outgo nor income. Such a situation is economically unheard-of, absurd," thundered an outraged Adams. Ham-fisted regulation at the federal level was only part of the problem. State statutes decreed drastic rate reductions, applied rigid regulation of rates, demanded "full crew laws" in some instances, and imposed a policy of disproportionate taxes on railroads.[16]

All of this was reflected locally by dreary profit-and-loss statements at a number of Minneapolis railroads. Chicago Great Western ducked in and out of receivership in 1908–9, but continued to struggle thereafter. In 1913, CGW's Samuel M. Felton pleaded with NP's Howard Elliott for additional overhead traffic (interline business—neither originated on or terminated on an intermediate carrier). "We cannot sustain ourselves without some help confined as we are to the Missouri River and the Twin Cities." Indeed, admitted Felton, "without your support as a feeder, we cannot hope to exist." Felton especially coveted NP's assistance in routing to CGW "Pacific Coast lumber, fruits, salmon and other products of the Northwest, wool and ore originating in Montana, and local business from Minnesota." Felton also hit up Great Northern in the same way, confiding to Elliott that "it is from friendly interests such as you and Great Northern, that we look for our great assistance." But despite their common ownership of Chicago, Burlington & Quincy and other important properties, NP and GN were increasingly intense rivals, and Elliott noted with some irritation that CGW in the previous year had delivered proportionately more traffic to GN than to NP. Felton persisted, but Elliott would guard NP's prerogatives. Minneapolis & St. Louis similarly found itself supplicant before giants Northern Pacific and Great Northern, doing all it could to lobby for overhead business employing its "Peoria gateway" instead of risking great delay to lading trying to slog through congested Chicago. In 1914 M&StL incurred a net deficit and failed to settle interline accounts with connecting roads, frustrating GN, NP, and others and sending a shudder through the investment community. Short-term notes were floated, but they were bid down, signaling unattractiveness. In 1916, M&StL dodged the bullet through an unusual reorganization without receivership. Owners of stock surrendered their holdings and paid $20 per share in cash for a new $78 par value issue. This brought in funds adequate to reestablish the road's credit—barely and temporarily. Much larger Chicago, Rock Island & Pacific was not as fortunate, sliding into the courts on April 20, 1915, and the Luce Line and Dan Patch were anemic from the outset.[17]

The experience of the local roads was mirrored nationally. By 1915, one-sixth of railroad mileage in the United States was in the hands of receivers. Fewer miles of line were built that year than in any since 1864, and more miles of road were in receivership than ever before. And, cynics must have noted, this was in a period of general prosperity. American route mileage peaked at 254,036 in 1916.[18]

There were other clouds of an even more ominous nature. Events growing out of the assassination of Archduke Franz Ferdinand on June 28, 1914, quickly escalated into the Great War—World War I as it eventually would be called. Europe at war soon craved American production; industrial and agricultural activity swelled traffic on the nation's rails. That swell only increased when the United States itself declared to war early in April 1917. The railroad

industry moved immediately to deal with new challenges by creating the Railroads' War Board, pledging to support the war effort by running the country's manifold independent carriers as a "continental system," by organizing car pools, and by eliminating duplication of service. But problems were great. War traffic tended to move only in one direction—east—and when Atlantic port facilities and ocean transport proved inadequate, rail cars simply piled up as unintended warehouses. A severe car shortage was the predictable consequence.[19]

Problems persisted and even worsened. Federal law and federal bureaucracy were at the heart of the matter. Unification of operation to promote efficiency was suspect under antitrust legislation, and car pooling was prohibited under ICC provisions. Congress was unwilling to change positions on either issue, the needs of war notwithstanding. At the same time the ICC was unwilling to authorize increased rates to compensate for heightened costs of labor and material. Under the circumstance, railroads were reluctant to seek capital to expand plant, and when they did, bankers were reluctant to lend. Gridlock was at hand. President Wilson, to complete mobilization of the country's resources required of war, took possession of the railroads by proclamation issued on December 26, 1917; control passed to the United States Railroad Administration (USRA) and to William D. McAdoo, director general, effective at noon on December 28 but for accounting purposes on January 1, 1918.[20]

Railroad owners and managers were properly nervous and perplexed by this revolutionary turn of events. There was nothing in the history of American railroading parallel to this new federal control, but neither was there anything in the American experience like

LEFT: Medium-sized Chicago Great Western, like Minneapolis-based Minneapolis & St. Louis, was dependent on good graces of larger roads for overhead or bridge traffic that neither originated nor terminated on its lines. CGW's depot and freight station at Washington Avenue and Tenth Avenue South looked bleak in this view from 1912 (and so did the road's profit and loss statement). Opposite the depot is the block that now houses the Open Book Center for reading, writing, and book arts. Photograph courtesy of the Minnesota Historical Society.

its participation in a war on the European continent. For his part, McAdoo took a firm stance. It was a matter of patriotism. Railroaders, he affirmed, were "just as important . . . in winning the war as the men in uniform who are fighting in the trenches." Only through "united effort, unselfish service, and effective work" could the war be won and "America's future be secured."[21]

The Railroad Control Act provided that the federal government would make annual compensation to the carriers on the basis of net operating income for the three years preceding and ending June 30, 1917. It also promised adequate maintenance of their property during the time of government operation. Regional federal directors were appointed to oversee general operations with local federal managers assigned to on-the-job responsibilities, but final authority rested in Washington with the tall, thin-lipped, and long-nosed McAdoo.[22]

Railroad managers at Minneapolis and across the land must have gazed at each other in utter amazement, categoric disbelief. The powerful ICC in addition to the entire body of antitrust law had

**BELOW:** Great Northern spent lavishly to improve plant and to increase efficiency, as with its multitrack thoroughfare between St. Paul and Minneapolis. Small wonder that GN owners and managers blanched when control of the property passed to the U.S. Railroad Administration in 1917. Van Cleve Park in southeast Minneapolis is visible on the left of this view looking toward St. Paul. Photograph by Charles P. Gibson; courtesy of the Minnesota Historical Society.

**FOLLOWING SPREAD:** Great Northern dominated southeast Minneapolis but Northern Pacific, Great Western, and Milwaukee Road were important contenders. Map from *Atlas of Minneapolis, Hennepin County, Minnesota* (Minneapolis: Minneapolis Real Estate Board, 1914); courtesy of the Minneapolis Public Library.

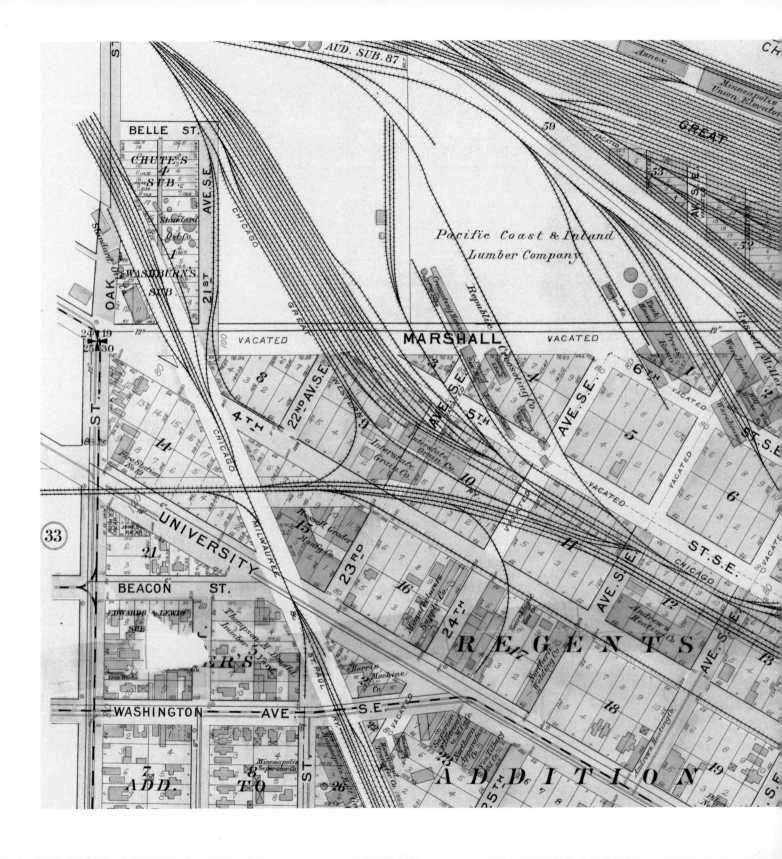

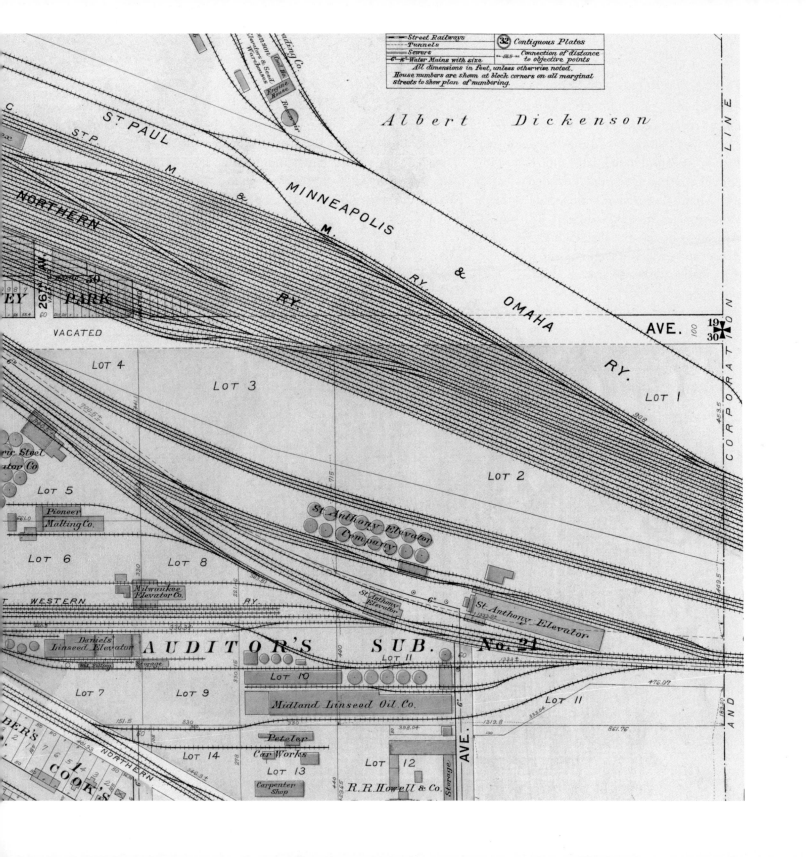

Albert    Dickenson

ST. PAUL

NORTHERN

STP

M

&

MINNEAPOLIS

M.

RY.

RY.

&

OMAHA

RY.

PARK

26TH AV. N.

VACATED

AVE.

19
30

LOT 4

LOT 3

LOT 1

LOT 2

LOT 5

Pioneer
Malting Co.

LOT 6

LOT 8

St. Anthony Elevator
Company

Milwaukee
Elevator Co.

WESTERN

RY.

St. Anthony
Elevator

6"

St. Anthony Elevator

Daniels
Linseed Elevator

AUDITOR'S    SUB.    No. 21

Storage

LOT 11

LOT 7

LOT 9

LOT 10

Midland Linseed Oil Co.

LOT 11

NORTHERN

COOK'S

Peteler
Car Works

LOT 13

Carpenter
Shop

LOT 14

LOT 12

AVE.

Storage

R.R.Howell & Co.

been summarily shunted aside, USRA's sweeping authority eclipsing both. ICC and antitrust had obliged railroads to compete with one another; USRA obliged them to cooperate.[23]

Cooperation meant change at various levels and of several types. For instance, USRA mandated consolidated ticket offices (in Minneapolis at 202 Sixth Street South) and closing individual local offices (mostly on Nicollet Avenue), cancellation of certain through routes (for instance Minneapolis–Chicago via M&StL/IC), curtailment of advertising campaigns directed at discretionary travelers, termination of immigration and agricultural efforts, and locally the move of M&StL out of its shabby passenger station into GN's modern facility on Hennepin Avenue.[24]

Traffic in freight and passengers mushroomed, although government-mandated policies of concentration favored some roads against others. American railroads handled more passengers in 1916 than ever before, but those records were eclipsed in 1917 and fell again in 1918. Military movements were a necessary and predictable part of the mix. Recruits bound for Europe to make the world safe

for democracy were loaded at outlying stations, and entire trainloads mustered in at Minneapolis and then shipped to Camp Cody, New Mexico, or Camp Dodge, Iowa, or elsewhere for training. Heavy demand for passenger transport notwithstanding, most area railroads made their greatest contributions to the war effort by hauling heavy tonnage related to agriculture—grain, flour, packinghouse products, and general foodstuffs. Coal volumes held steady, but billings

---

**BELOW LEFT:** Wartime did not interrupt most basic activities in the area. Pole treating in North Minneapolis, for instance, continued apace—good news for carriers that brought in the raw materials and carried away the finished product. In this scene a steam-powered derrick is dipping poles at the Page & Hill plant. Photograph by Charles J. Hibbard; courtesy of the Minnesota Historical Society.

**BELOW RIGHT:** Coal volumes delivered to Minneapolis yards held steady during the war years as coal remained the primary fuel for industrial use, electrical generating, and heating. These piles pictured in 1918 were for use at the Minneapolis General Electric's Riverside Station in northeast Minneapolis. Photograph by Charles J. Hibbard; courtesy of the Minnesota Historical Society.

in cement, lumber, and all building materials slumped as a result of wartime restrictions. So did traffic in motor vehicles, likewise a reflection of production restrictions caused by the war. The growing enthusiasm for prohibition explained the loss of revenue from transportation of alcoholic beverages. State prohibition laws were merely forerunners of the Eighteenth Amendment, passed by Congress late in 1917 and ratified in 1919, which shut down breweries at Minneapolis and most others to deny railroads shipments of barley, hops, bottles, and boxes inbound as well as outbound cases and barrels of beer. Even earlier, on August 12, 1918, USRA's William McAdoo had perfunctorily declared that "the sale of liquors and intoxicants of every character in dining cars, restaurants, and railroad stations under federal control shall be discontinued immediately."[25]

In a well-ordered world, general prosperity would be reflected in railroad traffic statistics and income accounts. That proved not

Most area railroads made their greatest contribution to the war effort by handling prodigious volumes of agricultural produce. This view is from Washington Avenue South across what is now Portland Avenue. The surviving remnants of the Washburn "A" Mill Complex are a National Historic Landmark and have been restored to include residential developments and the Mill City Museum. Photograph by Charles J. Hibbard; courtesy of the Minneapolis Public Library, Minneapolis Collection.

necessarily the case. Operating revenues did go up every year but so did operating expenses—dramatically in 1918, staying high in 1919 and 1920. This was instantly and alarmingly reflected in operating ratios (ratio of operating expenses to operating revenues) of individual roads as this chart shows:[26]

| Road | 1916 | 1917 | 1918 | 1919 | 1920 |
|---|---|---|---|---|---|
| C&NW | 66.46 | 72.75 | 86.02 | 85.96 | 94.82 |
| CB&Q | 59.74 | 64.27 | 77.73 | 78.24 | 90.51 |
| CGW | 69.74 | 76.32 | 93.02 | 87.24 | 110.00 |
| CM&StP | 66.69 | 74.90 | 91.75 | 92.15 | 97.94 |
| CRI&P | 68.14 | 74.07 | 86.21 | 86.95 | 94.63 |
| CStPM&O | 65.25 | 73.76 | 84.00 | 84.08 | 88.98 |
| GN | 58.35 | 66.92 | 83.84 | 81.41 | 91.23 |
| M&StL | 66.29 | 71.51 | 94.53 | 97.16 | 103.81 |
| NP | 53.85 | 60.41 | 69.50 | 75.61 | 89.30 |
| Soo | 55.82 | 66.49 | 80.49 | 80.65 | 90.66 |
| Class Ones Nationwide | 65.73 | 70.48 | 81.88 | 85.11 | 94.38 |

All of the country's major railroads (those under USRA control) were clamped solidly in a vise—powerful labor interests that had a most sympathetic ear in the Wilson administration on the one side, and on the other an equally powerful block of agricultural and industrial shipper groups that effortlessly convinced the government to deny rate increases. Accelerating wages mandated by USRA were an especially perplexing problem. For average hourly earnings of American railroad workers, officers excepted, the index number (1915 = 100) stood at 129 in 1917, at 198 a year later, and at 225 early in 1920. The inability of railroads to offset such rapidly escalating costs with an equal increase in the revenue stream was, of course, immediately apparent in the operation ratios.[27]

Meanwhile, the United States raised, trained, and deployed an army, ready in 1918 to bear the full weight of a war that sucked life and treasure from all parties. Then, after fifty-one months of deadly fighting—after nine million combatants and five million civilians had died—it was over, the result of an armistice. Many of the Minnesota troops arrived back home and marched in a great parade at St. Paul on May 8, 1919, before being mustered out of the service.[28]

The "war to end all wars," the war "to make the world safe for democracy" accomplished neither laudable goal. America's involvement in this cataclysmic international conflict had proved unsettling and dissatisfying, the end of hostilities through armistice was ambiguous, and combat had been so grisly that many Americans and others concluded that Western civilization itself must be deeply, inherently flawed. Not surprisingly, most citizens in response nostalgically yearned for an earlier mystical and mythical time when issues and answers had been more clearly apparent, when life had

Railroads faced a changing competitive landscape. In 1920, Northern Pacific's "A" line remained a vibrant thoroughfare between Minneapolis and St. Paul, but vehicular traffic on University Avenue Southeast soon would eclipse volumes on the rail. In the background Pillsbury Hall and the Armory on the University of Minnesota campus can be seen. The tracks in the foreground would soon make way for Memorial Stadium, completed in 1925. Photograph courtesy of the Minnesota Historical Society.

been simpler. A "return to normalcy" had great allure; "progressivism" was on the wane.[29]

It was in this milieu that a strenuous debate occurred regarding the disposition of the nation's railroads. At issue was the proper relationship of private to public power and responsibility in the American context. President Wilson in 1917 had promised that the country's railroads would be returned to their owners as soon as the "emergency" had passed, but one month after the armistice, the phenomenally forceful and ambitious McAdoo proposed continuing government operations for another five months before returning properties to individual companies. More frightening by far were the notions of Glenn E. Plumb, representing labor, who vigorously advocated purchase of railroad properties by the federal government, the creation of an operating company, and lease of these lines to it.[30]

Senator Albert Cummins, chairman of the Interstate Commerce Committee, would be at the vortex of these debates and would have a hand in any forthcoming legislation. Indeed, his task, not easy, would be to frame a plan of solid economics but capable of political passage. Cummins, a Republican, had the advantage of dealing in a Congress controlled by that party, although Woodrow Wilson, a Democrat, would hold the presidency until March 1921. Yet Cummins would have his hands full with fellow Republicans. For that matter, railroad managers were not uniform in their views. But M&StL's Charles Hayden likely spoke for the majority. "The greatest problems of your company, like so many other railway companies, is to obtain needed capital for expansion of facilities," Hayden told M&StL stockholders in 1920. "Under private ownership, this can only be done by fixing rates so that railway securities will offer to the average citizen, as an investor, an attractive investment." But what were the odds of getting compensatory rates if the carriers were delivered back to their owners? Anything but good. If managers could not control the income side of the ledger, they had but one alternative: control the expense side. Only by driving down the operating ratio could there be salvation for "our insolvent railroads," wrote one dry-eyed but pessimistic observer.[31]

Among other things, the Transportation Act of 1920 established 5.5 percent as a fair return on the aggregate value of railroad property. If this were accomplished, railroads could justify capital expenditures like this one in the west-bank milling district; otherwise, their future looked bleak. Photograph courtesy of the Minnesota Historical Society.

---

**UNITED STATES RAILROAD ADMINISTRATION**

OFFICE OF THE DIRECTOR GENERAL

———

WASHINGTON, AUGUST 12, 1918.

———

**GENERAL ORDER NO. 39.**

The sale of liquors and intoxicants of every character in dining cars, restaurants and railroad stations under Federal control shall be discontinued immediately.

W. G. McADOO,
*Director General of Railroads.*

76172—18

Senator Cummins recognized that there was unequal earning power in the family of railroads, and this led him to counsel "a series of consolidations which will merge weak roads with strong ones, to the end that the resulting systems, and they will be comparatively few in number, may do business on substantially even terms." Railroad consolidation would be a hallmark of what became the Esch-Cummins bill, or the Transportation Act of 1920. Pulling and hauling added other important elements including, critically, the return of railroads to their owners, a labor board with authority to arbitrate labor issues, establishing 5.5 percent as a fair return on the aggregate value of railroad property, allowing the pooling of traffic if found to be in the public interest, and variously strengthening an already powerful ICC. Esch-Cummins represented shipper interests more than railroad interests, but given the political landscape of the moment, it was about all that railroad managers and owners could hope for.[32]

"On December 24, 1919, the President of the United States issued a proclamation relinquishing control of the railroads of the United States which he had taken over on December 28, 1917, such relinquishment to be effective at midnight February 29, 1920." This was the terse announcement of Chairman Howard Elliott to Northern Pacific shareholders. "Thereafter," Elliott continued, "Congress enacted a law, approved February 28, 1920, known as the 'Transportation Act,' providing that Federal control should terminate in the President's proclamation." And, Elliott dryly concluded, "pursuant to this proclamation and this legislation, your Company resumed possession and control of its property at midnight February 29, 1920." Elliott claimed that "relations between the United States Railroad Administration and your Company have been cordial and cooperative." He was not entirely candid, for the result of USRA policies and administration at NP (as with most railroads under USRA control) had not been positive. In the case of NP, Elliott simply laid the below data before shareholders, who could draw their own conclusions.

Railroads passed back to their owners at midnight on February 29, 1920. Into what kind of a future was the industry steaming? Owners and managers at Chicago, Milwaukee & St. Paul—like all others of the time—had no clear view. A Milwaukee Road freight train trundled out of town at James Avenue South in the summer of 1920 along what is now the Midtown Greenway. Photograph courtesy of the Minnesota Historical Society.

|  | 1917 (before USRA) | 1919 (USRA) |
| --- | --- | --- |
| Railway Operating Income | $88,225,726 | $100,739,353 |
| Railway Operating Expense | $53,297,861 | $76,179,714 |
| Net Operating Income | $34,927,865 | $24,559,639 |
| Net Income | $31,379,565 | $17,279,912 |

NP'S circumstance, sad to say, was hardly unique. Indeed, it was typical.[33]

FACING PAGE: Railroad managers during the early 1920s were shaken and nervous. The scene at M&StL's Cedar Lake shop and engine facility in this wintry view implies an obscure future for that company and the industry at large. Photograph courtesy of the Minneapolis Public Library, Minneapolis Collection.

# An Uncertain Future

# 16

Minneapolis is the commercial and trade center of a larger territory than any other interior city in the country . . . in natural resources, agricultural and mineral, this territory is rich beyond description. . . . The channels through which it does now and will continue to find the way to market, are so fully developed by the system of railroads already constructed, penetrating all this Northwest country, that they will not be materially changed.

*MINNEAPOLIS CHAMBER OF COMMERCE ANNUAL REPORT*, 1889

As the United States moved into the third decade of the twentieth century it became apparent that the age of railways had slipped away. The nation's rail carriers remained critical to the nation's life and time, true enough, but they did not dominate the landscape as they had for a half century.

What of the future? Managers and owners of roads serving Minneapolis were typical of the industry at the time—shaken and nervous. As they gazed into a rather foggy crystal ball, they likely recalled an especially glorious time, 1897–1907—the belle époque of the steamcar civilization—and may have wondered if that heady past—before onslaught of the most ham-fisted regulation, before

massive labor unrest, and before real modal competition—might somehow be replicated in years to come. And local leaders may have dreamily recalled that back in 1881, the Minneapolis Board of Trade had offered a pleasantly upbeat and accurate assessment of the city's hinterland. "The tide of immigrant settling in this new Northwestern country has been in full flood . . . [and] . . . this immigration may continue to pour its tide into Minnesota, Dakota, Montana, and Manitoba for years, and still there will be room for more." At the same time, the board noted, the city's industrial sector supplemented important lumber and flour milling with iron works and manufacturing concerns turning out stoves, farm machinery, linseed oil products, fabrics, clothing, boots and shoes, furniture, cooperage and millwork, brooms, soap, paper, candy, crackers, and more. The city's simultaneous growth in jobbing was the understandable sequence of its importance as a manufacturing center. Railroads provided the essential transportation link—hauling in raw materials, fuel, and manufactured goods, taking away lumber and flour as well as locally manufactured items, groceries, dry goods, harnesses, wine, liquor, beer, hardware, "queensware," drugs, agricultural implements, wagons, carriages, commission produce, and much more. Had all of that changed, disappeared, evaporated over the intervening years? No, the pattern continued into the new century, slowed some by the Great War, but picked up thereafter. Indeed, Great Northern, reflecting all of this, in 1920 handled 2,940,000 tons of manufactured goods and miscellaneous commodities over its rails—up by 372,000 tons over 1919—and delivered 1,233 carloads of immigrant movables to its Minnesota stations (up from 670 a year earlier). And railroads remained central to the local as well as national economy. CM&StP, as an example, operated 10,267 miles of route (1,230 in Minnesota), and owned 1,979 locomotives

and 67,238 pieces of rolling stock. Its total assets were valued at $658,157,161—a big business, indeed. Milwaukee in 1920 handled 45,041,277 revenue tons and transported 15,919,200 passengers.[1]

But appearances were deceiving. The year 1920, stated one close observer of the industry, provided "the greatest traffic in railway history; the greatest operating revenues; the greatest operating expenses; the greatest wage aggregate; the greatest taxes; and the smallest net operating income in more than 30 years." Marvelous rate increases authorized by the Interstate Commerce Commission in 1920 mostly evaporated when special interest groups favoring agriculture got tariffs on hay, grain, and grain products knocked down and when carriers voluntarily reduced rates to stimulate business as the country slumped toward a postwar depression. And the Transportation Act of 1920 that returned the railroads to their owners had ominously reaffirmed the authority of the ICC—seeming to replace the powerful one-man federal control by USRA with what one analyst caustically labeled "indirect, halting, defective, and inefficient federal control by a commission of eleven quasi-judicial deliberators." But in its wake USRA had saddled the industry with a 16 percent larger work force and a payroll expanded by a startling 86 percent. Moreover, the economy was unstable when the conflict ended; it was precarious as 1920 approached. The downturn began in January and reached a trough during the summer of 1921. By then industrial production had fallen to only 65 percent of the recent high, and unemployment jumped from 1.4 percent to 11.7 percent. The agricultural economy was particularly devastated after spectacularly prosperous years before and during the conflict. The postwar depression was striking for its brevity but also for its severity.[2]

LEFT: The west-side milling district and attendant rail yards remained vibrant in the aftermath of the Great War, but change was afoot. Photograph courtesy of the Minnesota Historical Society.

FACING PAGE: This view looks downstream. The Omaha yards are on the left, Northern Pacific's in the center, and Soo Line's on the right. Left center next to the Mississippi River is Great Northern's passenger station. Photograph courtesy Minnesota Historical Society.

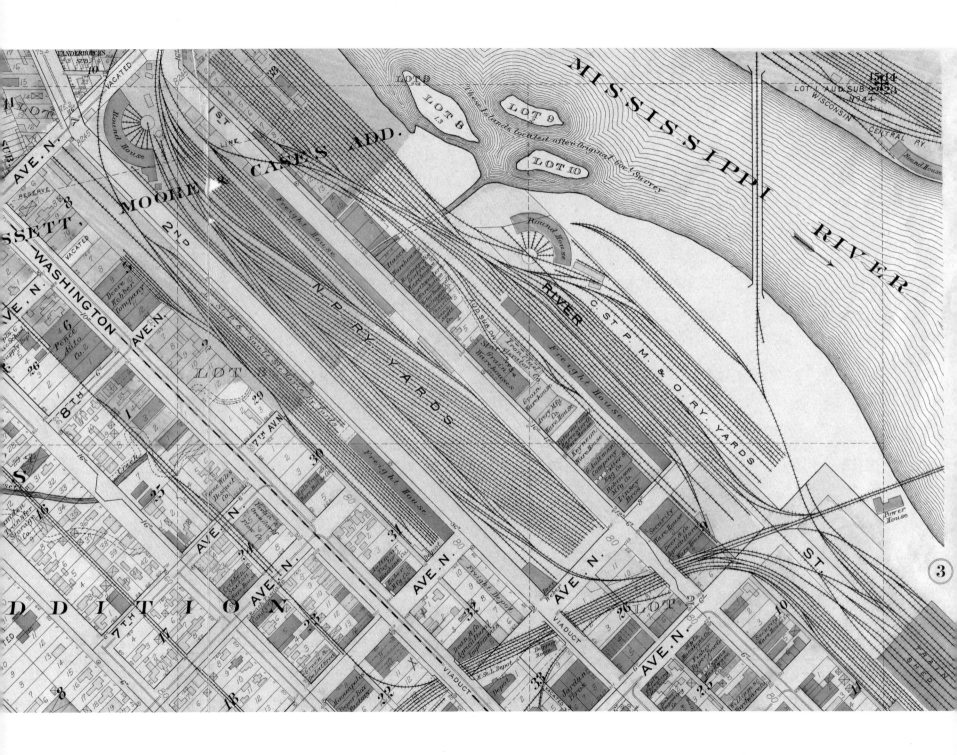

Of problems facing railroads in the wake of the USRA experience and the Transportation Act of 1920, none loomed larger than labor conditions—the size of the work force, wages, and work rules. Woodrow Wilson, gentle by nature and humanitarian by inclination, had taken a generally favorable attitude toward labor, and that posture was well reflected by McAdoo and USRA. The results were predictable: labor's power during the Wilson years grew tremendously. USRA, arguing with merit that railroad workers were being squeezed by increased costs of living and courted by other industries that paid better, had determined to raise wages across the board in order to retain railroaders and keep the trains running. At the same time, McAdoo instituted rules and regulations affecting conditions of employment that were uniform for all roads under his control; these were adopted without reference to local conditions or the financial health of individual companies. Among other effects was a dramatic increase in the number of workers required, with all employees covered by national agreements drawn with individual unions representing specific crafts and jurisdictions. In sum, railroads in 1920 were saddled with many more workers who were much better paid than they had been in 1917. And they were segregated rigidly by craft to restrict employer flexibility. (NP's payroll in 1920 was 95 percent over 1917; at M&StL, compensation of employees had risen by 125 percent.) Then, in 1920, the Labor Board, established as part of the Transportation Act, granted a substantial wage increase to nearly all rail employees. The ICC tried to offset these additional expenses and to secure a 5.5 percent return on the property of carriers by authorizing sizable rate increases, but depressed business conditions left railroads with high rates and reduced traffic. To this the ICC responded by lowering rates, especially on grain and livestock, but for railroads it had the effect of increasing volume while decreasing gross revenues. The only solution, they concluded, was to bring down operating costs, and since the most significant operating cost was wages (60 percent of total in 1920), managers quickly turned to that area.[3]

Workers understandably were unwilling to give up recently won gains, but managers were determined to cut the labor bill; strikes were certain. The worst occurred in 1922 when shop men responded to wage reductions and changes in work rules with a nationwide walkout effective July 1. In the Twin Cities, approximately ten thousand shop men left their jobs, seven hundred in Minneapolis

---

FACING PAGE: Above the Hennepin Avenue bridge lay Great Northern's passenger station and beyond were the substantial yards of Omaha, Northern Pacific, and Soo Line. M&StL's shabby passenger station (abandoned in 1918) was located at Washington and Fourth Avenues North. Map from *Atlas of Minneapolis, Hennepin County, Minnesota* (Minneapolis: Minneapolis Real Estate Board, 1914); courtesy of the Minneapolis Public Library.

RIGHT: This heavily ladened Northern Pacific freight getting a roll out of Northtown for the west gave the impression of stolidity. Was it an illusion? NP and the rest of the industry were saddled with greater labor costs coming out of the USRA experience. Could the industry adjust and prosper? Photograph courtesy of the Minnesota Historical Society.

at M&StL, as an example. Ultimately the strike ran its course. In February 1923, members of the Federated Shop Crafts called off the strike, but by that time many roads had signed agreements with new organizations that were much weaker. Were there winners? Many men lost both their jobs and their pensions, fissures erupted among the several crafts—especially between the operating crafts and the nonoperating crafts—and were difficult to paste over, and a serious spike was driven between management and labor. For the companies, much needed revenue had been lost during the strike, some business was lost to trucks, which had stood forth to demonstrate their versatility during this time of national trial, and the government even considered the use of aircraft to move the mails. On the positive side, carriers did get control of labor costs, but arguing that there were winners in this conflict would be a challenge at best.[4]

Unfortunately for Minneapolis railroads and the industry at large, labor costs were only one of several thorny problems faced during the early 1920s. Thin net earnings provided a double whammy: inadequate monies for betterment of plant and frightened lenders who either denied carrier requests or provided capital only at steep rates. The USRA experience for some roads had been merely distasteful, for others it was disastrous. In nearly all cases, however, a carrier's physical plant and its financial condition were not as strong as prior to USRA. That made capital infusion all the more critical. But lenders were appropriately chary. "The business is a hazardous one owing to political interference," was the blunt conclusion of the authoritative Moody's Investors Service. Government restrictions and regulations had become so burdensome since 1910, said Moody's, "as to deprive railways of a reasonable earning power." Specifically, argued Moody's, recent receiverships had been brought about "by legal restrictions preventing roads from adjusting their freight charges to the cost of the service" they provided. The prestigious New York investor service was mildly surprised as a consequence to note that railway facilities had consistently increased "in proportion to the growth of needs of traffic" despite "the lack of fair return on the capital invested." Indeed, from 1890 to 1920, railroad ton miles (one ton carried one mile) increased 443 percent against a 68 percent rise in domestic population; passenger miles (one passenger carried one mile) grew by 300 percent. "Yet," concluded Moody's, "the investment in road and equipment increased only 156 percent, thus showing that capital has not grown nearly as fast as the service rendered." It spoke more to a glorious past than a promising future.[5]

President Theodore Roosevelt years before had advocated continuous, informed, and expert regulation that only the federal government could properly undertake. Nonsense exclaimed historian Albro Martin. "An administrative body that innovates is a contradiction in terms." Martin's equally caustic but accurate assessment was that the Interstate Commerce Commission stupidly denied carriers rate increases even as Congress passed legislation restricting managerial prerogative. The cumulative effect was capital malnourishment and a stultifying atmosphere that drove the spirit of enterprise from the railroad sector. Policymakers, Martin correctly claimed, simply misunderstood: "Railroad problems of the Progressive Era were not those of the Gilded Age." Regulation, Martin concluded, simply failed. Why? Because the "philosophies of archaic Progressivism were applicable to problems and conditions which no longer existed . . . [and] . . . because the Commission simply did not constitute the fearless, impartial, and wise body which regulation presupposed. It was a boy on a man's errand."[6]

A later historian, Steven W. Usselman, asserted that railroads "often balked at introducing . . . complex novelties into their operations," and that explained, at least in part, the decline in railways. Yes, in part. As the industry matured, it certainly did tend toward a counterproductive "this-is-the-way-we-have-always-done-it" mentality that resisted innovation, and stifling government intervention

---

contributed to further encrustation and ossification among managers. This had the effect of further dampening the spirit of enterprise and making rail an even less attractive investment opportunity—a downward spiral ad nauseam. And all of it collected just as other industries—motor vehicle, steel, electrical appliances, radio, real estate, construction, and even aviation among them—beckoned brightly, ever more brightly, against rails. Activity on Wall Street reflected as much. "The market yesterday illustrated the completeness with which the standard railway issues have been eclipsed in the favor of traders by the industrials," explained the *New York Times* for September 22, 1915. "There was not a single transaction in . . . [CM&StP] . . . but extraordinary activity of motor issues."[7]

"Motor issues," of course, referred to manufacturers of motor vehicles. Not one automobile had been displayed at Chicago's great Columbian Exposition in 1893, but in 1904 modern transportation was a hallmark of the St. Louis World's Fair, and not fewer than 140 motor vehicles were among the most popular exhibits. It was a powerful omen. The Federal Highway Act of 1921 required that states design a system of interstate and intercounty roads for which federal dollars might be made available. Minnesota established a trunk highway network of 6,877 miles a year later. The *Minneapolis Journal* in 1928 urged a policy of paving "main roads" first, many of them paralleling the state's primary rail lines. "There should be no division of funds to roads of lesser importance, no slackening of the energetic push for the main traveled roads," said the *Journal*. Costs were staggering for the time—$30,000 per mile in the 1920s, paid for usually by license fees, fuel tax, state-issued bonds in some instances, and federal aid on occasion.[8]

The use of motor trucks during the Great War had greatly excited those who advocated their use in commercial transportation, but in the mid-1920s the place of over-the-road trucking was not yet assured. There were 2.4 million trucks registered across the nation in 1925, used in local operation and regarded mostly as useful feeders for the railways. Trucks nevertheless already were nibbling at rail revenues, and there was a clear correlation between the rise in motor truck registrations and the drop in railroad ton miles.[9]

There was not so much as a tad of ambiguity as to the impact of automobiles. Ownership of autos in the 1920s was no longer a class distinction, as had been the case earlier. By 1920, Minnesota registered 300,166 automobiles; there were 8.22 million registered

"Motor issues" had a different meaning on Nicollet Avenue in downtown Minneapolis, as this view from 1926 suggests.

to "motor-minded Americans" across the land. And by 1925 Ford Motor Company was turning out 9,000 cars daily, its Model T selling for only $290. Two years later Ford unveiled its famous Model A, but General Motors' Chevrolet increasingly was a popular competitor. In 1929, the automobile industry produced a record 4.5 million passenger cars; nationwide registration reached 23.1 million.[10]

Automobiles and buses cut into passenger volumes, especially for short hauls. The result was fewer persons frequenting the city's passenger terminals. Here, Milwaukee Road depot in 1925. Photograph courtesy of the Minnesota Historical Society.

"Jitneys," too, were part of the roadway mix. Intercity buses initially engaged in short-haul operation, averaging about 30 miles, but in the late 1920s a few companies began long-haul service. In 1927, 85,636 motor buses were employed on 635,609 miles of route, carrying 2.52 million passengers. "Greyhounds travel over 70,000 miles each day," claimed that company in 1928, and Minneapolis-based Northland Transportation Company offered service throughout Minnesota.[11]

Rail passenger service, especially local and intermediate distance, was especially vulnerable to vehicular attack. Indeed, the number of revenue passengers and revenue passenger miles for

the nation's carriers peaked in 1920 and then turned downward. At M&StL, for instance, revenue passengers declined by 18 percent in 1922 alone, down another 12 percent in 1923, "due principally to increased competition of automobiles and motor busses, made possible through the continued development of hard-surfaced highways," said a crestfallen company spokesman. In 1923, the nation's railroads transported approximately the same number of passengers as they

**LEFT:** Great Northern replaced its *Oriental Limited* with a new train, the *Empire Builder,* offering premier service between Chicago and Puget Sound. The new train went on display at Minneapolis in 1929. Photograph courtesy of the Minnesota Historical Society.

**BELOW:** Volumes remained steady or increased on the best trains, such as M&StL's *North Star Limited,* here crossing the Mississippi River and passing by the University of Minnesota on Northern Pacific's "A" line bridge, now a bicycle and pedestrian trail linking the east and west banks. Photograph from the collection of Aaron Isaacs.

had in 1912, and the ICC later found that boardings on Class One roads declined by nearly one-third between 1920 and 1926. This dramatic shrinkage was almost totally in shorter-distance business, sleeping car and parlor car numbers increasing during the same period by over one-quarter.[12]

Minneapolis railroads faced yet another imposing enemy: a stubborn depression in the agricultural sector that stood in marked contrast to the booming general economy. "The repeated crop failures of previous years, on top of low prices obtained for what was harvested caused a very severe business and agricultural depression

Sleeping car business remained strong, and space on Great Northern's marvelous new *Empire Builder* was at a premium. Photograph courtesy of Burlington Northern Santa Fe.

The "smart set" chose name trains such as Northern Pacific's fashionable *North Coast Limited* for long-distance travel. Photograph courtesy of Burlington Northern Santa Fe.

in our territory," sighed Soo Line's president in 1924. "Many farmers were so discouraged that they made no effort to retain their farms, so that the number of foreclosures and vacant farms was constantly increasing." It was much the same in the service areas of other roads, especially in western Minnesota and the Dakotas.[13]

Farm prices plummeted in 1920, stabilized the next year, but were flat through 1929. Foreign markets went slack and domestic demand fluctuated. Consumption of cereals declined by about one-third while meat consumption remained constant. Prohibition dried up demand for barley and hops; changing styles and synthetic fabrics reduced the need for wool; and the move from horse-drawn vehicles cut requirements for hay and oats. The national farm population, as a percent of the total, slid from 28.2 in 1923 to 25.2 in 1929, although average acreage per farm rose from 144 to 150. By 1930, there would be 160,000 fewer farms in the country than in 1920, and agriculture contributed progressively less to the national economy on a percentage basis.[14]

None of this meant that farmers were categorically disengaged from the economy, but there were clear alterations and adjustments. The value of farm property dropped steadily during the 1920s, but mortgage debt went up as owners substituted long-term mortgages for short-term debt that they had incurred during the earlier boom period. Predictable ripple effect flowed from these collective changes. All too often money was rashly borrowed or rashly loaned with the unfortunate consequence of failure, foreclosure, or bankruptcy for borrower and lender alike. In all, five thousand banks fell during the 1920s, most of them in grain-producing states. Early in 1929, reports from the Federal Reserve Bank of Minneapolis showed 1,177 bank failures in Minnesota, South Dakota, North Dakota, and

Montana since 1920, "wiping out the entire capital and surplus of the failed banks"—restricting, in train, "the buying and general development of these states."[15]

All of this was set against the backdrop of changes in the local flour milling industry. Indeed the place of Minneapolis among milling centers eroded throughout the 1920s; Buffalo, New York, assumed top rank in 1929. Three years earlier, locals roads, led by M&StL, had attempted to rectify a rate structure that disadvantaged

---

FACING PAGE: Soo Line shop forces at Shoreham received fewer orders to service locomotives during the dreary agricultural recession of the 1920s. Photograph courtesy of the Minnesota Historical Society.

RIGHT: Cereals and row crops continued to pour into Minneapolis from country elevators, whose spouts noisily spewed grain to bulkhead ends of boxcars.

Minneapolis, earning the adulation of city millers but the enmity of others. The ICC bowed to pressure from other milling centers and larger carriers elsewhere, local efforts going for naught. In fairness, however, analysts pointed out that Minneapolis millers also were increasingly handicapped by short supplies of wheat, and

that some of the large Minneapolis firms had, in fact, transferred export milling to Buffalo. An important aside: Washburn-Crosby in 1923 created a new division to manufacture Softasilk cake flour and Wheaties, a ready-to-eat breakfast cereal, later adding Kix and Cheerios and other packaged products such as Bisquick. All of this helped counter the dwindling demand for baking flour, and in 1928 Washburn-Crosby metamorphosed into General Mills, the world's largest miller.[16]

These collective variables predictably had an effect on railroad companies. Net income for all Class One railroads in 1921 was less than in 1915, and less than half of what it had been in 1916. Hard

A passenger station at Hoag Avenue and North Seventh Street served the needs of Dan Patch, Minnesota Western (Luce Line), and Anoka Lines. By the 1930s passengers were scarce, but team tracks to the left served the needs of shippers of perishables, who loaded and unloaded refrigerator cars in great numbers. Photograph courtesy of the Minneapolis Public Library, Minneapolis Collection.

numbers and dry-eyed analysis of them shook the industry to its foundations, but, of course, some companies were healthier than others. Among local roads, Chicago Great Western and Minneapolis & St. Louis earned inadequately in 1920 to cover fixed charges, while Omaha, C&NW, and Soo Line experienced that trauma in 1921. A year later railroad bonds amounting to $109 million were in default, and most rail securities were trading lower than before the war. Business then picked up, however, and some Class One carriers regained strength and confidence. But increased traffic volumes did not automatically translate into net profit or, in the case of M&StL, to service debt. That road headed to the courts in 1923. CM&StP followed two years later.[17]

But this was the "decade of prosperity," the Roaring Twenties. Indeed, from early 1923 until late 1929 the nation at large did experience unparalleled prosperity. Prices were stable, unemployment was negligible, real wages rose nicely, inflation was insignificant, and worker productivity soared. Corporate profits rocketed by 62 percent; dividends followed at 65 percent. The gross national product in 1929 was 22 percent higher than in 1922, 62 percent higher than in 1914. The prosperity label for the 1920s was real enough in most quarters but not for the railroad industry at large, which turned in a sluggish performance. Sprawling western giant Southern Pacific, for example, earned a mere 3.98 percent on investment during the boom year 1926. Nearer at hand, the return for Northern Pacific ranged from 1.45 in 1920 to 4.02 in 1928, 3.20 for the decade.[18]

That was context for the Great Depression and the "Dirty Thirties." Milwaukee Road, now out of receivership and restyled Chicago, Milwaukee, St. Paul & Pacific, reported the obvious: "The unprecedented industrial depression which began in the latter part of 1929 continued with increasing severity throughout 1931." NP was more subdued, referring to hard times as "unfavorable business conditions," but C. T. Jaffray at Soo Line got right to the point. "The year 1930 was a disastrous one," he bluntly told shareholders, and with no improvement in the months following he was compelled to say, "The year 1931 was a very disastrous one for this property." Milwau-

kee in 1931 reported "freight revenue lowest since 1917," and Rock Island in the same season also showed gross revenues that were "the lowest since 1917." NP's gross revenue slipped from $27.1 million in 1924 to $16.1 million in 1933. All of it mirrored an unalterable reality: the health of its customer base always found reflection on a railroad's profit-and-loss statement. That pointed to another truism. Cities and towns had created each other, and rails provided the umbilical lifeline linking each. Soo's Jaffray, in explaining his road's poor showing for 1933, pointed to the symbiotic relationship attaching to Minneapolis, its hinterland, and its railroads. The depressing decrease in manufacturing was "due in part," he said, "to the low purchasing power of the farmer and the communities serving them."

Ordered before the stock market crashed in 1929, Northern Pacific took delivery of new dining cars for its famous *North Coast Limited* in May 1930. To introduce the cars and to promote its marvelous cuisine, NP invited Minnesota Governor Theodore Christianson (*left*) and Minneapolis Mayor W. F. Kunze (*right*) for a sneak preview. Photograph courtesy of the Minneapolis Public Library, Minneapolis Collection.

The health of one hinged on the health of others. Mother Nature then added insult to injury, throwing a devastating drought over much of the outcountry. It was, said Jaffray in 1934, "the most serious drought in recent history, resulting in an almost complete failure in grain, feeds, hay crops, and pasturage." Conditions improved

**LEFT:** The Municipal River Terminal, long promised, finally was completed during the 1930s. It was served exclusively by M&StL. Inbound coal and outbound scrap were early primary commodities handled, but on this day in 1937 locally manufactured tractors were transloaded from flat cars to barge. Photograph by the *Minneapolis Star & Tribune*; courtesy of the Minnesota Historical Society.

**BELOW:** "The year 1930 was a disastrous one," Soo Line president C. T. Jaffray bluntly told company stockholders. The Great Depression had settled in with a vengeance, depriving Soo Line of much needed revenue. The result was predictable: fewer calls for switch crews such as this one in Minneapolis. Photograph by the *Minneapolis Star & Tribune*; courtesy of the Minnesota Historical Society.

not at all. "Because of unprecedented heat and continued drought," Jaffray told shareholders in 1936, "there was an almost complete failure of grain and agricultural crops of the territory tributary to our" road. "The results for 1936 were very disappointing," confessed the plainspoken president at Soo.[19]

Modal competition during the Great Depression became pronounced. "The continually increasing competition of the motor truck and the loss of passenger traffic to the automobile" partially explained Rock Island's woes. And, frankly, admitted Milwaukee, "no effective way has been found to meet the drift from rail to highway." Local or short-distance passenger volumes had been falling for years, of course, but severe competition by trucks for freight lading was new. Truckers, however, had distinct advantages. They were not tethered to arbitrary schedules, were not affected by connections, and could expeditiously accommodate small consignments. Trucks sliced deeply into less-than-carload traffic and then, frighteningly, into historically important commodity classes—agriculture, petroleum, and merchandise. Moreover, public policy during the depression looked to road construction as a means of trimming unemployment and stimulating the economy. And, predictably, as better roads were built, truckers gained greater load capacity as well as greater range, increased speed, and reliability. Moreover, it was easy to get into the trucking business. Unregulated "gypsy" truckers proliferated, some even hauling freight for "gas money."[20]

The cumulative effect was financial distress among the carriers. Northern Pacific's return on investment during the 1930s ranged from a low of .32 percent in 1933 to a high of 2.25 in 1930, averaging 1.33 for the decade. NP, like neighbors GN and CB&Q, stayed out of the courts, but Milwaukee Road, which recorded a wretched .90 percent return on investment for the 1930s, did not, again seeking bankruptcy refuge in 1935. Rock Island already was there, as

BELOW LEFT AND RIGHT: Hard times further depressed passenger numbers. The great waiting room of Great Northern's Minneapolis station and the nearby Milwaukee road train shed reflected as much. Photograph on right by the *Minneapolis Star & Tribune*; courtesy of the Minnesota Historical Society.

was M&StL (since 1923); CGW and C&NW both succumbed in 1935. Soo Line filed under Chapter 77 on December 31, 1937, and Wisconsin Central, long under lease to Soo, already had stumbled into receivership. In the aggregate, more than half of the mileage owned by roads serving Minneapolis was under the jurisdiction of courts—truly an accurate index of the symbiotic relationship between carriers and their service areas.[21]

Railroads, under the circumstance, fought back with surprising pluck. M&StL beat back a concerted effort to dismember that road,

**FACING PAGE:** Looking west, in the foreground are the recently completed Cedar Avenue bridge, the Minneapolis Western bridge, the old Tenth Avenue wagon bridge, and the western end of the Stone Arch Bridge. On the left are the M&StL and Minneapolis Western yards. New to the skyline was the marvelous Foshay Tower, completed in 1929. Photograph by Norton & Peel; courtesy of the Minnesota Historical Society.

**BELOW:** Looking across the Mississippi River from the east bank toward the Minneapolis skyline: in the foreground is Nicollet Island and across the river the newly completed Minneapolis post office flanked by the Third Avenue bridge and the Great Northern depot. Approaching the station is an Omaha passenger train.

M&StL, GN, and others embraced aggressive pick-up-and-delivery campaigns to hold LCL traffic, and CB&Q introduced high-speed, diesel-powered, light-weight streamliners—the *Zephyrs*—in a bold and successful attempt to stem the tide of passenger losses. "Service is still inadequate to demand" between Chicago and Minneapolis, exclaimed a delighted Burlington in 1935; two six-car trains on seven-hour schedules entered service late the next year. Milwaukee was not far behind in the same market with steam-powered *Hiawathas*. Between May 29, 1935, and the end of 1936, CMStP&P's celebrated "high steppers" handled 394,594 revenue passengers, and the road proudly if quietly announced that the "trains have been very successful and the earnings substantial."[22]

The "dark decade" finally ended, the rains returned, and the economy improved, but the world again was gripped by a cataclysmic world war. All of this registered quickly enough on demand for transportation, and, happy to say, railroads—despite recent vicissitudes—were remarkably able to respond. In 1941, a much relieved

Great Northern announced that its operating revenues had reached that of 1929. But a booming economy and wartime demand for a two-front effort taxed the capacity of GN and all other roads. As during the Great War, railroads of Minneapolis and the upper Midwest handled prodigious tonnage of agricultural and food products, but in this war, unlike the last, it was done without an onerous United

---

BELOW LEFT: CB&Q introduced its *Twin Cities Zephyr* on April 15, 1935, with a ceremony at Chicago Union Station. The train was an instant success. Passengers here are detraining at Great Northern's Minneapolis station after a swift ride aboard this sleek streamliner. Photograph by the *Minneapolis Star & Tribune*; courtesy of the Minnesota Historical Society.

BELOW RIGHT: Milwaukee Road's *Hiawatha* was so spectacularly successful that the company soon ordered more and even more impressive equipment for the train, including elegant streamlined 4-6-4 Hudsons as motive power. On September 28, 1938, Milwaukee put the *Hi* on display at its Minnehaha station. Photograph courtesy of the Minneapolis Public Library, Minneapolis Collection.

**ABOVE LEFT:** On this brisk wintry day, passengers have just detrained from Rock Island's pedestrian *Mid-Continent Special*. On the left is Milwaukee Road's resplendent *Morning Hiawatha* about to depart for Chicago. Photograph by the *Minneapolis Star & Tribune*; courtesy of the Minnesota Historical Society.

**ABOVE RIGHT:** Passenger volumes turned upward during the late 1930s, especially during the summer months, when travelers headed westward to places such as Yellowstone National Park. Passengers here waited to board the second section of Northern Pacific's crack *North Coast Limited* at Great Northern's Minneapolis station. Photograph by the *Minneapolis Star & Tribune*; courtesy of the Minnesota Historical Society.

**RIGHT:** Fortunes for the railroad industry improved in 1941. On October 8, 1941, a photographer for the *Minneapolis Star Journal* recorded this view of a Milwaukee Road Mikado-type locomotive performing a switching move. Just beneath the locomotive is a streetcar emerging from the viaduct over Washington Avenue South approaching Park Avenue. Photograph courtesy of the Minnesota Historical Society.

FACING PAGE: Passengers, many of them military personnel, lined up at Milwaukee's Minneapolis station to board outbound evening trains including Milwaukee's *Olympian Hiawatha* and *Pioneer Limited* and Rock Island's *Short-Line Express*. Photograph ca. 1943 by the *Minneapolis Star & Tribune*; courtesy of the Minnesota Historical Society.

ABOVE LEFT: War brought increased demands for locally produced foodstuffs such as Land O' Lakes butter, packed in Minneapolis and shipped by rail to destinations near and far. Photograph courtesy of the Library of Congress.

ABOVE RIGHT: The war effort could take many forms. This huge butane fractioning tower for the petroleum industry was produced by Williams Brothers Boiler Manufacturing Company in 1943 and served as a huge rolling billboard with a patriotic message as it moved out of Minneapolis to a distant destination. Photograph courtesy of the Minneapolis Public Library, Minneapolis Collection.

RIGHT: Fort Snelling from 1940 through 1945 again swelled with recruits, this time to fight a nasty two-front war. Photograph by the *St. Paul Dispatch-Pioneer Press*; courtesy of the Minnesota Historical Society.

States Railroad Administration. Labor and equipment shortages were epidemic. Employees put off retirement or returned from retirement, and women picked up jobs never before open to them. New and modern motive power and rolling stock were hard to come by; elderly locomotives and creaky cars, some previously consigned to scrap, were recalled, patched and painted, and thrust into emergency service. Passenger miles and ton miles escalated; net profit returned; companies (even woebegone M&StL) emerged from receivership. Burlington "provided more transportation in 1944 than in any previous year," beamed that road's Ralph Budd. Passenger miles at CB&Q exceeded by 69 percent the previous high of 1920.

Between December 7, 1941, and the end of hostilities on V-J Day 1945, the country's railways handled 97 percent of domestic troop movements and approximately 90 percent of domestic movement of military freight equipment and supplies. "It was our privilege

Rationing of gasoline and rubber tires took travelers off roadways just as military demand for transportation mushroomed. Railroads consequently were flooded with passengers. That was reflected by Omaha/C&NW's eastbound *Viking,* which on this day in 1942 was doubleheaded out of Minneapolis. The Chicago-bound day train would add an RPO and other headend cars at St. Paul. Photograph courtesy of the Minnesota Historical Society.

and responsibility to devote our manpower, equipment and facilities, primarily to the war effort," said Budd, who might have been speaking for the entire industry.[23]

The nation's railways, like the country itself, had been on a roller-coaster ride for a decade and a half. They had experienced their darkest days during the Great Depression and their finest hour during World War II. Their leaders could but wonder as to the future.

Except for occasional blips, prosperity continued in the immediate postwar period. New or refurbished equipment appeared on passenger trains of all roads. Milwaukee's *Hiawathas* and Burlington's *Zephyrs* were upgraded and matched in the Chicago–Minneapolis trade by North Western's *400s*; Great Northern's resplendent *Empire Builder* was equaled by Northern Pacific's elegant *North Coast Limited* and Milwaukee's sparkling *Olympian Hiawatha* to the

Appropriately named *Victory,* Omaha/Chicago & North Western's train number 514 left Great Northern's Minneapolis station each evening at 7:20 P.M. for the overnight run to Chicago via Madison, Wisconsin. Omaha and C&NW (and indeed all American railroads) had ample reason for pride in their accomplishments during World War II. Photograph courtesy of the Minneapolis Public Library, Minneapolis Collection.

Major railroads serving Minneapolis that had long-distance passenger offerings invested heavily in new equipment, such as these sleepers assigned to Great Northern's *Empire Builder.* Photograph courtesy of Burlington Northern Santa Fe.

Pacific Northwest. Rock Island *Rockets* zipped all the way from the North Star state to the Lone Star state. And high-capacity freight cars replaced older and smaller rolling stock; diesel-electric locomotives replaced steam; huge capital infusion flowed into advanced signaling, Centralized Traffic Control, heavier rail, and deeper ballast. Railroad managers and investors bet on continued prosperity, and for a while it appeared that their high-stakes wager was well placed. But tonnage nationwide peaked in 1948, earnings in 1953; five years later "the railroad problem" again was a hot topic among policy analysts and others.[24]

In fact, difficulties faced by railroads before the war had not disappeared during that conflict; they had only diminished, to reappear in spades thereafter. Detroit barely met demand for new motor vehicles, whose drivers in 1956 celebrated passage of the Interstate Highway Act authorizing 41,000 miles of controlled-access, multiple-lane expressways. A year later air carriers captured one-third of domestic passenger miles, a figure sure to rise with sophisticated jet planes soon to make obsolete propeller-driven craft. And air carriers since 1925 had authority to move mail. Competitive factors facing

rail freight were equally stark. Pipelines captured nearly all petroleum products, by 1965 water carriers skimmed off 18 percent of intercity ton miles, and trucks had run off with much of the highly rated merchandise traffic. By 1966, American railroads moved only 18 percent of intercity passengers and 44 percent of intercity freight.[25]

Railroads responded by trimming capacity—dumping local passenger trains, abandoning branches, and reducing crew size. Then they focused on long-distance passenger trains. Completion of the interstate highway system quickly drained off coach customers, and jets claimed lucrative commercial traffic from sleepers and parlor cars. The decision by the Post Office Department during the 1960s to terminate en route sorting of mail on Railway Post Office cars and to otherwise divert mail from passenger trains was the coup de grâce. By 1971 only two RPO routes remained on the few passenger trains running to, from, or through Minneapolis. They, too, would

LEFT: Milwaukee's famous *Hiawatha* passenger trains featured "sky-top" parlor observation cars such as this one, just arrived from Chicago at the Minneapolis passenger station. Photograph courtesy of the Minnesota Historical Society.

ABOVE: The engine crew of Northern Pacific's *Mainstreeter* saw a "clear track" over the historic Stone Arch Bridge. Was there similarly a clear track for the American railroad industry in the postwar period? Photograph courtesy of Burlington Northern Santa Fe.

pass in 1971 when Amtrak began operation of a greatly truncated national passenger net that provided but one train daily (Chicago–Seattle) through the city. The Milwaukee station fell silent and into decay but would be redeveloped later. But Great Northern's newer station was not as fortunate, falling to the wrecker's ball when Amtrak chose a new station site between Minneapolis and St. Paul.[26]

Merger was another nostrum administered in a campaign to revitalize the industry. One by one the Minneapolis railroads disappeared to reflect a national pattern. Omaha was fully absorbed into Chicago & North Western, which in 1960 gobbled up Minneapolis & St. Louis, the home road, the local favorite of long ago, and the enterprise on which Minneapolis had pinned its hopes early in the age of railways. In the same year Minneapolis, St. Paul & Sault Ste. Marie merged with Wisconsin Central and another to form a "new" Soo Line which eventually took in Minneapolis, Northfield & Southern. In 1968 C&NW further expanded by acquiring Chicago Great Western. The granddaddy amalgamation, however, came in 1970 when Chicago, Burlington & Quincy, Great Northern, Northern Pacific, and others combined to create a Burlington Northern colossus. The merger train rolled on through the 1970s, a particularly grim decade as far as railroads were concerned. Rock Island stumbled, fell, and was dismembered or abandoned; C&NW picked up the important Kansas

City–Des Moines–Minneapolis tendril. Milwaukee, too, dropped to its knees and abandoned much of its Pacific extension and others of its lines to emerge with a much abbreviated system serving only the Midwest. Still weak, it went into play, and in the mid-1980s rather surprisingly was acquired by Soo Line; not long thereafter, however, Canadian Pacific took complete stock ownership of Soo. Before that, and curiously as it turned out, Soo shed itself of many lines including those which once had constituted Wisconsin Central. New owners reclaimed that ancient moniker, but those properties subsequently passed to Canadian National in 2001. That was not the end of change.

LEFT: The remnant of Milwaukee Road's once famous *Olympian Hiawatha* about to depart Milwaukee's Washington Avenue station. By 1967, at the time of this view, service extended west only to Aberdeen, South Dakota, on an overnight round-trip schedule. Photograph by Don L. Hofsommer.

ABOVE: Milwaukee Road conductor Gerald J. Lund had a lonely outpost at the Minneapolis station on August 8, 1970; passengers for the famed *Pioneer Limited* were scarce. Photograph by Don L. Hofsommer.

Minnesota Transfer earlier had restyled itself as Minnesota Commercial; Union Pacific grabbed Chicago & North Western; and Burlington Northern and Atchison, Topeka & Santa Fe merged to become Burlington Northern Santa Fe.[27]

Even as the city's railways evolved and their local place contracted, so, too, was the area shipper base changing, evolving, and slenderizing. Sawmills were long gone, and pole treating and creosote works gradually disappeared. So did linseed oil processing facilities and much of the city's manufacturing sector, for example, farm machinery and woolen mills. Perhaps most prominent was the long slide in flour milling and the need for huge satellite grain elevators in and about the city. Industrial activity ceased on both sides of the Mississippi River below what had been the roaring falls at St. Anthony before arrival of the twenty-first century. Gone also were the maze of tracks and railroad support facilities that so long had proudly and efficiently provided the essential transportation link between producers spread throughout the city's broad hinterland and consumers of value-added goods from Minneapolis manufacturers that found market outlets across the country and beyond.

BELOW: By January 1970, Burlington's *Afternoon Zephyr* had shrunk to four cars. CB&Q would disappear into Burlington Northern two months later. Amtrak would take over intercity passenger operations on May 1, 1971, and the *Zephyr* would not be part of the package. The Minneapolis station from whence this train departed would fall to wreckers after Amtrak took a new terminal site between Minneapolis and St. Paul in 1978. Photograph by Don L. Hofsommer.

By mid-passage in the first decade of the new century, a much slimmed down but more financially vibrant rail industry served the needs of Minneapolis and the nation. The Staggers Act of 1980 finally gave railroads partial deregulation and restored to the industry a spirit of enterprise long absent. In 1998, the country's rails moved more tonnage than ever before, accounting for 40.2 percent of domestic intercity ton miles. Amtrak moved almost 1 percent of intercity passengers, and its presence in the area remained spartan, but area policy makers seriously studied rail commuter service northwestwardly to or toward St. Cloud over Burlington Northern Santa Fe, and 2004 would see light-rail commuter operation from downtown to the airport with the prospect of expansion elsewhere in time. Collectively the signs indicated that rail would continue to play an important part in a balanced transportation package serving private and public needs near at hand and across the land.[28]

Northern Pacific, like Great Northern and Milwaukee Road, maintained classy standards for its premier passenger trains to the bitter end. The kitchen crew on NP's crack *North Coast Limited* met every standard for excellence on this wintry night in February 1970. Photograph by Don L. Hofsommer.

But even as smokestack industry faded, other jobs appeared in private and public sectors alike. All of this happened collaterally with the continuing movement of people off the farms and out of small towns to the city as well as a surge of migration from foreign lands. The collective result was an escalation of population in the Twin Cities metropolitan area—a population in need of a plethora of items requiring transportation. This was mirrored in railroad traffic statistics—more inbound deliveries than outbound billings. Roadway salt to keep streets and highways clear in winter, coal for electrical generating plants, lumber and building materials, food stuffs, beer, and motor vehicles were among other elements of the traffic mix. Finished goods often found convenient delivery by intermodal transport, trailer-on-flat-car or container-on-flat-car, blending the advantages of rail and highway.

# EPILOGUE

There is a weary old story that has one fellow soon joined by another on the platform of a railway station at some mythical location. "Has the train gone?" asked the new arrival of the first. "Yes," was the instant reply. "How do you know?" wondered the second. "Because it left its tracks," smiled the first. This yarn, in a homely way, sums up the experience of Minneapolis and its railways. They grew up together—each influencing and nurturing the other. The needs of one were the needs of the other; the prosperity of one was the prosperity of the other; each left an unmistakable imprint on the other.

The experience of Minneapolis and its railways cannot, of course, be understood in a vacuum. Indeed, that experience must be placed within the context of trends and events regionally, nationally, and even internationally. The rise of Minneapolis and the evolution of rail service occurred as the United States evolved from a society and economy mostly rural and agrarian to one mostly urban and industrial. Attendant phenomena included massive migration from foreign to American shores, "conquering" of the West, and the ascent of great cities—particularly in the interior. At center stage were railways—the nation's first big business, acting very much like a piston in a cylinder, pushing against the frontier and pulling, in its wake, a sophisticated market economy.

Minneapolis reflected all of this. Its leaders fully understood the industrial potential at the Falls of St. Anthony; the area soon sprouted lumber mills, grist and flouring mills, and an assortment of additional enterprises. And while they understood, at least in the

abstract, the benefits of the all-weather, efficient transportation afforded by railways, they were surprisingly slow to act on their own behalf in the embrace of the steamcar civilization. Indeed, they reacted, moving only on their own account when finally perceiving the ominous nature of iron tentacles emanating from the Lake Michigan port cities of Chicago and Milwaukee—both of them early

M&StL certainly left its "tracks"—its imprint—on Minneapolis. In 1960 this switch job was doing heavy duty in the historic west-bank milling district near South Second Street and Third Avenue South. Photograph courtesy of the Minnesota Historical Society.

and marvelously successful practitioners of urban economic imperialism using railways as weapons of choice.

Railways, by their very nature, demand concentration in urban areas, the clustering of "built environment" including factories, warehouses, grain elevators, storage sheds, and the like. The "energizing spine" of that "metropolitan corridor," as Harvard's respected

**BELOW:** Minneapolis and its railways grew up together.

**FACING PAGE:** The metropolitan corridor. The Minneapolis Western bridge shows at the very bottom of this view. Above that is the famous Stone Arch Bridge. The long bridge up from that is Third Avenue, and just up from that is Nicollet Island, which is joined to the west bank by a bridge carrying Hennepin Avenue and then a Great Northern bridge with GN's passenger station on the left.

John R. Stilgoe correctly argues, was the railway and its handmaiden, the trackside telegraph line.[1]

The built environment that characterized a metropolitan corridor offered an abundance of outbound business to its powerful spine just as that spine delivered an equal abundance of traffic to the plethora of customers along its urban route. An easy example locally is Milwaukee Road's pioneer route parallel with today's Hiawatha Avenue.

But of course metropolitan corridors do not end at the city limit, extending, as they do, to all corners of the country. For the "hardy pioneer who had left all the comforts and conveniences of civilized life," observed the Dakota Railroad Commission in 1885, "the whistle of the locomotive would be the sweetest music" possible, for that whistle implied procurement of "communication with the civilized world." The *Lutheran Observer* a couple years later chimed similarly: "It is a wonderful transformation a railroad will make in a country in a few months, changing trackless prairie into settled farms, fields of grain, and prosperous towns." A writer for Chicago, Milwaukee & St. Paul was equally expansive. "The remarkable development of the Minnesota prairies, and following that, the opening of the broad Dakota wheat fields . . . was a constant stimulus to railroad effort, and railroad activities boomed." And the historian of one Minnesota village said simply, ". . . the railroad was a cure for stagnation and a charm against decline and failure. . . . A small town in rural Minnesota served by a railroad meant being connected with big cities like Minneapolis. . . ."[2]

The built environment along railroad rights-of-way in tiny rural communities replicated those of huge cities—if on a greatly abbreviated scale. Cresbard, served by Minneapolis & St. Louis in Faulk County, South Dakota, provides a representative example. Between

the main line switches at that place early in the twentieth century could be found a stockyard, several coal sheds, a lumberyard, a loading platform, a warehouse, four grain elevators, and the railroad company's depot. M&StL's metropolitan corridor through Cresbard derived from Minneapolis, and, predictably, goods for the depot's freight house, nearby warehouse, loading platform, and lumberyard arrived primarily from Minneapolis suppliers and manufacturers; grain billed from trackside elevators mostly found market at Minneapolis. The relationship between Minneapolis and Cresbard was simply one example illustrating the tight connection of the city with its huge hinterland. It also demonstrated the critical bond provided by roads of rail to create the metropolitan corridor—linking city and town as one.[3]

Not to be forgotten in all of this was nearby arch rival St. Paul, territorial and then state capital, head of navigation on the Mississippi River, and headquarters city for important regional railroad

By the last quarter of the twentieth century the west-bank milling district had lost much of its luster, but there remained pockets of activity and the place still rumbled with railroad activity. This view from 1976 is of the Ceresota Elevator, a familiar historic landmark on South Second Street. Photograph courtesy of the Minnesota Historical Society.

# NOTES

## 1. STEAMCARS AT LAST

1. Street designation changed over time so that today the hotel would be located at Kellogg and Exchange.

2. Minnesota Historical Society, "Scrapbook" (Biography), 50:25–26; *St. Paul Pioneer*, June 14, 1849; Minutes of Minnesota Western Rail Road, Constituting Minute Book of Minneapolis & St. Louis to 8-28-80. Entries are by date, not page numbers. November 26, 1853; *United States Biographical Dictionary* (New York: American Biographical Publishing, 1879), 104–6, 235–36, 598–99; William Watts Folwell, *A History of Minnesota*, 4 vols. (St. Paul: Minnesota Historical Society, 1921), 3:256–57; Isaac Atwater, ed., *History of the City of Minneapolis, Minnesota* (New York: Munsell & Co., 1893), 287–390. Another director, one B. Allen, appears on the census rolls of 1850 as a citizen of St. Paul; nothing more is known of him or of Otis Hogh, last of the eight. This is hardly surprising given the fluid nature of frontier life in very early Minnesota.

3. Theodore C. Blegen, *Minnesota: A History of the State* (Minneapolis: University of Minnesota Press, 1963), 159–73; *St. Paul Daily Minnesotan*, May 14, 1858.

4. Blegen, *Minnesota*, 164.

5. Joseph A. A. Burnquist, *Minnesota and Its People*, 4 vols. (Chicago: S. J. Clarke Publishers, 1924), 1:209–54; Christopher Columbus Andrews, *History of St. Paul with Illustrations and Biographical Sketches of Its Prominent Men and Pioneers* (Syracuse, NY: D. Mason & Co., 1890), 392–407; Blegen, *Minnesota*, 180; Burnquist, *Minnesota and Its People*, 2:517–31, 553–55.

6. Emory R. Johnson, *American Railway Transportation* (New York: D. Appleton Co., 1905), 24; John F. Stover, *Iron Road to the West: American Railroads in the 1850s* (New York: Columbia University Press, 1978), ix, 13, 16, 116.

7. Thomas A. Bailey and David M. Kennedy, *The American Pageant: A History of the Republic*, 6th ed., 2 vols. (Lexington, MA: D. C. Heath, 1979), 1:29; George Rogers Taylor, *The Transportation Revolution, 1815–1860* (New York: Holt, Rinehart & Winston, 1951), vii, 396–98.

8. Taylor, *The Transportation Revolution*, 388–89; James Neal Primm, *Lion of the Valley: St. Louis, Missouri*, 2nd ed. (Boulder, CO: Pruett Publishing, 1990), 9, 49, 73, 107, 113, 165–69; Mentor L. Williams, "The Chicago River and Harbor Convention, 1847," *Mississippi Valley Historical Review* 35 (March 1949): 607–26; William Cronon, *Nature's Metropolis: Chicago and the Great West* (New York: Norton, 1991), 26–29, 60–68, 110–15.

9. Taylor, *The Transportation Revolution*, 48–50, 68, 96; John F. Stover, *History of the Illinois Central Railroad* (New York: Macmillan, 1975), 15–21; Edward C. Kirkland, *A History of American Economic Life*, 4th ed. (New York: Appleton-Century-Crofts, 1969), 165, 168, 274–76.

10. Rasmus S. Saby, "Railroad Legislation in Minnesota, 1849 to 1875," *Collections of the Minnesota Historical Society* 15 (1915): 1–49, especially 8, 30–32; *Records of the St. Paul, Minneapolis & Manitoba Railway Company of Minnesota up to April 1886* (St. Paul: Pioneer Press, 1886), 9–20; *The Frontiersman* [Sauk Rapids, MN], April 8, 1854; Andrews, *History of St. Paul*, 409; Burnquist, *Minnesota and Its People*, 233, 534–39.

11. John H. Randall, "The Beginning of Railroad Building in Minnesota," *Collections of the Minnesota Historical Society* 15 (1915): 215–20; Ralph W. Hidy, Muriel E. Hidy, Roy V. Scott, and Don L. Hofsommer, *The Great Northern Railroad: A History* (Boston: Harvard Business School Press, 1988), 2–5; Burnquist, *Minnesota and Its People*, 539–43; *St. Paul Daily Press*, June 29, 1862.

12. *Handbook of St. Paul 1900* (St. Paul: St. Paul Chamber of Commerce, 1900), 73.

13. Lucile M. Kane, *The Falls of St. Anthony: The Waterfall That Built Minneapolis* (St. Paul: Minnesota Historical Society Press, 1987), 9–11. Ray

Allen Billington, *Westward Expansion: A History of the American Frontier,* 4th ed. (New York: Macmillan, 1974), 281–86. See also Jocelyn Wills, *Boosters, Hustlers, and Speculators: Entrepreneurial Culture and the Rise of Minneapolis and St. Paul* (St. Paul: Minnesota Historical Society Press, 2004).

14. Kane, *The Falls of St. Anthony,* 12–29; Burnquist, *Minnesota and Its People,* 292, 296–97.

15. Burnquist, *Minnesota and Its People,* 305–6; Kane, *The Falls of St. Anthony,* 30–41; *St. Paul Daily Press,* April 14, 1863.

16. *St. Anthony Express,* March 22, April 26, 1853; Dwight L. Agnew, "Beginnings of the Rock Island Lines, "*Journal of the Illinois State Historical Society* 46 (Winter 1953): 407–24; *Iowa Board of Railroad Commissioners Report 1879,* 87; William J. Peterson, *Steamboating on the Upper Mississippi* (Iowa City: State Historical Society of Iowa, 1968), 271–86; Benedict K. Zobrist, "Steamboat Men versus Railroad Men: The First Bridging of the Mississippi River," *Missouri Historical Review* 59 (January 1965): 160–72; G. H. Crosby, *History of CRI&P* (Chicago: Chicago, Rock Island & Pacific Railway, n.d., 1902?), 9; *Iowa Board of Railroad Commissioners Report 1879,* 92; *Des Moines Tribune,* September 9, 1967; Chicago, & Rock Island, *Annual Report,* 1870, 5. Chicago & Rock Island became Chicago, Rock Island & Pacific in 1866. Early work in Iowa was done by surrogate Mississippi & Missouri.

17. Richard C. Overton, *Burlington Route: A History of the Burlington Lines* (New York: Alfred A. Knopf, 1965), 60–61; CB&Q, *Annual Report,* 1867, 56–57; Don L. Hofsommer, "A Chronology of Iowa's Railroads," *Railroad History,* Spring 1975, 72–74.

18. *Yesterday and Today: A History of the Chicago & North Western Railway System,* 3rd ed. (Chicago: C&NW, 1910), 164–65, 186; Hofsommer, "A Chronology of Iowa's Railroads," 80.

19. Hofsommer, "A Chronology of Iowa's Railroads," 72–76.

20. Frank H. Dixon, *State Railroad Control, with a History of Its Development in Iowa* (New York: Crowell, 20–23); John Lauritz Larson, *Bonds of Enterprise: John Murray Forbes and Western Development in America's Railway Age* (Boston: Harvard University, 1984), 41, 105, 115; CB&Q, *Annual Report,* 1867, 57.

21. James Neal Primm, *Lion of the Valley: St. Louis, Missouri,* 2nd ed. (Boulder, CO: Pruett Publishing, 1990), 270–71; C&RI, *Annual Report,* 1861, 17–18; ibid., 1862, 10; Mildred Lucile Hartsough, *The Twin Cities as a Metropolitan Market: A Regional Study of the Economic Development of Minneapolis and St. Paul* (Minneapolis: University of Minnesota, 1925), 12–13, 36–37, 75–76; Cronon, *Nature's Metropolis,* 296–309; John S. Wright, *Chicago: Past, Present, Future Relations to the Interior, and to the Continent* (Chicago: 1870), 347; *Iowa Railroad Commissioners Report 1881,* 76.

22. Hidy et al., *The Great Northern Railroad,* 318; Andrews, *History of St. Paul,* 412–14; August J. Veenendaal Jr., *Slow Train to Paradise: How Dutch Investment Helped Build American Railroads* (Stanford, CA: Stanford University Press, 1996), 169; Col. William Crooks, "The First Railroad in Minnesota," *Collections of the Minnesota Historical Society* 10 (1900–1904): 445–48; *St. Paul Pioneer,* May 27, June 24, July 25, September 2, 1866; *Minneapolis Tribune,* January 7, 1868, June 3, July 9, 1869; *St. Paul Daily Press,* November 17, 1869.

23. Saby, "Railroad Legislation in Minnesota," 49–60; 417–19; Atwater, *History of the City of Minneapolis,* 329–30, 334–35; *Compendium of History and Biography of Carver and Hennepin Counties, Minnesota* (Chicago: H. Taylor, 1915), 134–35; Edward Vernon, *American Railroad Manual* (New York: American Railroad Manual Co., 1873), 536; John C. Luecke, *Dreams, Disasters, and Demise: The Milwaukee Road in Minnesota* (Eagan, MN: Grenadier Publications, 1988), 53–73; Burnquist, *Minnesota and Its People,* 543–44; A. D. Emery, "The Twin Cities, St. Paul and Minneapolis," *Milwaukee Magazine* 13 (May 1925): 1–9, especially 4–5; A. D. Emery, "When the Milwaukee Road First Reached Minneapolis," *Milwaukee Magazine* September 1925, 7–8; *St. Paul Daily Press,* September 9, 1866; Stan Mailer, *The Omaha Road: Chicago, St. Paul, Minneapolis & Omaha* (Mukilteo, WA: Hundman Publishing, 2004), 23–24.

24. Judson W. Bishop, "History of the St. Paul & Sioux City Railroad, 1864–1881," *Collections of the Minnesota Historical Society* 10 (1905): 399–415; Andrews, *History of St. Paul,* 418–19; C&NW, *Annual Report,* 1878, 22; *Yesterday and Today,* 77; Atwater, *History of the City of Minneapolis,* 329, 334–35; Vernon, *American Railroad Manual,* 536; Burnquist, *Minnesota and Its People,* 544.

25. *Yesterday and Today,* 61, 62, 71, 88, 165–66.

26. NP, Original Tracklaying Record, March 15, 1933; Lester B. Shippee, "The First Railroad between the Mississippi and Lake Superior," *Mississippi Valley Historical Review* 5 (1918–19): 121–42.

27. *Minneapolis Tribune,* May 25, 1867; *Poor's Manual of the Railroads, 1869–1870,* 421–23; *Boston Transcript,* February 4, 1871; *New York Times,* October 13, 1891; Ellis Paxton Oberholzer, *Jay Cooke: Financier of the Civil War,* 2 vols. (Philadelphia: George W. Jacobs, 1907), 2:106–11, 244–45; Eugene V. Smalley, *History of the Northern Pacific Railroad* (New York: G. P. Putnam's Sons, 1883), 159–70, 186–87, 380–83; John L. Harnsberger, *Jay Cooke and Minnesota: The Formative Years of the Northern Pacific Railroad, 1868–1873* (New York: Arno Press, 1981), 70–72, 90; Burnquist, *Minnesota and Its People,* 544–46.

28. Alfred D. Chandler Jr., *The Railroads: The Nation's First Big Business* (New York: Harcourt, Brace & World, 1965), 3–12, 21–24; Andrews, *History of St. Paul,* 411.

29. Andrews, *History of St. Paul*, 411.

30. Kane, *The Falls of St. Anthony*, 57–59; *Minneapolis Tribune*, May 27, 1867; F. H. Jackson, prep., *The Milwaukee Road, 1847–1939: Brief Record of the Milwaukee Road from Chartering of Its First Predecessor Company in 1847 to Date—August 1939* (Chicago: CMStP&P, 1939), 22.

31. *Minneapolis Tribune*, May 27, 1867.

## 2. LATE TO THE PARTY

1. Thomas C. Cochran, "Did the Civil War Retard Industrialization?" *Mississippi Valley Historical Review* 47 (September 1961): 199–200.

2. Alfred D. Chandler Jr., *The Visible Hand: The Managerial Revolution in American Business* (Cambridge: Harvard University Press, 1977), 58–78, 240–57; Cochran, "Did the Civil War Retard Industrialization?" 200. See also, Alfred D. Chandler Jr., "The Beginnings of 'Big Business' in American Industry," *Business History Review* 35 (Spring 1959): 88–101.

3. Chandler, *The Visible Hand*, 188–94; Cochran, "Did the Civil War Retard Industrialization?" 202; Merle Curti and Kendall Birr, "The Immigrant and the American Image in Europe, 1860–1914," *Mississippi Valley Historical Review* 37 (September 1950): 203–30; Harold F. Peterson, "Early Minnesota Railroads and the Quest for Settlers," *Minnesota History* 13 (March 1932): 25–44; Carlton C. Qualey, "A New El Dorado: Guides to Minnesota, 1850s–1880s," *Minnesota History* 42 (Summer 1971): 215–24.

4. Agnes Larson, *History of the White Pine Industry in Minnesota* (Minneapolis: University of Minnesota Press, 1949), 14–19, 36; Mildred Lucile Hartsough, *The Twin Cities as a Metropolitan Market: A Regional Study of the Economic Development of Minneapolis and St. Paul* (Minneapolis: University of Minnesota, 1925), 26–27; Joseph A. A. Burnquist, *Minnesota and Its People*, 4 vols. (Chicago: S. J. Clarke Publishers, 1924), 2:441–60; Michael Williams, *Americans and Their Forests: A Historical Geography* (New York: Cambridge University Press, 1989), 197–220.

5. *St. Paul Pioneer*, February 7, 1852; *Minneapolis Tribune*, August 31, 1873; Larson, *History of the White Pine Industry*, 36; *Compendium of History and Biography of Carver and Hennepin Counties, Minnesota* (Chicago: H. Taylor, 1915), 152–60; Larson, *History of the White Pine Industry*, 51; Burnquist, *Minnesota and Its People*, 2:461–65.

6. Charles B. Kuhlmann, "The Influence of the Minneapolis Flour Mills upon the Economic Development of Minnesota and the Northwest," *Minnesota History* 6 (June 1925): 142–43; George D. Rogers, "History of Flour Manufacturing in Minnesota," *Collections of the Minnesota Historical Society* 10 (February 1905): 36–40; Paul Wallace Gates, *The Farmer's Age: Agriculture, 1815–1860* (New York: Harper & Row, 1960), 166; William C. Edgar, *The Medal of Gold: A Story of Industrial Achievement* (Minneapolis: Bellman Company, 1925), 17–33; Burnquist, *Minnesota and Its People*, 2:415–20, 468–72.

7. Gates, *The Farmer's Age*, 157, 165, 167; Henrietta M. Larson, *The Wheat Market and the Farmer in Minnesota, 1858–1900* (New York: Columbia University, 1926), 55; Charles Byron Kuhlmann, *The Development of the Flour Milling Industry in the United States with Special Reference to Minneapolis* (Boston: Houghton Mifflin, 1929), 117.

8. Larson, *The Wheat Market*, 68; Marion Daniel Shuttes, *History of Minneapolis: Gateway to the Northwest*, 2 vols. (Chicago: S. J. Clarke Publishing Co., 1923), 2:353–54.

9. James Neal Primm, *Lion of the Valley: St. Louis, Missouri*, 2nd ed. (Boulder, CO: Pruett Publishing, 1990), 201–2, 346–47; Edgar, *The Medal of Gold*, 31–32; Larson, *The Wheat Market*, 66, William Cronon, *Nature's Metropolis: Chicago and the Great West* (New York: Norton, 1991), 110–15; Chandler, *The Visible Hand*, 209–13; Carlton J. Corliss, *Main Line of Mid-America: The Story of the Illinois Central* (New York: Creative Age Press, 1950), 61, 77–79; Cronon, *Nature's Metropolis*, 65–73, 181; D. C. Brooks, "Chicago and Its Railways," *Lakeside Monthly*, October 1872, 264–80.

10. Larson, *The Wheat Market*, 66–69.

11. Larson, *The Wheat Market*, 66–69; *Chicago Tribune*, December 15, 1865; *Minneapolis Tribune*, May 6, 7, 1869.

12. *Minneapolis Tribune*, January 7, 1868.

13. Christopher Columbus Andrews, *History of St. Paul with Illustrations and Biographical Sketches of Its Prominent Men and Pioneers* (Syracuse, NY: D. Mason & Co., 1890), 411; quoted in Ellis Paxton Oberholzer, *Jay Cooke: Financier of the Civil War*, 2 vols. (Philadelphia: George W. Jacobs, 1907), 245; *Handbook of St. Paul 1900* (St. Paul: St. Paul Chamber of Commerce, 1900), 73; Henry A. Castle, *A History of St. Paul and Vicinity: A Chronicle of Progress and Narrative Account of the Industries, Institutions, and People of the City and Its Tributary Territory*, 3 vols. (Chicago: Lewis Publishing, 1912), 1:229.

14. Quoted in Richard C. Overton, *Burlington Route: A History of the Burlington Lines* (New York: Alfred A. Knopf, 1965), 103; quoted in Cronon, *Nature's Metropolis*, 91.

15. Clare Leslie Marquette, "The Business Activities of C. C. Washburn," unpublished Ph.D. diss., University of Wisconsin, 1940, 323–27; *Minneapolis Journal*, November 16, 1938.

16. GN, *Annual Report*, 1912, 11; Rendigs Fels, *American Business Cycles, 1865–1897* (Chapel Hill: University of North Carolina Press, 1959), 96; Emory R. Johnson, *American Railway Transportation* (New York: D. Appleton Co., 1905), 27; Castle, *History of St. Paul*, 219; Andrews, *History of St. Paul*, 411.

17. L. O. Leonard, "The Founders and Builders of the Rock Island: Article 16—Charles J. Ives," *Rock Island Magazine* 22 (April 1927): 10–11; *Cedar Falls Gazette*, July 21, 1865 and November 30, 1866; *Poor's Manual of the Railroads, 1869–1870*, 222–28; BCR&M, Map with Prospectus for 7% First Class Gold Bonds, in AC; *Cedar Falls Gazette*, August 11, 1871.

18. *Iowa Railroad Commissioners Report*, 1880, 246–47; L. U. Reavis, *The Railway and River Systems of the City of St. Louis* (St. Louis: Woodward, Tiernan & Hale, 1879), 212–25; William Swartz, "The Wabash Railroad," *Railroad History*, Fall 1975, 1–25.

19. *Iowa Railroad Commissioners Report*, 1896, 221; *Cedar Falls Gazette*, May 4, 1866, May 15, 1868, and November 12, December 31, 1869; Don L. Hofsommer, "A Chronology of Iowa's Railroads," *Railroad History*, Spring 1975, 74.

20. Don L. Hofsommer, "The Grandest Railroad Project of the Age," *Annals of Iowa* 44 (Fall 1977): 118–36; *Cedar Falls Gazette*, March 20, April 27, June 1, 1866; *Report to the Board of Directors of the North Missouri Railroad to the Stockholders* (St. Louis: George Knapp & Co., 1866), 16. The Iowa Central *Railroad* should not be confused with the Iowa Central *Railway* of a later date.

21. Don L. Hofsommer, "The Railroad and an Iowa Editor: A Case Study," *Annals of Iowa* 41 (Fall 1972): 1073–1103; Hofsommer, "A Chronology of Iowa's Railroads," 74.

22. *American Railroad Journal*, January 7, 1832; James A. Ward, *Railroads and the Character of America, 1820–1887* (Knoxville: University of Tennessee Press, 1986), 10, 93–95; *St. Anthony Democrat*, January 14, 1870.

23. Marquette, "The Business Activities of C. C. Washburn," 326; August J. Veenendaal Jr., *Slow Train to Paradise: How Dutch Investment Helped Build American Railroads* (Stanford, CA: Stanford University Press, 1996), 169.

24. Marquette, "The Business Activities of C. C. Washburn," 327–28; Isaac Atwater, ed., *History of the City of Minneapolis, Minnesota* (New York: Munsell & Co., 1893), 330.

25. Minutes of the Minnesota Western Rail Road Constituting Minute Book of the Minneapolis & St. Louis Railroad to 8-28-80. Entries are by date; August 26, December 27, 1869; *Minnesota Executive Documents 1872*, 1:143–44; *Journal of the . . . Minnesota . . . Senate* (1870), 42; *Minneapolis Tribune*, February 11, 1870.

## 3. Of Champagne and Panic

1. Isaac Atwater, ed., *History of the City of Minneapolis, Minnesota* (New York: Munsell & Co., 1893), 491, 578–81, 591–96, 628–30, 738–40, 973–77, 994–99; Edward D. Neill and J. Fletcher Williams, *History of Hennepin County and the City of Minneapolis, Including the Explorers and Pioneers of Minnesota and Outlines of the History of Minnesota* (Minneapolis: North Star Publishing Co., 1881), 503; Charles E. Flandrau, *Encyclopedia of Biography of Minnesota* (Chicago: Century Publishing and Engraving Co., 1900), 190–91; Minnesota Historical Society, "Scrapbook" (Biography), 1:60, 74; R. I. Holcombe and William H. Bingham, eds., *Compendium of History and Biography of Minneapolis and Hennepin County, Minnesota* (Chicago: Henry Taylor & Co., 1914), 230–31, 264–65, 323–24.

2. Atwater, *History of the City of Minneapolis*, 391–94; Neill and Williams, *History of Hennepin County*, 655; Holcombe and Bingham, *Compendium of History and Biography of Minneapolis*, 248–49.

3. Atwater, *History of the City of Minneapolis*, 393.

4. All of the boys gained prominence. Israel was elected to Congress in 1850 and served five terms before becoming governor of Maine in 1860; Elihu served as congressman from Illinois for the period 1853 to 1869, when he was appointed secretary of state by President Grant; Cadwallader was in Congress before and after the Civil War, was a general in the Union Army, and in 1871 was elected governor of Wisconsin; Charles was editor of the *San Francisco Daily* and later minister to Paraguay; Samuel was a distinguished naval officer; and Algernon was a banker.

5. Neill and Williams, *History of Hennepin County*, 654; Flandrau, *Encyclopedia of Biography of Minnesota*, 135–42; Atwater, *History of the City of Minneapolis*, 545–51; James Gray, *Business without Boundary: The Story of General Mills* (Minneapolis: University of Minnesota Press, 1954), 14; Minutes of the Minnesota Western Rail Road Constituting Minute Book of M&StL to 8-28-80, August 26, September 4, December 27, 1869. Entries are by date, not page number. Hereinafter cited as M&StL MB.

6. Flandrau, *Encyclopedia of Biography of Minnesota*, 167–69; Atwater, *History of the City of Minneapolis*, 264–69; Gray, *Business without Boundary*, 6–13; William C. Edgar, *The Medal of Gold: A Story of Industrial Achievement* (Minneapolis: Bellman Company, 1925), 3–13, 34–65.

7. M&StL MB, October 29, November 5, 1870.

8. John L. Harnsberger, *Jay Cooke and Minnesota: The Formative Years of the Northern Pacific Railroad, 1868–1873* (New York: Arno Press, 1981), 13–23; Henry A. Castle, *Minnesota: Its Story and Biography*, 3 vols. (Chicago: Lewis Publishing Co., 1915), 1:440; Henry A. Castle, *A History of St. Paul and Vicinity: A Chronicle of Progress and Narrative Account of the Industries, Institutions, and People of the City and Its Tributary Territory*, 3 vols. (Chicago: Lewis Publishing, 1912), 1:61, 340; Flandrau, *Encyclopedia of Biography of Minnesota*, 436; *St. Paul City Directory for 1875* (St. Paul: St. Paul Pioneer Press, 1975), 382–83, 389.

9. Francis M. Carroll, *Crossroads in Time: A History of Carlton County, Minnesota* (Cloquet: Carlton County Historical Society, 1987), 96, 102–7.

10. Ellis Paxton Oberholzer, *Jay Cooke*: *Financier of the Civil War*, 2 vols. (Philadelphia: George W. Jacobs, 1907), 2:101–2, 186; Henrietta M. Larson, *Jay Cooke: Private Banker* (Cambridge: Harvard College, 1936), 246–53.

11. Harnsberger, *Jay Cooke and Minnesota*, 22–29; Oberholtzer, *Jay Cooke*, 2:106–20; "A Week at Duluth," *Atlantic Monthly* 25 (May 1870): 605–13.

12. Oberholtzer, *Jay Cooke*, 2:107–8, 130–31; NP, Original Tracklaying Record, March 15, 1933; *St. Paul Pioneer*, August 2, 1870; *St. Anthony Democrat*, September 1, 1870.

13. Lake Superior & Mississippi Directors Minute Book Number One, 146, MHS.

14. Larson, *Jay Cooke*, 272, 332, 368; Joseph A. A. Burnquist, *Minnesota and Its People*, 4 vols. (Chicago: S. J. Clarke Publishers, 1924), 1:320, 457, 531; 2:244, 247; Castle, *History of St. Paul*, 1:61, 95–97, 169, 340; 3:105; Castle, *Minnesota*, 1:103, 222, 363, 429, 441, 453, 456; *St. Paul City Directory for 1875*, 291, 400, 425; Bishop, "History of the St. Paul & Sioux City Railroad," 399–407.

15. "A Week at Duluth," 605–13; *St. Anthony Democrat*, September 1, 1870; advertising flyer, office of Charles H. Graves, Real Estate Agent, Duluth, April 2, 1870, in AC; *St. Paul Pioneer*, June 12, 1870; Larson, *Jay Cooke*, 272.

16. Lester B. Shippee, "Steamboating on the Upper Mississippi after the Civil War: A Mississippi Magnate," *Mississippi Valley Historical Review* 6 (March 1920): 470–502; Larson, *Jay Cooke*, 331–35; Harnsberger, *Jay Cooke and Minnesota*, 32–36; Clare Leslie Marquette, "The Business Activities of C. C. Washburn," unpublished Ph.D. diss., University of Wisconsin, 1940, 301–28; LS&M, *Annual Report*, 1872, 5; Edwin C. Washburn, "*The 17*" (Englewood, NJ: Washburn, 1929), 119–34; Karel D. Bicha, *C. C. Washburn and the Upper Mississippi Valley* (New York: Garland Publishing, 1995), 168–77; *Minneapolis Tribune*, October 13, 1895; *Minneapolis Journal*, November 16, 1938.

17. David Maldwyn Ellis, "The Forfeiture of Railroad Land Grants, 1867–1894," *Mississippi Valley Historical Review* 33 (June 1946): 27–60; *St. Anthony Democrat*, February 11, 18, 25, 1870; *Minneapolis Tribune*, February 17, March 6, 1870; M&StL MB to 8-28-80, April 1, 1871.

18. Atwater, *History of the City of Minneapolis*, 335; *Minneapolis Tribune*, December 15, 1870, February 2, July 18, August 9, 1871.

19. *Executive Documents . . . State of Minnesota . . . 1872*, 1:142–43; *St. Anthony Democrat*, November 2, 1871; *Poor's Manual of the Railroads, 1872*, 443–44; Harnsberger, *Jay Cooke and Minnesota*, 146.

20. *Minneapolis Tribune*, July 23, 1871; Atwater, *History of the City of Minneapolis*, 330, 335; *St. Anthony Democrat*, January 14, March 11, 1870.

21. *Minneapolis Tribune*, July 23, 1871; Atwater, *History of the City of Minneapolis*, 330–35; *St. Anthony Democrat*, January 14, March 11, 1870.

22. M&StL MB to 8-28-80, April 15, 1871; M&StL Contract File 215, August 27, 1874, C&NW; *Minneapolis Tribune*, May 27, 31, 1870; *St. Anthony Democrat*, November 17, 1870.

23. *Minneapolis Tribune*, April 16, June 4, 22, July 18, 19, August 15, 17, 1871.

24. *Minneapolis Tribune*, July 18, August 15, November 15, 1871.

25. *Minneapolis Tribune*, November 26, 1871; *St. Anthony Falls Democrat*, November 30, 1871.

26. *Minneapolis Tribune*, November 26, 29, 1871.

27. *St. Anthony Democrat*, March 11, 1870.

28. *New York Times*, October 31, 1891; *St. Paul Press*, February 16, 1870; Holcombe and Bingham, *Compendium of History and Biography of Minneapolis*, 216–17; Atwater, *History of the City of Minneapolis*, 545–51; Oberholtzer, *Jay Cooke*, 2:245; Harnsberger, *Jay Cooke and Minnesota*, 74; *St. Paul Pioneer*, February 17, 1871; Larson, *Jay Cooke*, 281.

29. *St. Anthony Democrat*, March 18, 1870; M&StL MB to 8-28-80, May 1, 3, 1871; *Minneapolis Tribune*, May 2, 1871; *St. Anthony Democrat*, November 2, 1871; *Minneapolis Tribune*, July 23, 1871; M&D Minute Book 1, 1, 3, 30, MHS; LS&M, *Annual Report*, 1872, 12.

30. Atwater, *History of the City of Minneapolis*, 994–98; August J. Veenendaal Jr., *Slow Train to Paradise*: *How Dutch Investment Helped Build American Railroads* (Stanford, CA: Stanford University Press, 1996), 234; Marquette, "The Business Activities of C. C. Washburn," 387; F. K. Bennett and J. S. McLintock, *The M&StL Railroad Co. History* (M&StL, 1921), 13; *St. Anthony Democrat*, November 30, 1871; *Poor's Manual of the Railroads, 1872–1873*, 230–31; LS&M, Minute Book No. 2, 90, 99, MHS 136. D.11, Box 1; Edward Vernon, *American Railroad Manual* (New York: American Railroad Manual Co., 1873), 531; H. T. Welles, *Autobiography and Reminiscences*, 2 vols. (Minneapolis: Marshall Robinson, 1899), 2:139; Larson, *Jay Cooke*, 365–66. LS&M, *Annual Report*, 1872, 19; ibid., 1871, 10–11.

31. LS&M, *Annual Report*, 1872, 19; ibid., 1871, 10–11.

32. Ralph W. Hidy, Muriel E. Hidy, Roy V. Scott, and Don L. Hofsommer, *The Great Northern Railroad*: *A History* (Boston: Harvard Business School Press, 1988), 18–29; Robert L. Reid, ed., "From Duluth to Bismarck in 1872: Travels with Artist Alfred R. Ward," *Minnesota History* 54 (Summer 1994): 69–86.

33. *Minneapolis Tribune*, February 17, 1870, August 8, 1871.

34. *Minneapolis Tribune*, August 8, 15, 16, 1871; *St. Anthony Falls Weekly Democrat*, February 16, August 23, 1870.

35. *St. Anthony Falls Weekly Democrat*, November 16, 1871; *Minneapolis Tribune*, June 23, July 18, August 8, 1871.

36. *St. Anthony Falls Weekly Democrat*, December 7, 1871.

37. *Minneapolis Tribune*, September 8, 19, 21, 1872.

38. *St. Paul Pioneer*, March 14, 1871; Carroll, *Crossroads in Time* 108–15; LS&M, *Annual Report*, 1872, 9; Oberholtzer, *Jay Cooke*, 2:334–49; Larson, *Jay Cooke*, 334–69; *St. Paul Pioneer*, March 31, 1872; E. V. Smalley, *Northern Pacific Railroad Book of Reference* (New York: E. Wells Sackett & Rankin, 1883), 86, 90, 92, 114; Oberholtzer, *Jay Cooke*, 2:421–39, 511–14.

39. William Watts Folwell, *A History of Minnesota*, 4 vols. (St. Paul: Minnesota Historical Society, 1921), 3:72; Oberholtzer, *Jay Cooke*, 2:400; Marquette, "The Business Activities of C. C. Washburn," 405–6; Eugene V. Smalley, *History of the Northern Pacific Railroad* (New York: G. Putnam's Sons, 1883), 198–203; Rendigs Fels, *American Business Cycles, 1865–1897* (Chapel Hill: University of North Carolina Press, 1959), 98–102; Robert Heilbroner and Aaron Singer, *The Economic Transformation of America: 1600 to the Present* (San Diego: Harcourt Brace Jovanovich, 1984), 229; Vincent Carosso, *The Morgans: Private Bankers, 1854–1913* (Cambridge: Harvard University Press, 1987), 219; Mansel G. Blackford and K. Austin Kerr, *American Enterprise in American History* (Boston: Houghton Mifflin, 1986), 208–9.

40. Andrews, *History of St. Paul*, 411; Atwater, *History of the City of Minneapolis*, 342.

41. LS&M, Directors Minute Book No. 2, 209, MHS; Smalley, *Northern Pacific Railroad Book of Reference*, 116, 118, 120, 124.

42. M&D Minute Book No. 1, 80, 231, MHS; LS&M, *Annual Report*, 1873, 9; Smalley, *Northern Pacific Railroad Book of Reference*, 116.

## 4. THE ST. LOUIS ROAD

1. Minutes of Minnesota Western Rail Road Constituting Minute Book of M&StL to 8-28-80, January 3, May 2, 1874. Entries are by date, not page number. Hereinafter cited as M&StL MB.

2. *Minnesota Railroad Commission Report*, 1874, 6; *Minneapolis Tribune*, October 28, 31, 1874.

3. Clare Leslie Marquette, "The Business Activities of C. C. Washburn," unpublished Ph.D. diss., University of Wisconsin, 1940, 341; *Minneapolis Tribune*, April 3, 1872; *St. Paul Weekly Press*, April 1, 1875; BCR&N, *Annual Report*, 1877, 1.

4. Quoted in Richard C. Overton, *Burlington Route: A History of the Burlington Lines* (New York: Alfred A. Knopf, 1965), 87, 117; Richard C. Overton, "The Burlington's Struggle for a Chicago-Twin Cities Lines, 1870–1890," a paper delivered at Vancouver, B.C., June 12, 1965, AC; Thomas C. Cochran, *Railroad Leaders, 1845–1890: The Business Mind in Action* (Cambridge: Harvard University Press, 1953), 133; Marquette, "The Business Activities of C. C. Washburn," 341.

5. Southern Minnesota Rail Road, *Annual Report*, 1875, 13, 20–22, 24; ibid., 1876, 5, 8, 20–23.

6. *Executive Documents . . . State of Minnesota . . . 1875*, vol. 3, 3; *Minnesota Railroad & Warehouse Commission Report*, 1890, 577.

7. Richard Hofstadter, *The Age of Reform: From Bryan to F.D.R.* (New York: Vintage Books, 1955), 6–12; George H. Miller, *Railroads and the Granger Laws* (Madison: University of Wisconsin Press, 1971), 161–71; John Lauritz Larson, *Bonds of Enterprise: John Murray Forbes and Western Development in America's Railway Age* (Boston: Harvard University, 1984), ix–xi, xv; *St. Anthony Democrat*, September 1, 1870.

8. Frank L. Kement, "Middle Western Copperheadism and the Genesis of the Granger Movement," *Mississippi Valley Historical Review* 38 (March 1952): 679–94; Mildred Throne, *Cyrus Clay Carpenter and Iowa Politics, 1854–1898* (Iowa City: State Historical Society of Iowa, 1974), 156–85; Frank H. Dixon, *State Railroad Control, with a History of Its Development in Iowa* (New York: Crowell, 20–23), 19–30; Martin Ridge, "Ignatius Donnelly and the Granger Movement in Minnesota, "*Mississippi Valley Historical Review* 42 (March 1956): 693–709; William Watts Folwell, *A History of Minnesota*, 4 vols. (St. Paul: Minnesota Historical Society, 1921), 3:32–57; *Minneapolis Tribune*, August 1, 1874.

9. Larson, *Bonds of Enterprise*, 152–55; Miller, *Railroads and the Granger Laws*, 17–23.

10. Rasmus S. Saby, "Railroad Legislation in Minnesota, 1849 to 1875," *Collections of the Minnesota Historical Society* 15 (1915): 68; *Executive Documents . . . State of Minnesota . . . 1875*, vol. 2, 4; *Minnesota Railroad Commission Report*, 1874, 6.

11. E. L. Godkin, "The Farmer's Clubs and the Railroads," *The Nation* 16 (April 10, 1873): 250.

12. *Biographical Directory of Railway Officials of America* (Chicago: Railway Age, 1887), 39; *Executive Documents . . . State of Minnesota . . . 1873*, vol. 2, 136, 360–61; ibid., 1874, vol. 1, 66, 223, 226; ibid., 1875, vol. 2, 176–78; ibid., 1876, vol. 2, 673.

13. *Minneapolis Tribune*, June 7, 1872; November 13, December 29, 1874; *Traveler's Official Guide* (January 1875), schedule 273; Tabular data from M&StL operations, 1873–1960, derives from *Poor's Manuals*, Minnesota and Iowa railroad commission annual reports, and M&StL annual reports. Hereinafter cited as M&StL tabular data.

14. M&StL tabular data.

15. Warren Upham, *Minnesota Geographic Names: Their Origins and Historic Significance* (St. Paul: Minnesota Historical Society, 1920), 81; *Minneapolis Tribune*, December 29, 1874; *Annual Report of the Board of Trade of Minneapolis*, 1877, 67–75.

16. *Minneapolis Tribune*, December 11, 1873; Minneapolis & Duluth Railroad Co. to the Holders of the first Mortgage Bonds of the Minneapolis & Duluth Railroad Co., January 30, 1874, AC; *Executive Documents . . . State of Minnesota . . . 1876*, vol. 2, 619; *Minnesota Railroad Commission Report, 1877*, 339; ibid., 1873, 331; Richard S. Prosser, *Rails to the North Star*: *One Hundred Years of Railroad Evolution in Minnesota* (Minneapolis: Dillon Press, 1966), 142.

17. Isaac Atwater, ed., *History of the City of Minneapolis, Minnesota* (New York: Munsell & Co., 1893), 337; *Annual Report of the Board of Trade of Minneapolis*, 1877, i-iii.

18. Atwater, *History of the City of Minneapolis*, 264–69; Robert M. Frame, "William Drew Washburn," in *Railroads in the Nineteenth Century*, ed. Robert L. Frey (New York: Facts on File, 1988), 425–28; *Minneapolis Tribune*, June 8, 28, July 15, 1873; Marquette, "The Business Activities of C. C. Washburn," 265, 385, 400; William C. Edgar, *The Medal of Gold*: *A Story of Industrial Achievement* (Minneapolis: Bellman Company, 1925), 61; Lucile M. Kane, *The Falls of St. Anthony*: *The Waterfall That Built Minneapolis* (St. Paul: Minnesota Historical Society Press, 1987), 88; C. C. Washburn to W. D. Hale, December 27, 1875, and February 18, 1876, William De la Barre Collection, MHS.

19. *Annual Report of the Board of Trade of Minneapolis*, 1877, 54–63; M&StL MB to 8-28-80, passim.

20. *Rock Island Magazine* 17 (October 1922): 34; CB&Q, *Annual Report*, 1872, 66; ibid., 1875, 29; Overton, *Burlington Route*, 151, 165; W. W. Baldwin, preparer, *Corporate History of the Chicago, Burlington & Quincy Railroad Company and Affiliated Companies* (Chicago: CB&Q, 1921), 144, 284–85, 296–99; Overton, *Burlington Route*, 174, 231–32.

21. *St. Paul Weekly Press*, April 1, 1875; *St. Paul Weekly Pioneer*, January 1, 1875; W. D. Washburn to W. D. Hale, January 12, 13, 1877, W. D. Hale papers, MHS; First Consolidated Mortgages Minneapolis & St. Louis Railroad Company to Central Trust Company of New York, Trustee, November 2, 1894, 18, AC.

22. *Minneapolis Tribune*, April 11, 1877; Upham, *Minnesota Geographic Names*, 198–205, 300–305, 507–12, 564–67; *Minneapolis Tribune*, August 21, October 13, 17, 23, 1877; *Minneapolis Tribune*, August 21; James E. Child, *Child's History of Waseca County, Minnesota* (Waseca: Privately published by the author, 1905), 225, 291–94, 321, 324–26.

23. *Albert Lea Enterprise*, August 23, September 6, 13, November 15, 1877; Edward D. Neill, *History of Freeborn County* (Minneapolis: Minnesota Historical Company, 1882), 355, 377; Franklyn Curtiss-Wedge, *History of Freeborn County Minnesota* (Chicago: H. C. Cooper & Co., 1911), 168.

24. *Albert Lea Enterprise*, November 15, 1877; *Minneapolis Tribune*, November 12–15, 1877.

25. *Annual Report of the Minneapolis Board of Trade, 1877*, advertising section; *Traveler's Official Railway Guide*, May 1878, 425–28; ibid., June 1878, xxxiv, 468–69; *Railroad Gazette* 11 (March 8, 1878): 130.

26. Marquette, "The Business Activities of C. C. Washburn," 352–54; M&StL, *Annual Report*, 1878, 7–8.

27. Folwell, *A History of Minnesota*, 3:73, 141; *Minneapolis Tribune*, October 17, 1877; *Annual Report of the Board of Trade of Minneapolis, 1877*, 51; Christopher Columbus Andrews, *History of St. Paul with Illustrations and Biographical Sketches of Its Prominent Men and Pioneers* (Syracuse, NY: D. Mason & Co., 1890), 410–12.

## 5. Pulling and Hauling

1. W. D. Hale diary, November 15, 1877, MHS; *Minneapolis Tribune*, December 26, 1877; C. C. Washburn to W. D. Hale, July 31, 1877. W. D. Hale diary, November 15, 1877, MHS; W. D. Hale papers, MHS.

2. John McAuley Palmer, "Railroad Building as a Mode of Warfare," *North American Review* 175 (December 1902): 844–52.

3. George H. Miller, *Railroads and the Granger Laws* (Madison: University of Wisconsin Press, 1971), 150–51; *Yesterday and Today*: *A History of the Chicago and North Western Railway System* (Chicago: C&NW, 1910), 71, 77, 164–66; *Railroad Gazette* 5 (October 11, 1873): 413.

4. H. Roger Grant, "Alexander Mitchell," *Railroads in the Nineteenth Century*, ed. Robert L. Frey (New York: Facts on File, 1988), 260–62; *History of the Chicago, Milwaukee & St. Paul Railway Company and Representative Employees* (Chicago: Railroad Historical Company, 1901), 159; John W. Cary, *The Organization and History of the Chicago, Milwaukee & St. Paul Railway Company* (Chicago: Cramer, Aikens & Cramer, 1893), 305; Richard S. Prosser, *Rails to the North Star*: *One Hundred Years of Railroad Evolution in Minnesota* (Minneapolis: Dillon Press, 1966), 137; *Minneapolis Tribune*, April 30, July 20, 1877; *Annual Report of the Minneapolis Board of Trade, 1877*, 48–49.

5. Cary, *The Organization and History of the Chicago, Milwaukee & St. Paul*, 170–71; Ralph W. Hidy, Muriel E. Hidy, Roy V. Scott, and Don L. Hofsommer, *The Great Northern Railroad*: *A History* (Boston: Harvard Business School Press, 1988), 32–34; Cary, *The Organization and History of the Chicago, Milwaukee & St. Paul*, 182–83, 267; Julius Grodinsky, *Transcontinental Railway Strategy, 1869–1893*: *A Study of Businessmen* (Philadelphia: University of Pennsylvania Press, 1962), 126–28; August Derleth, *The Milwaukee Road*: *Its First 100 Years* (New York: Creative Age Press, 1948), 124.

6. M&StL, *Annual report*, 1878, 9.

7. *Corporate History of the Chicago, St. Paul, Minneapolis & Omaha*

Railway Company (April 1, 1940), 1, 8, 13–23; *Yesterday and Today*, 81, 170; Judson W. Bishop, "History of the St. Paul & Sioux City Railroad, 1864–1881," *Collections of the Minnesota Historical Society* 10 (1905): 399–415.

8. *Minnesota Railroad Commission Report, 1878*, 504; ibid., 1879, 22; *Minneapolis Tribune*, July 6, 11, 12, 15, October 23, November 8, 1878; Minutes of Minnesota Western Railroad Constituting Minute Book of M&StL to 8-28-80, August 26, 1878. Entries are by date, not page number. Hereinafter cited as M&StL MB.

9. *St. Paul Pioneer Press*, October 24–25, 1878; *Minneapolis Tribune*, October 28, November 1, 2, 1878; *Corporate History of the Chicago, St. Paul, Minneapolis & Omaha Railway Company* (April 1, 1940), 20; *Minneapolis Tribune*, July 26, 29, 1879, April 21, 1880; M&StL MB, July 2, October 18, 1879.

10. Tabular data from LS&M Annual Reports, 1873–76; *Minnesota Railroad Commission Report, 1875*, 41–42; NP, *Annual Report*, 1876, 10–11; Eugene V. Smalley, *History of the Northern Pacific Railroad* (New York: G. Putnam's Sons, 1883), 295; E. V. Smalley, *Northern Pacific Railroad Book of Reference* (New York: E. Wells Sackett & Rankin, 1883), 147.

11. *Railroad Gazette* 2 (July 18, 1879): 39; ibid. (July 25, 1879): 404; ibid. (August 1, 1879), 421; ibid. (August 8, 1879), 433; *St. Paul Dispatch*, July 24, August 25, 1879; *Minnesota Railroad Commission Report, 1879*, 39; M&StL MB, August 2, 1879.

12. Clare Leslie Marquette, "The Business Activities of C. C. Washburn," unpublished Ph.D. diss., University of Wisconsin, 1940, 353.

13. Leland L. Sage, *A History of Iowa* (Ames: Iowa State University Press, 1974), 12–17, 310; John Lauritz Larson, *Bonds of Enterprise: John Murray Forbes and Western Development in America's Railway Age* (Boston: Harvard University, 1984), 162; *Iowa Railroad Commission Report, 1880*, 53; *Iowa: The Home for Immigrants* (Des Moines: Iowa Board of Immigration, 1870), 28–29; *Annual Report of the Minneapolis Board of Trade, 1877*, 18; *Railway World* 6 (August 7, 1880): 746; John R. Stilgoe, *Metropolitan Corridor: Railroads and the American Scene* (New Haven: Yale University Press, 1983), 3.

14. Marquette, "The Business Activities of C. C. Washburn," 344–50; H. T. Welles, *Autobiography and Reminiscences*, 2 vols. (Minneapolis: Marshall Robinson, 1899), 1:142–43; *History of Kossuth and Humboldt Counties, Iowa* (Springfield: 1884), 661; Clyde Clarkson Way, ed., *Biography and Memoirs of Thomas Asbury Way* (Privately published, 1946), 24–25; *Iowa Railroad Commission Report, 1880*, 244–46; Mortgage, Minneapolis & St. Louis Railway to Central Trust Company to New York; M&StL MB, October 14, 1879; *Minneapolis Tribune*, March 20, 1880; *Britt News-Tribune*, January 26, 1949; *Corwith, Iowa "Then" and "Now"* (Corwith: Corwith Centennial Committee, 1980), 13; *Minneapolis Tribune*, June 29, 1880.

15. *Railway World* 5 (June 14, 1879): 564; *Minneapolis Tribune*, June 12, 1878.

16. James J. Hill to Hamilton Browne, August 25, 1878, James J. Hill Letter Book, 4-11-78/1-16-79, 257, JJHRL; *Minneapolis Tribune*, July 26, 29, August 20, 1879; James J. Hill to S. S. Merrill, July 12, 1879, James J. Hill Letter Book, 1-4/9-11-79, 431, JJHRL; Don L. Hofsommer, "A Chronology of Iowa's Railroads," *Railroad History*, Spring 1975, 70–93.

17. *Railway Age* 5 (September 23, 1880): 503; *Railway World* 6 (August 4, 1880): 781; *Minneapolis Tribune*, August 24, November 23, 1880; Hubert L. Olin, *Coal Mining in Iowa* (Des Moines: State Mining Board, 1965), 40, 80; James H. Lees, "History of Coal Mining in Iowa," *Iowa Geological Survey* 22 (1913): 582–83; *Iowa*, 23; E. R. Landis, *Coal Resources of Iowa* (Des Moines: Iowa Geological Survey, 1965), table 15; *Corwith, Iowa "Then" and "Now,"* 13; *Iowa Railroad Commission Report*, 1880, 574–75, 582–85.

18. StP&D, Stockholders Minute Book No. 1, 1, MHS; *Minnesota Railroad Commission Report, 1878*, 576; ibid., 1879, 39; *St. Paul Dispatch*, July 24, 1879; *St. Paul Pioneer Press*, July 15, 16, 18, 1879; *Railroad Gazette* 2 (August 1, 1879): 421.

19. *Railroad Gazette* 2 (August 8, 1879), 433; *St. Paul Dispatch*, July 24, 1879; M&StL MB, August 2, 1879.

20. John L. Harnsberger, *Jay Cooke and Minnesota: The Formative Years of the Northern Pacific Railroad, 1868-1873* (New York: Arno Press, 1981), 147.

21. *Special Laws of Minnesota*, 1875, 278–79; ICC, *Valuation Reports*, No. 25 (1929), 582; *Minnesota Railroad Commission Report, 1876*, 750; *Minneapolis Tribune*, July 17, September 13, 1879; *St. Paul Dispatch*, July 23, 24, August 15, October 29, 1879; William D. Washburn to James J. Hill, October 23, 1879, GN papers, MHS.

22. *St. Paul Pioneer Press*, February 10, 20, 25, 1880; *Railway Age* 5 (April 29, 1880): 227; *Minneapolis Tribune*, February 10, April 28, 29, 1880; StP&D, Stockholders Minute Book No. 1, 1, MHS; Taylor's Falls & Lake Superior, Stock Book, passim, MHS; M&StL MB, March 20, May 8, 1880.

23. *Minneapolis Tribune*, May 15, November 5, 10, 1880; *The* [St. Croix Falls, Wisconsin, and Taylors Falls, Minnesota] *Dalles Visitor*, Summer 1972.

24. Lucile M. Kane, *The Falls of St. Anthony: The Waterfall That Built Minneapolis* (St. Paul: Minnesota Historical Society Press, 1987), 160; Smalley, *History of the Northern Pacific*, 318–19.

## 6. Optimism and Realism

1. Gordon Carruth, *What Happened When: A Chronology of Life and Events in America* (New York: Harper & Row, 1989), 490–94.

2. Alfred D. Chandler Jr., *The Visible Hand: The Managerial Revolution in American Business* (Cambridge: Harvard University Press, 1977), 5–6, 79, 240–45, 288–91, 308–14, 485; Thomas C. Cochran, "Did the Civil War Retard Industrialization?" *Mississippi Valley Historical Review* 47 (September 1961): 199–200.

3. William Watts Folwell, *A History of Minnesota*, 4 vols. (St. Paul: Minnesota Historical Society, 1921), 3:138–41; Leland L. Sage, *A History of Iowa* (Ames: Iowa State University Press, 1974), 201.

4. Lucile M. Kane, *The Falls of St. Anthony: The Waterfall That Built Minneapolis* (St. Paul: Minnesota Historical Society Press, 1987), 106–13; *Annual Report of the Board of Trade of Minneapolis*, 1877, 65–66; Agnes Larson, *History of the White Pine Industry in Minnesota* (Minneapolis: University of Minnesota Press, 1949), 110–24; William G. Rector, *Log Transportation in the Lake States Lumber Industry* (Glendale, CA: Arthur H. Clark Co., 1953), 31–32, 44–45; Michael Williams, *Americans and Their Forests: A Historical Geography* (New York: Cambridge University Press, 1989), 222–30.

5. Henrietta M. Larson, *The Wheat Market and the Farmer in Minnesota, 1858–1900* (New York: Columbia University, 1926), 127; Kane, *The Falls of St. Anthony*, 106–13; *Annual Report of the Board of Trade of Minneapolis*, 1877, 54–64.

6. James Gray, *Business without Boundary: The Story of General Mills* (Minneapolis: University of Minnesota Press, 1954), 34–35; Charles Byron Kuhlmann, *The Development of the Flour Milling Industry in the United States with Special Reference to Minneapolis* (Boston: Houghton Mifflin, 1929), 125–33; George D. Rogers, "History of Flour Manufacturing in Minnesota," *Collections of the Minnesota Historical Society* 10 (February 1905): 44–52; William C. Edgar, *The Medal of Gold: A Story of Industrial Achievement* (Minneapolis: Bellman Company, 1925), 58–71.

7. Edgar, *The Medal of Gold*, 77–79; Marion Daniel Shuttes, *History of Minneapolis: Gateway to the Northwest*, 2 vols. (Chicago: S. J. Clarke Publishing Co., 1923), 1:365–67; *Minneapolis Tribune*, April 19, May 15, 1881.

8. *St. Paul Pioneer Press*, February 2, 1880; Shuttes, *History of Minneapolis*, 357–61; Kuhlman, *The Development of the Flour-Milling Industry*, 131–32; Kane, *The Falls of St. Anthony*, 104.

9. Rogers, "History of Flour Manufacturing," 53; Edgar, *The Medal of Gold*, 73; Chandler, *The Visible Hand*, 207–8, 250–53, 293–94; Gray, *Business without Boundary*, 36; Edgar, *The Medal of Gold*, 106.

10. John C. Hudson, *Making the Corn Belt: A Geographical History of Middle-Western Agriculture* (Bloomington: Indiana University Press, 1994), 152–55.

11. Ralph W. Hidy, Muriel E. Hidy, Roy V. Scott, and Don L. Hofsommer, *The Great Northern Railroad: A History* (Boston: Harvard Business School Press, 1988), 5–49; *Minneapolis Tribune*, December 13, 1880; W. D. Washburn to James J. Hill, April 2, 1881, James J. Hill Papers, JJHRL; StPM&M, *Annual Report* 1881, 5–6.

12. James J. Hill to A. C. Morrill, February 4, 1880, Microfilm R-2:556. James J. Hill Papers, JJHRL; Hidy et al., *The Great Northern Railway*, 45–46.

13. NP, *Annual Report*, 1877, 6–7; *Minneapolis Tribune*, July 10, 11, 1878; NP, *Annual Report*, 1877, 9–12; Agreement between St. Paul, Minneapolis & Manitoba Railway Company and Northern Pacific Railroad Company, August 1, 1879, AC.

14. *Minneapolis Tribune*, July 10, 11, 1878; NP, *Annual Report*, 1879, 7–8, 17–18; Eugene V. Smalley, *History of the Northern Pacific Railroad* (New York: G. Putnam's Sons, 1883), 215, 235–36, 296–301.

15. August Derleth, *The Milwaukee Road: Its First 100 Years* (New York: Creative Age Press, 1948), 134–35; *Brief Record of the Development of the Milwaukee Road from Chartering of Its First Predecessor Company in 1847 to Date—August 1939* (Chicago: CMStP&P, 1939), 22–23, 26–27; *Minneapolis Tribune*, January 16, April 19, August 15, 1880, and January 25, 1881; M&StL, *Annual Report*, 1878, 9; *Commercial & Financial Chronicle* 30 (May 22, 1880): 532–33; *Railroad Gazette* 13 (May 27, 1881): 292–93; *Minneapolis Tribune*, January 1, 1882.

16. *Yesterday and Today: A History of the Chicago & North Western Railway System*, 3rd ed. (Chicago: C&NW, 1910), 97, 166; *Railway World* 6 (August 7, 1880): 756; H. Roger Grant, *The North Western: A History of the Chicago & North Western Railway System* (De Kalb: Northern Illinois University Press, 1996), 58–61; *Railroad Gazette* 14 (August 11, 1882): 498.

17. William Cronon, *Nature's Metropolis: Chicago and the Great West* (New York: Norton, 1991), 97–206; *Northwestern Lumberman*, March 27, 1880; *Railroad Gazette* 14 (March 31, 1882): 199; Larson, *History of the White Pine Industry*, 110–11, 122; Christopher Columbus Andrews, *History of St. Paul with Illustrations and Biographical Sketches of Its Prominent Men and Pioneers* (Syracuse, NY: D. Mason & Co., 1890), 410.

18. *Minnesota Railroad Commission Report, 1880*, 775; *Iowa Railroad Commission Report*, 1881, 146–50; Minute Book of the Fort Dodge & Fort Ridgely R. R. & Telegraph Co. 7-28-1876/7-28-1881, September 15, 1880, and April 20, 1881. Entries are by date, not page number. C&NW.

19. Albro Martin, *James J. Hill and the Opening of the Northwest* (New York: Oxford University Press, 1976), 113, 232; James J. Hill to William C. Van Horne, June 23, 1880, JJH Letter Book 9-24-79.9-20-82, 44; James J. Hill to Hamilton Browne, August 5, 1880, JJH Letter Book 9-24-79/9-20-82, 62; James J. Hill to William C. Van Horne, December 16, 1880, StPM&M Letter Book 4:380 10-4-80/4-21-81, JJHRL.

20. Mortgage, Minneapolis & St. Louis Railway Company to Central

Trust Company of New York, January 5, 1881, AC; *St. Paul Pioneer Press*, January 7, 1881; *Railroad Gazette* 14 (November 11, 1881): 640.

21. *Minneapolis Tribune*, November 30, 1881; Eugene V. Hastie, *History of Perry, Iowa* (Perry: self-published, 1962), 100–101; Hubert L. Olin, *Coal Mining in Iowa* (Des Moines: State Mining Board, 1965), 39–40, 43; James H. Lees, "History of Coal Mining in Iowa," *Iowa Geological Survey* 22 (1913): 579–80; StPM&M, *Annual Report*, 1882, 10.

22. *Special Laws of the Territory of Minnesota for 1853*, 28; *General Laws of the State of Minnesota*, 1869, 340–41; *Minnesota Railroad Commission Report*, 1873, 331; *Special Laws of the State of Minnesota for 1874*, 326; *Executive Documents of the State of Minnesota for the Year 1876*, 2:619; *Minnesota Railroad Commission Report*, 1879, 26; *Minneapolis Journal*, August 25, 1907; *Minneapolis Tribune*, November 7, 13, 1877; *Minneapolis Journal*, January 13, 22, 28, 1879; Mildred Lucile Hartsough, *The Twin Cities as a Metropolitan Market: A Regional Study of the Economic Development of Minneapolis and St. Paul* (Minneapolis: University of Minnesota, 1925), 29.

23. *Railway Age* 4 (March 13, 1879): 131; *Minneapolis Tribune*, January 28, 31, February 2, 6, 28, April 21, June 24, December 11, 1880.

24. Hallie Farmer, "The Economic Background of Frontier Populism," *Mississippi Valley Historical Review* 10 (March 1924): 406; C&NW, *Annual Report*, 1878, 11; *Railway Age* 5 (July 29, 1880): 405; Chandler, *The Visible Hand*, 216; *Annual Report of the Minneapolis Board of Trade*, 1877, 67.

25. *Minneapolis Tribune*, April 5, 19, 20, 1881; *Railroad Gazette* 13 (April 22, 1881): 226; *Railway Age* 4 (May 12, 1881): 263; Mortgage, Minneapolis & St. Louis Railway to Central Trust Company of New York, June 20, 1881, AC; *Sibley County Independent* [Henderson, MN], January 28, February 4, April 8, July 29, November 18, 1881; *Winthrop News*, October 8, 1931; Frank Curtiss-Wedge, *History of Redwood County*, 2 vols. (Chicago: H. C. Cooper, Jr. Co., 1916), 4, 233–34; *Railroad Gazette* 13 (July 27, 1881): 407; ibid. (October 14, 1881): 562; ibid. (November 11, 1881): 640; ibid. (December 23, 1881): 175; Warren Upham, *Minnesota Geographic Names: Their Origins and Historic Significance* (St. Paul: Minnesota Historical Society, 1920), 83–84, 221–25, 518–20.

26. *Poor's Manual of the Railroads, 1882*, 731–32; tabular data from M&StL annual reports and other sources, AC; *Railway World* 7 (January 22, 1881): 77; *Minneapolis Tribune*, August 24, 1880, January 18, 1881; *Railroad Gazette* 13 (October 28, 1881): 610.

27. Minutes of Minnesota Western Rail Road Constituting Minute Book of M&StL to 8-28-80, March 20, 1878. Entries are by date, not by page number, C&NW; tabular data; *Minneapolis Tribune*, April 22, 1879, October 2, 1880; *Traveler's Official Guide*, January 1882, 241; ibid., February 1882, 247.

28. *Traveler's Official Guide*, November 1881, 188–94, 198–99, 204–5, 217, 220.

29. *Minneapolis Tribune*, June 28, July 17, August 5, 9, September 5, 1878; *Britt News-Tribune*, January 26, 1949; *Minneapolis Tribune*, July 12–25, 1878.

30. *Minneapolis Tribune*, October 13, 16, 21, 1881; *Iowa Railroad Commission Report*, 1878, 45–46; *Railroad Gazette* 11 (July 11, 1879): 377.

31. LS&M, poster, June 14, 1869, AC; *St. Paul Daily Press*, March 26, 1869; Harold F. Peterson, "Early Minnesota Railroads and the Quest for Settlers," *Minnesota History* 18 (March 1932): 25–44; Lars Ljungmark, *For Sale—Minnesota* (Stockholm: Scandinavian University Books, 1971), 70–262; Sig Mickelson, *The Northern Pacific Railroad and the Settling of the West* (Sioux Falls, SD: Center for Western Studies, 1993), 1–44.

32. Larson, *History of the White Pine Industry*, 111; *Railroad World* 6 (August 1880): 771; M&StL, *Annual Report*, 1878, 23–31; ibid., 1879, 23–33; *Minnesota Executive Documents, 1881*, 3 vols., 2:799–803, 831–32, 861–62.

33. *Railroad World* 6 (August 14, 1880): 777; M&StL, *Annual Report*, 1879, 16–18, 25–31; ibid., 1878, 23–31.

## 7. NEW PLAYERS

1. Alfred D. Chandler Jr., *The Visible Hand: The Managerial Revolution in American Business* (Cambridge: Harvard University Press, 1977), 120; Vincent Carosso, *The Morgans: Private Bankers, 1854–1913* (Cambridge: Harvard University Press, 1987), 246.

2. Chandler, *The Visible Hand*, 88; John Lauritz Larson, *Bonds of Enterprise: John Murray Forbes and Western Development in America's Railway Age* (Boston: Harvard University, 1984), 177; James A. Ward, "Railroads in the American Context," *Railroad History*, Autumn 1994, 12–13.

3. Chandler, *The Visible Hand*, 147–48; *Railway Age* 5 (September 2, 1880): 456; quoted in Thomas C. Cochran, *Railroad Leaders, 1845–1890: The Business Mind in Action* (Cambridge: Harvard University Press, 1953), 133; ibid., 132.

4. Julius Grodinsky, *Transcontinental Railway Strategy, 1869–1893: A Study of Businessmen* (Philadelphia: University of Pennsylvania Press, 1962), 122–34; Chandler, *The Visible Hand*, 162–63; August Derleth, *The Milwaukee Road: Its First 100 Years* (New York: Creative Age Press, 1948), 126–28, 133–37.

5. Quoted in Cochran, *Railroad Leaders*, 159; Richard C. Overton, *Burlington Route: A History of the Burlington Lines* (New York: Alfred A. Knopf, 1965), 169.

6. Rendigs Fels, *American Business Cycles, 1865–1897* (Chapel Hill: Uni-

versity of North Carolina Press, 1959), 125–26; *Railroad Gazette* 14 (March 17, 1882): 174–75; ibid. (March 24, 1882): 187; *Minneapolis Tribune*, February 12, March 18, 1882; *Railroad Gazette* 14 (July 21, 1882): 449.

7. Frank P. Donovan Jr., *Mileposts on the Prairie: The Story of the Minneapolis & St. Louis Railway* (New York: Simmons Boardman, 1950), 69–76; *Railway Age* 6 (June 16, 1881): 330; *Official Guide* (November 1881), 253; Joyce Quinn, ed., *Lydia Ferguson Diary: 1854–1886* (Excelsior, MN: Excelsior–Lake Minnetonka Historical Society, 1981), 5; *Minneapolis Journal*, May 23, 1937; *Minneapolis Star Journal*, August 26, 1940; Kathryn H. Moody, "The Reminiscences of Lowell Henderson Moody," *Hennepin County History*, Winter 1967, 7–12; *Minneapolis Journal*, September 1, 1882.

8. Ralph W. Hidy, Muriel E. Hidy, Roy V. Scott, and Don L. Hofsommer, *The Great Northern Railroad: A History* (Boston: Harvard Business School Press, 1988), 44–45; *St. Paul Globe*, August 24, 1881 and July 16, 1882; *Minneapolis Tribune*, August 30, 1883.

9. James Gray, *Business without Boundary: The Story of General Mills* (Minneapolis: University of Minnesota Press, 1954), 34–35; R. I. Holcombe and William H. Bingham, eds., *Compendium of History and Biography of Minneapolis and Hennepin County, Minnesota* (Chicago: Henry Taylor & Co., 1914), 546; William Watts Folwell, *A History of Minnesota*, 4 vols. (St. Paul: Minnesota Historical Society, 1921), 3:388–400; William C. Edgar, *The Medal of Gold: A Story of Industrial Achievement* (Minneapolis: Bellman Company, 1925), 59.

10. Henrietta M. Larson, *The Wheat Market and the Farmer in Minnesota, 1858–1900* (New York: Columbia University, 1926), 322, 139–55, 211; Charles Byron Kuhlmann, *The Development of the Flour Milling Industry in the United States with Special Reference to Minneapolis* (Boston: Houghton Mifflin, 1929), 141–54; *Minnesota Railroad Commissioner Report, 1883*, 273–74; ibid., 1882, 36.

11. Gray, *Business without Boundary*, 40; Theodore C. Blegen, *Minnesota: A History of the State* (Minneapolis: University of Minnesota Press, 1963), 356–57.

12. *St. Paul Pioneer Press*, July 15, 16, 18, 1879; *Minnesota Railroad Commissioner Report*, 1879, 39.

13. *St. Paul Pioneer Press*, July 15, 1879; *Railroad Gazette* 11 (July 18, 1879): 390; ibid. (July 25, 1879): 404; Karel D. Bicha, *C. C. Washburn and the Upper Mississippi Valley* (New York: Garland Publishing, 1995), 173–75; *St. Paul Dispatch*, July 24, August 25, 1879.

14. *Railroad Gazette* 11 (August 29, 1879): 463; *Minneapolis Tribune*, October 28, 1873.

15. *Minnesota Railroad Commissioner Report 1880*, 853–55; J. S. Kennedy to James J. Hill, February 26, 1881, General correspondence; James J.

Hill to J. S. Kennedy, April 7, 1881, StPM&M Letter Book 4:802 (1880–1881), JJHRL; *Minneapolis Tribune*, July 8, 10, 14, 22, 1879; *St. Paul Daily Globe*, December 31, 1881; StPM&M, *Annual Report*, 1880–1881, 506; Hidy et al., *The Great Northern Railway*, 40–41.

16. *Minneapolis Tribune*, December 2, 1881; Hidy et al., *The Great Northern Railway*, 45–46; StPM&M, *Annual Report*, 1882, 11–12; ibid., 1883, 13.

17. *Minneapolis Tribune*, May 25, 1867; *St. Paul Dispatch*, July 15, 1879; E. V. Smalley, *Northern Pacific Railroad Book of Reference* (New York: E. Wells Sackett & Rankin, 1883), 184, 197; NP, *Annual Report*, 1880, 28–29; Grodinsky, *Transcontinental Railway Strategy*, 132.

18. NP, *Annual Report*, 1882, 42.

19. Smalley, *Northern Pacific Railroad Book of Reference*, 237; Eugene V. Smalley, *History of the Northern Pacific Railroad* (New York: G. Putnam's Sons, 1883), 299–301; Louis Tuck Renz, *The History of the Northern Pacific Railroad* (Fairfield, WA: Ye Galleon Press, 1980), 93–94; T. F. Oakes to Gen. H. Haupt, March 4, 1882, NP New York Office, Letters and Reports 1882–1883, AC; *Poor's Manual, 1882*, 733; Cochran, *Railroad Leaders*, 163.

20. Cochran, *Railroad Leaders*, 126–28; Derleth, *The Milwaukee Road*, 134–37; Agnes Larson, *History of the White Pine Industry in Minnesota* (Minneapolis: University of Minnesota Press, 1949), 118; *Railroad Gazette* 14 (December 1, 1882): 733–34.

21. *Corporate History of the Chicago, St. Paul, Minneapolis & Omaha Railway Company* (St. Paul: CStPM&O, 1940), 19, 22, 24, 30–31; *Yesterday and Today*, 82–84; *Poor's Manual, 1882*, 727–30; *Biographical Directory of the Railway Officials of America* (Chicago: Railway Age, 1896), 378–79; compilation of data from annual reports of C&NW, CStPM&O, and CRI&P for 1880; Stan Mailer, *The Omaha Road: Chicago, St. Paul, Minneapolis & Omaha* (Mukilteo, WA: Hundman Publishing, 2004), 35–57.

22. *Minneapolis Tribune*, April 21, 1880; Larson, *History of the White Pine Industry*, 117.

23. Fred. Taylor to the Bondholders and Stockholders of the Burlington, Cedar Rapids & Northern Railway Company, January 17, 1877, AC; BCR&N, *Annual Report*, 1878, 10, 13; *Official Guide* (April 1878), 454–55; *Rock Island Magazine* 17 (December 1922): 21.

24. *Minneapolis Tribune*, August 25, 1879; *St. Paul Pioneer Press*, August 26, 1879; *Railroad Gazette* 11 (August 29, 1879): 462–63; *New York Times*, September 4, 1879; *Railroad Gazette* 11 (September 5, 1879): 478; *Minneapolis Tribune*, September 8, 10, 15, 20, 1879; Larson, *Bonds of Enterprise*, 166–67; Overton, *Burlington Route*, 151, 165, 169.

25. CB&Q, *Annual Report*, 1879, 24; *Iowa Board of Railroad Commissioners Report*, 1879, 104–5; *Rock Island Magazine* 17 (December 1922): 21; ICC, *Valuation Docket 715*, Chicago, Burlington & Quincy Railroad (1927),

240–41; ICC, *Valuation Docket 152*, Chicago, Rock Island & Pacific Railway (1929), 936–38; *Minneapolis Tribune*, September 6, 1879.

26. Stuart Daggett, *Railroad Reorganization* (New York: Augustus M. Kelley, 1967), 311–15; August J. Veenendaal Jr., *Slow Train to Paradise: How Dutch Investment Helped Build American Railroads* (Stanford, CA: Stanford University Press, 1996), 96–97; *Commercial & Financial Chronicle* 30 (June 26, 1880): 663–65; William E. Hayes, *Iron Road to Empire: The History of the Rock Island Lines* (New York: Simmons-Boardman, 1953), 81–82, 102–3; *Railroad Gazette* 13 (October 7, 1881): 561; Chandler, *The Visible Hand*, 134–35; Fels, *American Business Cycles*, 125–27.

27. CRI&P, "From Iowa-Minnesota State Line to Saint Paul-Minneapolis, Minnesota," Volume E. Public Relations Department, E-14; Hayes, *Iron Road to Empire*, 70, 76–77; Cochran, *Railroad Leaders*, 135.

28. Quoted in Overton, *Burlington Route*, 169; Bicha, *C. C. Washburn*, 186.

29. Clare Leslie Marquette, "The Business Activities of C. C. Washburn," unpublished Ph.D. diss., University of Wisconsin, 1940, 357–60, 367; *Railway Age* 4 (September 11, 1879): 460; *Minneapolis Tribune*, January 21, 1881; *Railroad Gazette* 13 (February 4, 1881): 75.

30. Bicha, *C. C. Washburn*, 175–76; Minutes of the Minnesota Western Rail Road, Constituting Minute Book of Minneapolis & St. Louis to 8-28-80. Entries for July 29, October 14, 1879 and May 22, 1880; *Minneapolis Tribune*, February 14, March 5, 1881; *St. Paul Pioneer Press*, January 25, 28–31, February 3, 1881; Gray, *Business without Boundary*, 40.

31. Larson, *History of the White Pine Industry*, 116–17, 120; M&StL, *Annual Report*, 1879, 25–31; *Minnesota Railroad Commissioner Report, 1881*, 60, 64–65; *Minneapolis Tribune*, February 28, 1880.

32. *Poor's Manual*, 1882, 732; William D. Washburn to James J. Hill, January 22, 1882, General Correspondence, JJHRL; *Minneapolis Tribune*, February 12, 14, March 20, 24, April 20, 30, 1882; CRI&P, *Annual Report*, 1882, 13–14; *Railroad Gazette* 14 (April 28, 1882): 262; *Railway Age* 7 (March 23, 1882): 164.

33. *Minneapolis Tribune*, May 2, 1882; *Railway Age* 7 (March 30, 1882): 169; ibid. (May 4, 1882): 248.

34. Cochran, *Railroad Leaders*, 136; *Minneapolis Tribune*, May 3–5, 7, 12, 1882; *Railroad Gazette* 14 (May 5, 1882): 278; ibid. (May 12, 1882): 294; ibid. (July 21, 1882): 447; *Railway Age* 7 (May 18, 1882): 276; *Minneapolis Tribune*, July 30, November 24, 1882.

35. *Minneapolis Tribune*, September 11, 1877, July 30, 1879, January 1, 1883, January 8, 1873; Gray, *Business without Boundary*, 45.

## 8. DANCING WITH THE GIANTS

1. CRI&P, "From Iowa-Minnesota State Line to Saint Paul-Minneapolis, Minnesota." Volume E, Public Relations Department, E-14-15. Hereinafter cited as Volume E; Don L. Hofsommer, *Prairie Oasis: The Railroads, Steamboats, and Resorts of Iowa's Spirit Lake Country* (Des Moines: Waukon & Mississippi Press, 1975), 13; CRI&P, *Annual Report*, 1882, 13–14.

2. *Rock Island Magazine* 17 (December 1922): 22; Richard S. Prosser, *Rails to the North Star: One Hundred Years of Railroad Evolution in Minnesota* (Minneapolis: Dillon Press, 1966), 150, 171–72; *Minneapolis Tribune*, March 1, May 20, 23, 1882 and January 7, 9, 1883; H. Roger Grant, *The Corn Belt Route: A History of the Chicago Great Western Railroad Company* (De Kalb: Northern Illinois University Press, 1984), 50–51; *Railway Age* 6 (December 1, 1881): 680; ibid. 7 (September 28, 1882): 543; Roger Bee, Gary Browne and John Luecke, *The Chicago Great Western in Minnesota* (Anoka, MN: Blue River Publications, 1984), 3–9; John L. Relf, *The Man Whose Dream Came True: A Biography of A. B. Stickney* (Dellwood, MN: Privately published by the author, 1992), 47–48.

3. Quoted in Ellis Paxton Oberholzer, *Jay Cooke: Financier of the Civil War*, 2 vols. (Philadelphia: George W. Jacobs, 1907), 2:113; W. B. Hazen, "The Great Middle Region of the United States and Its Limited Space of Arable Lane," *North American Review*, January 1875, 27–30; Herbert S. Schell, *History of South Dakota* (Lincoln: University of Nebraska Press, 1968), 158–59.

4. *Minneapolis Tribune*, January 1, 1882; *Yesterday and Today: A History of the Chicago & North Western Railway System*, 3rd ed. (Chicago: C&NW, 1910), 166; Roger Grant, *The North Western: A History of the Chicago & North Western Railway System* (Dekalb: Northern Illinois University Press, 1996), 58–59.

5. Schell, *History of South Dakota*, 158–59; John N. Vogel, *Great Lakes Lumber on the Great Plains: The Laird, Norton Company in South Dakota* (Iowa City: University of Iowa Press, 1990), 15, 22, 26; *Railroad Gazette* 14 (August 11, 1882): 497; Harold E. Briggs, "The Great Dakota Boom, 1879 to 1886," *North Dakota Historical Quarterly* 4 (January 1930): 78–108; James F. Hamberg, "Railroads and the Settlement of South Dakota during the Great Dakota Boom, 1878–1887," *South Dakota History* 5 (Spring 1975): 165–78.

6. Thomas C. Cochran, *Railroad Leaders, 1845–1890: The Business Mind in Action* (Cambridge: Harvard University Press, 1953), 162, 170; Julius Grodinsky, *Transcontinental Railway Strategy, 1869–1893: A Study of Businessmen* (Philadelphia: University of Pennsylvania Press, 1962), 126–34; Alfred D. Chandler Jr., *The Visible Hand: The Managerial Revolution in American Business* (Cambridge: Harvard University Press, 1977), 134–42; *Minnesota Railroad Commissioner Report, 1882*, 41–42.

7. Cochran, *Railroad Leaders*, 170; *Minnesota Railroad Commissioner Report*, 1882, 27.

8. *Minneapolis Tribune*, September 16, October 3, 6, 1882.

9. *Minnesota Railroad Commissioner Report*, 1882, 75.

10. *Railroad Gazette* 13 (November 11, 1881): 640; *Minneapolis Tribune*, November 30, 1881; *Railway Age* 6 (November 17, 1881): 656–57; *Railroad Gazette* 14 (January 1, 1882): 34; *Minneapolis Tribune*, June 13, July 30, 1882; *Railroad Gazette* 14 (August 11, 1882): 496; StP&D, Stockholders Minute Book No. 1, 29, 45–46, 49–50, MHS; StP&D, *Annual Report*, 1883, 23–24; *Minnesota Railroad Commissioner Report*, 1881, 62–65.

11. M&StL, Contract File 4310, C&NW; *Corporate History of Chicago, St. Paul, Minneapolis, & Omaha Railway Company*, 29; StPM&M and NP, General Contract, October 1, 1882, 7, 12–13, AC; *Minneapolis Tribune*, October 6, 21, 1882.

12. John S. Kennedy to James J. Hill, November 4, 1882, General Correspondence, JJHRL; *Railway Age* 7 (October 26, 1882): 600; *Minneapolis Tribune*, October 26, November 11, 12, 15, 21, 22, 1882.

13. *Minnesota Railroad Commissioner Report*, 1882, 40–43; *Minneapolis Tribune*, November 22, 1882; James A. Ward, "Image and Reality: The Railway Corporate-State Metaphor," *Business History Review* 55 (Winter 1981): 491–516.

14. *Minneapolis Tribune*, December 14, 1882.

15. *Minneapolis Tribune*, September 1, November 22, 24, December 14, 1882 and January 1, 1883; *Railroad Gazette* 16 (December 29, 1882): 804–5; *Yesterday and Today*, 99; C&NW, *Annual Report*, 1883, 22–24.

16. *Minneapolis Tribune*, December 14, 1882 and January 1, 1883.

17. *Minneapolis Tribune*, March 30, December 31, 1883.

18. *Grand Opening of the Northern Pacific Railway Celebration at St. Paul, Minnesota September 3, 1883* (St. Paul: Compliments of the City, 1883), passim; *St. Paul Pioneer Press*, September 3, 1883; *St. Paul Globe*, September 10, 1883; *The Nation* 37 (September 13, 1883): 218; *Railroad Gazette* 15 (September 14, 1883): 606.

19. Louis Tuck Renz, *The History of the Northern Pacific Railroad* (Fairfield, WA: Ye Galleon Press, 1980), 93–94.

20. *Minneapolis Tribune*, December 31, 1883; *Railroad Gazette* 15 (April 25, 1884): 330; *Minneapolis Tribune*, August 31, 1884 and April 27, 1885; StPM&M, *Annual Report*, 1885, 13; Ralph W. Hidy, Muriel E. Hidy, Roy V. Scott, and Don L. Hofsommer, *The Great Northern Railroad: A History* (Boston: Harvard Business School Press, 1988), 45–46.

21. *Minneapolis Tribune*, April 7, 1873; MStPM&SteM, *Annual Report*, 1959, 1; H. T. Welles, *Autobiography and Reminiscences*, 2 vols. (Minneapolis: Marshall Robinson, 1899), 2:144–47; Isaac Atwater, ed., *History of the City of Minneapolis, Minnesota* (New York: Munsell & Co., 1893), 335–36.

22. MStP&SteM, *Annual Report*, 1900, 5–8; *Poor's Manual of Railroads*, 1887, 816; *Minnesota Railroad and Warehouse Commission Report*, 1899, 587; John A. Gjevre, *Saga of the Soo: West from Shoreham* (Moorhead, MN: Gjevre Books, 1990), 13–19; Agnes Larson, *History of the White Pine Industry in Minnesota* (Minneapolis: University of Minnesota Press, 1949), 115; Charles B. Kuhlmann, "The Influence of the Minneapolis Flour Mills upon the Economic Development of Minnesota and the Northwest," *Minnesota History* 6 (June 1925): 145; *Minneapolis Tribune*, December 31, 1883.

23. *Railroad Gazette* 14 (December 29, 1882): 804–5; Rendigs Fels, *American Business Cycles, 1865-1897* (Chapel Hill: University of North Carolina Press, 1959), 124–26; Ron Chernow, *The House of Morgan: An American Banking Dynasty and the Rise of American Finance* (New York: Atlantic Monthly Press, 1990), 54–56.

24. *New York Times*, June 7, 1883.

25. *New York Times*, February 6, 15, 16, 17, 18, 23, 1884; *Chicago Tribune*, February 8, 21, 1884; *Railway Age* 9 (March 20, 1884): 181; Hugh Riddle, David Dows, R. R. Cable, F. H. Tows, to the Stockholders of the Chicago, Rock Island & Pacific Railway (1884), AC.

26. *Chicago Tribune*, February 21, 1884; *New York Times*, October 26, 1883 and February 16, 18, 1884.

27. Fels, *American Business Cycles*, 127–30; *Railroad Gazette* 14 (December 29, 1882): 805; *Railway Review*, August 16, 1884, 428.

28. Grant, *The North Western*, 58–61; Hamburg, "Railroads and the Settlement of South Dakota," 165–78; *Minneapolis Tribune*, March 23, April 4, May 11, June 1, 1884; Schell, *History of South Dakota*, 165; Vogel, *Great Lakes Lumber*, 26–27; Gilbert C. Fite, *The Farmers: Frontier, 1865-1900* (New York: Holt, Rinehart & Winston, 1966), 99–100; *St. Paul: The Commercial Emporium of the Northwest* (St. Paul: Pioneer Press, 1886), 46–47.

29. *St. Paul*, 40–44; Fite, *The Farmers*, 102; *Railroad Gazette* 15 (August 17, 1883): 549.

30. *Minneapolis Tribune*, December 31, 1883; BCR&N, Consolidated First Mortgage to Secure "Consolidated First Mortgage Five Per Cent Bonds," April 1, 1884–April 1, 1934, 22, 25, AC; *Minnesota Railroad Commissioner Report*, 1884, 586; Stuart Daggett, *Railroad Reorganization* (New York: Augustus M. Kelley, 1967), 315; *Railroad Gazette* 16 (April 4, 1884): 271; ibid. (April 11, 1884): 288; ibid. (April 18, 1884): 309; *Railway Age* 8 (December 13, 1883): 795; ibid. 9 (March 20, 1884): 189; *Minneapolis Tribune*, March 23, 1884; ICC, Chicago, Rock Island & Pacific Railway, *Valuation Docket 152* (February 12, 1929), 997.

31. R. R. Cable to James J. Hill, May 14, 1883, GN Executive Department Vault 15 B Box 25 C, AC.

32. *Minneapolis Tribune*, May 1, 1884; Warren Upham, *Minnesota Geographic Names: Their Origins and Historic Significance* (St. Paul: Minnesota Historical Society, 1920), 288–92, 448–54, 593–98; Frank Curtiss-Wedge, *History of Redwood County*, 2 vols. (Chicago: H. C. Cooper, Jr. Co., 1916), 1:4, 232–35; L. R. Moyer and O. G. Dale, eds. *History of Chippewa and Lac qui Parle Counties Minnesota*, 2 vols. (Indianapolis: B. F. Bowen & Co., 1916), 1:477–87, 557–65.

33. *Minneapolis Tribune*, August 1, 14, September 13, 1884; *Railroad Gazette* 16 (September 19, 1884): 692; ibid. (September 26, 1884): 709; *New York Times*, September 14, 25, 27, 1884; *Railway Age* 9 (September 18, 1884): 591.

34. Upham, *Minnesota Geographic Names*, 595, 597; *Railway Age* 9 (September 1, 1884): 577; *Railroad Gazette* 16 (September 26, 1884): 709; *Minneapolis Tribune*, July 3, August 14, 17, October 5, 28, 1884; BCR&N, *Annual Report*, 1884, x.

35. *Minneapolis Tribune*, October 5, 28, 1884.

## 9. Falling Rates and Encroachment

1. Norm Cohen, *Long Steel Rail: The Railroad in American Folk Song* (Champaign: University of Illinois Press, 1981), 374–75; *Minneapolis Tribune*, July 27, 1883; M&StL, Time Table (July 1884), 3; *Official Guide* (May 1885), 244–47, 327–29.

2. *Official Guide* (May 1885), 244, 247; *Minneapolis Tribune*, July 24, 1884.

3. *Official Guide* (June 1883), 296–97; M&StL, Time Table (July 1884), 6, 10.

4. *Minneapolis Tribune*, December 31, 1883; *Grand Opening of the Northern Pacific Railway Celebration at Saint Paul, Minnesota*, September 3, 1883 (Compliments of the City of St. Paul, 1883), 66–68; Mark Twain, *Life on the Mississippi* (New York: Modern Library, 1993), 427; Christopher Columbus Andrews, *History of St. Paul with Illustrations and Biographical Sketches of Its Prominent Men and Pioneers* (Syracuse, NY: D. Mason & Co., 1890), 422; Walter G. Berg, *Buildings and Structures of American Railroads* (New York: John Wiley & Sons, 1900), 426–31. See also Mary Lethert Wingerd, *Claiming the City: Politics, Faith, and the Power of Place in St. Paul* (Ithaca, NY: Cornell University Press, 2001).

5. CRI&P, Summer Resorts of Northern Iowa and Minnesota Reached by the Albert Lea Route (Chicago: Rand McNally, 1883), 3, 20–29, 59–63; *Minneapolis Tribune*, June 22, 1884; *Railroad Gazette* 19 (June 24, 1887): 427.

6. Tabular data from M&StL annual reports and annual reports of the Railroad Commissions of Minnesota and Iowa.

7. Ibid.

8. *Minneapolis Chamber of Commerce Annual Report, 1884*, 39, 48–50; ibid. (1886), 41–42, 117.

9. *Minneapolis Tribune*, January 9, 1883; *National Cyclopedia of American Biography*, vol. 14 (New York: J. T. White & Co., 1917), 450; Slason Thompson, *A Short History of American Railways* (Chicago: Bureau of Railway News and Statistics, 1925), 432–33.

10. Quoted in Mildred Lucile Hartsough, *The Twin Cities as a Metropolitan Market: A Regional Study of the Economic Development of Minneapolis and St. Paul* (Minneapolis: University of Minnesota, 1925), 90; *Minnesota Railroad Commissioner Report, 1884*, 593; *Minnesota Railroad and Warehouse Commission Report, 1915*, 91.

11. E. C. Lindley to Carl R. Gray, June 7, 1913, GN President File 5828; W. H. Truesdale to James J. Hill, July 31, August 8, 9, 1886, GN Executive Department, Box 42, MHS; Henry D. Minot to John S. Kennedy, March 28, 1886, Minot Letter Book, vol. 28–29, James J. Hill Collection, JJHRL; *Railway Age* 10 (June 11, 1885): 380; ibid. (October 1, 1885): 632; Frank P. Donovan Jr., *Mileposts on the Prairie: The Story of the Minneapolis & St. Louis Railway* (New York: Sinman Boardman, 1950), 83–85.

12. *Minnesota Railroad Commissioner Report, 1883*, 242; ibid. (1884), 564–65; *St. Paul Chamber of Commerce Annual Report, 1886*, 35; ibid. (1888), 84; Andrews, *History of St. Paul*, 421; Frank P. Donovan Jr., *Gateway to the Northwest: The Story of the Minnesota Transfer Railway* (Minneapolis: Privately published by the author, 1954), passim.

13. Rendigs Fels, *American Business Cycles, 1865–1897* (Chapel Hill: University of North Carolina Press, 1959), 137–39.

14. *Minneapolis Chamber of Commerce Annual Report, 1884*, 43; ibid. (1885), 130; *Poor's Manual, 1888*, 1118; *Official Guide* (May 1885), 262–63.

15. *Biographical Directory of the Railway Officials of America* (Chicago: Railway Age 1901), 520; H. Roger Grant, *The Corn Belt Route: A History of the Chicago Great Western Railroad Company* (De Kalb: Northern Illinois University Press, 1984), 1–21; *Corporate History of the Chicago Great Western Railway Company as of Date of Valuation, June 30, 1916* (Chicago: CGW, n.d.), 1–2, AC; Roger Bee, Gary Browne, and John Luecke, *The Chicago Great Western in Minnesota* (Anoka, MN: Blue River Publications, 1984), 13–16; *Minneapolis Chamber of Commerce Annual Report, 1885*, 121; Don L. Hofsommer, "A Chronology of Iowa's Railroads," *Railroad History*, Spring 1975, 74, 77.

16. *Boston Transcript*, July 8, August 31, 1885; Henry D. Minot to John S. Kennedy, May 28, 1886, Minot Letter Book, vol. R28–20, James J. Hill Collection, JJHRL; StPM&M, *Annual Report*, 1886, 13; *Chicago Tribune*, February 20, 1886; H. Roger Grant, "A. B. Stickney Builds a Railroad: The Saga of the Minnesota & Northwestern," *Midwest Review* 6 (Spring 1984): 13–26.

17. Soo Line, Construction Dates (n.d.), 2–4, AC; *Minneapolis Tribune*, November 8, 1884; Soo Line, *Annual Report*, 1957, 1; *Minneapolis Chamber of Commerce Annual Report, 1886*, 130; H. D. Minot to John S. Kennedy, November 12, 1886, General Correspondence, James J. Hill Collection, JJHRL; Soo Line, *Annual Report*, 1900, 5; Memorandum of Agreement, Canadian Pacific Railway and Minneapolis, Sault Ste. Marie & Atlantic Railway, October 7, 1886, AC; *Chicago Tribune*, February 10, 1886.

18. Julius Grodinsky, *Transcontinental Railway Strategy, 1869–1893: A Study of Businessmen* (Philadelphia: University of Pennsylvania Press, 1962), 270–77, 312–13; Richard C. Overton, *Burlington Route: A History of the Burlington Lines* (New York: Alfred A. Knopf, 1965), 190–98; *Chicago Tribune*, February 3, 1886; James J. Hill to John S. Kennedy, June 8, July 13, 1885; John S. Kennedy to James J. Hill, July 3, 18, 1885, General Correspondence, James J. Hill Collection, JJHRL; Ralph W. Hidy, Muriel E. Hidy, Roy V. Scott, and Don L. Hofsommer, *The Great Northern Railroad: A History* (Boston: Harvard Business School Press, 1988), 53–54; CB&Q, *Annual Report*, 1886, 20.

19. *Boston Transcript*, September 24, 1885; *Commercial & Financial Chronicle*, August 29, 1885; *Boston Transcript*, August 5, 1885; CB&Q, *Annual Report*, 1885, 20–22; C. E. Perkins to John Murray Forbes, November 1, 1883, NP President File 197-21-4, AC; CB&Q, *Annual Report*, 1871, 18.

20. Henry D. Minot to John S. Kennedy, June 5, 1886, Minot Letter Book, vol. 28–29, James J. Hill Collection, JJHRL; *Chicago Tribune*, January 30, February 2, 5, 16, 26, 1886; *Boston Transcript*, August 24, 1885; *Bradstreet's* 13/14 (April 7, 1886): 242; Overton, *Burlington Route*, 195; *Railroad Gazette* 18 (June 25, 1886): 452; *Bradstreet's* 13/14 (July 3, 1886): 488.

21. *Boston Transcript*, August 5, 11, 1886; *Commercial & Financial Chronicle*, August 29, 1885; O. H. Holt, *Dakota: Behold I Show You a Delightsome Land* (Chicago: Rand McNally, 1885), 88; *Chicago Tribune*, February 18, 1886; CRI&P, *The Western Trail* 5 (February 1886): 2; *Railroad Gazette* 18 (October 22, 1886): 732; John S. Kennedy to James J. Hill, June 28, 1886, General Correspondence, James J. Hill Collection, JJHRL.

22. *New York Times*, August 13, 14, 15, 1885; *Boston Transcript*, August 14, 15, 22, 1885; *Railway Age* 10 (September 3, 1885): 561; W. H. Truesdale to H. Haupt, March 10, June 4, August 2, 1883, NP General Manager Files, 137A.3.2F Box 8, MHS.

23. NP, *Annual Report*, 1884, 10; Louis Tuck Renz, *The History of the Northern Pacific Railroad* (Fairfield, WA: Ye Galleon Press, 1980), 128; NP, *Annual Report*, 1886, 10; Grant, *The Corn Belt Route*, 193; *Railway Age* 10 (June 11, 1885): 380; *Iowa Railroad Commissioners Report, 1886*, 348; *Minnesota Railroad Commissioner Report, 1886*, 951; *Chicago Tribune*, January 11, 19, 1886; NP, Annual Report of the Vice President and General Manager to the President and Board of Directors, 1886, 24; H. D. Minot to John S.

Kennedy, May 28, 1886, Minot Letter Book, vol. R28–29, James J. Hill Collection, JJHRL; *Chicago Tribune*, February 18, 1886.

24. *Railroad Gazette* 18 (February 26, 1886): 155; ibid. (June 25, 1886): 451, 454; ibid. (November 12, 1886): 786; *Railroad Gazette* 19 (August 5, 1887): 520; *Railway Age* 13 (March 9, 1888): 151; ibid. (December 9, 1888): 789; Hidy et al., *The Great Northern*, 61–66; NP, *Annual Report*, 1887, 23.

25. CRI&P, *The Western Trail*, 5 (February 1886), 2; James J. Hill to J. S. Kennedy, July 8, 1886, JJH Letter Book 3-22-86/10-22-86, 268, James J. Hill Collection, JJHLR.

26. *Bradstreet's* 13/14 (April 17, 1886): 242; tabular data taken from *Minneapolis Chamber of Commerce Annual Reports, 1884–89*.

27. *Minneapolis Tribune*, December 24, 1884; *Chicago Tribune*, February 19, 1886; *Railroad Gazette* 18 (June 25, 1886): 453.

28. *Commercial & Financial Chronicle* 42 (June 12, 1886): 706–8.

29. G. H. Crosby, *History of CRI&P* (Chicago: Chicago, Rock Island & Pacific Railway, n.d., 1902?), 34; Overton, *Burlington Route*, 196–98.

30. Charles E. Perkins to John Murray Forbes, November 1, 1883, NP President File 197-21-4, AC; *Chicago Tribune*, February 16, 1886; Map of Rock Island Lines Showing Lines Built and Acquired, April 29, 1922, AC; Stuart Daggett, *Railroad Reorganization* (New York: Augustus M. Kelley, 1967), 314–17; William E. Hayes, *Iron Road to Empire: The History of the Rock Island Lines* (New York: Simmons-Boardman, 1953), 127; CRI&P, *Annual Report*, 1889, 13–16; *Chicago Tribune*, August 11, 1885.

31. Quoted in Saul Engelbourg and Leonard Bushkoff, *John Stewart Kennedy and the Financing of the Western Railroads* (East Lansing: Michigan State University Press, 1996), 120; quoted in *Minneapolis Tribune*, July 29, 1879; CM&StP, *Annual Report*, 1887, 14; Hartsough, *The Twin Cities as a Metropolitan Market*, 84–112; James A. Ward, *Railroads and the Character of America, 1820–1887* (Knoxville: University of Tennessee Press, 1986), 144; quoted in Richard C. Overton, *Perkins/Budd: Railway Statesmen of the Burlington* (Westport, CT: Greenwood Press, 1982), 48; W. M. Ackworth, *The Elements of Railway Economics* (Oxford Clarendon Press, 1905), 76–77.

32. *Minnesota Railroad and Warehouse Commission Report, 1885*, 9–14; ibid. (1888), 31; *Iowa Railroad Commission Report, 1878*, 58; Leland L. Sage, *A History of Iowa* (Ames: Iowa State University Press, 1974), 204–7; *Railroad Gazette* 13 (November 2, 1888): 722.

33. Fels, *American Business Cycles*, 142–43; Harold E. Briggs, "The Great Dakota Boom, 1879 to 1886," *North Dakota Historical Quarterly* 4 (January 1930): 78–108; John N. Vogel, *Great Lakes Lumber on the Great Plains: The Laird, Norton Company in South Dakota* (Iowa City: University of Iowa Press, 1990), 134–37; Gilbert C. Fite, *The Farmers: Frontier, 1865–1900* (New York: Holt, Rinehart & Winston, 1966), 106–9.

34. *Minnesota Railroad & Warehouse Commission Report*, 1888, 390; *Winthrop News*, March 10, 1888; *New York Times*, January 14, 1888; *Minneapolis Tribune*, January 14, 1888; W. H. Truesdale to Bondholders of the Minneapolis & St. Louis Railway Company, May 26, 1888, AC; *New York Times*, June 2, 29, 1888; *Railway Age* 8 (June 15, 1888): 374; ibid. (July 6, 1888): 438.

## 10. ADRIFT

1. M&StL, *Annual Report*, 1890, 10–11; CRI&P, Annual Report, 1889, 13–17; *Official Guide* (December 1889), 318; *Rock Island Magazine* 21 (November 1926): 19–20; BCR&N, *Annual Report*, 1884, ix; ibid., 1888, 3; *Minneapolis Tribune*, February 25, 25, June 11, 1890.

2. *Minneapolis Tribune*, June 11, 1890 and July 7, 1891.

3. *Commercial & Financial Chronicle* 46 (June 16, 1888): 752–54; *Minneapolis Tribune*, December 21, 1888; *New York Times*, June 26, 27, 1888; June 18, 1890; June 4, 1891.

4. *Chicago Tribune*, July 30, 1890; William V. Allen, "Western Feelings toward the East," *North American Review* 162: 590; Hallie Farmer, "The Economic Background of Frontier Populism," *Mississippi Valley Historical Review* 10 (March 1924): 406–27; Hallie Farmer, "The Railroads and Frontier Populism," *Mississippi Valley Historical Review* 13 (December 1926): 387–97; Philip D. Jordan, *Ohio Comes of Age, 1873–1900* (Columbus: Ohio State Archaeological and Historical Society, 1943), 121.

5. Jack T. Johnson, *Peter Anthony Dey: Integrity in Public Service* (Iowa City: State Historical Society of Iowa, 1939), 184–89; *St. Paul Chamber of Commerce, Annual Report, 1888*, 25; CB&Q, *Annual Report*, 1888, 19–23; *Minneapolis Tribune*, July 12, 1888, 25; CB&Q, *Annual Report*, 1888, 19–23; *Minneapolis Tribune*, July 12, 1888; ibid., February 26 and March 6, 1889; ibid., February 21, 26, July 2, 1890; *Iowa, Report of Railroad Commissioners, 1889*, 494; CRI&P, *Annual Report*, 1889, 17–20. See also Richard C. Cortner, *The Iron Horse and the Constitution: Railroads and the Transformation of the Fourteenth Amendment* (Westport, CT: Greenwood Press, 1993).

6. CStP&KC, *Annual Report*, 1890, 2; *Minneapolis Tribune*, June 29, 1888; *Bradstreet's*, April 26, 1890, 265; *Minneapolis Tribune*, August 8, December 3, 11, 12, 1888; ibid., March 8, 1889; ibid., February 14, 1890.

7. *Minneapolis Tribune*, March 6, 1889; Agnes Larson, *History of the White Pine Industry in Minnesota* (Minneapolis: University of Minnesota Press, 1949), 229–46, 374–77; *Annual Report of the Minneapolis Chamber of Commerce*, 1888, 43; ibid., 1890, 42; ibid., 1892, 225–26.

8. *Annual Report of the Minneapolis Chamber of Commerce*, 1888, 42; *Minneapolis Tribune*, September 16, 1888; ibid., January 1, 1889; ibid., January 28, 1890; ibid., August 21, 1891; Isaac Atwater, ed., *History of the City of Minneapolis, Minnesota* (New York: Munsell & Co., 1893), 1:331–32; Charles Byron Kuhlmann, *The Development of the Flour Milling Industry in the United States with Special Reference to Minneapolis* (Boston: Houghton Mifflin, 1929), 165.

9. Minneapolis Railway Transfer Minute Book #1, March 31, 1883; *Minnesota, Report of the Railroad and Warehouse Commission, 1904*, Entry "1," Railway Transfer Company of Minneapolis.

10. 133 ICC 356–365; *Minneapolis Tribune*, January 6, 1890; Samuel Hill to James J. Hill, November 12, 15, 18, 1889, and Charles A. Pillsbury to James J. Hill, November 22, 1889, James J. Hill Papers, General Correspondence, JJHRL; *Minneapolis Tribune*, August 25, 1895; William C. Edgar, *The Medal of Gold: A Story of Industrial Achievement* (Minneapolis: Bellman Company, 1925), 154–55, 275–76.

11. *Minneapolis Tribune*, May 8, 17, 1889.

12. *Minneapolis Tribune*, November 27, 1888; ibid., May 21, 25, 1889.

13. James J. Hill to F. P. Olcott, June 6, 1889, James J. Hill Letter Book, vol. P-13, 319–21, JJHRL; *Minneapolis Tribune*, April 15, 22, May 10, 25, September 5, 1890; M&StL, *Annual Report*, 1890, 8–9; ibid., 1891, 6; ibid., 1893, 7.

14. M&StL, *Annual Report*, 1893, 5–7; ibid., 1892, 7; ibid., 1890, 2, 8; *Railroad Gazette* 24 (April 18, 1892), 257; *Minneapolis Tribune*, November 25, 27, 1890.

15. Lucile M. Kane, *The Falls of St. Anthony: The Waterfall That Built Minneapolis* (St. Paul: Minnesota Historical Society Press, 1987), 147; *Census of Minnesota*, 1890, 2–3; *Annual Report of the Saint Paul Chamber of Commerce, 1888*, 51, 83.

16. *American Heritage* 40 (November 1989): 11–14; Leland L. Sage, *A History of Iowa* (Ames: Iowa State University Press, 1974), 201; tabular data from annual reports of M&StL, CGW, and CM&StP for 1893; *Iowa Report of Railroad Commissioners, 1890*, 14; *Minneapolis Tribune*, August 2, 1890; M&StL, *Annual Report*, 1890, 4–5.

17. M&StL, *Annual Report*, 1892, 4; ibid., 1895, 5.

18. StP&D, *Annual Report*, 1888, 8, 60–61; M&StL, *Annual Report*, 1895, 5; tabular data derived from StP&D annual reports, 1890–94.

19. *Commercial & Financial Chronicle*, June 18, 1887, 769; August Derleth, *The Milwaukee Road: Its First 100 Years* (New York: Creative Age Press, 1948), 136–37; John W. Cary, *The Organization and History of the Chicago, Milwaukee & St. Paul Railway* (Chicago: Cramer, Atkins & Cramer, 1893), 184; W. D. Washburn to James J. Hill, January 24, 1890, General Correspondence, James J. Hill Papers, JJHRL; *Minneapolis Tribune*, June 5, August 6, 1890 and April 22, 1891; Stenographer's Minutes, ICC Valuation Docket 326 (May 3, 1926), 47–53 with addenda including contracts dated 1886, 1890, and 1899, exhibits part of testimony by Thomas E. Sands, AC.

20. *Minneapolis Tribune*, September 10, 1889 and October 1, 1890; *New York Times*, February 12, 1891.

21. James J. Hill to John S. Kennedy, January 7, 1888; James J. Hill to E. T. Nichols, September 4, 7, 9, 11, 1889; C. H. Warren to E. T. Nichols, September 17, 1889, James J. Hill papers, Letter Books and General Correspondence, JJHRL.

22. *Minneapolis Tribune*, June 18, July 10, 11, August 4, 1891; "Glimpse of a Marvelous City . . . Watertown in 1889" (Watertown City Council, 1889), 16–17 and advertising following; Gilbert C. Fite, *The Farmers: Frontier, 1865–1900* (New York: Holt, Rinehart & Winston, 1966), 108–9.

23. *Bradstreet's*, April 26, 1890, 265; Rendigs Fels, *American Business Cycles, 1865–1897* (Chapel Hill: University of North Carolina Press, 1959), 159, 179–92; *Official Guide*, June 1894, xxii.

24. Emory R. Johnson, *American Railway Transportation* (New York: D. Appleton Co., 1905), 78–96, 400–407; *The Manual of Statistics: Stock Exchange Hand Book, 1906* (New York: The Manual of Statistics, 1906), 338; Slason Thompson, *Railway Statistics of the United States of America for the Year Ending June 30, 1910* (Chicago: Gunthorp-Warreen, 1911), 117; E. G. Campbell, *The Reorganization of the American Railroad System, 1892–1900* (New York: Columbia University Press, 1938), 26–27; Peter Trefano, "Business Failures, Judicial Intervention, and Financial Innovation: Restructuring U.S. Railroads in the Nineteenth Century," *Business History Review* 71 (Spring 1997): 1–40; Albro Martin, "Railroads and the Equity Receivership: An Essay on Institutional Change," *Journal of Economic History* 34 (September 1974): 685–709.

25. Vincent Carosso, *The Morgans: Private Bankers, 1854–1913* (Cambridge: Harvard University Press, 1987), 219–67, 364–71; Ron Chernow, *The House of Morgan: An American Banking Dynasty and the Rise of American Finance* (New York: Atlantic Monthly Press, 1990), 66–69; William Z. Ripley, *Railroad Finance and Organization* (New York: Longmans, Green & Co., 1920), 371–411. See also Stuart Daggett, *Railroad Reorganization* (New York: Augustus M. Kelley, 1967).

26. CB&Q, *Annual Report*, 1879, 19; *New York Times*, January 14, 1888; *Minnesota, Railroad and Warehouse Commission Annual Report*, 1888, 30.

27. *Railroad Gazette* 23 (November 27, 1891): 850; M&StL, *Annual Report*, 1891, 7; ibid., 1892, 4–9; ibid., 1893, 8, 16; *New York Times*, August 13, 1892; *New York Times*, September 3, 1892 and April 7, May 8, 1893; W. S. Mellen to T. F. Oakes, November 1, 1892, NP General Manager Files 134.F.1.5, MHS; James J. Hill to W. H. Truesdale, August 30, 1892, GN President Files 479, Box 2477, MHS; *Poor's Manual of the Railroads*, 1893, 403–4; ibid., 1892, 153; M&StL, *Annual Report*, 1893, 9.

28. *New York Times*, June 7, September 1, 28, 1894; *Railroad Gazette* 26 (August 24, 1894): 588; *Minneapolis Tribune*, September 1, October 4, 12, 1894; *Record Containing Proceedings Held in the District Court of Hennepin County, State of Minnesota, in the Case of Henry Seibert, Trustee, Against the Minneapolis & St. Louis Railway and Others. June 28, 1888 to September 1, 1892*, 2 vols. and supplements, passim.

29. *Railway Age* 6 (May 19, 1881): 272; 137 ICC 814-816; *Minneapolis Tribune*, November 3, 1894; *National Cyclopedia of American Biography*, vol. 14 (New York: J. T. White & Co., 1917), 450–51.

30. *Minneapolis Tribune*, October 12, 1894.

31. Martin, "Railroads and the Equity Receivership," 689; Alfred D. Chandler Jr., *The Visible Hand: The Managerial Revolution in American Business* (Cambridge: Harvard University Press, 1977), 204–5.

## 11. THREE CENTS PER MILE

1. *Railway Age* 88 (June 14, 1930): 1459; Maury Klein, *Union Pacific: Birth of Railroad, 1862–1893* (Garden City: Doubleday & Company, 1987), 572; *Who Was Who in America* (Chicago: Marquis Who's Who, 1943), 1:163–64; Louis Tuck Renz, *The History of the Northern Pacific Railroad* (Fairfield, WA: Ye Galleon Press, 1980), 164–80.

2. *Minneapolis Tribune*, October 13, 1895.

3. Gerald G. Eggert, *Railroad Labor Disputes, The Beginnings of Federal Strike Policy* (Ann Arbor: University of Michigan Press, 1967), 136–46; GN, *Annual Report*, 1894, 17; *St. Paul Pioneer Press*, September 3, 5, 1894; Ralph W. Hidy, Muriel E. Hidy, Roy V. Scott, and Don L. Hofsommer, *The Great Northern Railroad: A History* (Boston: Harvard Business School Press, 1988), 139–43.

4. *Minneapolis Tribune*, September 27, 1895.

5. Theodore C. Blegen, *Minnesota: A History of the State* (Minneapolis: University of Minnesota Press, 1963), 390–98; St. Paul Chamber of Commerce, *Annual Report*, 1898, 82–84; *St. Paul Union Stockyards: 1886 Centennial Year 1986* (St. Paul: Fahey & Associates, 1986), 14–17.

6. Allan G. Bogue, *From Prairie to Corn Belt: Farming on the Illinois and Iowa Prairie in the Nineteenth Century* (Chicago: Quadrangle Books, 1963), 216–40, 285; Fred A. Shannon, *The Farmer's Last Frontier: Agriculture, 1860–1897* (New York: Harper & Row, 1945), 163, 165, 257–58; David B. Danbom, *Born in the Country: A History of Rural America* (Baltimore: Johns Hopkins University Press, 1995), 132–33.

7. John R. Borchert, *America's Northern Heartland* (Minneapolis: University of Minnesota Press, 1987), 3–4, 40–49; St. Paul Chamber of Commerce, *Annual Report*, 1900, 82.

8. *Minneapolis Tribune*, September 8, 1895; James B. Hedges, "The Col-

onization Work of the Northern Pacific Railroad," *Mississippi Valley Historical Review* 13 (December 1926): 311–42; Harold F. Peterson, "Some Colonization Projects of the Northern Pacific Railroad," *Minnesota History* 10 (June 1929): 127–44; Sig Michelson, *The Northern Pacific Railroad and the Selling of the West* (Sioux Falls, SD: Center for Western Studies, 1993), 27–154; Hidy et al., *The Great Northern Railway*, 99–102; Charles Dudley Warner, "Studies of the Great West," *Harper's New Monthly Magazine* 76 (March 1888): 556–69; tabular data from StPM&M annual reports, 1880–90.

9. *Railway Age* 86 (February 16, 1929): 397–98; Tabular data from annual reports of CM&StP, NP, CGW, Omaha, GN, and M&StL.

10. Richard C. Overton, *Burlington Route: A History of the Burlington Lines* (New York: Alfred A. Knopf, 1965), 196; M&StL, Time Table (June 1886), 3, 6; *Official Guide* (September 1891), 388, 417, 420, 423, 442, 445, 451, 465, 488, 505.

11. *Minneapolis Tribune*, March 2, August 19, 21, November 20, 1895, June 9, 1896; *Excelsior Cottager*, January 31, 1896; Lucile A. Kane and John A. Dougherty, "Movie Debut: Films in the Twin Cities, 1894–1909," *Minnesota History* 54 (Winter 1995): 342–85; *Jordan Independent*, May 26, 1886; *Lake Mills Graphic*, October 4, 1899.

12. William Cronon, *Nature's Metropolis: Chicago and the Great West* (New York: Norton, 1991), 341–43; Phil Patton, "'Sell the Cookware If Necessary, but Come to the Fair,'" *Smithsonian* 24 (June 1993): 38–50; *Official Guide* (October 1893), xix; ibid. (November 1893), xxix; M&StL, Time Table (October 1893), 2–5; *Railroad Gazette* 26 (January 19, 1894): 47.

13. Hidy et al., *The Great Northern Railway*, 44–45.

14. *Minneapolis Tribune*, July 4, 17, 18, 26, August 31, 1889, May 18, June 10, July 4, 12, 19, 1890, July 14, 21, 25, 1895; *Official Guide* (September 1896), 578; CM&StP, Time Table (August 1, 1890), 47.

15. *Minneapolis Tribune*, July 8, 27, September 1, 3, 7, 1895.

16. *Waconia, Paradise of the Northwest: The Lake and Its Island* (Waconia, MN: Waconia Heritage Association, 1986, 61–64, 73–76; *Minneapolis Tribune*, July 27, August 8, 1889, July 4, 1890; *Watertown* [South Dakota] *Kampeskian*, June 25, 1897.

17. St. Paul & Northern Pacific, Certificate of the Fulfillment of . . . Contract . . . St. Paul & Northern Pacific and Northern Pacific, February 15, 1887, AC; Cass Gilbert Collection, MHS; M. C. Byers, Memorandum October 8, 1913, GN President File 6092, MHS; M&StL, Time Table (October 1893), 2.

18. St. Paul & Northern Pacific, Certificate of the Fulfillment of . . . Contract . . . St. Paul & Northern Pacific and Northern Pacific, February 15, 1887, AC; *Minneapolis Journal*, December 6, 1886; *Official Guide* (October 1886), 345; St. Paul Chamber of Commerce, *Annual Report*, 1888, 77.

19. *St. Paul Pioneer and Democrat*, July 3, 6, 1862; *St. Paul Pioneer*, March 19, 1863, May 4, 11, November 10, 1866, April 7, 1867; *Minneapolis Tribune*, May 25, 1867, July 18, 1869, November 29, December 7, 1880; *Official Guide* (November 1881), 191, 199; ibid. (May 1883), 226, 238; ibid. (May 1885), 258, 266; ibid. (September 1891), 449; ibid. (June 1893), 501; *Railroad Gazette* 19 (July 8, 1887): 454.

20. *Minneapolis Tribune*, January 2, May 6, July 1, 1888, February 17, 27, September 10, 12, 1889, December 10, 1890, February 6, June 14, October 16, 1891; St. Paul Chamber of Commerce, *Annual Report*, 1898, 65; Edward W. Solberg, "The Minneapolis Street Railway: Emergence and Disappearance," unpublished master's thesis, St. Cloud State University, 1999, 39; CM&StP, Time Table (May 1893), 9, 23; ibid. (June 1893), 9, 23.

21. Kenneth T. Jackson, *Crabgrass Frontier: The Suburbanization of the United States* (New York: Oxford University Press, 1985), 102–3; George W. Hilton and John F. Due, *The Electric Interurban Railways in America* (Stanford: Stanford University Press, 1960), 4–7, 86–87; Isaac Atwater, ed., *History of the City of Minneapolis, Minnesota* (New York: Munsell & Co., 1893), 336–44; St. Paul Chamber of Commerce, *Annual Report*, 1900, 75–76.

22. *The Compendium of Passenger Rates and Divisions* (Chicago: W. F. Bailey, 1897), 46, 84, 112, 118, 169, 220, 221, 252, 329, 347.

23. *The American Magazine* 70 (May 1910): 47; Isaac F. Marcosson, "The Coming Railroad Ruler," *Saturday Evening Post*, October 2, 1909, 6.

24. Marcosson, "The Coming Railroad Ruler," 6; Frank P. Donovan Jr., "Edwin Hawley," *Trains* 12 (September 1952), 53; *New York Times*, March 2, 1990.

25. *New York Times*, February 2, 1912; Marcosson, "The Coming Railroad Ruler," 6–7; Muriel O. Fuller, *John Muir of Wall Street* (New York: The Knickerbockers Press, 1927), 232–34; Bernard M. Baruch, *Baruch: My Own Story* (New York: Henry Holt & Company, 1957), 167.

26. Parker Morell, *Diamond Jim* (Garden City, NY: Garden City Publishing, 1934), 180.

27. *New Ulm Daily Journal*, August 13, 1954; *Minneapolis Tribune*, September 15, 1889; *Railroad Gazette* 23 (February 27, 1891): 154; 137 ICC 845; M&StL, *Annual Report*, 1896, 8; *Official Guide* (December 1896), 572; M&StL, AFE Index, Mankato Division, AC; *Yesterday and Today*, 166; *Winthrop News*, March 13, 1975; *Minneapolis Tribune*, June 27, 1896; M&StL/MNU&SW, Time Table No. 1 (July 6, 1896); *Official Guide* (September 1896), 578; *Railroad Gazette* 27 (November 1895): 731.

28. Rendigs Fels, *American Business Cycles, 1865–1897* (Chapel Hill: University of North Carolina Press, 1959), 193–208; George M. Stephenson, *John Lind of Minnesota* (Minneapolis: University of Minnesota Press, 1935), 137; Joseph A. A. Burnquist, *Minnesota and Its People*, 4 vols. (Chicago: S. J. Clarke Publishers, 1924), 2:174–77.

29. M&StL, *Annual Report*, 1912, 13; Fuller, *John Muir of Wall Street*, 212; Marcosson, "The Coming Railroad Ruler," 7; W. B. Davids, interview by Frank P. Donovan Jr., undated, AC; Morell, *Diamond Jim*, 181; Baruch, *Baruch*, 139; C. M. Keys, "Harriman: The Building of His Empire," *World's Work* 13 (February 1907): 8548; Don L. Hofsommer, *The Southern Pacific: 1901-1985* (College Station: Texas A&M University Press, 1986), 9.

30. *Spirit Lake Beacon*, February 3, 1899; *St. James Plaindealer*, February 21, 28, March 7, 14, 21, 1899; *Watonwan County Plaindealer*, June 11, 1970; Don L. Hofsommer, *Prairie Oasis: The Railroads, Steamboats, and Resorts of Iowa's Spirit Lake Country* (Des Moines: Waukon & Mississippi Press, 1975), 105-11; *Iowa Railroad Commission Report*, 1900, 145; *Railroad Gazette* 31 (March 3, 1899): 161.

31. Earle D. Ross, *Iowa Agriculture: An Historical Survey* (Iowa City: State Historical Society of Iowa, 1951), 8-9, 61-62, 72-91; Leonard K. Eaton, *Gateway Cities and Other Essays* (Ames: Iowa State University Press, 1989), 8-9.

32. 137 ICC 798; *Minneapolis Tribune*, January 7, 1900; *Iowa Railroad Commission Report, 1900*, 144; *St. James Plaindealer*, July 25, September 5, 1899; *New Ulm Journal*, August 12, 1899, August 13, 1954; *St. James Gazette*, October 6, 1899; Shirley Knudson, ed., *History of Watonwan County* (Dallas: Curtis Media, 1995), T127; *St. James Plaindealer*, August 1, 1899; *Emmet County* [Estherville, Iowa] *Republican*, October 7, 1899; Iowa & Minnesota Land & Townsite Company advertising handbill, AC; M&StL, Right-of-Way and Track Maps, AC.

33. *St. James Plaindealer*, December 12, 1899; *Spencer News*, November 15, 29, 1899; *Railroad Gazette* 31 (November 10, 1899): 701; *Emmet County* [Estherville, Iowa] *Republican*, November 9, December 21, 1899, January 18, 1900; *Sioux Rapids Press*, January 25, March 8, 29, April 12, June 28, July 10, August 16, 1900; M&StL, *Annual Report*, 1900, 1-12; *Spencer News*, April 26, 1899; Knudson, *History of Watonwan County*, 11; C. H. Wegerslev and Thomas Walpole, *Past and Present of Buena Vista County Iowa* (Chicago: S. J. Clarke Publishers, 1909), 135; *Sioux Rapids Press*, April 19, 1900; Walter Carlson, *Happenings in Our Neighborhood*, 3 vols. (Trimont, MN: Trimont Progress, 1969), 2:37; *Hanska, A Century of Tradition: 1901-2001* (Hanska, MN: Hanska Centennial Committee, 2001), 106-7; John Gross, *LaSalle: Whistle-Stop on the Prairie* (Medford, MN: Privately published by the author, 1999), 17; *Storm Lake Pilot-Tribune*, July 27, August 3, 10, 17, 1900.

34. *St. James Courier*, November 18, 1969; *Sioux Rapids Press*, August 9, 16, September 20, 1900; Julia Becken to the author, November 10, 1971; *Watonwan County Plaindealer*, June 11, 1970; Carlson, *Happenings in Our Neighborhood*, 38; *New Ulm Journal*, August 13, 1954; *Spencer News*, November 15, 1899; *Storm Lake Pilot-Tribune*, March 30, 1900; M&StL maps, ca. 1900.

## 12. RUMORS AND REALITY

1. Don L. Hofsommer, "The Nation's Arteries," in *Rails Across America*, ed. William L. Withuhn (New York: Smithmark Publishers, 1993), 90-109; Slason Thompson, *Railway Statistics of the United States of America for the Year Ending June 30, 1910* (Chicago: Gunthorp-Warreen, 1911), 123; Emory R. Johnson, *American Railway Transportation* (New York: D. Appleton Co., 1905), 29-32.

2. Alfred D. Chandler Jr., *The Visible Hand: The Managerial Revolution in American Business* (Cambridge: Harvard University Press, 1977), 145-87, especially 151, 154-55, 168-69, 174-75.

3. NP, *Annual Report*, 1900, 15, 21, 39, 51, 59; GN, *Annual Report*, 1900, 30, 36, 37, 40, 41; Soo Line, *Annual Report*, 1900, 9, 14-16.

4. Ralph W. Hidy, Muriel E. Hidy, Roy V. Scott, and Don L. Hofsommer, *The Great Northern Railroad: A History* (Boston: Harvard Business School Press, 1988), 92-93; H. T. Newcomb, "The Recent Great Railroad Combinations," *Review of Reviews* 24 (August 1901): 163-74; M. G. Cunniff, "Increasing Railroad Consolidation," *World's Work* 3 (Fall 1902): 1775-80; Collis P. Huntington, "A Plea for Railroad Consolidation," *North American Review* 153 (July 1891): 272-82.

5. Quoted in Thomas C. Cochran, *Railroad Leaders, 1845-1890: The Business Mind in Action* (Cambridge: Harvard University Press, 1953), 433; *Railroad Gazette* 276 (September 6, 1895): 590; *New York Times*, July 4, 1895; *Wall Street Journal*, July 5, 1895; Carosso, *The Morgans: Private Bankers, 1854-1913* (Cambridge: Harvard University Press, 1987), iv-vi; "The 'Great Northern' and Its Builder," *Review of Reviews* 8 (July-December 1893): 11-12; *Railroad Gazette* 27 (May 24, 1895): 338; *Engineering News and American Railway Journal* 34 (August 8, 1895): 88.

6. Balthasar H. Meyer, *A History of the Northern Securities Case* (Bulletin of the University of Wisconsin, No. 142. Madison, 1906), 225-36; Richard C. Overton, *Burlington Route: A History of the Burlington Lines* (New York: Alfred A. Knopf, 1965), 246-63; George Kennan, *E. H. Harriman: A Biography*, 2 vols. (Boston: Houghton Mifflin, 1922), 1:286-87; Jean Strouse, *Morgan: American Financier* (London: Harvill Press, 1999), 239-41; NP, *Annual report*, 1901, 13; GN, *Annual Report*, 1901, 9-10; ibid., 1912, 17.

7. Henry Irving Dodge, "The Epoch-Making Struggle for Northern Pacific," *Woman's Home Companion*, January 1903, 9, 43-44; Strouse, *Morgan*, 418-27, 431-34; Ron Chernow, *The House of Morgan: An American Banking Dynasty and the Rise of American Finance* (New York: Atlantic Monthly Press, 1990), 88-94; Carosso, *The Morgans*, 363-68, 383-86, 474-79.

8. *Railway Age* 33 (March 14, 1902): 310; *Railroad Gazette* 34 (April 4, 1902): 247-48; ibid. (April 18, 1902): 281.

9. Chernow, *The House of Morgan*, 106–9; Russell Sage et al., "Industrial and Railroad Consolidation," *North American Review* 531 (May 1901): 641–700; *Minneapolis Times*, December 21, 1901; Carosso, *The Morgans*, 528–30; *Railway Age* 37 (March 18, 1904): 403–4, 409–12; ibid. 39 (March 17, 1905): 352; Richard Wagner, "A Falling Out: The Relationship between Oliver Wendell Holmes and Theodore Roosevelt," *Journal of Supreme Court History* 27 (2002): 119–37; Robert L. Cutting, "The Northern Securities Company and the Sherman Anti-Trust Law," *North American Review* 174 (1902): 528–35; Edmund Morris, *Theodore Rex* (New York: Random House, 2001), 59–62, 87–92, 303–5, 313–15; Strouse, *Morgan*, 440–43, 460–61, 533–35.

10. George E. Mowry, *The Era of Theodore Roosevelt and the Birth of Modern America, 1900–1912* (New York: Harper & Row, 1958), 130–33, 164.

11. Iowa Central, *Annual Report*, 1900, 2; *Railroad Gazette* 32 (July 6, 1900): 458; *New York Times*, June 21, 1900; M. G. Cunniff, "Increasing Railroad Consolidations," *World's Work* 3 (February 1902): 1775–80; 137 ICC *Valuation Reports* 848–851; CRI&P, Abstract to Important Contracts Affecting Operations (1965), RI Secretary's No. 2261, 20, AC.

12. Edward W. McGrew, *Corporate History of the Illinois Central Railroad Company and Its Controlled and Affiliated Companies Up to June 30, 1915* (Chicago: Illinois Central, 1915), 236–37; *Official Guide* (June 1900), 616; Dow, Jones & Co., New Bulletin, February 16, 1898.

13. CRI&P, *Annual Report*, 1899, 10, 18; H. H. Hollister to C. J. Ives, December 23, 1899; R. R. Cable to C. J. Ives, February 1, 1900; M. J. Stohr to Robert Williams, April 14, 1900; Charles E. Perkins to C. J. Ives, May 11, 1900; R. R. Cable to C. J. Ives, July 16, 17, 1900; J. M. Hannaford to Robert Williams, September 12, 1900; Albert N. Harbert Collection (MsC 434), Special Collections, University of Iowa Library (hereafter cited as Harbert Collection); *Emmet County* [Estherville, Iowa] *Republican*, January 18, 1900.

14. J. T. Harahan to C. J. Ives, June 2, 1900; J. F. Wallace to C. J. Ives, August 9, 23, 1900; R. R. Cable to Robert Williams, August 27, 1900, Harbert Collection; McGrew, *Corporate History of the Illinois Central*, 234–235.

15. *Minneapolis Tribune*, February 21, 1888; *Fort Dodge Messenger*, May 12, 1897; *Peoria Journal*, August 29, 1899; *New York Times*, March 9, July 2, October 2, 1901; *Storm Lake Pilot-Tribune*, August 2, 1901; *Sioux Rapids Press*, September 5, 1901; *Railroad Gazette* 33 (April 5, 1901): 238; ibid. (July 12, 1901): 492; ibid. (July 19, 1901): 508; ibid. (August 9, 1901): 568; IC, *Annual Report*, 1899, 4; ibid., 1900, 3–4; ibid., 1901, 1–3.

16. BCR&N, *Annual Report*, 1900, 1; C. J. Ives to J. W. Kendrick, January 3, 1901; J. W. Kendrick to C. S. Mellen, March 16, 1901; C. J. Ives to E. H. McHenry, April 19, 1901; NP General Manager Files, MHS; BCR&N, *Annual Report*, 1901, 1–2; H. H. Field, *History of Milwaukee Road, 1891–1940* (Chicago: CMStP&P, 1941?), 205–8.

17. NP, Index Diagram and Original Tracklaying Record, May 15, 1933, AC; Hidy et al., 321–23; *Yesterday and Today: A History of the Chicago & North Western Railway System*, 3rd ed. (Chicago: C&NW, 1910), 166–70.

18. Soo Line, *Annual Report*, 1905, 6; ibid., 1906, 6; ibid., 1907, 6; ibid., 1909, 5; *Official Guide* (August 1905), 618–21.

19. August Derleth, *The Milwaukee Road: Its First 100 Years* (New York: Creative Age Press, 1948), 294–98; CM&StP, *Annual Report*, 1909, 16.

20. *New York Times*, March 27, 1903; Maury Klein, *History of the Louisville & Nashville Railroad* (New York: Macmillan, 1972), 311–12; Bernard M. Baruch, *Baruch: My Own Story* (New York: Henry Holt & Company, 1957), 168–76; George Kennan, *The Chicago & Alton Case: A Misunderstood Transaction* (New York: The Country Life Press, 1916), 3, 8, 38; Cyrus Adler, *Jacob H. Schiff: His Life and Letters*, 2 vols. (Garden City, NY: Doubleday, Doran & Co., 1928), 1:131–38; C. M. Keys, "As Many Methods as Railroad Kings," *World's Work* 10 (September 1905): 6652–59; C. M. Keys, "The Newest Railroad Power," *World's Work* 10 (June 1905): 6302–12; C. M. Keys, "Harriman: The Building of His Empire," *The World's Work* 13 (February 1907): 8537–52; Carl Snyder, *American Railways as Investments* (New York: The Moody Corporation, 1907): 167–76; *New York Times*, June 24, September 19, 1904; Kennan, *Edward H. Harriman*, 2:228–310; Maury Klein, *Life and Legend of Edward H. Harriman* (Chapel Hill: University of North Carolina Press, 2000), 323.

21. BCR&N, Time Table (January 1900), 18–24; ibid. (September 1900), 53; Doane Robinson, "Close of a Great Decade," *Dacotah Magazine* (December 1907): 88–89; Slason Thompson, *Railway Statistics of the United States of America for the Year Ending June 30, 1907* (Chicago: Gunthorp-Warreen, 1908), 8; Donald J. Pisani, "George Maxwell, the Railroads, and American Land Policy, 1894–1904," *Pacific Historical Review* 63 (May 1994): 177–90; Mildred Lucile Hartsough, *The Twin Cities as a Metropolitan Market: A Regional Study of the Economic Development of Minneapolis and St. Paul* (Minneapolis: University of Minnesota, 1925), 174; *South Dakota Railway Commission Report, 1902*, 131.

22. M&StL, *Annual Report*, 1906, 11; *McPherson County* [Leola, SD] *Herald*, December 27, 1906; R. C. Lathrop, "Watertown and West—M&StL's Final Expansion," *North Western Lines* 21 (Spring 1994): 50, 56; *Minneapolis Journal*, August 4, September 1, 1907; *Minneapolis Tribune*, June 20, 1907; *Minneapolis Journal*, September 3, 1907; *Official Guide* (September 1907), xxxviii; *Brown County History* (Aberdeen, SD: Brown County Historical Society, 1980), 387–91; *Watertown Public Opinion*, September 9, 1907; *New York Times*, October 27, 1909; *Minneapolis Tribune*, October 27, 1909; *Dakota Magazine*, January–February 1909, 94; Doane Robinson, "Thousands Seek South Dakota," *Dacotah Magazine* (August 1908): 1–5; Henry G. Durand, "The Railroads of Tomorrow," *World's Work* 13 (January 1907):

8465–70; 137 ICC 886–888; M&StL Contract 1257 with Franklin Floete et al., January 17, 1906, AC; Clyde Clarkson Way, ed., *Biography and Memoirs of Thomas Asbury Way* (Westchester, PA: Privately published by the editor, 1946), 42; Clyde C. Way to Frank P. Donovan Jr., September 19, 1949, AC; *Minneapolis Journal*, June 30, July 30, August 5, 11, 12, 1907; Way, *Biography and Memoirs of Thomas Asbury Way*, 26, 30, 32, 34, 41–44, 64; James Frederic Hamburg, *The Influence of Railroads upon the Processes and Patterns of Settlement in South Dakota* (New York: Arno Press, 1981), 310–18; *Brown County History*, 48–49; Don L. Hofsommer, "Boosterism and Townsite Development along the Minneapolis & St. Louis Railroad in South Dakota," *Journal of the West* 42 (Fall 2003): 8–16.

23. *Official Shippers Guide and Directory of the Minneapolis & St. Louis and Iowa Central Railroad* (Chicago: Perk-Hill, 1909), passim; Jimmy M. Skaggs, *Prime Cut: Livestock Raising and Meatpacking in the United States, 1607–1983* (College Station: Texas A&M University Press, 1986), 60–129; *Railway World* (August 7, 1880): 751; Howard C. Hill, "The Development of Chicago as a Center of the Meat Packing Industry," *Mississippi Valley Historical Review* 10 (December 1923): 253–73; William Cronon, *Nature's Metropolis: Chicago and the Great West* (New York: Norton, 1991), 207–59; *Dacotah Magazine*, December 1907, 6; ibid., January 1908, advertising section; M. M. Dealy, "Farm Life," *Dacotah Magazine*, January-February 1909, 33–37; James D. McLaird, "From Bib Overalls to Cowboy Boots: East River/West River Differences in South Dakota," *South Dakota History* 19 (Winter 1989): 458–61; *Minneapolis Tribune*, June 30, 1907; *St. Paul Union Stockyards, 1886–1986* (St. Paul: St. Paul Union Stockyards, 1986), passim; Don L. Hofsommer, "A Promise Broken: LeBeau and the Railroad," *South Dakota History* 33 (Spring 2003): 1–17.

24. *Official Shippers Guide and Directory of the Minneapolis & St. Louis and Iowa Central Railroad*, passim; D. Jerome Tweeton, "The Business of Agriculture," in *Minnesota in a Century of Change: The State and Its People since 1900*, ed. Clifford E. Clark Jr. (St. Paul: Minnesota Historical Society, 1989), 261–94, especially 267–68.

25. *LeBeau Phenix*, August 20, September 24, October 27, November 5, 1908, April 29, May 6, 20, 27, June 17, 24, July 22, August 2, September 9, October 14, 1909; M&StL AFE 3102.

26. Ross R. Cotroneo, "Colonization of the Northern Pacific Land Grant, 1900–1920," *North Dakota Quarterly* 38 (Summer 1970): 33–48; Stanley N. Murray, "Railroads and the Agricultural Development of the Red River Valley of the North, 1870–1890" *Agricultural History* 31, 4 (October 1957): 57–66; GN, Time Table (June 9, 1907), 3–4; CM&StP, Time Table (March 1904), 26, 51; *Railroad Gazette* 32 (April 6, 1900): 224; GN, *Annual Report*, 1900, 26; ibid., 1902, 22.

27. Arthur D. Dubin, *Some Classic Trains* (Milwaukee: Kalmbach Publications, 1964), 294–331; Arthur D. Dubin, *More Classic Trains* (Milwaukee: Kalmbach Books, 1974), 356–67; NP, Time Table (June 2, 1904), 51–54; NP, *Annual Report*, 1900, 32; *Official Guide* (August 1905), 623.

28. CM&StP, Time Table (March 1904), 15–16; Dubin, *Classic Trains*, 158–67, 250–61; *Official Guide* (August 1905), 652.

29. McGrew, *Corporate History of the Illinois Central*, 235–37; *Cosmopolitan*, March 1900, 88; IC, Western Lines Train Service (February 22, 1900), 7, 12; *Official Guide* (August 1905), 875; *Official Guide* (April 1901), 761; ibid. (June 1902), 644–45; ibid. (July 1902), 644–45; M&StL, *Annual Report*, 1902, 9; Frank P. Donovan Jr., "Passenger Trains of Yesteryear on the Minneapolis & St. Louis," *Minnesota History* 30 (September 1949): 232–41; M&StL, *Annual Report*, 1903, 10; *Official Guide* (November 1902), xxxix, *Minneapolis Tribune*, October 31, November 1–4, 11, 15, 1902; *St. Paul Chamber of Commerce Annual Report*, 1900, 88, 90.

30. *Official Guide* (August 1905), 598, 621, 626, 630, 663, 783; GN, Time Table (February 1905), 54.

31. Carlos A. Schwantes, *Going Places: Transportation Redefines the Twentieth-Century West* (Bloomington: Indiana University Press, 2003), 137; *Minneapolis Tribune*, November 24, 1902, June 13, November 15, 1904; David R. Frances, *The Universal Exposition of 1904*, 2 vols. (St. Louis: Louisiana Purchase Exposition Company, 1913), 1:255–56, 259–60, 280, 452–58, 620–21, 627; H. Roger Grant, Don L. Hofsommer, and Osmund Overby, *St. Louis Union Station: A Place for People, a Place for Trains* (St. Louis: St. Louis Mercantile Library, 1994), 22–25.

32. *St. James Plaindealer*, May 8, 22, June 12, 26, August 8, 1900; *Storm Lake Pilot-Tribune*, August 2, October 12, 1900; *Sioux Rapids Press*, June 13, 1901; *Winthrop News*, August 14, 1902, April 2, 1903; *South Dakota Railroad Commission Report*, 1902, 18–19.

33. *Jordan Independent*, August 13, September 18, 1902, June 11, July 16, 1903, July 7, September 1, 1904.

34. *Minneapolis Tribune*, September 19, November 17, 19, 1902; *Official Guide* (August 1905), 722.

35. NP, *Annual Report*, 1900, 39; GN, *Annual Report*, 1900, 33; Soo Line, *Annual Report*, 1900, 14; tabular data from M&StL annual reports, 1890–1905; CM&StP, *Annual Report*, 1909, 14.

36. *Minneapolis Tribune*, December 24, 1885, and August 21, September 8, 27, 1895; *Minnesota Railroad and Warehouse Commission Report*, 1886, 777–78; Henrietta M. Larson, *The Wheat Market and the Farmer in Minnesota, 1858–1900* (New York: Columbia University, 1926), 222, 230–33, 245; *Minneapolis Chamber of Commerce Annual Report*, 1902, 50.

37. Charles Byron Kuhlmann, *The Development of the Flour Milling In-*

*dustry in the United States with Special Reference to Minneapolis* (Boston: Houghton Mifflin, 1929), 166; George D. Rogers, "History of Flour Manufacturing in Minnesota," *Collections of the Minnesota Historical Society* 10 (February 1905): 53; *Minneapolis Chamber of Commerce Annual Report*, 1901, 55–56; ibid., 1902, 56; *Minneapolis Tribune*, September 8, 1895; William C. Edgar, *The Medal of Gold: A Story of Industrial Achievement* (Minneapolis: Bellman Company, 1925), 210–17; James Gray, *Business without Boundary: The Story of General Mills* (Minneapolis: University of Minnesota Press, 1954), 52–62.

38. Agnes Larson, *History of the White Pine Industry in Minnesota* (Minneapolis: University of Minnesota Press, 1949), 229–46, 376–77; *Minneapolis Chamber of Commerce Annual Report*, 1895, 48; ibid., 1901, 55–56; ibid., 1902, 56.

39. Tabular data from M&StL annual reports, 1890–1905; *Carver County* [Waconia] *News*, June 3, 1892; *Minneapolis Journal*, July 2, September 8, 1907.

## 13. Shifting Winds

1. Paul S. Boyer et al., *The Enduring of a Vision: A History of the American People* (Lexington: D. C. Heath & Co., 1990), 751–88.

2. William V. Allen, "Western Feelings toward the East," *North American Review* 162: 588–93; Alfred D. Chandler Jr., *The Visible Hand: The Managerial Revolution in American Business* (Cambridge: Harvard University Press, 1977), 497–99; Carl H. Chrislock, *The Progressive Era in Minnesota, 1899–1918* (St. Paul: Minnesota Historical Society, 1971), 22–36; Henry S. Haines, *Restrictive Railway Legislation* (New York: Macmillan & Co., 1905), 222–30.

3. CB&Q, *Annual Report*, 1888, 20; A. L. Mohler to C. J. Ives, February 5, 1895; A. J. Earling to C. J. Ives, February 19, 1900, Albert N. Harbert Collection (MsC434), Special Collections University of Iowa Library.

4. Theodore Roosevelt, First Annual Message to Congress, December 3, 1901; John F. Stover, *American Railroads*, 2nd ed. (Chicago: University of Chicago Press, 1997), 129–31.

5. Phillip Longman, "Scientific Management," *Audacity* 5 (Summer 1997): 40–49.

6. *Minnesota Board of Railroad Commissioners Annual Report*, 1897, 302–24; James W. Ely Jr., "The Railroad Equation Revisited: Chicago, Milwaukee & St. Paul v. Minnesota and Constitutional Limits on State Regulation," *Great Plains Quarterly* 12 (Spring 1992), 121–34.

7. Charles E. Perkins and David C. Shepard to President and Board of Directors, April 22, 1907; Howard Elliott to Charles E. Perkins, May 3, 1907, NP Presidents' File 1397, MHS; *Minneapolis Journal*, September 4, 1907; *Washington Post*, March 24, 1908; U.S. Supreme Court Decision Regarding Decrees in Nos. 291, 292, and 293 (June 9, 1913); Northern Pacific, *Annual Report*, 1908, 18; ibid., 1910, 21–22; ibid., 1911, 20; ibid., 1912, 21; ibid., 1913, 20; James W. Ely Jr., *Railroads and American Law* (Lawrence: University Press of Kansas, 2001), 233–34.

8. Slason Thompson, *Railway Statistics of the United States of America for the Year Ending June 30, 1910* (Chicago: Gunthorp-Warreen, 1911), 84–85; "Railway Rates," an address by A. B. Stickney at St. Paul, February 2, 1907, AC; *Commercial and Financial Chronicle*, June 30, 1906, August 17, 1907; *Bankers Magazine* 74 (April 1907): 506; Howard Elliott, "The Work of the Farmer and the Railroad in Minnesota," an address before the Minnesota Agriculture Society, St. Paul, January 7, 1912, AC.

9. M&StL, *Annual Report*, 1907, 8, 13; ibid., 1908, 8–9; *Minneapolis Journal*, July 4, 11, 1907; *Wall Street Journal*, September 13, 1910; M&StL, *Annual Report*, 1911, 11–12.

10. *Minneapolis Journal*, December 15, 16, 1911; *Manual of Statistics: Stock Exchange Handbook, 1906* (New York: Manual of Statistics, 1906), 932–35; L. R. Moyer and O. G. Dale, eds., *History of Lac qui Parle County, Minnesota*, 2 vols. (Indianapolis: B. F. Bowen & Co., 1916), 1:487; *Fort Dodge Messenger*, September 17, 1897; Otis H. Moore, "Handling the Grain Crop of the Great Northwest," *Dacotah Magazine* (January 1908): 61–68; *Official Shippers' Guide and Directory of the Minneapolis & St. Louis Railroad and the Iowa Central Railway* (Chicago: Perk-Hill, 1909), 21–27, hereinafter cited as *Official Shippers' Guide*; *Minneapolis Journal*, September 1–30, 1907.

11. *Minneapolis Chamber of Commerce Annual Repot*, 1902, 131–34; Michael P. Malone and Richard W. Etulain, *The American West: A Twentieth-Century History* (Lincoln: University of Nebraska Press, 1989), 26–29; Ralph W. Hidy, Frank Ernest Hill, and Allan Nevins, *Timber and Men: The Weyerhaeuser Story* (New York: Macmillan Co., 1963), 115–16, 187; *Minneapolis Journal*, August 13, 1907; Agnes Larson, *History of the White Pine Industry in Minnesota* (Minneapolis: University of Minnesota Press, 1949), 377; *Official Shipper's Guide*, 38–40; GN, *Annual Report*, 1901, 10; NP, *Annual Report*, 1902, 17; George W. Hotchkiss, *History of the Lumber and Forest Industry of the Northwest* (Chicago: George W. Hotchkiss & Co., 1898), 545–48; William G. Rector, *Log Transportation in the Lake States Lumber Industry, 1840–1918* (Glendale: Arthur H. Clark Company, 1953), 217, 234, 265–66, 332.

12. H. H. Young, *St. Paul: The Commercial Emporium of the Northwest* (St. Paul: Pioneer Press Co., 1886), 106–7; *St. Paul Chamber of Commerce Annual Report*, 1898, 74; ibid., 1900, 75, 107; Mildred Lucile Hartsough, *The Twin Cities as a Metropolitan Market: A Regional Study of the Economic Development of Minneapolis and St. Paul* (Minneapolis: University of Min-

nesota, 1925), 66–67; *Official Shippers' Guide*, 50–52; *Minneapolis Journal*, September 1–October 31, 1907, October 1–December 31, 1911, January 1–March 1, 1912.

13. Theodore C. Blegen, *Minnesota: A History of the State* (Minneapolis: University of Minnesota Press, 1963), 390–96; Hartsough, *The Twin Cities as a Metropolitan Market*, 55; Chandler, *The Visible Hand*, 406–9; *Official Shipper's Guide*, 64–661; Kurt E. Leichtle, "Power in the Heartland: Tractor Manufacturers in the Midwest," *Agricultural History* 69 (Spring 1995): 314–325.

14. Martin Stack, "Local and Regional Breweries in America's Brewing Industry, 1865 to 1920," *Business History Review* 74 (Autumn 2000): 453–63; Manfred Friedrich and Donald Bull, *The Register of United States Breweries 1876–1976* (Trumbull, CT: Privately published by Donald Bull, 1976), 140–52; *Official Shippers' Guide*, 90–93; *Jordan Independent*, December 20, 1900.

15. *Official Shippers' Guide*, 90–93; Eric Sloane, "Natural Ice," *American Heritage* 18 (August 1966): 83–84; John Gruber, "Harvest of Cold," *Locomotive & Railway Preservation* (January-February 1996): 20–27; *Waconia, Paradise of the Northwest* (Waconia, MN: Waconia Heritage Association, 1986), 113–14; Stanley B. Fettl, "Ice Harvesting on Shady Oak Lane," *Hennepin County History* 32 (Fall 1977): 15–19; George W. Nassig, "Ice Harvesting, Storage, and Distribution," *Hennepin County History* 32 (Summer 1978): 14–22; *Minneapolis Journal*, December 18, 1911, January 28, 1912. See also Joseph C. Jones Jr., *America's Icemen: An Illustrative History of the United States Natural Ice Industry, 1665–1925* (Humble, TX: Jobeco Books, 1984).

16. M&StL, Time Table (Minnetonka Points), July 1, 1900; *Minneapolis Tribune*, May 24, 1896 Kenneth T. Jackson, *Crabgrass Frontier: The Suburbanization of the United States* (New York: Oxford University Press, 1985), 102; M&StL, Time Table No. 32, February 28, 1904, 3; Ellen Wilson Meyer, ed., *Picturesque Deephaven* (Excelsior, MN: Excelsior-Lake Minnetonka Historical Society, 1989), 88, 107; J. J. Hill to J. C. Eliel, January 30, February 6, 1899; J. J. Hill to George D. Hodges, February 21, 1899, GN President Letter File, AC; E. A. Holcombe to J. J. Hill, September 17, 1892, GN President File 214, AC.

17. M&StL AFEs 900, 1603, 1968, 2217, 3617; *Minneapolis Journal*, June 16, July 3, 1907; M&StL, Annual Reports, 1895–1905; Russell L. Olson, *The Electric Railways of Minnesota* (Hopkins: Minnesota Transportation Museum, 1976), 79–98; Goodrich Lowry, *Streetcar Man: Tom Lowry and the Twin City Rapid Transit Company* (Minneapolis: Lerner Publications, 1979), 68, 141, 143; Isaac Atwater, ed., *History of the City of Minneapolis, Minnesota* (New York: Munsell & Co., 1893), 336–44; Bob Williams, *Excelsior: An Historical Novel of Lake Minnetonka* (Minneapolis: James D. Thueson, Publisher, 1982), 230–31; M&StL, *Annual Report*, 1908, 12; CM&StP, Time Table (August 1, 1900), 47.

18. *Minneapolis Journal*, June 20, 29, 1907; M&StL, Popular Excursion flyer, October 13, 1906, AC: *Minneapolis Journal*, August 6, 1907; *Waconia*, 74; *Jordan Independent*, July 15, 1907.

19. Harlan F. Hall, "The Colossus of the Railroad World," *Northwest Magazine* 21 (1903): 12–14; NP, *Annual Report*, 1910, 5, 12, 34, 37, 41; GN, *Annual Report*, 1911, 27, 32, 36, 47. On Hill, see Joseph Gilpin Pyle, *The Life of James J. Hill* (Garden City: Doubleday & Company, 1916); Albro Martin, *James J. Hill and the Opening of the Northwest* (New York: Oxford University Press, 1976); and Michael P. Malone, *James J. Hill: Empire Builder of the Northwest* (Norman: University of Oklahoma Press, 1996).

20. H. Roger Grant, "A. B. Stickney," in *Railroads in the Age of Regulation, 1900–1980*, ed. Keith L. Bryant Jr. (New York: Facts on File, 1988), 418–21; H. Roger Grant, "A. B. Stickney Builds a Railroad: The Saga of the Minnesota & Northwestern," *Midwest Review* 6 (Spring 1984): 13–26; H. Roger Grant, "A. B. Stickney and James J. Hill: The Railroad Relationship," *Railroad History* (Spring 1982): 9–22; Robert L. Frey, "Howard Elliott," in *Railroads in the Age of Regulation, 1900–1980*, ed. Keith L. Bryant Jr. (New York: Facts on File, 1988), 131–34.

21. *Railway and Engineering Review* 42 (June 21, 1902): 480–84; *Minneapolis Journal*, August 24, 1907; *Minneapolis Tribune*, October 5–18, 1910; Isaac F. Marcosson, "The Coming Railroad Ruler," *Saturday Evening Post*, October 2, 1909, 6–7, 42–43; *New York Times*, December 20, 1908, April 14, July 9, 1910; Frank Escher, "The Rise of a Great System," *Harper's Weekly* 53 (October 30, 1909): 28; *American Review of Reviews* 40 (November 1909): 528–31; *American Magazine* 70 (May 1910): 43, 46–47; *New York Sun*, December 24, 1911.

## 14. THE STRUGGLING GIANT

1. Gordon Carruth, ed., *The Encyclopedia of American Facts and Dates* (New York: Thomas Y. Crowell, 1979), 424–27; *Minneapolis Journal*, January 5, 1912.

2. G. R. Stevens, *Canadian National Railways: Toward the Inevitable, 1896–1922* (Toronto: Clarke, Irwin & Co., 1962), 242, 251–53; Melanchthon W. Jacobs, *Connecticut Railroads . . . An Illustrated History* (Hartford: Connecticut Historical Society, 1989), 229–30; Don L. Hofsommer, *The Quanah Route: A History of the Quanah, Acme & Pacific Railway* (College Station: Texas A&M University Press, 1999), 29.

3. John F. Stover, *American Railroads*, 2nd ed. (Chicago: University of Chicago Press, 1997), 122–30.

4. Ibid., 115, 128–30, 168; *New York Times*, July 17, 1914; "What Breaks the Railroads," *Literary Digest* 51 (November 6, 1915): 998; *Railway Age*

578 (December 4, 1914): 1054; *New York Times*, December 31, 1915; Walker D. Hines, *War History of American Railroads* (New Haven: Yale University Press, 1928), 1–9; William Z. Ripley, "The Railroad Eight-Hour Law," *American Review of Reviews* 54 (October 1916): 389–93; Edwin J. Clapp, "The Adamson Law," *Yale Review* 6 (1916–17): 258–75; Samuel O. Dunn, "The Threatened Strike of the Railways," *North American Review* 204 (October 19, 1916): 575–88.

5. John Moody, *The Railroad Builders: A Chronicle of the Welding of the States* (New Haven: Yale University Press, 1916), 234–38; Don L. Hofsommer, *The Southern Pacific: 1901–1985* (College Station: Texas A&M University Press, 1986), 71. See Albro Martin, *Enterprise Denied: Origins of the Decline of American Railroads* (New York: Columbia University Press, 1971) for a masterful treatment.

6. "New Money for the Railroads," *American Review of Reviews* 48 (May 1912): 627–28; "The Pitiful Plight of the American Railroad," *Current Literature* 53 (November 1912): 527–30; "Our Starving Railroads," *Literary Digest* 24 (November 2, 1912): 772–73; Benjamin F. Yoakum, "What the Railroads Need," *Harper's Weekly* 58 (March 28, 1914): 24–25; "The Public and the Railroads," *Independent* 78 (May 25, 1914): 312–15; *New York Times*, April 7, 1914; M&StL, *Annual Report*, 1912, 12.

7. M&StL, *Annual Report*, 1912, 12; Walker D. Hines, *War History of American Railroads* (New Haven: Yale University Press, 1928), 1–9; William Z. Ripley, "The Railroad Eight-Hour Law," *American Review of Reviews* 54 (October 1916): 389–93; Edwin J. Clapp, "The Adamson Law," *Yale Review* 6 (1916–17): 258–75; Dunn, "The Threatened Strike of the Railways," 575–88.

8. NP, *Annual Report*, 1912, 20; Julius Grodinsky, *Railroad Consolidation: Its Economics and Controlling Principles* (New York: D. Appleton, 1930), 6.

9. NP, *Annual Report*, 1914, 20; C. M. Keys, "The Contest for Pacific Traffic," *World's Work* 10 (August 1905): 6503–09; "A Month's Traffic through the Canal," *The Independent* 82 (June 7, 1915): 333.

10. *Minneapolis Tribune*, September 11, 1895; *St. Paul Chamber of Commerce Annual Report, 1888*, advertising section; O. C. Gregg, ed., *Minnesota Farmers' Institutes Annual No. 8* (Minneapolis: 1895), 338; Carruth, *The Encyclopedia of American Facts and Dates*, 361, 387.

11. Edwin Wildman, "The City of the Automobile," *Munsey's Magazine* 22 (February 1900): 704–12; John B. Rae, *The Automobile Industry* (Boston: Twayne Publishers, 1984), 29–30; James J. Flink, *The Automobile Age* (Cambridge: MIT Press, 1988), 56–72, 86–111, 135–57; Alfred D. Chandler Jr., comp. and ed., *Giant Enterprise: Ford, General Motors, and the Automobile Industry* (New York: Harcourt, Brace & World, 1964), xi–xii, 9–20; William Leuchtenburg, *The Perils of Prosperity, 1914–1932* (Chicago: University of

Chicago Press, 1958), 6; *Minneapolis Journal*, February 18, 1912, 6; Bronson Batchelor, "Motorizing America: A Review and Forecast of America's Automobile Industry," *The Independent* 81 (March 1, 1915): 319–22.

12. Sylvester Stewart, "The Automobile and the Railway as Transport Agents," *Engineering Magazine* 25 (July 1903): 481–87.

13. *Minneapolis Journal*, November 30, December 15, 1911; Arthur J. Larson, *The Development of the Minnesota Road System* (St. Paul: Minnesota Historical Society, 1966), 330–79; Howard Elliott, "Minnesota Railways and Advertising," an address before the Minnesota Federation of Commercial Clubs, January 25, 1911, AC; *Railroad Gazette* (November 16, 1900): 761; Roy V. Scott, *Railroad Development Programs in the Twentieth Century* (Ames: Iowa State University Press, 1985), 41–43.

14. Carruth, *The Encyclopedia of American Facts and Dates*, 367, 399, 403, 415, 417; Harry B. Haines, "The Automobile and the Average Man," *American Monthly Review of Reviews* (January 1907): 74–83; *Minneapolis Tribune*, November 11, 1902, June 16, 1907; *Minneapolis Journal*, June 23, 26, 30, August 26, 1907; *Official Shippers' Guide and Directory of the Minneapolis & St. Louis and Iowa Central Railway* (Chicago: Perk-Hill Publishing, 1909), 64–66.

15. *Minneapolis Journal*, October 22, November 5, December 3, 1911; *New York Sun*, November 12, December 26, 27, 1911.

16. *Minneapolis Journal*, October 22, 1911, January 28, February 18, 1912.

17. *Minneapolis Journal*, February 13, 18, 21, 25, 1912.

18. *Minnesota Journal*, January 16, February 18, 1912; *Winthrop News*, August 16, 1917; Peter Fearon, *The U.S. Economy, 1917–1945* (Lawrence: University Press of Kansas, 1987), 61; Theodore C. Blegen, *Minnesota: A History of the State* (Minneapolis: University of Minnesota Press, 1963), 462–66.

19. S. M. Felton, "New Influences Affecting Passenger Traffic," *Railway Age* 61 (December 1, 1916): 997–998; Margaret Walsh, "Tracing the Hound: The Minnesota Roots of the Greyhound Corporation," *Minnesota History* 49 (Winter 1985): 314–25; "Getting Rid of Rails," *The Independent* 82 (May 31, 1915): 342; Isaac Don Levine, "The Jitney," *The Independent* 82 (May 31, 1915): 356–57.

20. NP, *Annual Report*, 1912, 20; tabular data from annual reports of railroads serving Minneapolis, 1910–20; *Literary Digest* 54 (January 20, 1917): 164–67.

21. CRI&P, *Annual Report*, 1915, 7; GN, *Annual Report*, 1915, 26; NP, *Annual Report*, 1915, 7; Hidy et al., *The Great Northern Railway*, 125; James A. Ward, "On Time: Railroads and the Temp of American Life," *Railroad History* (Autumn 1984): 87–95; *Minneapolis Journal*, January 15, 1911.

22. Ralph W. Hidy, Muriel E. Hidy, Roy V. Scott, and Don L. Hofsommer,

*The Great Northern Railroad: A History* (Boston: Harvard Business School Press, 1988), 124–25; *Proceedings of the Twenty-Fourth Annual Convention of the American Railway Engineering Association* 24 (1923), 862–63, 885–87, 892, 899–901, 910, 912, 916, 924; "New Great Northern Station at Minneapolis," *Railway Age* 56 (January 30, 1914): 227–37; *Official Guide* (June 1916), passim.

23. "A Former Railroad Commissioner's Views on Passenger Fares," *Railway Age* 58 (January 15, 1915): 102–3; John C. Luecke, *Dreams, Disasters, and Demise: The Milwaukee Road in Minnesota* (Eagan, MN: Grenadier Publications, 1988), 168–74; Arthur D. Dubin, *More Classic Trains* (Milwaukee: Kalmbach Books, 1974), 344–55; *Minneapolis Journal*, January 26, 1912; *Minneapolis Tribune*, May 4, 1912, June 1, 1914; *Official Guide* (June 1916), 699; *Railroad Gazette* 32 (January 19, 1900), 44.

24. William A. McKenzie, *Dining Car Line to the Pacific: An Illustrated History of the NP Railway's "Famously Good Food," with 150 Authentic Recipes* (St. Paul: Minnesota Historical Society Press, 1990), 23–30, 43–56, 62, 71–75; Lucius Beebe and Charles Clegg, *The Trains We Rode*, 2 vols. (Berkeley, CA: Howell-North, 1965–66), 2:466–83; *Official Guide* (June 1916), 636–40, 760–68; NP, *Annual Report*, 1912, 21; *New York Sun*, December 29, 1911.

25. Beebe and Clegg, *The Trains We Rode*, 1:228–37; Arthur D. Dubin, *Some Classic Trains* (Milwaukee: Kalmbach Publications, 1964), 244–303; Don L. Hofsommer, "The Maritime Enterprises of James J. Hill," *American Neptune* 47 (Summer 1987): 193–205.

26. Dubin, *More Classic Trains*, 356–67; *Official Guide* (June 1916), 725; Jim Scribbins, *Milwaukee Road Remembered: A Fresh Look at an Unusual Railroad* (Waukesha: Kalmbach Publishing, 1990), 47–52.

27. Dubin, *Some Classic Trains*, 282–93; *Official Guide* (June 1916), 687, 690.

28. "A Former Railroad Commissioner's View on Passenger Fares," 102–3; "Many Changes in Pullman Cars since 1858," *Railway Age* 88 (May 17, 1930): 1195–97; "Fifty Years of Pullman," *Railway Age* 129 (October 28, 1950): 164–66; Dubin, *More Classic Trains*, 93–105.

29. John R. Stilgoe, *Metropolitan Corridor: Railroads and the American Scene* (New Haven: Yale University Press, 1983) 68–70; Elting E. Morrison, "The Absolute All-American Civilizer," *American Heritage* 36 (June-July 1985): 54–57.

30. Peter T. Maiken, *Night Trains: The Pullman System in the Golden Years of American Rail Travel* (Chicago: Lakme Press, 1989), 277–81; Scribbins, *Milwaukee Road Remembered*, 66; *Schedule of Lines* (Chicago: The Pullman Company, July 15, 1915), passim; *Official Guide* (June 1916), 724–39, 763, 957–65.

31. *Schedule of Lines*, passim; *Official Guide* (June 1916), 637, 684, 698, 720.

32. *Official Guide* (June 1916), 636, 688; *Minneapolis Journal*, February 1, 1912; *Minneapolis Tribune*, June 1, 1914, June 2, 1915, July 1, 1916, June 7, 12, 16, July 4, 17, August 1, 1917.

33. A. B. Cutts to Our Agents, January 27, 1913, AC; A. B. Cutts to J. J. Thompson, June 8 1914, AC: M&StL, Advertising flyer, October 23, 1913, and June 6, 1914, AC; *Minneapolis Journal*, January 18, 1912.

34. Kendrick W. Brown, "Memories of a Commercial Traveler," *The Palimpsest* 52 (May 1971): 225–88; Susan Strasser, "'The Smile that Pays': The Culture of the Traveling Salesman, 1880-1920," in *The Mythmaking Frame of Mind: Social Imagination and American Culture*, ed. James Gilbert et al. (Belmont, CA: Wadsworth Publishing, 1993), 155–77; Don Marquis, "My Memories of the Old-Fashioned Drummer," *American Magazine* 107 (February 1929): 20–21, 152–54; Truman E. Moore, *The Traveling Man: The Story of the American Traveling Salesman* (Garden City, NJ: Random House, 1972), 21–39; "Drummers Accommodated: A Nineteenth-Century Salesman in Minnesota," *Minnesota History* 46 (Summer 1978): 59–65.

35. Stilgoe, *Metropolitan Corridor*, 193–211; George H. Douglas, "Down by the Depot." *Locomotive & Railway Preservation* (November-December 1992): 11–27; H. Roger Grant and Charles W. Bohi, *The Country Railroad Station in America* (Boulder, CO: Pruett Publishing, 1978), 3–10.

36. "A Century of Express Service," *Railway Age* 106 (March 4, 1939): 365–68; V. S. Roseman, *Railway Express: An Overview* (Denver: Rocky Mountain Publishing, 1992): 4–9.

37. Boris Emmet and John E. Jeuck, *Catalogues and Counters: A History of Sears, Roebuck & Company* (Chicago: University of Chicago Press, 1950), 18–46, 100–122, 169–70; Gordon L. Weil, *Sears, Roebuck, U.S.A.: The Greatest Catalogue Store and How It Grew* (New York: Stein and Day, 1977), 2–40; David B. Danbom, *Born in the Country: A History of Rural America* (Baltimore: Johns Hopkins University Press, 1995), 132–34, 149–50.

38. Leo A. McKee and Alfred L. Lewis, eds., *Railroad Post Office History* (Pleasantville, NY: Mobile Post Office Society, 1972), passim; *Railroad Age Gazette* 47 (October 1, 1909): 603; Guy M. Purington, "Rural Free Delivery," *Transit Postmark Collector* 47 (January-February 1996): 28–29; Joseph A. A. Burnquist, *Minnesota and Its People*, 4 vols. (Chicago: S. J. Clarke Publishers, 1924), 1:556–57; Henry A. Castle, *A History of St. Paul and Vicinity: A Chronicle of Progress and Narrative Account of the Industries, Institutions, and People of the City and Its Tributary Territory*, 3 vols. (Chicago: Lewis Publishing, 1912), 1:233–34; John R. Borchert, "The Heyday of the Railway Post Office in Minnesota," *Minnegazette* (Winter 1997): 19–34.

## 15. MIXED BLESSINGS

1. Gordon Carruth, *What Happened When*: *A Chronology of Life and Events in America* (New York: Harper & Row, 1989), 405–638; Paul S. Boyer et al., *The Enduring of a Vision: A History of the American People* (Lexington: D. C. Heath & Co., 1990), 2:568–673.

2. Albro Martin, *James J. Hill and the Opening of the Northwest* (New York: Oxford University Press, 1976), 613–15; Michael P. Malone, *James J. Hill: Empire Builder of the Northwest* (Norman: University of Oklahoma Press, 1996), 185, 229, 234, 248, 266, 268, 271–72; Soo Line, *Annual Report*, 1912, 11; *New York Times*, February 6, 9–11, 1912.

3. Dow, Jones & Co., Electric Page News Ticker Bulletin No. 21, November 29, 1909; ibid., Bulletin No. 66 (October 31, 1910); ibid., Bulletin No. 59, August 16, 1911; ibid., Bulletin No. 48, September 8, 1911; ibid., .Bulletin No. 6, October 18, 1911; ibid., Bulletin No. 30, December 22, 1911; *Minneapolis Journal*, October 13, November 1, 2, 13, 15, 19, 22, 24, December 4, 16, 20, 23, 1911, January 8, 10, 1912; M&StL, *Annual Report*, 1912, 5–6.

4. Soo Line, *Annual Report*, 1909, 6–7; *Yesterday and Today: A History of the Chicago & North Western Railway System*, 3rd ed. (Chicago: C&NW, 1910), 166–70; Ralph W. Hidy, Muriel E. Hidy, Roy V. Scott, and Don L. Hofsommer, *The Great Northern Railroad: A History* (Boston: Harvard Business School Press, 1988), 321–23; NP, Index Diagram and Original Tracklaying Record May 15, 1933.

5. August Derleth, *The Milwaukee Road: Its First 100 Years* (New York: Creative Age Press, 1948), 294–98; *Milwaukee Railway System Employees' Magazine*, June 1915, 18–20.

6. *Annual Report of the Minneapolis Board of Trade, 1881*, 13; A. D. Emery, "The Twin Cities, St. Paul and Minneapolis," *Milwaukee Magazine* 13 (May 1925): 3–9.

7. *Minneapolis Journal*, June 23, September 1, 22, 1907, December 11, 1911; George W. Hilton and John F. Due, *The Electric Interurban Railways in America* (Stanford, CA: Stanford University Press, 1960), 357–58; Richard S. Prosser, *Rails to the North Star: One Hundred Years of Railroad Evolution in Minnesota* (Minneapolis: Dillon Press, 1966), 47–48, 56, 102–4; MStPR&DET, Time Table, December 10, 1916, passim; Stan Mailer, "The Blue Dragon of Golden Valley," *Railfan & Railroad* 4 (July 1982): 48–57; *Dakota County Tribune*, June 20, 1974.

8. Edward W. Solberg, "The Minneapolis Street Railway: Emergence and Disappearance," unpublished master's thesis, St. Cloud State University, 1999, 39; Twin Cities Lines, Time Table, May 15, 1914, passim; Ellen Wilson Meyer, ed., *Picturesque Deephaven* (Excelsior: Excelsior-Lake Minnetonka Historical Society, 1989), 35; Hilton and Due, *The Electric Interurban Railways in America*, 359.

9. John R. Borchert, *America's Northern Heartland* (Minneapolis: University of Minnesota Press, 1987), 51–78; Don L. Hofsommer, "Boosterism and Townsite Development along the Minneapolis & St. Louis Railroad in South Dakota," *Journal of the West* (Autumn 2003): 8–16.

10. L. J. Bricker to Thomas Cooper, March 27, 1911; L. J. Bricker to J. M. Rockwell, April 8, 1914; L. J. Bricker to J. M. Hannaford, February 24, 1915, NP Presidents File, MHS; *Minneapolis Tribune*, May 5, 1914; GN, *Annual Report*, 1916, 20; M&StL, *Annual Report*, 1916, 8.

11. Howard Elliott, "The Work of the Farmer and of the Railroad in Minnesota," an address before the Minnesota Agricultural Society, St. Paul, January 9, 1912, AC; James J. Hill, "The Nation's Future," an address at the Minnesota State Fair, St. Paul, September 3, 1906, AC; Roy V. Scott, *Railroad Development Programs in the Twentieth Century* (Ames: Iowa State University Press, 1985), 38, 39, 41, 46, 53; *The Farmer: A Journal of Agriculture* 28 (June 25, 1910): passim; W. E. Alain to Thomas Cooper, June 18, 1910, NP President File, MHS. For a less flattering assessment, see Claire Strom, *Profiting from the Plains: The Great Northern Railway and Corporate Development of the American West* (Seattle: University of Washington Press, 2003).

12. *Minneapolis Chamber of Commerce Annual Report, 1889*, 40–41; ibid., 1900, 54–55, 129–34; Agnes Larson, *History of the White Pine Industry in Minnesota* (Minneapolis: University of Minnesota Press, 1949), 243–46, 399.

13. *Minneapolis Chamber of Commerce Annual Report, 1899*, 40; ibid., 1900, 10, 54, 55; ibid., 1920, 175; Marion Daniel Shuttes, *History of Minneapolis: Gateway to the Northwest*, 2 vols. (Chicago: S. J. Clarke Publishing Co., 1923), 1:373; Whitney Eastman, *The History of the Linseed Oil Industry in the United States* (Minneapolis: T. S. Denison & Co., 1968), 15–62, 123–53.

14. *Minneapolis Chamber of Commerce Annual Report*, 1900, 27, 54–55, 113–16, 124–28; ibid., 1910, 24–25, 116–17.

15. *Minneapolis Chamber of Commerce Annual Report*, 1920, 26–27, 39, 164–74; Shuttes, *History of Minneapolis*, 370; William C. Edgar, *The Medal of Gold: A Story of Industrial Achievement* (Minneapolis: Bellman Company, 1925), 218–23; Charles Byron Kuhlmann, *The Development of the Flour Milling Industry in the United States with Special Reference to Minneapolis* (Boston: Houghton Mifflin, 1929), 155–75; Victor A. Pickett and Roland S. Vaile, *The Decline of Northwestern Flour Milling* (Minneapolis: University of Minnesota Press, 1933), 5–15, 20–23, 34–35, 54–57; James Gray, *Business without Boundary: The Story of General Mills* (Minneapolis: University of Minnesota Press, 1954), 62–67, 82–89, 96–103, 130–35.

16. *Minneapolis Journal*, February 17, 1912; Carl H. Chrislock, *The Progressive Era in Minnesota, 1899–1918* (St. Paul: Minnesota Historical Society, 1971), 60, 200; *New York Times*, November 28, 1911; Otto H. Kahn, "What

American Railroads Need," *World's Work* 31 (February 1916): 451–60; Arthur Pound and Samuel Taylor Moore, *They Told Barron: Conversations and Revelations of an American Pepys in Wall Street* (New York: Harper & Row, 1930), 59–60; Richard Hoadley Tingley, "Lo, The Poor Railroads," *Current Opinion* 73 (July 1922): 11–13.

17. H. Roger Grant, *The Corn Belt Route: A History of the Chicago Great Western Railroad Company* (De Kalb: Northern Illinois University Press, 1984), 73–77; S. M. Felton to Howard Elliott, January 11, 23, February 12, 1913; Howard Elliott to S. M. Felton, January 27, 1913, NP President File 186, AC; *Wall Street Journal*, January 18, 1916; Great Northern President File 6092, Box 197, MHS, passim; *New York Times*, February 1, April 14, 1916; *Railway Age* 61 (September 8, 1916): 435; CRI&P, *Annual Report*, 1915, 9.

18. *New York Times*, July 17, 1914, December 31, 1915; "What Breaks the Railroads," *Literary Digest* 51 (November 6, 1915): 998; Walker D. Hines, *War History of American Railroads* (New Haven: Yale University Press, 1928), 1–9; NP, *Annual Report*, 1917, 16–17; ibid., 1918, 14–17.

19. John F. Stover, *American Railroads*, 2nd ed. (Chicago: University of Chicago Press, 1997), 181–86; Hines, *War History of American Railroads*, x–xv, 1–21; *The Independent*, December 13, 1915, 318–19.

20. John F. Stover, *Life and Decline of the American Railroad* (New York: Oxford University Press, 1970), 158–73; Hines, *War History of American Railroads*, 22–41.

21. Stover, *American Railroads*, 185–97; K. Austin Kerr, "Decision Federal Control: Wilson, McAdoo, and the Railroads, 1917," *Journal of American History* 3 (December 1967): 550–60; W. G. McAdoo, General Order No.1, December 29, 1917.

22. Stover, *American Railroads*, 187–97.

23. *Minneapolis Tribune*, April 5, 1917; M&StL, *Annual Report*, 1917, 13; Joseph A. A. Burnquist, *Minnesota and Its People*, 4 vols. (Chicago: S. J. Clarke Publishers, 1924), 2:179–86.

24. M&StL, Time Table, October 25, 1918, 16; *Official Guide* (March 1918), 1124–29; ibid. (October 1918), 521; *Minneapolis Tribune*, May 1, 1919; "New Great Northern Station at Minneapolis," *Railway Age* 56 (January 30, 1914): 227–33.

25. Hines, *War History of American Railroads*, 41, 55–56; M&StL, *Annual Report*, 1917, 8; ibid., 1918, 27; Cyrus W. Cornelius to the author, April 6, 1988; JWD to GPM, December 17, 1917, AC; tabular data from M&StL annual reports, 1917–18; JPM to All Agents, April 14, 1917, AC; Chrislock, *The Progressive Era in Minnesota*, 47, 133–41, 212–15; USRA, General Order No. 39, August 12, 1918, AC.

26. Tabular data from annual reports of the carriers cited.

27. *Moody's Analysis of Investments and Security Ratings: Railroad Investment* (New York: Moody's Investors Service, 1922), 899, 907; M&StL, *Annual Report*, 1918, 27; J. G. Woodworth to Howard Elliott, March 10, 1918, NP President File 2045, AC.

28. Chrislock, *The Progressive Era in Minnesota*, 244–75; Martin Gilbert, *The First World War: A Complete History* (New York: Henry Holt, 1994), xv, 503–41.

29. Gilbert, *The First World War*, 519.

30. Glenn E. Plumb, "Labor's Solution to the Railroad Problem," *The Nation* 109 (August 16, 1919): 200–220.

31. *New York Times*, December 9, 1918, June 6, 1919; M&StL, *Annual Report*, 1919, 6; Gerard C. Henderson, "Our Insolvent Railroads," *New Republic* 19 (July 2, 1919): 274–76.

32. Albert B. Cummins, "The Railway Problem," *Review of Reviews* 60 (July 1919): 61–66; James M. Herring, *The Problem of Weak Railroads* (Philadelphia: University of Pennsylvania Press, 1929), 40–43; Ari Hoogenboom and Olive Hoogenboom, *A History of the ICC: From Panacea to Palliative* (New York: W. W. Norton & Co., 1976), 94–118; M&StL, *Annual Report*, 1919, 5.

33. NP, *Annual Report*, 1919, 12, 16–17.

## 16. AN UNCERTAIN FUTURE

1. *Annual Report of the Minneapolis Board of Trade, 1878*, 50–63; ibid., 1881, 13; *Minneapolis Chamber of Commerce Annual Report, 1889*, 208–9; GN, *Annual Report*, 1920, 14; CM&StP, *Annual Report*, 1920, 10, 12, 23, 18, 34.

2. Julius H. Parmelee, "Railway Revenues and Expenses in the Year 1920," *Railway Age* 70 (January 7, 1921): 129; *New Republic* 22 (March 3, 1920): 6–8; *New York Times*, July 25, 1922; Peter Fearon, *War, Prosperity, and Depression: The U.S. Economy 1917–45* (Lawrence: University Press of Kansas, 1987), 8–9, 15–21, 84; Alfred D. Chandler Jr., *The Visible Hand: The Managerial Revolution in American Business* (Cambridge: Harvard University Press, 1977), 456–59; C&NW, *Annual Report*, 1922, 8.

3. Walker D. Hines, *War History of American Railroads* (New Haven: Yale University Press, 1928), 152–91, 226–29; *Moody's Analyses of Investments and Security Rating Books: Railroad Securities* (New York: Moody's Investors Service, 1923), xxxix; M&StL, *Annual Report*, 1920, 4–5; *New York Times*, July 24, 1922; Samuel O. Dunn, "What Has Happened to the Railroads?" *Review of Reviews* 63 (May 1921): 501–5; *Current Opinion* 70 (June 1921): 732–36; Robert H. Zieger, *America's Great War: World War I and the American Experience* (New York: Rowman & Littlefield, 2000), 122–23; W. Thomas White, "Railroad Labor Relations in the Great War and After, 1917–1921," *Journal of the West* 25 (April 1986): 36–43.

4. *New York Times*, October 16, 1921; *Minneapolis Tribune*, July 1, 7–9, 14, 17, 19, 1922; *Railway Age* 73 (September 16, 1922): 526; Colin J. Davis, *Power at Odds: The 1922 Shopmen's Strike* (Urbana: University of Illinois Press, 1997), 48–79; William Z. Ripley, "Why the Railroad Strike Failed and the Coal Miners Won," *Survey* 49 (January 1, 1923): 436–38, 470–71.

5. *Moody's Analyses of Investments: Railroad Securities* (New York: Moody's Investors Service, 1924), xxv, xxxvii.

6. Albro Martin, *Railroads Triumphant: The Growth, Rejection and Rebirth of a Vital American Force* (New York: Oxford University Press, 1992), 387; Albro Martin, *Enterprise Denied: Origins of the Decline of American Railroads* (New York: Columbia University Press, 1971), 354, 361, 369, 372–73.

7. Steven W. Usselman, *Regulating Railroad Innovation: Business, Technology, and Politics in America, 1840–1920* (Cambridge: Cambridge University Press, 2002), 1–12, 329–30, 346, 381–87.

8. Carlos A. Schwantes, *Going Places: Transportation Redefines the Twentieth-Century West* (Bloomington: Indiana University Press, 2003), 137; Edward Weiner, *Urban Transportation Planning in the United States: An Historical Overview* (Westport, CT: Prager, 1999), 7–8; Daniel J. Elazar, "A Model of Moral Government," *Minnesota in a Century of Change: The State and Its People Since 1900*, ed. Clifford E. Clark (St. Paul: Minnesota Historical Society, 1989), 345; *Minneapolis Journal*, January 28, 1927.

9. Victor W. Knaughth, "Railway vs. Truck: A Tug of War in Transportation," *World's Work* 50 (October 1925): 664–68; Edward G. Riggs, "Motor Trucks vs. Railroads," *Forum* 65 (June 1921): 609–18; *Moody's Manual of Investments: Steam Railroads* (New York: Moody's Investment Service, 1941), a43–a45; Arthur Pound and Samuel Taylor Moore, eds., *They Told Barron: Conversations and Revelations of an American Pepys in Wall Street* (New York: Harper & Brothers, 1930), 66–67; CRI&P, *Annual Report*, 1924, 9.

10. Kenneth T. Jackson, *Crabgrass Frontier: The Suburbanization of the United States* (New York: Oxford University Press, 1985), 161; *Railroad Facts No 7: A Yearbook of Railroad Information* (Chicago: Western Railways Committee on Public Relations, 1929), 33; Frederick Lewis Allen, *Only Yesterday: An Informal History of the Nineteen-Twenties* (New York: Harper & Row, 1931), 134–39.

11. Richard C. Overton, *Perkins/Budd: Railway Statesmen of the Burlington* (Westport, CT: Greenwood Press, 1982), 161–71; James M. Herring, *The Problem of Weak Railroads* (Philadelphia: University of Pennsylvania Press, 1929), 130–31; Greyhound, Time Table (December 20, 1928), 19; *Minneapolis Journal*, February 6, 1927.

12. *Moody's Manual of Investments: Railroads* (New York: Moody's Investors Service, 1945), a14; M&StL, *Annual Report*, 1922, 23; ibid., 1923, 24;

*Literary Digest* 54 (January 20, 1917): 164–67; *New York Times*, August 14, 1921; "Railroads Losing Their Passengers," *Literary Digest* 86 (September 26, 1925): 22; Ralph Budd, "The Trend in Passenger Travel," *Railway Age* 84 (April 28, 1928): 1025–27; Herring, *The Problem of Weak Railroads*, 131–32; "Deserting the Rails," *Literary Digest* 84 (January 10, 1925): 27; C&NW, *Annual Report*, 1923, 7–8; CRI&P, *Annual Report*, 1925, 7; GN, *Annual Report*, 1925, 9; Ralph Budd, "Railways and Highways," *Railway Age* 86 (March 1929): 740–41.

13. Soo Line, *Annual Report*, 1924, 14.

14. David B. Danborn, *Born in the Country: A History of Rural America* (Baltimore: Johns Hopkins University Press, 1995), 185–97; Fearon, *War, Prosperity, and Depression*, 28–41; Preston William Slosson, *The Great Crusade and After, 1914–1928* (New York: Macmillan, 1930), 166–68, 190–218; Lester V. Chandler, *America's Greatest Depression, 1929–1941* (New York: Harper & Row, 1970), 5–55.

15. Curtis L. Hosher to J. G. Hoodworth, May 24, 1929; J. G. Hoodworth to Charles Donnelly, May 24, 1929, NP President File 139–11, 1342–11, MHS; Fearon, *War, Prosperity, and Depression* 38; Slosson, *The Great Crusade and After*, 184–86.

16. *Minneapolis Journal*, February 11, 1927; Victor A. Pickett and Roland S. Vaile, *The Decline of Northwestern Flour Milling* (Minneapolis: University of Minnesota Press, 1933), 70; *New York Times*, August 5–7, 15, 1926; *Minneapolis Tribune*, February 28, 1927; Charles Byron Kuhlmann, *The Development of the Flour Milling Industry in the United States with Special Reference to Minneapolis* (Boston: Houghton Mifflin, 1929), 177–82; James Gray, *Business without Boundary: The Story of General Mills* (Minneapolis: University of Minnesota Press, 1954), 140–41, 152.

17. *Minneapolis Tribune*, February 28, 1922; *New York Times*, May 10, 1922; tabular data from annual reports of roads identified, 1920–23; *Wall Street Journal*, November 11, 1922; F. J. Lisman, "The Trouble with the Minneapolis & St. Louis," *Railway Age* 75 (August 25, 1923): 347–48; *New York Times*, March 18, 1925.

18. Chandler, *America's Greatest Depression*, 15–17; William Leuchtenburg, *The Perils of Prosperity, 1914–1932* (Chicago: University of Chicago Press, 1958), 178–93; Jonathan Hughes, *American Economic History*, 3rd ed. (Glenview, IL: Scott, Foresman/Little Brown, 1990), 448–51; Irving Bernstein, *The Lean Years: A History of the American Worker, 1920–1933* (Boston: Houghton Mifflin, 1960), 54; Don L. Hofsommer, *The Southern Pacific: 1901–1985* (College Station: Texas A&M University Press, 1986), 117; NP, *Annual Report*, 1929, 13.

19. CMStP&P, *Annual Report*, 1931, 3–4; NP, *Annual Report*, 1932, 13; ibid., 1933, 14; CRI&P, *Annual Report*, 1931, 7; Soo Line, *Annual Report*,

1930, 13; ibid., 1931, 13; ibid., 1933, 7; ibid., 1934, 6; ibid., 1936, 6, 12.

20. CRI&P, *Annual Report*, 1931, 7; CMStP&P, *Annual Report*, 1932, 4; GN, *Annual Report*, 1930, 8; ibid., 1931, 9; Soo Line, *Annual Report*, 1934, 8.

21. NP, *Annual Report*, 1939, 14; CRI&P, *Annual Report*, 1936, 1; Soo Line, *Annual Report*, 1937, 13; tabular data from CMStP&P annual reports, 1930–38.

22. CB&Q, *Annual Report*, 1935, 10; ibid., 1936, 9; CMStP&P, *Annual Report*, 1936, 10; ibid., 1939, 8; Jim Scribbins, *The Hiawatha Story* (Milwaukee: Kalmbach Publishing, 1970), 10–63.

23. GN, *Annual Report*, 1941, 3; John F. Stover, *American Railroads*, 2nd ed. (Chicago: University of Chicago Press, 1997), 203–9; Ralph W. Hidy, Muriel E. Hidy, Roy V. Scott, and Don L. Hofsommer, *The Great Northern Railroad: A History* (Boston: Harvard Business School Press, 1988), 218–30; CB&Q, *Annual Report*, 1944, 7.

24. *Moody's Transportation Manual* (New York: Moody's Investors Service, 1958), a9–a12.

25. Stover, *American Railroads*, 211–20; *Moody's Transportation Manual* (1958), a26–a35, a.62–a71.

26. Harold A. Edmonson, ed., *Journey to Amtrak: The Year History Rode the Passenger Train* (Milwaukee: Kalmbach Publishing, 1972), passim; Amtrak, Time Table (May 1, 1971), 25.

27. Don L. Hofsommer, *Grand Trunk Corporation: Canadian National Railways in the United States, 1971–1992* (East Lansing: Michigan State University Press, 1995), 95–112. On the subject of mergers, see Richard Saunders Jr., *Merging Lines: American Railroads, 1900–1970* (De Kalb: Northern Illinois University Press, 2001).

28. Stover, *American Railroads*, 245–62; Richard J. Saunders Jr., *Main Lines: Rebirth of the North American Railroads, 1970–2002* (De Kalb: Northern Illinois University Press, 2003), passim; Eno Transportation Foundation, *Transportation in America 1999: A Statistical Analysis of Transportation in the United States* (Washington, DC: Eno Transportation Foundation, 2000), 11, 46–47.

## EPILOGUE

1. John R. Stilgoe, *Metropolitan Corridor: Railroads and the American Scene* (New Haven: Yale University Press, 1983), 3.

2. *Dakota Railroad Commission Report, 1885*, 1; quoted in Carlos A. Schwantes, *Going Places: Transportation Redefines the Twentieth-Century West* (Bloomington: Indiana University Press, 2003), 75–76; J. T. Conley, "The Twin Cities," *Milwaukee Road Employees Magazine* (September 1913): 11–12; John Gross, *LaSalle: Whistle-Stop on the Prairie* (Medford, MN: Privately published by the author, 1999), 9.

3. M&StL, Track and Station Map, Cresbard, Faulk County, South Dakota (1921), AC.

4. H. H. Young, *St. Paul: The Commercial Emporium of the Northwest* (St. Paul: Pioneer Press Co., 1886), 40–78, 101; *St. Paul Chamber of Commerce Annual Report, 1886*, 33–35; *Minneapolis Chamber of Commerce Annual Report, 1886*, 41–42.

5. Joseph A. A. Burnquist, *Minnesota and Its People*, 4 vols. (Chicago: S. J. Clarke Publishers, 1924), 2:609.

6. Soo Line remains a corporate shell, doing business as Canadian Pacific.

# INDEX

## ABOUT THE AUTHOR

Don L. Hofsommer is professor of history at St. Cloud State University. He is the author and coauthor of several books, including *The Tootin' Louie: A History of the Minneapolis & St. Louis Railway*, *The Hook & Eye: A History of the Iowa Central Railway*, and *The Great Northern Railway: A History*, all published by the University of Minnesota Press.

## ALSO PUBLISHED BY THE UNIVERSITY OF MINNESOTA PRESS

*The Great Northern Railway* by Ralph W. Hidy, Muriel E. Hidy, Roy V. Scott, and Don L. Hofsommer

*The Hook & Eye: A History of the Iowa Central Railway* by Don L. Hofsommer

*The Tootin' Louie: A History of the Minneapolis & St. Louis Railway* by Don L. Hofsommer

*Minnesota Logging Railroads* by Frank A. King

*The Missabe Road: The Duluth, Missabe and Iron Range Railway* by Frank A. King

*Dining Car to the Pacific: The "Famously Good" Food of the Northern Pacific Railway* by William A. McKenzie

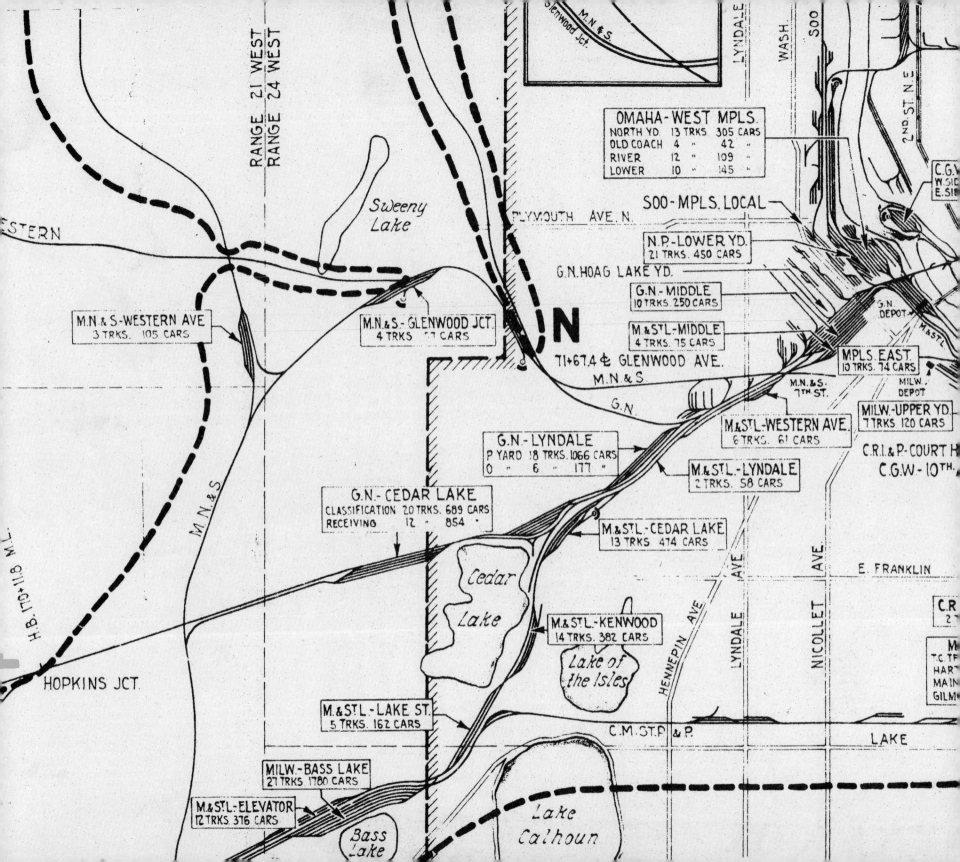

RANGE 21 WEST
RANGE 24 WEST

*Sweeny Lake*

Glenwood Jct.
M.N.&S.

WESTERN

PLYMOUTH AVE. N.

**OMAHA - WEST MPLS.**

| | | |
|---|---|---|
| NORTH YD. | 13 TRKS. | 305 CARS |
| OLD COACH | 4 " | 42 " |
| RIVER | 12 " | 109 " |
| LOWER | 10 " | 145 " |

LYNDALE
WASH.
SOO
2ND ST. N.E.

C.G.W.
W. SIDE
E. SIDE

SOO - MPLS. LOCAL

**N.P.- LOWER YD.**
21 TRKS. 450 CARS

G.N. HOAG LAKE YD.

**G.N.- MIDDLE**
10 TRKS. 250 CARS

**M.N.& S.-WESTERN AVE**
3 TRKS. 105 CARS

**M.N.& S.- GLENWOOD JCT.**
4 TRKS. 57 CARS

N

71+67.4 ℄ GLENWOOD AVE.
M.N. & S.

**M.&STL-MIDDLE**
4 TRKS. 75 CARS

G.N.
DEPOT
M.&STL.

**MPLS. EAST.**
10 TRKS. 74 CARS

MILW.
DEPOT

M.N.&S.
7TH ST.

**M.&STL-WESTERN AVE.**
6 TRKS. 61 CARS

**MILW-UPPER YD.**
7 TRKS. 120 CARS

C.R.I.& P.- COURT H.
C.G.W.- 10TH.

G.N.

**G.N.- LYNDALE**

| | | |
|---|---|---|
| P YARD | 18 TRKS. | 1066 CARS |
| O " | 6 " | 177 " |

**M.&STL-LYNDALE**
2 TRKS. 58 CARS

M.N. & S.

**G.N.- CEDAR LAKE**

| | | |
|---|---|---|
| CLASSIFICATION | 20 TRKS. | 689 CARS |
| RECEIVING | 12 " | 854 " |

**M.&STL-CEDAR LAKE**
13 TRKS. 474 CARS

E. FRANKLIN

H.B. 170+11.8 M.L.

*Cedar Lake*

HENNEPIN AVE.
LYNDALE AVE.
NICOLLET AVE.

C.R.

**M.&STL-KENWOOD**
14 TRKS. 382 CARS

*Lake of the Isles*

M.
T.C. TF
HART
MAIN
GILM

HOPKINS JCT.

**M.&STL-LAKE ST.**
5 TRKS. 162 CARS

C.M. ST.P. & P.

LAKE

**MILW-BASS LAKE**
27 TRKS. 1780 CARS

**M.&STL-ELEVATOR**
12 TRKS. 376 CARS

*Bass Lake*

*Lake Calhoun*